A-Z PORTSMOUTH

CONTENTS

Key to Map Pages
Large Scale City Centre
Map Pages   58-88

REFERENCE

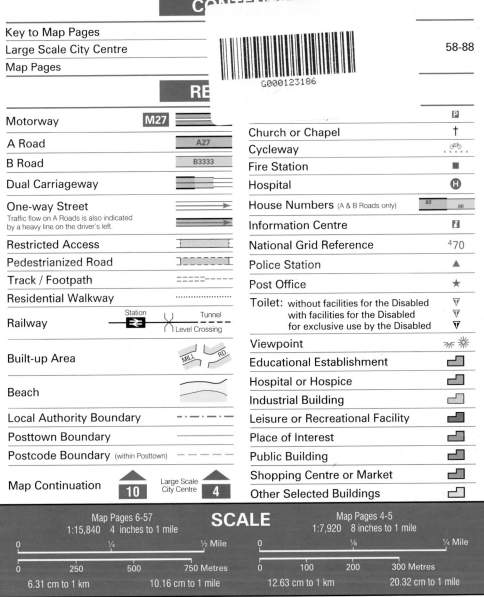

Motorway	M27		
A Road	A27		
B Road	B3333		
Dual Carriageway			
One-way Street			
Traffic flow on A Roads is also indicated by a heavy line on the driver's left.			
Restricted Access			
Pedestrianized Road			
Track / Footpath			
Residential Walkway			
Railway	Station	Tunnel	Level Crossing
Built-up Area	MILL RD.		
Beach			
Local Authority Boundary			
Posttown Boundary			
Postcode Boundary (within Posttown)			
Map Continuation	10	Large Scale City Centre	4

	P
Church or Chapel	†
Cycleway	☁
Fire Station	■
Hospital	H
House Numbers (A & B Roads only)	83 96
Information Centre	i
National Grid Reference	470
Police Station	▲
Post Office	★
Toilet: without facilities for the Disabled	▽
with facilities for the Disabled	▽
for exclusive use by the Disabled	▽
Viewpoint	
Educational Establishment	
Hospital or Hospice	
Industrial Building	
Leisure or Recreational Facility	
Place of Interest	
Public Building	
Shopping Centre or Market	
Other Selected Buildings	

SCALE

Map Pages 6-57	Map Pages 4-5
1:15,840 4 inches to 1 mile	1:7,920 8 inches to 1 mile
0 ¼ ½ Mile	0 ⅛ ¼ Mile
0 250 500 750 Metres	0 100 200 300 Metres
6.31 cm to 1 km 10.16 cm to 1 mile	12.63 cm to 1 km 20.32 cm to 1 mile

Copyright of Geographers' A-Z Map Company Limited

Fairfield Road, Borough Green, Sevenoaks, Kent TN15 8PP
Telephone: 01732 781000 (Enquiries & Trade Sales)
01732 783422 (Retail Sales)
www.a-zmaps.co.uk

Ordnance Survey®

This product includes mapping data licensed from Ordnance Survey® with the permission of the Controller of Her Majesty's Stationery Office.

KEY TO MAP PAGES

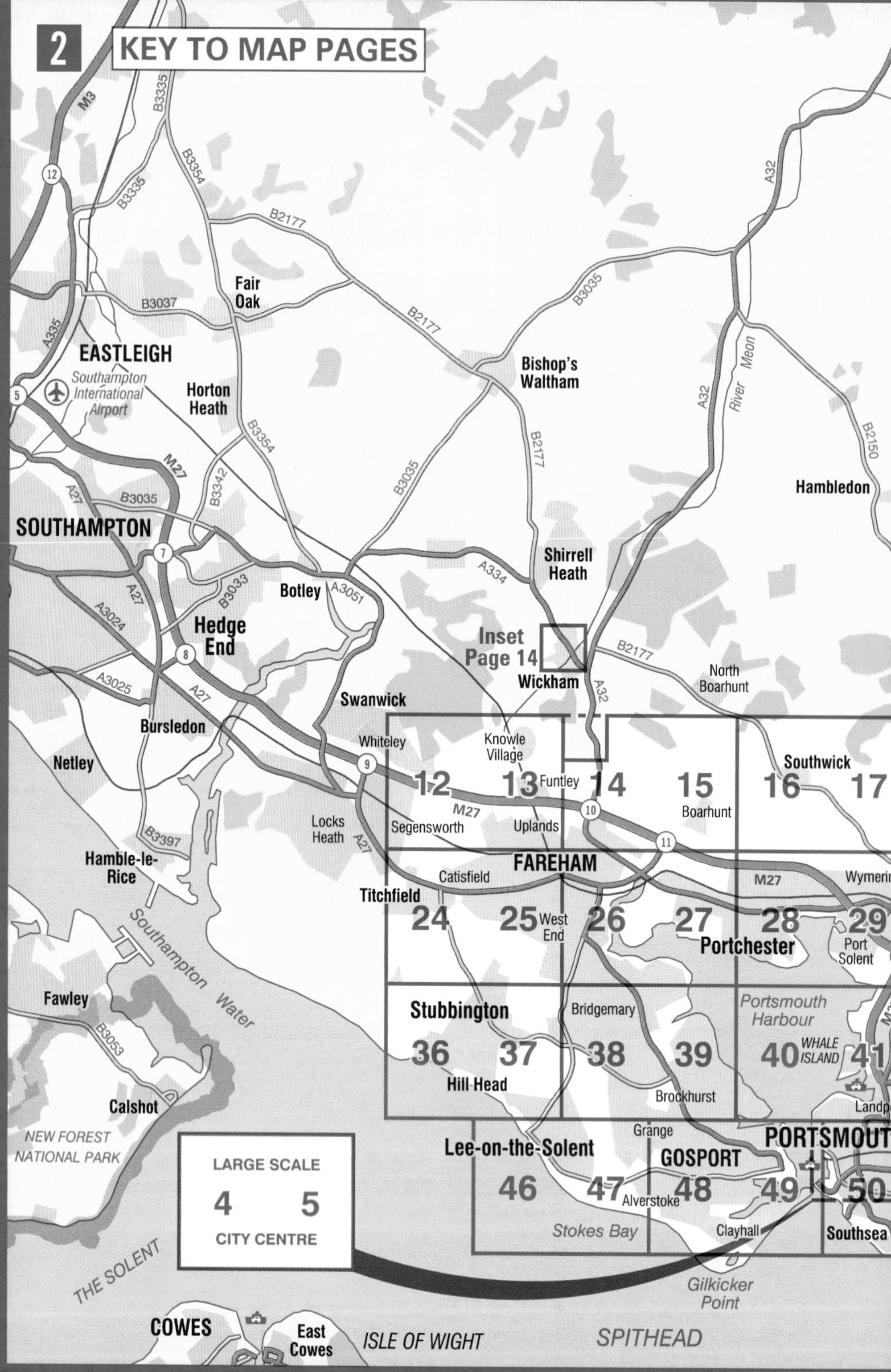
M3
B3335
B3354
B2177
B3037
A335
Fair Oak
EASTLEIGH
Southampton International Airport
Horton Heath
B3354
M27
A27
B3035
B3342
SOUTHAMPTON
A27
B3033
A3024
Hedge End
Botley
A3051
A3025
A27
Bursledon
Netley
Swanwick
Whiteley
B3397
Hamble-le-Rice
Locks Heath
A27
Titchfield
Southampton Water
Fawley
B3053
Calshot
NEW FOREST NATIONAL PARK
THE SOLENT
COWES
East Cowes
ISLE OF WIGHT
SPITHEAD
B3035
B2177
Bishop's Waltham
B2177
A334
Shirrell Heath
Inset Page 14
Wickham
A32
B2177
North Boarhunt
A32
River Meon
B2150
Hambledon
Knowle Village
Funtley
12
13
14
15
16
17
Southwick
M27
Segensworth
Uplands
Boarhunt
FAREHAM
Catisfield
M27
Wymering
24
25
West End
26
27
28
29
Portchester
Port Solent
Stubbington
Bridgemary
Portsmouth Harbour
36
37
38
39
40
WHALE ISLAND
41
Hill Head
Brockhurst
Landport
Grange
Lee-on-the-Solent
GOSPORT
PORTSMOUTH
46
47
Alverstoke
48
49
50
Stokes Bay
Clayhall
Southsea
Gilkicker Point
LARGE SCALE
4
5
CITY CENTRE

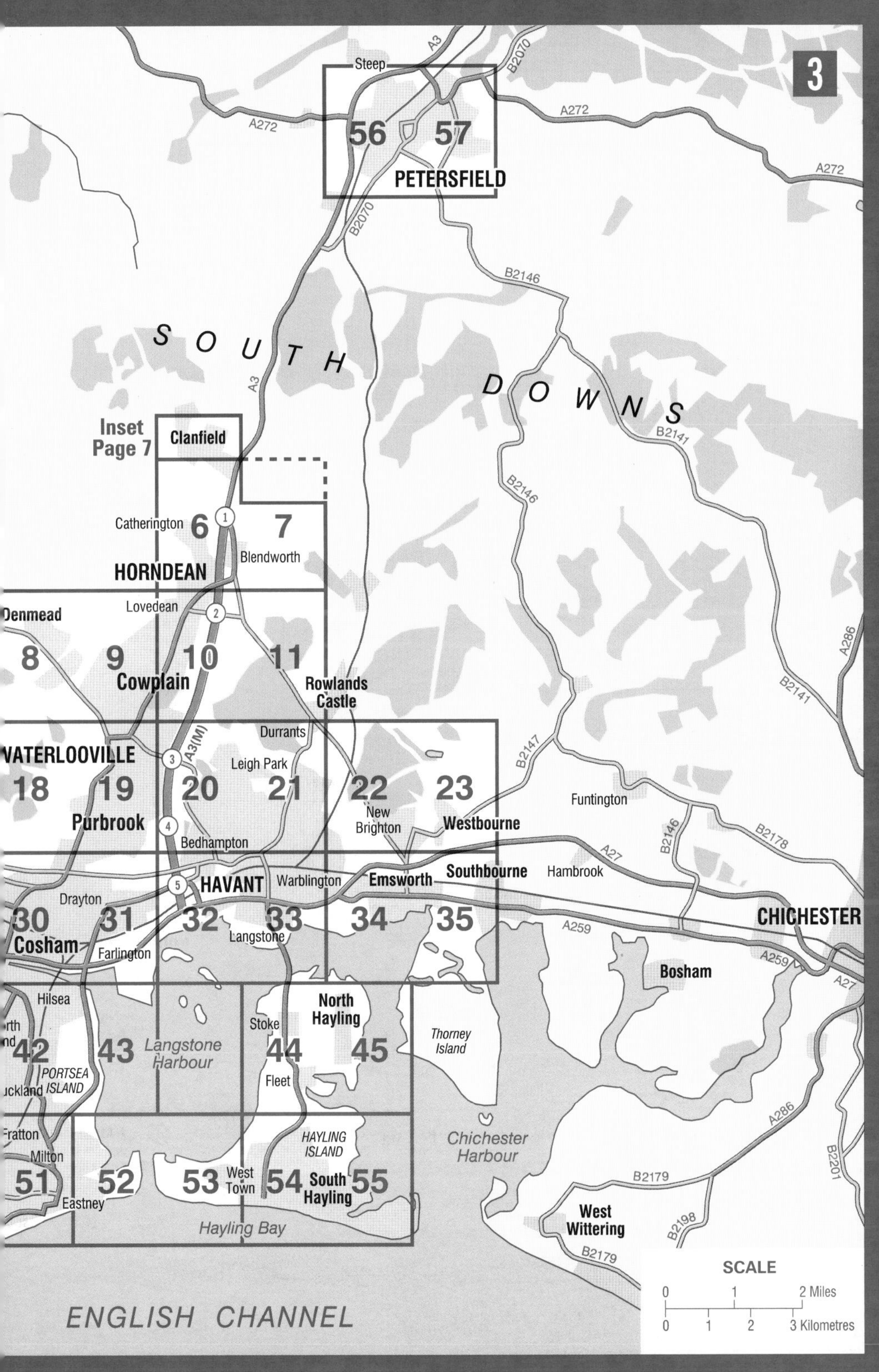

Steep
A3
B2070
A272
56
57
PETERSFIELD
A272
A272
B2070
B2146
S O U T H
D O W N S
A3
B2141
Inset Page 7
Clanfield
B2146
Catherington
6
7
Blendworth
HORNDEAN
Denmead
Lovedean
8
9
10
11
Cowplain
Rowlands Castle
A286
B2141
Durrants
WATERLOOVILLE
A3(M)
Leigh Park
B2147
18
19
20
21
22
23
Funtington
New Brighton
Purbrook
Westbourne
B2146
B2178
Bedhampton
A27
HAVANT
Warblington
Emsworth
Southbourne
Hambrook
Drayton
30
31
32
33
34
35
CHICHESTER
A259
Cosham
Farlington
Langstone
A259
Bosham
A27
Hilsea
North Hayling
Stoke
42
43
Langstone Harbour
44
45
Thorney Island
PORTSEA ISLAND
Fleet
A286
Fratton
HAYLING ISLAND
Chichester Harbour
Milton
B2201
B2179
51
52
53
West Town
54
South Hayling
55
Eastney
West Wittering
B2198
Hayling Bay
B2179
SCALE
0
1
2 Miles
0
1
2
3 Kilometres
ENGLISH CHANNEL

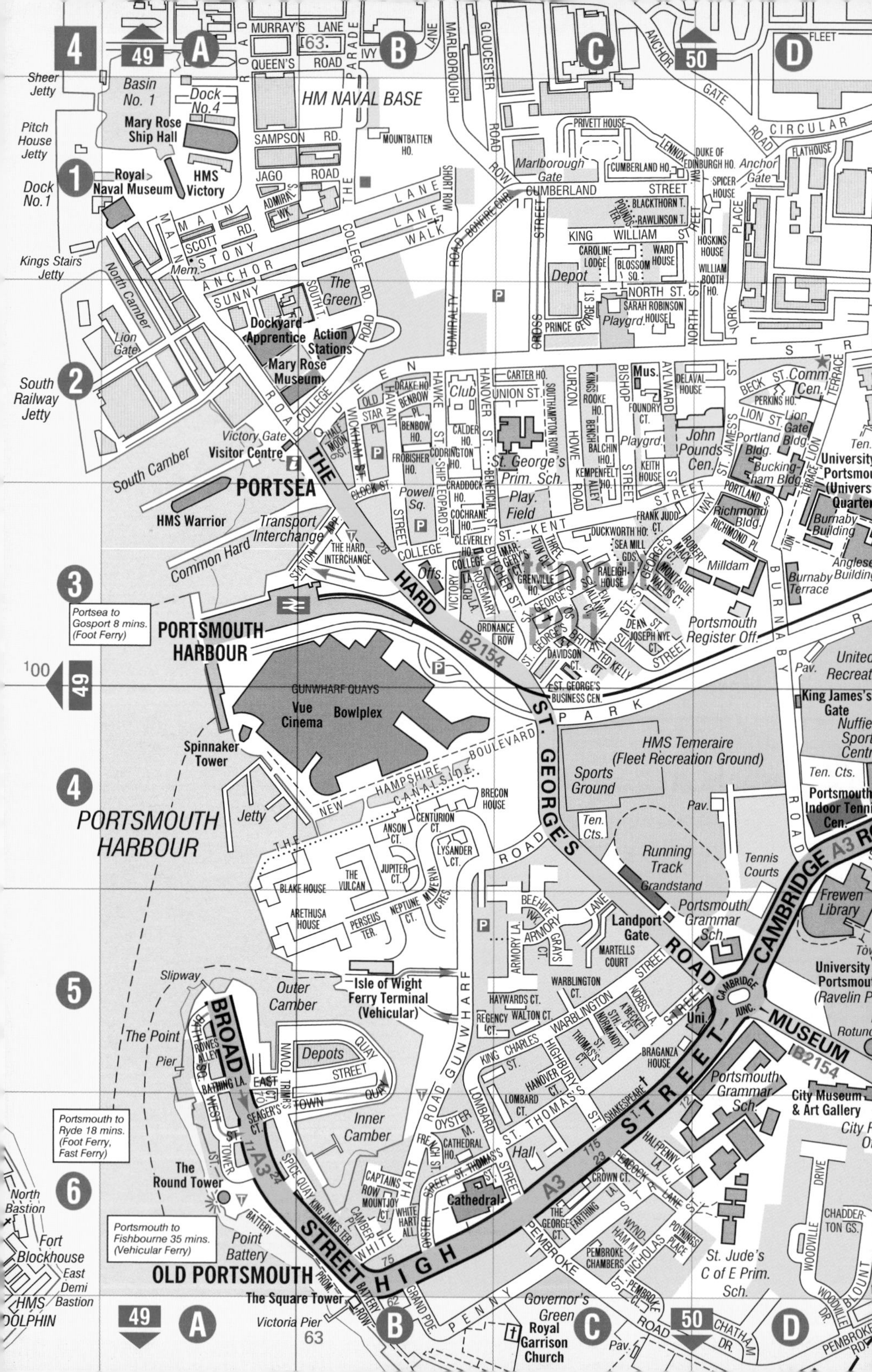
4
HM NAVAL BASE
Mary Rose Ship Hall
Royal Naval Museum
HMS Victory
Dockyard Apprentice
Action Stations
Mary Rose Museum
Victory Gate
Visitor Centre
PORTSEA
HMS Warrior
Transport Interchange
Portsea to Gosport 8 mins. (Foot Ferry)
PORTSMOUTH HARBOUR
GUNWHARF QUAYS
Vue Cinema
Bowlplex
Spinnaker Tower
PORTSMOUTH HARBOUR
HMS Temeraire (Fleet Recreation Ground)
Sports Ground
Running Track
Grandstand
Portsmouth Grammar Sch.
Landport Gate
Isle of Wight Ferry Terminal (Vehicular)
Outer Camber
Inner Camber
The Point
Portsmouth to Ryde 18 mins. (Foot Ferry, Fast Ferry)
The Round Tower
Portsmouth to Fishbourne 35 mins. (Vehicular Ferry)
Point Battery
OLD PORTSMOUTH
The Square Tower
Victoria Pier
Cathedral
Governor's Green
Royal Garrison Church
St. Jude's C of E Prim. Sch.
City Museum & Art Gallery
John Pounds Cen.
St. George's Prim. Sch.
Portsmouth Register Off.
King James's Gate
Portsmouth Indoor Tennis Cen.
Frewen Library
Fort Blockhouse
HMS DOLPHIN
QUEEN STREET
THE HARD
ST. GEORGE'S ROAD
CAMBRIDGE ROAD
HIGH STREET
BROAD STREET
MUSEUM ROAD
PARK ROAD
GUNWHARF ROAD
CUMBERLAND STREET
ANCHOR GATE ROAD
CIRCULAR ROAD

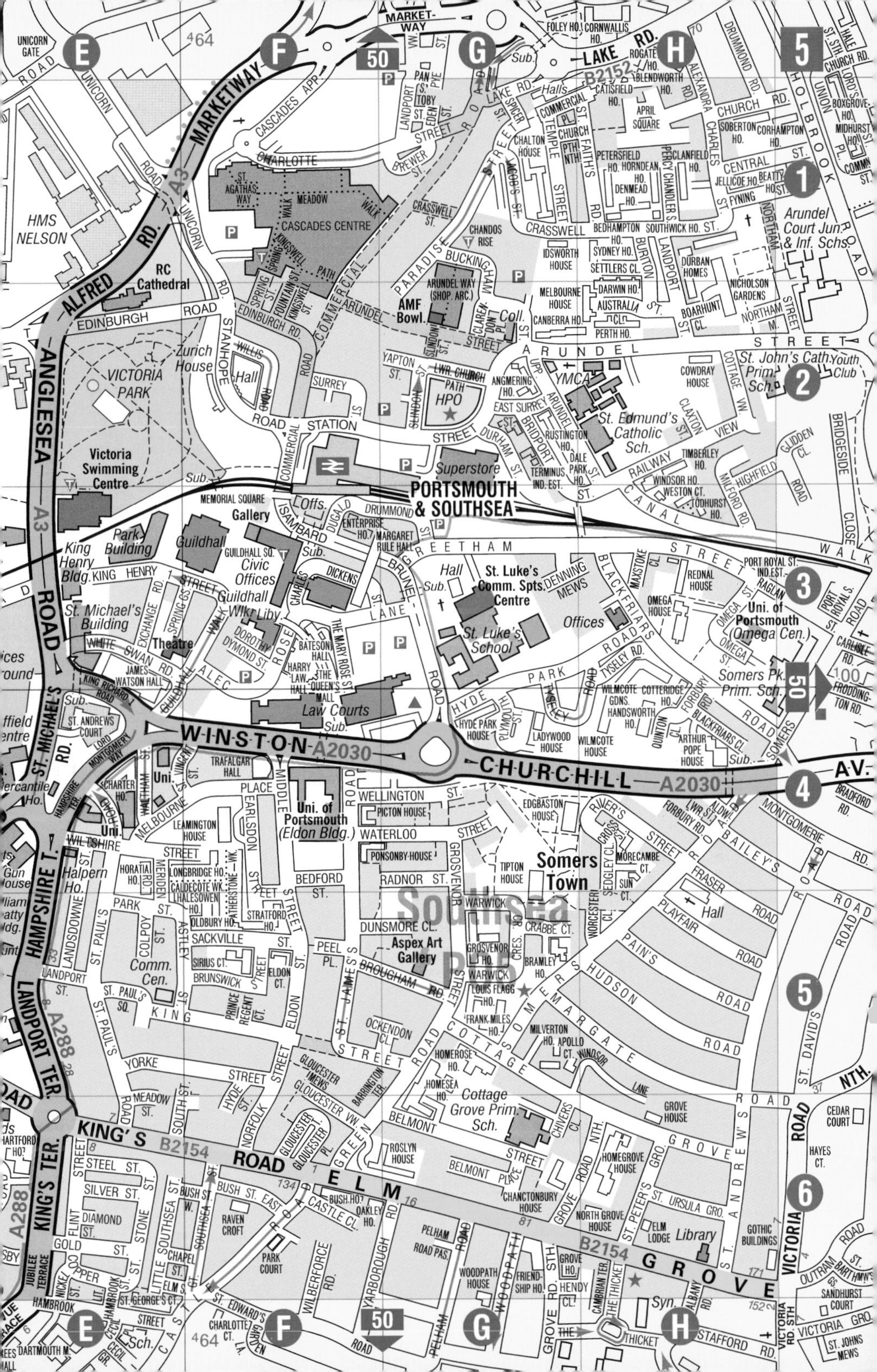

5
E
F
G
H
1
2
3
4
5
6
50
464
UNICORN GATE
MARKET-WAY
MARKETWAY
FOLEY HO.
CORNWALLIS HO.
LAKE RD.
B2152
ROGATE HO.
BLENDWORTH HO.
CATISFIELD HO.
DRUMMOND RD.
HOLBROOK ROAD
HALE ST. STH.
CHURCH RD.
LORD'S ST.
UNION PL.
BOXGROVE HO.
MIDHURST HO.
COMMN. ST.
ALEXANDRA CHARLES ST.
CHURCH RD.
SOBERTON HO.
CORHAMPTON HO.
CENTRAL ST.
BEATTY HO.
JELLICOE HO.
FYNING ST.
APRIL SQUARE
CLANFIELD HO.
PETERSFIELD HO.
HORNDEAN HO.
DENMEAD HO.
PERCY CHANDLER ST.
COMMERCIAL PL.
CHURCH PTH. NTH.
TEMPLE ST.
FAITH'S ST.
CHALTON HOUSE
Halls
Sub.
SPICER ST.
JACOB'S ST.
LAKE RD.
PAN ST.
TOBY ST.
EDEN ST.
PYE ST.
LANDPORT ST.
BREWER ST.
CASCADES APP.
CHARLOTTE ST.
UNICORN ROAD
ST. AGATHA'S WAY
MEADOW WALK
CASCADES CENTRE
KINGSWELL PATH
SPRING ST.
FOUNTAIN ST.
KINGSWELL ST.
CRASSWELL ST.
CRASSWELL ST.
BEDHAMPTON HO.
SOUTHWICK HO.
BURITON ST.
LANDPORT ST.
NORTHAM ST.
Arundel Court Jun. & Inf. Schs.
CHANDOS RISE
PARADISE ST.
BUCKINGHAM ST.
IDSWORTH HOUSE
SYDNEY HO.
SETTLERS CL.
DURBAN HOMES
NICHOLSON GARDENS
MELBOURNE HOUSE
DARWIN HO.
AUSTRALIA CL.
CANBERRA HO.
PERTH HO.
BOARHUNT CL.
NORTHAM M.
ARUNDEL WAY (SHOP. ARC.)
AMF Bowl.
CLARENDON PL.
Coll.
HMS NELSON
RC Cathedral
ALFRED RD.
A3
EDINBURGH ROAD
EDINBURGH RD.
STANHOPE RD.
COMMERCIAL RD.
ARUNDEL STREET
ARUNDEL STREET
ANGLESEA ROAD
VICTORIA PARK
Zurich House
WILLIS ST.
Hall
YAPTON ST.
LWR. CHURCH PATH
HPO
SLINDON ST.
SURREY ST.
STATION ROAD
ANGMERING HO.
UPP. ARUNDEL ST.
YMCA
COWDRAY HOUSE
COTTAGE VW.
St. John's Cath. Prim. Sch.
Youth Club
EAST SURREY ST.
RUSTINGTON HO.
BRIDPORT ST.
St. Edmund's Catholic Sch.
CLAYTON ST.
VIEW
BRIDGESIDE CLOSE
GLIDDEN CL.
HIGHFIELD ROAD
Victoria Swimming Centre
Sub.
STREET
DURHAM ST.
Superstore
DALE PARK HO.
TERMINUS IND. EST.
RAILWAY
TIMBERLEY HO.
WINDSOR HO.
WESTON CT.
TODHURST HO.
MILFORD RD.
CANAL WALK
PORTSMOUTH & SOUTHSEA
MEMORIAL SQUARE
Offs.
DUGALD DRUMMOND ST.
Gallery
ISAMBARD BRUNEL RD.
ENTERPRISE HO.
MARGARET RULE HALL
Park Building
Guildhall
King Henry Bldg.
GUILDHALL SQ.
Civic Offices
Sub.
GREETHAM STREET
Hall
St. Luke's Comm. Spts. Centre
DENNING MEWS
BLACKFRIARS RD.
MAXSTOKE CL.
REDNAL HOUSE
PORT ROYAL ST. IND. EST.
PORT ROYAL ST.
RAGLAN ST.
KING HENRY 1 STREET
EXCHANGE RD.
SPRING GS.
CHARLES ST.
DICKENS
Guildhall Wlk.
Liby.
ST. LANE
OMEGA HOUSE
Uni. of Portsmouth (Omega Cen.)
OMEGA ST.
St. Michael's Building
WHITE SWAN RD.
Theatre
DOROTHY DYMOND ST.
ROSE ST.
BATESON HALL
THE MARY ROSE ST.
St. Luke's School
Offices
TYSELEY RD.
PARK ROAD
CARLISLE RD.
Somers Pk. Prim. Sch.
100
FRODDINGTON RD.
JAMES WATSON HALL
GUILDHALL WALK
ALEC ROSE
HARRY LAW HALL
THE QUEEN'S MALL
HYDE PARK ROAD
WILMCOTE GDNS.
COTTERIDGE HO.
HANDSWORTH HO.
FORBURY RD.
BLACKFRIARS CL.
KING RICHARD 1 ROAD
Sub.
ST. ANDREWS COURT
LORD MONTGOMERY WAY
Law Courts
Sub.
HYDE PARK HOUSE
PLYMOUTH ST.
LADYWOOD HOUSE
WILMCOTE HOUSE
QUINTON CL.
ARTHUR POPE HOUSE
SOMERS ROAD
Sub.
WINSTON
A2030
CHURCHILL
A2030
AV.
ST. MICHAEL'S RD.
WALTHAM ST.
Uni.
ST. VINCENT ST.
TRAFALGAR HALL
MIDDLE ST.
CHARTER HO.
PLACE
Uni. of Portsmouth (Eldon Bldg.)
WELLINGTON ST.
PICTON HOUSE
EDGBASTON HOUSE
RIVER'S ST.
LWR. FORBURY RD.
ALDWICH RD.
BRADFORD RD.
MONTGOMERIE RD.
HAMPSHIRE TER.
MELBOURNE PL.
LEAMINGTON HOUSE
EARLSDON ST.
WATERLOO STREET
CROSS ST.
BAILEY'S ROAD
Uni.
WILTSHIRE ST.
STREET
PONSONBY HOUSE
GROSVENOR ST.
TIPTON HOUSE
Somers Town
SEDGLEY CL.
MORECAMBE CT.
SUN CT.
FRASER ROAD
Halpern Ho.
HORATIA HO.
MERIDEN RD.
LONGBRIDGE HO.
CALDECOTE WK.
HALESOWEN HO.
ATHERSTONE WK.
RADNOR ST.
BEDFORD ST.
Hall
PLAYFAIR ROAD
HAMPSHIRE T.
PARK ST.
OLDBURY HO.
STRATFORD HO.
WARWICK CRES.
CRABBE CT.
WORCESTER CL.
LANDSDOWNE ST.
ST. PAUL'S RD.
COLPOY ST.
ASTLEY ST.
SACKVILLE ST.
DUNSMORE CL.
Aspex Art Gallery
GROSVENOR HO.
BRAMLEY HO.
PAIN'S ROAD
HUDSON ROAD
Comm. Cen.
SIRIUS CT.
BRUNSWICK ST.
ELDON CT.
PEEL PL.
BROUGHAM RD.
WARWICK
LOUIS FLAGG HO.
SOMERS RD.
MARGATE ROAD
LANDPORT ST.
ST. PAUL'S SQ.
KING ST.
PRINCE REGENT CT.
ELDON ST.
ST. JAMES'S STREET
OCKENDON CL.
FRANK MILES HO.
MILVERTON HO.
APOLLO CT.
WINDSOR LANE
ST. DAVID'S RD.
LANDPORT TER.
A288
ST. PAUL'S RD.
YORKE STREET
GLOUCESTER MEWS
BARRINGTON TER.
COTTAGE GROVE
HOMEROSE HO.
HOMESEA HO.
Cottage Grove Prim. Sch.
CHIVERS CL.
37
NTH.
ROAD
MEADOW ST.
SOUTH ST.
HYDE ST.
NORFOLK ST.
GLOUCESTER VW.
BELMONT ST.
GROVE HOUSE
CEDAR COURT
KING'S TER.
KING'S ROAD
B2154
STEEL ST.
GLOUCESTER PL.
GREEN ROAD
ROSLYN HOUSE
BELMONT PLACE
HOMEGROVE HOUSE
ST. ANDREW'S RD.
HAYES CT.
SILVER ST.
BUSH ST. W.
BUSH ST. EAST
ELM GROVE
CASTLE CL.
BUSH HO.
OAKLEY HO.
CHANCTONBURY HOUSE
GROVE ROAD NTH.
ST. PETER'S GRO.
ST. URSULA GRO.
VICTORIA ROAD
FLINT ST.
DIAMOND ST.
STONE ST.
RAVEN CROFT
SOUTHSEA TER.
PELHAM ROAD PAS.
NORTH GROVE HOUSE
ELM LODGE
Library
GOTHIC BUILDINGS
GOLD ST.
JUBILEE TERRACE
COPPER ST.
NICKEL ST.
HAMBROOK ST.
LITTLE SOUTHSEA ST.
CHAPEL ST.
ELM ST.
PARK COURT
WILBERFORCE RD.
YARBOROUGH RD.
WOODPATH HOUSE
FRIENDSHIP HO.
GROVE RD. STH.
GROVE HO.
CAMBRIAN TER.
THE THICKET
B2154
OUTRAM RD.
BARTHMW'S GDNS.
SANDHURST COURT
HAMBROOK ST.
ST. GEORGE'S CT.
STREET
CASTLE RD.
ST. EDWARD'S RD.
CHARLOTTE CT.
GARDEN LA.
PELHAM RD.
HENDY CL.
Syn.
ALBANY RD.
THE THICKET
STAFFORD RD.
VICTORIA RD. STH.
VICTORIA GRO.
ST. JOHNS MEWS
DARTMOUTH M.
CECIL GR.
Sch.

6
69
470
INSET
A
B
C
D
16
15
14
13
1
2
3
4
5
6
Down House
Reservoir (covered)
Hinton Heights
Hinton Manor
HINTON MANOR LANE
DOWNHOUSE ROAD
DRIFT ROAD
TRAFALGAR PL.
FARM VIEW
SUNDERTON LA.
ST. DAVID'S RD.
Nursery
Charity Farm
Greylands Farm and Kennels
PINE DR.
STORRINGTON RD.
GORING AV.
BLACKBERRY CL.
WALBURTON WAY
HARTING WAY
MIDDLETON RI.
CHILWORTH GDS.
ST. JAMES CL.
SINGLETON GDS.
HEYSHOTT GS.
ELDERBERRY CL.
LODSWORTH CL.
TILLINGTON GS.
Petersgate Inf. Sch.
FIELDFARE CL.
KESTREL CL.
REDWING RD.
REDWING CL.
RIDGE CL.
NEW ROAD
GREEN LANE
MEON CL.
ARLE CL.
VALLEY PARK DR.
GODWIN CRES.
WHITE DIRT LA.
SAXON CL.
FIRST AVENUE
CHALK RIDGE RD.
HILLSIDE CL.
HILLTOP GDS.
Snell's Corner
NEW BARN FARM
LONDON ROAD
A3
DRAYCOTE RD.
VIKING WAY
WESSEX RD.
Butser Ct.
WODE CL.
FRANCIS RD.
BLACKTHORN RD.
BELMONT CL.
MOBILE HOME PK.
ROMSEY RD.
White Dirt Farm
WHITE DIRT LANE
WREXHAM GRO.
GLAMORGAN ROAD
CATHERINGTON HILL
Kingswood
Lawrence Row
Munday's Row
Coombs Copse
SOUTHDOWN RISE
SOUTHDOWN ROAD
DERWENT CL.
THORNFIELD CL.
The Hollies
NORTHFIELD CL.
ST. HILDA AV.
ESKDALE CL.
ENNERDALE CL.
TARN RD.
ST. GILES WY.
WASDALE CL.
ST. ANDREW CL.
ST. MICHAELS WAY
ST. HUBERT RD.
CLAIRE GS.
NORTH ROAD
HAWTHORN
OLD LANE
Reservoir (covered)
Vicarage
Church House
Playing Field
Catherington C of E Inf. Sch.
Hall
St. Catherines
Catherington Down Nature Reserve
Kinches Farm
LOVEDEAN LANE
SOUTH RD.
SOUTH ROAD
THE VALE
DOWNWOOD WAY
COOMBS CL.
MUNDAYS RW.
WELL COPSE CL.
HOLDENHURST CL.
CHERVIL CLOSE
JUNIPER R.
DOWN RD.
LITH LANE
Junction 1
LOVAGE WY.
COMFREY CL.
DOWN FARM PL.
HORNDEAN CARAVAN SITE
HILLSIDE IND. EST.
A3(M)
Catherington Lith
LITH CRESCENT
LITH LANE
Blendworth Lith
Catherington
HILL ROADS
Kingscourt School
Waterlooville
PO8
FIVE HEADS ROAD
White Gate Farm
Strip Lychets
Randells
LUCKY LITE FARM CARAVAN PARK
LITH LANE
CATHERINGTON BUSINESS PARK
CATHERINGTON LANE
LITH AVENUE
ENTERPRISE RD.
ENTERPRISE IND. EST.
HIGHCROFT IND. EST.
HIGHCROFT LANE
CHALK HILL RD.
DURLAND RD.
BENTLEY CL.
Highcroft Row
A3(M) MOTORWAY
TAGDELL
PATH
BRIDLE
Football Ground
Pavilion
Recreation Ground
LYCHGATE DR.
CHANTRY RD.
MAYNARD PL.
WENTWORTH DR.
HORNDEAN
CROUCH LANE
COLDHILL LANE
AVOCET WAY
TEAL CL.
WALDEN GS.
Horndean Technology College
PRINCESS GDNS.
ST. ANN'S RD.
STAGSHORN RD.
HIGHCROFT LA.
TARBERY CR.
LARBERT
BRIDGET CL.
CRESCENT
THE YEWS
A3 ROAD
Crookley Park Ho.
Blendworth
WESTFIELD IND. EST.
Brewery
Meadowdown Farm
WARBLER CL.
GOLDCREST CL.
CROSSBILL CL.
SWIFT CL.
CHERITON CL.
HEATH CLOSE
Drill Hall
Horndean C of E Jun. Sch.
Horndean Inf. Sch.
JODREL CL.
BENBOW CL.
Lib.
Horndean Pct.
BLENDWORTH LANE
FALCON RD.
HARRIER CL.
JAY CL.
SANDPIPER CL.
LAPWING CL.
SHANK RD.
BARTON CROSS
BOWES-LYON CT.
QUEENS
NELSON CR.
CUNNINGHAM RD.
Knighton Cnr.
PORTSMOUTH RD.
HAVANT RD.
B2149
KILDERKIN DR.
FROGMORE LANE
STONECHAT
NIGHTJAR CL.
WAGTAIL RD.
MERCHISTOUN ROAD
Rosecott
Yoells Copse
PENTERE RD.
SHEPPARD CL.
RODNEY
MURRAY RD.
10
DORSET CL.
NAPIER ROAD
WESSEX GATE INDUSTRIAL EST.
ORCHARD
AVENUE
ST. VINCENT CRES.
CHURCH

7
INSET
E
F
G
H
1
2
3
4
5
6
470
71
72
73
17
16
14
13
11
CLANFIELD
Waterlooville
PO8
Sunnyfields
Clanfield Chase
Clanfield Jun. Sch.
Manor Farm
Downs View
Recreation Ground
Pav.
Swallow Ct.
Hall
Down Farm
Meadow Croft Farm
Barnfield
Down House
EAST MEON ROAD
LITTLE HYDEN LA.
BRAMBLE LA.
NORTH LANE
PETERSFIELD ROAD
CHALTON LANE
IVY
ORCHARD ROAD
CHURCH CL.
KINGSBURY CT.
POND LA.
NICKLEBY RD.
WILKINS CL.
HOMEFIELD WY.
HAMBLEDON ROAD
SOUTH LANE
GREEN LANE
WINDMILL CL.
NEW ROAD
MAPLE CRESCENT
BEECH ROAD
SYCAMORE CL.
OAK RD.
WHITE BEAM RISE
HAZEL RD.
HAZEL GROVE
ROSEWOOD GDS.
SANDLEWOOD CL.
ALDRIDGE CL.
JACOBS CL.
JASMINE WAY
PINE DR.
STORRINGTON
DUNCTON RD.
REDWING RD.
GORING AV.
PEAK RD.
PIPERS MEAD
SWORD CL.
MANOR LANE
HINTON
DOWNHOUSE RD.
DRIFT ROAD
TRAFALGAR PL.
FARM VIEW AV.
SUNDERTON LANE
ST. DAVID'S RD.
LONDON RD.
LONDON-A3-RD.
Hawquins
New Barn Farm
BARN LANE
FARM LANE
SOUTH LANE
Netherley Down
Crabden Row
CRABDEN LANE
DUCKSTILE
(DUCKPOND LA.)
Blendworth Farm
Six Bells Farm
Southview Farm
Broxburn House
Play. Fld.
HORNDEAN ROAD
BOYES LANE
St. Giles Farm
LANE
WICK HANGER
Wick Farm
Murrants
Idsworth House
The New Blendworth Centre
Cadlington House
Hook Cottage
Nobles Farm
PATTERSONS LANE
WOODHOUSE LA.
Idsworth Villa
IDSWORTH PARK

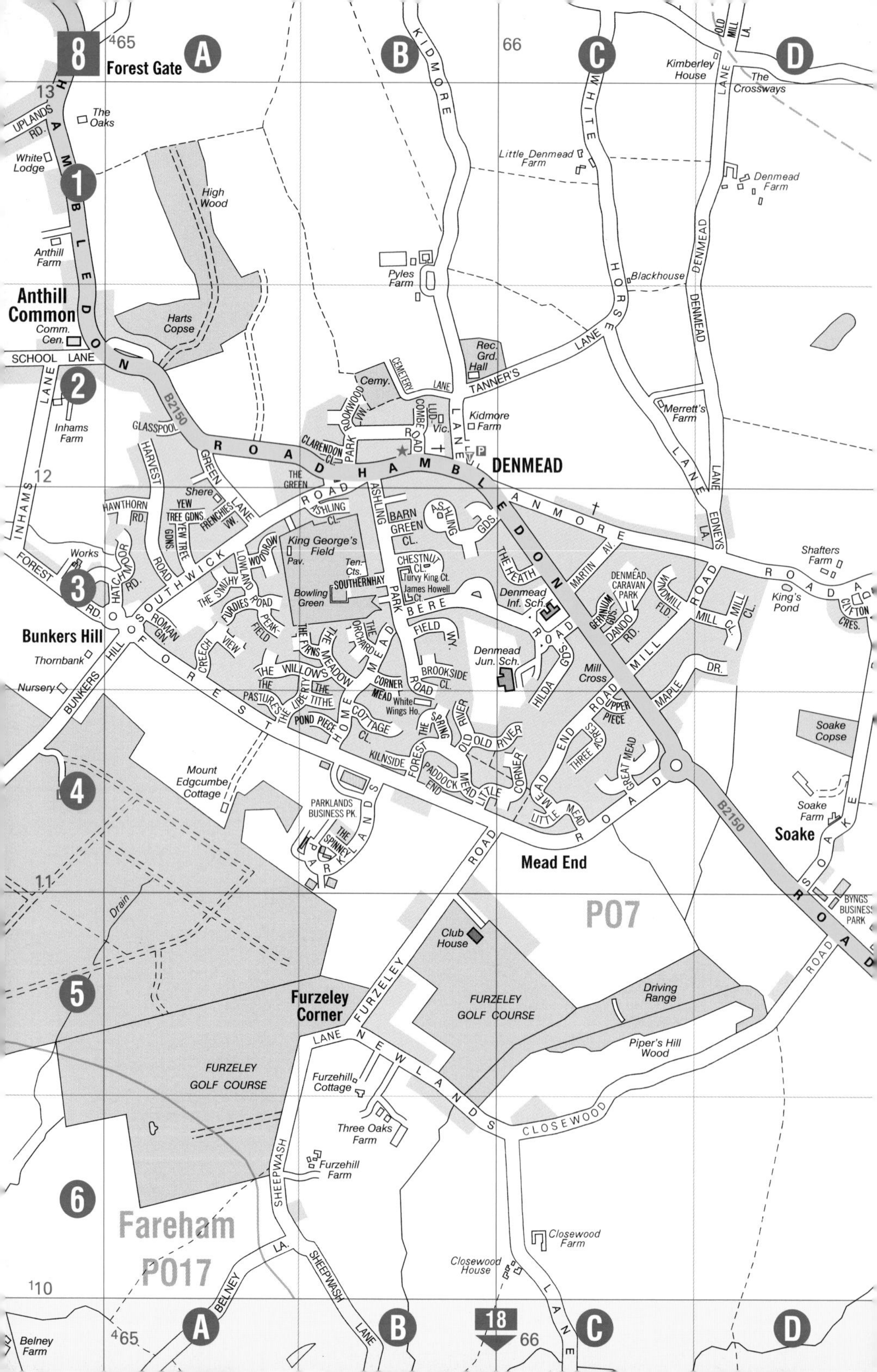

Forest Gate
Anthill Common
Comm. Cen.
School Lane
Hambledon Road
B2150
Uplands Rd.
The Oaks
White Lodge
Anthill Farm
High Wood
Harts Copse
Inhams Farm
Inhams Lane
Glasspool
Harvest Road
Green Lane
The Green
Shere
Yew Tree Gdns.
Frenchies Vw.
Hawthorn Rd.
Hatchmoor Rd.
Works
Forest Rd.
Bunkers Hill
Thornbank
Nursery
Southwick Road
Ashling Cl.
Woodrow
Lowland Road
The Smithy
Furdies
Peak Field
Roman Gn.
Creech View
King George's Field
Pav.
Ten. Cts.
Southernhay
Bowling Green
The Firns
The Meadow
The Orchard
Mead
The Willows
The Pastures
The Liberty
The Tithe
Pond Piece
Home Cottage Cl.
Corner Mead
White Wings Ho.
Forest Road
Kilnside
Forest End
Paddock Mead
The Spring
River
Old River
Little Corner
Mead End Road
Little Mead
Three Acres
Upper Piece
Great Mead
Mount Edgcumbe Cottage
Parklands Business Pk.
Parklands
The Spinney
Mead End
P07
Club House
Furzeley Golf Course
Furzeley Corner
Furzeley Lane
Newlands
Closewood Road
Driving Range
Piper's Hill Wood
Furzehill Cottage
Three Oaks Farm
Furzehill Farm
Sheepwash Lane
Belney La.
Belney Farm
Fareham
P017
Closewood Farm
Closewood House
Closewood Lane
Kidmore Lane
Pyles Farm
Cemetery Lane
Cemy.
Rookwood Vw.
Ludcombe
Clarendon Cl.
Park Road
Vic.
Kidmore Farm
Rec. Grd. Hall
Tanner's Lane
DENMEAD
Ashling Park Road
Barn Green Cl.
Ashling Gds.
Chestnut Cl.
Turvy King Ct.
James Howell Ct.
Bere Road
Field Wy.
Brookside Road
Brookside Cl.
Denmead Inf. Sch.
Denmead Jun. Sch.
The Heath
Hilda Gds.
Anmore Road
Martin Av.
Mill Cross
Mill Road
Geranium Gds.
Dando Rd.
Windmill Fld.
Denmead Caravan Park
Mill Cl.
Maple Dr.
White Horse Lane
Little Denmead Farm
Blackhouse
Merrett's Farm
Kimberley House
Old Mill La.
The Crossways
Denmead Farm
Denmead Lane
Edneys La.
Shafters Farm
King's Pond
Clifton Cres.
Soake Copse
Soake Farm
Soake
Soake Road
Byngs Business Park
465
66
13
12
11
10

18

9
Lovedean
Eastland Gate
PO8
EAST HAMPSHIRE
HAVANT
Wecock
Waterlooville
COWPLAIN
WINCHESTER
EAST HAMPSHIRE
THE QUEEN'S INCLOSURE
Yoells Copse
James's Copse
Coldhill Copse
Broadway Farm House
Little ...enmead Farm
Lower Chapters
The Arrows
Eastland Gate Cottages
Yewtree Cottage
Shrover
Woodcroft Farm
Woodcroft
Clarendon Farm
Meadowlands Jun. Sch.
Meadowlands Inf. Sch.
Rec. Grd.
Comm. Cen.
Patrick Howard Dobson Ct.
Recreation Ground
Rachel Madocks Sch.
Woodlands Education Centre
Wecock Common
Woodlands Prim. Sch.
Conners Keep
Sundridge School
Cowplain Comm. Sch.
South Downs College
Hart Plain Inf. Sch.
Playing Fields
Hart Plain Jun. Sch.
Hambledon Parade
Old Park Farm
Works
THE BRAMBLES ENTERPRISE CENTRE
Waterlooville Leisure Cen.
Cherry Tree Apartments
CHURCHILL YARD IND. ESTATE
Playground
Bowling Grn.
Waterlooville Rec. Grd.
Pav.
Tennis Courts
Park Wood
Highfield Pde.
Weir
THE BRAMBLES BUS. CEN.
BRAMBLES FARM INDUSTRIAL
PARKWOOD CENTRE
Mission Lane
Fernwood Ho.
HAMBLEDON ROAD
B2150
LONDON ROAD
A3
BROADWAY LANE
LOVEDEAN LANE
HART PLAIN AVENUE
MILTON ROAD
SILVESTER ROAD
KING'S ROAD
LONGWOOD AVENUE
EAGLE AVENUE
FLAG AVENUE
WOODCROFT LANE
FROGMORE LANE
HIGHFIELD ROAD
WALLIS ROAD
ROWLANDS AVENUE
SUNNYMEAD DRIVE
HASLAR CRESCENT
CRESCENT ROAD
CHAUCER CL.
68
69
10
11
12
13
19
E
F
G
H
1
2
3
4
5
6

10
69
A
B
C
D
6
470
13
Yoells Copse
1
2
3
4
5
6
12
11
110
Horndean Inf. Sch.
BOWES-LYON CT.
BARTON CROSS
CATHERINGTON
MERCHISTOUN
ROAD
FALCON RD.
HARRIER CL.
JAY CL.
LAPWING CL.
SHANK RD.
WAGTAIL
STONECHAT
PENTERE RD.
SHEPPARD CL.
PIPIT CL.
QUAIL WAY
RODNEY WAY
MURRAY ROAD
Comm. Cen.
DORSET CL.
BOURNE CL.
NAPIER ROAD
Ten. Cts.
ROOKES CL.
ST. VINCENT CRES.
AVENUE
VICTORY
EPERSTON R.
ELMESWELLE RD.
APPLE GATE PL.
CHURCHILL CT.
COPPICE
THE SPINNEY
BIRDLIP CL.
COPSE LANE
WEST-BROOKE
BRIARFIELD GDNS.
KINGS MEDE
ACORN GDS.
LYNE PL.
CAUSEWAY FM.
OAKS COPPICE
MURRAY LANE
BULLS COPSE LANE
TILFORD RD.
YOELLS LANE
LENSYD GDS.
YOELLS CR.
WELCHWOOD
FROGMORE
ROSE HILL
ASH COPSE
CRICKET DR.
ELAINE GS.
GYPSY LA.
LOVEDEAN LANE
WOODSTOCK AVENUE
BLENHEIM ROAD
BLENHEIM RD.
WILTON DRIVE
KINGS CROSS LA.
WINKFIELD ROW
HERRIOTT CL.
ROSELANDS
NURSERY GS.
FARM-HOUSE WY.
BEVAN RD.
ASPEN WY.
CYPRESS CRES
KEYDELL CL.
KEYDELL AVENUE
PARKLANDS
WODBURY GRO.
HUNTSMAN
PUMP LA.
THISTLEDOWN
PORTSMOUTH ROAD
A3
166
120
145
30
DELL PIECE WEST
B2149
HAZLETON
LAKESMERE ROAD
HAZLETON IND. EST.
Superstore
WESSEX GATE INDUSTRIAL EST.
ORCHARD
A3(M)
A3(M) — MOTORWAY
Rosecott
HAVANT ROAD
SHEEPWASH ROAD
Rushmore Cottages
Redcroft Row
DELL PIECE EAST
Junction 2
Hazelton Farm
WELLINGTON CL.
WHITEHAVEN
CHURCH
ROWLANDS
BRIAR CLOSE
ACACIA GDS.
DEEP DELL
LINDEN WY.
CEDAR
WHITEBEAM CL.
LARCHFIELD WY.
FIR TREE GS.
HILLVIEW
GREENFIELD CRESCENT
CHESTNUT AV.
MAPLETREE AV.
HOLLYBANK CL.
Hazleton Wood
PO8
ALMOND CL.
LAUREL RD.
CRESCENT
BEECH WAY
VALE WAY
ROSEMARY WAY
WYNDHAM CL.
PROCHURCH RD.
AVENUE CRESCENT
VERBENA CRESCENT
FURZE WY.
ELDERBERRY WY.
EGLANTINE
MAGNOLIA WAY
Waterlooville
BOWERS CLOSE
KENDAL CL.
LINCOLN RISE
CL. ROAD
SPRING VALE
COTWELL
GRANADA CL.
GALAXIE RD.
ERICA WY.
ERICA CL.
CELANDINE
MARJORAM CRES.
HAZLETON
FAIRMEAD WALK
MEADOW RISE
GREENFIELD
GREENFIELD CR.
CRESTLAND CL.
GREENFIELD RISE
Padnell Cuts Wood
SHEEPWASH
EAST HAMPSHIRE
HAVANT
BLENDWORTH COMMON
FLAG WK.
Thames Ct.
CROMBIE CL.
Hamble Ct.
Avon Ct.
Itchen Ct.
Rec. Grd.
PASSINGHAM WALK
HARCOURT CL.
Courtlands Ter.
PYLE CL.
HEMSLEY WK.
WESTERMARSH RD.
KEATS
RUSKIN WAY
CRESCENT
GLADYS AVENUE
DORRITA AV.
ASHINGTON CL.
DENE GS.
South Vw.
LONGWOOD AVENUE
MORLEY CRES.
BREWSTER CL.
FOREST CL.
COWPLAIN
MILBECK CL.
LATCHMORE FOREST GRO.
SUMMERHILL ROAD
GLADES AV.
DURLEY AV.
LINDA GRO.
KING'S ROAD
Mission Lane
Vicarage
PADNELL ROAD
LONDON ROAD
Padnell Jun. Sch.
Herriot House
Cowplain Pav. Recreation Ground
Cowplain Activity Centre
Padnell Inf. Sch.
Bowl. Grn.
Ten. Ct.
PADNELL AVENUE
PADNELL PL.
CHERRY TREE AV.
Padnell Grange
WATERLOOVILLE GOLF COURSE
THE OAKS
Fernwood Ho.
HOLMAN CL.
WINSCOMBE AV.
CONIFER CL.
PINE TREE GDS.
WILLOW TREE AV.
DUDLESTON HEATH DR.
HURST GN. CL.
FAIRY CROSS WY.
YEW TREE AV.
ROWAN AV.
CHERRY TREE
Club House
PARK LANE
THE QUEEN'S INCLOSURE
IDSWORTH
STEPHEN
GLENEAGLES DR.
PINEHURST CL.
GRASSMERE WAY
MOOR PARK
MEADOWSWEET
ANVIL CL.
FARRIERS WY.
GOODWOOD CL.
LAVANT CL.
FONTWELL M.
CHEPSTOW CL.
HAYDOCK M.
Comm. Cen.
SHIRE CL.
BARN FOLD
ACRE LA.
CORNBROOK GRO.
Queen's Inclosure Prim. Sch.
AINTREE DR.
RIPON GRO.
THE WESTBROOK CENTRE
Playing Field
PLUMPTON GRO.
WINCANTON WY.
KEMPTON PK.
GRASSMERE
DAMASK GS.
BRACKEN HEATH
RAMBLERS
THRESHER CL.
EDGEFIELD GRO.
HITHER-WOOD CL.
BELL'S COPSE
BURNSIDE
INHURST AV.
HIGHFIELD CL.
HIGHFIELD
Highfield Pde.
MEADOWLANDS
LINK
PRINCES DR.
PO7
CARDINAL DR.
HATHAWAY
CORNELIUS
DORCAS
JESSICA CL.
SENTINEL GS.
TEMPEST AV.
CORALIN GRO.
SALET WY.
NERISSA CL.
CELIA CL.
SONNET WY.
Beech Wood
LYSANDER
STARINA GDS.
TUSCANY
HARKNESS
ROUNDWAY
FERNDALE
THE GLADE
20

E
F
G
H
7
72
73
11
13
Nobles Farm
Hook Cottage
PATTERSONS LANE
WOODHOUSE LANE
Idsworth House
Idsworth Villa
IDSWORTH PARK
Treadwheel Farm
1
CASTLE ROAD
TREADWHEEL ROAD
Idsworth Lodge
Eastlands
Wood-house
Woodhouse Farm
PYLE LANE
Pyle Farm
Soakfield Row
Deadman's Dell
BROAD
Motleys Copse
Ring and Bailey
Earthwork
MAGPIE ROAD
LANE
2
Magpie
THE HOLT
Holt Pond
WALK
12
Magpie Cottages
WALK MAGPIE
BROAD
3
WOODHOUSE
Woodhouse Ashes Farm
B2149
THE HOLT
STEIN WOOD
WALK
LANE
BOWES
Little Woodhouse
WELLSWORTH LA.
MEADOW-LANDS
4
HOLT GDNS.
Loscott's Plain
GREATFIELD WAY
THE
HILL
Horsefoot Hill
11
ROWLANDS CASTLE GOLF COURSE
LINKS
PEAK
ROWLANDS CASTLE
Recreation Ground
HAVANT THICKET
ROAD
Tennis Cts.
Pav.
FAIRWAY
Swallow Holes
5
THE GREEN
Club House
LINKS LANE
THE GREEN
The Forest
CASTLE
Motte and Bailey
MANOR
KINGS CL.
Long Wood
Works
STANSTED CL.
The Avenue
ROYAL GS.
NIGHTINGALE CL.
Rowlands Castle
ROAD
COLLEGE
B2149
Kings Way
Red Hill
KINGFISHER CL.
DUNNOCK CL.
PO9
COLLEGE CL.
YARDLEA CL.
CLOSE
HAVANT THICKET
BLACKCAP CL.
BRAMBLING RD.
THE
DRIFT
6
Furzy Plain
LODGE
MALLARD RD.
HILL BROW CL.
Red Hill Farm
Monument
NUTHATCH CL.
HAZELDEAN CT.
Lodge
Oaklands House
HAZELDEAN DR.
Upper Lake
Bettina
Hall
REDHILL
STAUNTON COUNTRY PARK
10
Mem.
ROAD
21
72
Rowlands Castle St. John's C of E Prim. Sch.
73
Gipsies

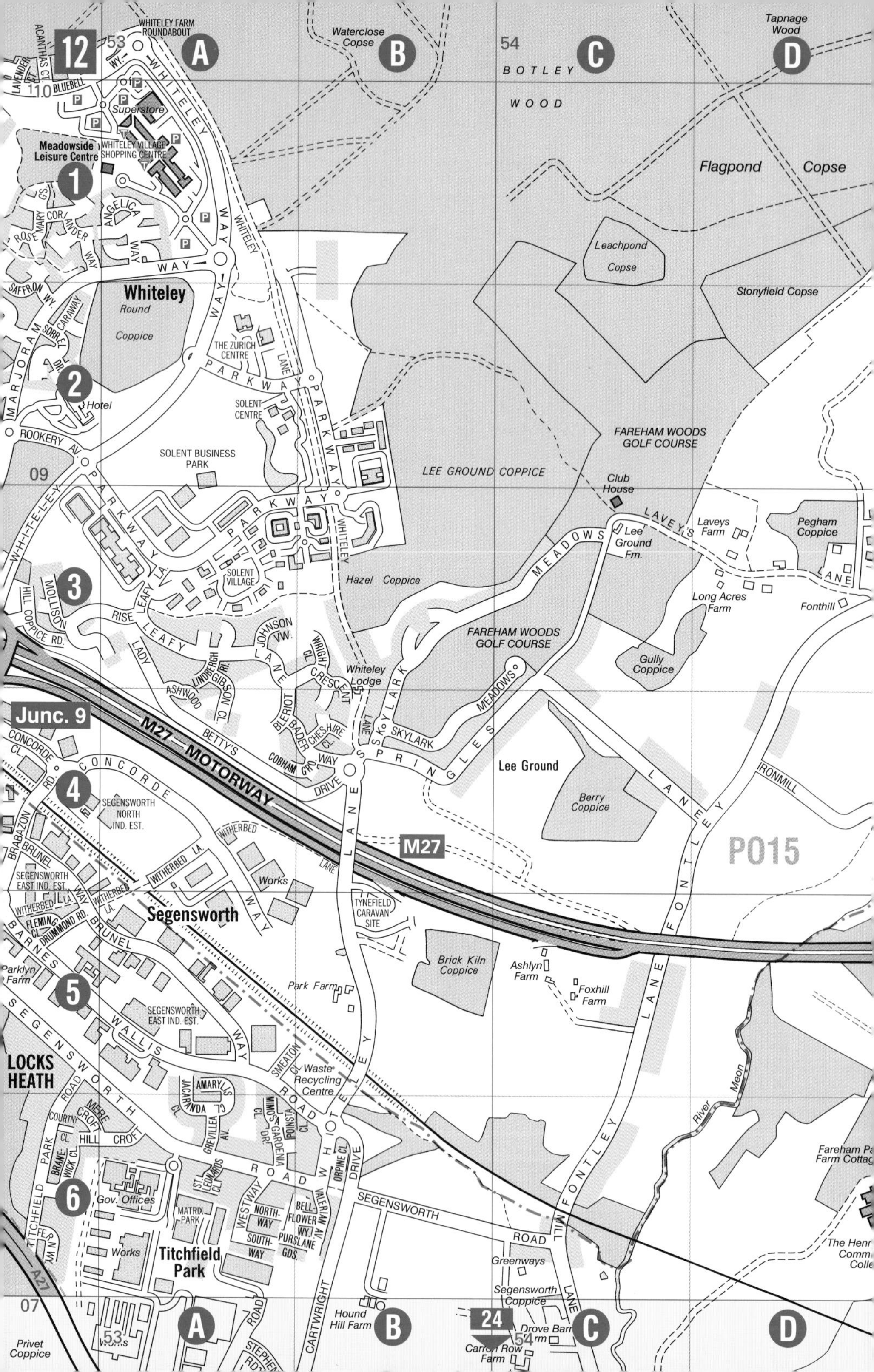
12
A
B
C
D
53
54
09
07
1
2
3
4
5
6
Whiteley Farm Roundabout
Waterclose Copse
Botley Wood
Tapnage Wood
Flagpond Copse
Leachpond Copse
Stonyfield Copse
Meadowside Leisure Centre
Superstore
Whiteley Village Shopping Centre
Whiteley
Round Coppice
The Zurich Centre
Solent Centre
Solent Business Park
Solent Village
Hotel
Fareham Woods Golf Course
Lee Ground Coppice
Club House
Laveys Farm
Pegham Coppice
Lee Ground Fm.
Long Acres Farm
Fonthill
Hazel Coppice
Gully Coppice
Whiteley Lodge
Lee Ground
Berry Coppice
Junc. 9
M27 Motorway
M27
PO15
Segensworth North Ind. Est.
Segensworth East Ind. Est.
Segensworth
Works
Tynefield Caravan Site
Brick Kiln Coppice
Ashlyn Farm
Foxhill Farm
Park Farm
Parklyn Farm
Waste Recycling Centre
Locks Heath
River Meon
Fareham Park Farm Cottages
Gov. Offices
Matrix Park
Titchfield Park
Greenways
Segensworth Coppice
The Henry Cort Community College
Hound Hill Farm
24
Drove Barn Farm
Carron Row Farm
Privet Coppice
A27
Whiteley Way
Parkway
Whiteley Lane
Rookery Av.
Marjoram
Laveys Lane
Meadows
Skylark
Springles Lane
Fontley Lane
Ironmill Lane
Concorde Way
Brabazon Rd.
Brunel Way
Witherbed La.
Barnes Way
Wallis Way
Segensworth Road
Cartwright Drive
Mill Lane
Titchfield Park Road
Hill Croft
Westway
North-Way
South-Way
Leafy Lane
Lady Betty's Drive
Coppice Rd.
Rise
Mollison
Johnson Vw.
Wright Cl.
Crescent
Bader Way
Cheshire Cl.
Cobham Gro.
Saffron Wy.
Bluebell Wy.
Angelica Way
Coriander Way
Caraway
Sorrel Dr.
Lindbergh Ri.
Gibson Cl.
Ashwood
Bleriot
Fleming Cl.
Drummond Rd.
Smeaton Cl.
Amaryllis Cl.
Jacaranda Cl.
Grevillea Av.
Mimosa Dr.
Gardenia Dr.
Poinsta Cl.
Orpine Cl.
Valerian Av.
Bell-flower Wy.
Purslane Gds.
St. Leonards Cl.
Courtney Cl.
Mere Croft
Brane-wick Cl.
Stephen Rd.

13
E
F
G
H
55
56
57
110
09
08
07
1
2
3
4
5
6
14
25
Dandy Copse
Dash Wood
Aytesbury Copse
Ravens Wood
Everett's Coppice
Spring
Lone Cottage
The Lodge
Long Pond
Works
Cemy.
Knowle Hatches Viaduct
Mushes Plantation
Mushes Coppice
RAVENSWOOD HOUSE
NORTH PARK BUS. CEN.
Mayles Cnr.
KNOWLE VILLAGE BUS. PK.
TITCHFIELD
KNOWLE ROAD
KNOWLE AVENUE
HORSESHOE WY.
BOUNDARY WK.
PARK APP.
CHARITY VW.
CONSORT M.
ORCHID CL.
North Sq.
East M.
West M.
South Sq.
Victoria M.
Saxe Ct.
Regents Ct.
POTINE CL.
Kingswood Pl.
Fareham
River Meon
The Lodge
Knowle Village
Park Cotts.
Totsome Cotts.
Dean Villas
Great Funtley Farm
TITCHFIELD LA.
Overway
Funtley Cotts.
WINCHESTER
FAREHAM
PO17
Long Water Bridge
RIVER LANE
MAYLES
FUNTLEY
ROEBUCK AV.
STAG WAY
DEER LEAP
HONEY LANE
Football Ground
Recreation Ground
Funtley
FUNTLEY LA.
LAKESIDE
ROAD
THE WATERS
FUNTLEY HILL
Fontley House Farm
Three Meadows
Great Beamond Coppice
Courts of the Morning
Woodleigh Farm
Hookhouse Coppice
Little Beamond Coppice
Mill Coppice
Dean Farm Cottages
M27
M27 MOTORWAY
COURT
Oak Lea
Funtley Ct.
LECHLADE GS.
THE COPSE
THE GLADE
KINGSTON GS.
RUNNYMEDE
WALTON CT.
THAMES
DRIVE
RED BARN LANE
MARLOW CL.
HENLEY GDS.
SUNBURY CT.
HILL
WINNINGTON
Greendale Cl.
GREENDALE
PARK
BEAUMONT
Orchard Lea Inf. & Jun. Schs.
Fareham Tunnel
HOLLY GROVE
White Lodge Gs.
KILN ROAD
KNELLER
Fareham Common
PO16
GREEN HOLLOW CL.
THE CEDARS
WAKEFIELD AV.
ROAD
BURNHAM
SAVILLE GDS.
FAREHAM PARK
WHINCHAT CL.
CORT
AVENUE
HILLSON
THORNI
PARK FARM AV.
ATKINS PL.
IRON MILL CL.
Hayes Close
PENNINGTON
HILLBROW CL.
BEAUMONT CL.
KENNEDY AV.
HIGH MEAD
HOLLYCROSS
WOODHALL WAY
MARY ROSE CL.
Green Wk.
FROSTHOLE
BRAEMAR
Miller Dr.
MILLER
LYNTON
ODELL CL.
CRAWFORD
LONGSTAFF GDNS.
FARM
MORSHEAD
IRVINE CL.
Rec. Grd. Comm. Cen.
Day Centre
WYNTON WAY
HENRY CORT DR.
Oak Mdw. C of E Prim. Sch.
TEWKESBURY AV.
Recreation Ground
Oak Meadow Childcare Cen.
Playing Field
Hillson Ho.
Nashe Ho.
OAK COPPICE
Hill Park
Chantrell Wk.
BUCKINGHAM CT.
BARTLETT CL.
RANNOCH CL.
Hill Drive
FROSTHOLE CL.
HIGHLDS PK.
INVERNESS
Stirling Ct.
AVENUE
ANGUS CL.
DUNDEE CL.
BALMORAL RD
ABERDEEN CL.
CRES
BEAUFORT
MAYLINGS
SOMERVELL
CRESCENT
Uplands Prim. Sch.
Play. Fld.
VALENTINE CL.
PRIVETT RD.
Menin Ho.
NASHE
Arras Ho.
NASHE WY.
Gaza Ho.
Caroline
NORSET ROAD
NEPTUNE RD.
HIGH
GUDGE HEATH LA.
HEATHER GDS.
CRAVEN CT.
GIFFORD CL.
Hollingwood Ho.
GLENESHA GS.
CULLODEN CL.
ARGYLE CRES.
ELGIN CL.
Depot
BLAIR
HILLARY AV.
FUNTLEY CRES.
DRIVE
OXFORD CL.
DENBIGH
HAMMOND
Uplands

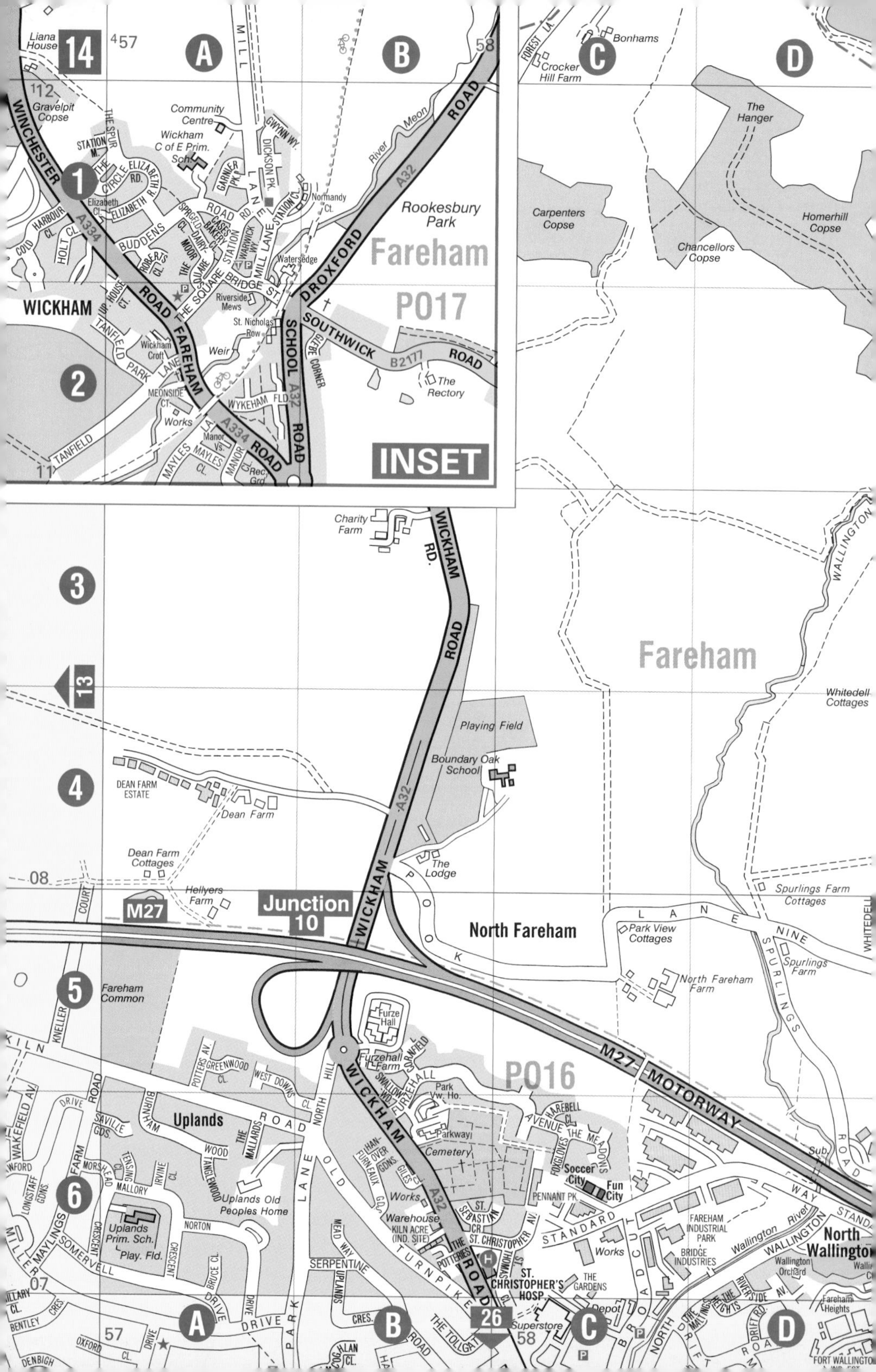

INSET
WICKHAM
Fareham
PO17
Rookesbury Park
Community Centre
Wickham C of E Prim. Sch.
Gravelpit Copse
Liana House
Normandy Ct.
Watersedge
Riverside Mews
St. Nicholas Row
Wickham Croft
Weir
Works
The Rectory
WINCHESTER ROAD
FAREHAM ROAD
DROXFORD ROAD
SCHOOL ROAD
SOUTHWICK ROAD
B2177
A334
A32
Crocker Hill Farm
Bonhams
The Hanger
Carpenters Copse
Chancellors Copse
Homerhill Copse
Charity Farm
WICKHAM RD.
WICKHAM ROAD
Playing Field
Boundary Oak School
The Lodge
DEAN FARM ESTATE
Dean Farm
Dean Farm Cottages
Hellyers Farm
M27
Junction 10
North Fareham
POOK LANE
NINE
Park View Cottages
Spurlings Farm Cottages
Spurlings Farm
North Fareham Farm
Whitedell Cottages
WALLINGTON
Fareham Common
Furze Hall
Furzehall Farm
Park Vw. Ho.
Parkway
Cemetery
PO16
M27 MOTORWAY
Uplands
Uplands Old Peoples Home
Uplands Prim. Sch.
Play. Fld.
Soccer City
Fun City
FAREHAM INDUSTRIAL PARK
BRIDGE INDUSTRIES
Works
Warehouse
KILN ACRE (IND. SITE)
ST. CHRISTOPHER'S HOSP.
THE GARDENS
Depot
Superstore
North Wallington
Wallington Orchard
Wallington River
Fareham Heights
STANDARD WAY
BROADCUT
NORTH HILL
OLD PARK LANE
TURNPIKE
THE TOLLGATE
SOMERVELL DRIVE
MAYLINGS FARM ROAD
WAKEFIELD AV.
KNELLER COURT
SERPENTINE
13
26

15
Orchard Copse
Wine Cross
Jack o' Tooles Row
B2177
Yewtree Row
Staversash Copse
Staple Cross
Staplecross Copse
Carmans Copse
WINCHESTER
FAREHAM
BERE FARM LANE
BLACKHOUSE LANE
Prior's Hold Farm
Bucks Copse
Bere Farm House
Bere Farm
Carmans Farm
Pigeonhouse Copse
Gravelhole Copse
Boarhunt Mill
Grub Coppice
Mill Coppice
RIVER
Moor Coppice
Dirtystile Copse
P017
Dell Row
16
Manor Farm
ROAD
Ashley Down Farm
Boarhunt
MONUMENT LANE
Ashleydown Cottages
ELMS LANE
BOARHUNT ROAD
Damson Row
SWIVELTON LANE
Monument Farm
Gas Valve Compound
Reservoir (covered)
The Royal Armouries Museum of Artillery
Fort Nelson
Nelson Monument
M27
Junction 11
Depot
PORTSDOWN HILL ROAD
NELSON LA.
DOWNEND RD.
27
A27
LANE
Chalk Pit
Solent View

16
A
B
C
D
61
62
Tylers Copse
Walton Heath Plantation
Ashlands Plantation
Mitchelland Copse
SOUTHWICK
Yewtree Row
Staple Cross
Staplecross Copse
Lodge Moor
Walton Heath Cott.
Walton Heath
B2177
COMMON
Walton Heath Cottages
Vernons Farm
Mitchelland
Lodge Farm
Carmans Farm
LANE
Lodge Coppice
Friar's Coppice
Fareham
PO17
ROAD
SOUTHWICK
09
Great Breach Row
Ham Coppice
BRIDGE
Snow Hill
COMMON
Castle Farm
Bridge House
BERRY-MEADOW COTTS.
LANE
CASTLE RD.
NORTON
NORTON CL.
ROAD
Royal Naval Cotts.
Newman's Bridge
STREET
BACK
The Elms
Ham Farm
Sewage Works
WEST
STREET
HIGH
Playground
Old Vicarage
ROAD
Southwick
NORTH
The Wild
15
Ashleydown Coppice
Newport Farm
Cheeseman's Bridge
FAREHAM
Rook's Bridge
Collier Row
B2177
BY-PASS
SOU
Boarhunt
Ashley Down Farm
LANE
Perrige's Coppice
MONUMENT
Marl Rows
Stroud Coppice
Ashleydown Cottages
08
LANE
Watercress Beds
Offwell Farm
Row
WALK
New Barns
PORTCHESTER
CROOKED
Reservoir (covered)
Mountemoor's Coppice
LANE
Nelson Monument
Research Establishment
FORT SOUTHWICK
PORTSDOWN
HILL
ROAD
07
NELSON LA.
61
28
62
JAMES
Solent View
Westmore House
High
Tor
1
2
3
4
5
6

E
F
G
H
64
465
110
Jays Hummock
Jays Copse
Wynn's Copse
Little Belney Copse
Belney Farm
Great Belney Copse
BELNEY LANE
1
PLACE WOOD
Assells Coppice
Assells Row
Wanstead Farm
Hazelhook Coppice
2
Ring Work & Bailey Castle
Tennis Courts
Sheep Park Plantation
Lyeheath Farm
09
Rooks Row
Pav.
Playing Field
LANE
Hobern Coppice
NORTH RD. WEST
WOOD
NORTH RD. EAST
WEST RD.
Sports Ground
Roman Road
(Course of)
DRIVE SOUTH
ROAD
RD.
PRIORY RD.
3
Lye Heath
Southwick House
EAST
HMS DRYAD
Littlehunts Cop
Tennis Court
DRIVE
18
Comphouse Moor Coppice
Comphouse Common
LANE
PIGEON HOUSE
SOUTHWICK PARK GOLF COURSE
Club House
Comphouse Farm
The Slopes
Sawyer's Wood
4
Hookheath Farm
WICK
08
ROAD
PITYMOOR
Pitymoor Coppice
Pinsley Coppice
Miller's Coppice
Tree Coppice Plantation
Tree Coppice
Venables Coppice
5
Potwell Farm
Pinsley Lodge
Pinsley Plantation
POTWELL
DROVE
Ford
LANE
Bushy Coppice
New Barns House
Waterlooville
PO7
B2177
Moat & Bailey
6
PIGEONHOUSE
Pigeon House Farm
07
Sewage Works
WORKSHOP
NORTH
DSTL Portsdown West
29
ROAD NORTH
EASTFIELD RD.
HILLTOP
ROAD
465

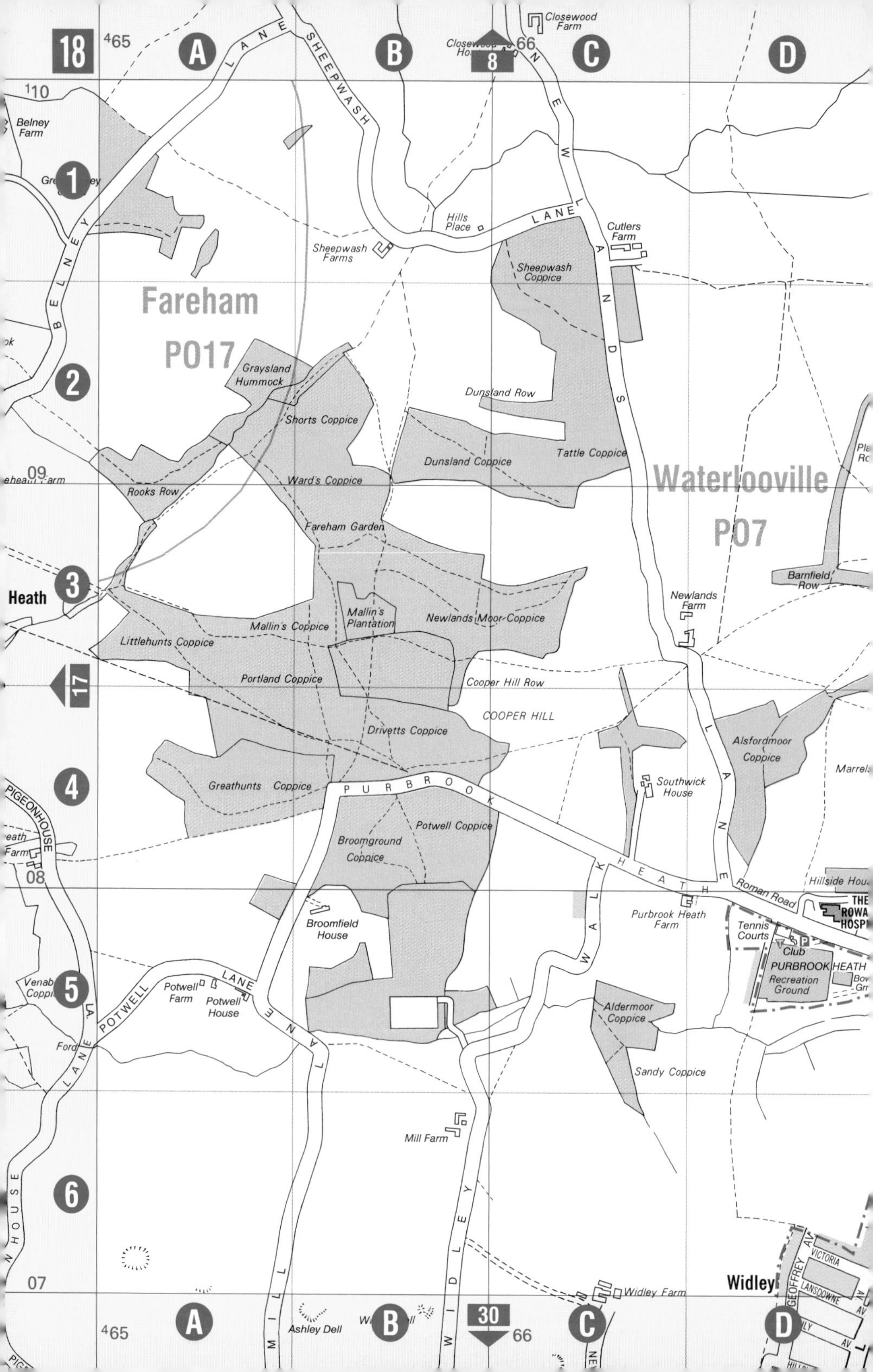
465
A
B
C
D
8
66
110
Belney Farm
1
2
3
4
5
6
09
08
07
Heath
17
Fareham
PO17
Waterlooville
PO7
BELNEY LANE
SHEEPWASH
NEWLANDS LANE
LANE
Closewood Farm
Hills Place
Sheepwash Farms
Cutlers Farm
Sheepwash Coppice
Graysland Hummock
Shorts Coppice
Dunsland Row
Dunsland Coppice
Tattle Coppice
Ward's Coppice
Rooks Row
Fareham Garden
Barnfield Row
Newlands Farm
Mallin's Plantation
Mallin's Coppice
Newlands Moor Coppice
Littlehunts Coppice
Portland Coppice
Cooper Hill Row
COOPER HILL
Drivetts Coppice
Alsfordmoor Coppice
Marrels
Greathunts Coppice
PURBROOK
Southwick House
PIGEONHOUSE
Potwell Coppice
Broomground Coppice
HEATH
Roman Road
Hillside House
WALK
Purbrook Heath Farm
Tennis Courts
Club
PURBROOK HEATH
Recreation Ground
Broomfield House
POTWELL LANE
Potwell Farm
Potwell House
Aldermoor Coppice
LA.
Ford
LANE
MILL LANE
Sandy Coppice
Mill Farm
WIDLEY
Widley Farm
Widley
GEOFFREY AV
VICTORIA
LANSDOWNE AV
Ashley Dell
30

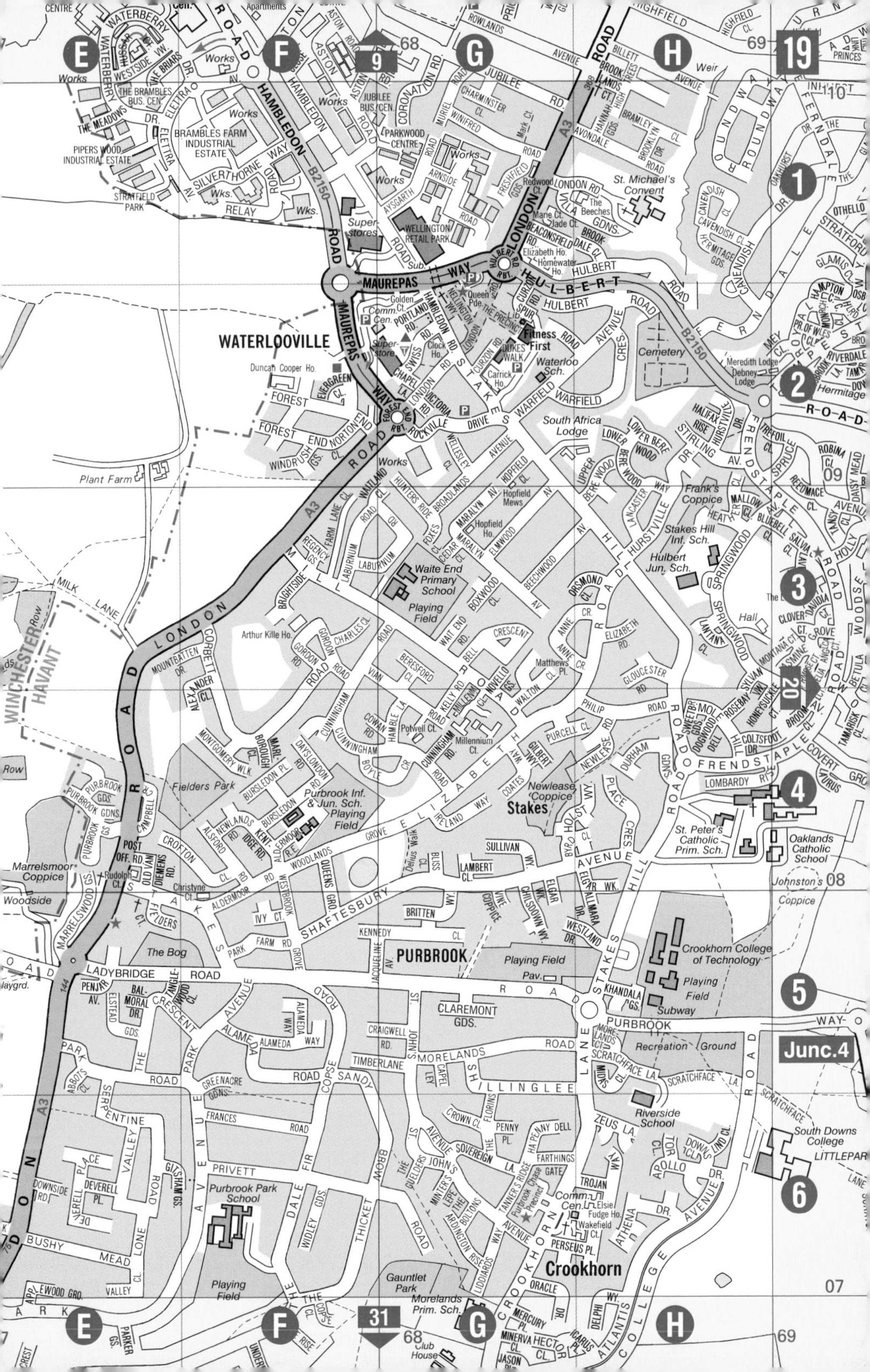
19
E
F
G
H
9
68
69
110
1
2
3
4
5
6
08
09
07
20
31
Junc.4
WATERLOOVILLE
PURBROOK
Stakes
Crookhorn
HAMBLEDON ROAD
B2150
MAUREPAS WAY
LONDON ROAD
A3
HULBERT ROAD
FRENDSTAPLE ROAD
STAKES ROAD
STAKES HILL ROAD
MILL ROAD
MILK LANE
LADYBRIDGE ROAD
PURBROOK WAY
ELIZABETH GROVE
SHAFTESBURY AVENUE
WOODLANDS AVENUE
CROOKHORN LANE
COLLEGE AVENUE
PRIVETT ROAD
HIGHFIELD AVENUE
JUBILEE RD.
RELAY RD.
SILVERTHORNE WAY
HAMBLEDON RD.
PORTLAND RD.
SWISS RD.
CHAPEL LA.
LONDON RD.
VICTORIA RD.
ROCKVILLE DRIVE
WARFIELD AVENUE
FOREST END
NORTON CL.
WINDRUSH GS.
EVERGREEN CL.
FOREST END RBT.
HULBERT RD. RBT.
Super-stores
WELLINGTON RETAIL PARK
BRAMBLES FARM INDUSTRIAL ESTATE
PIPERS WOOD INDUSTRIAL ESTATE
THE BRAMBLES BUS. CEN.
JUBILEE BUS. CEN.
PARKWOOD CENTRE
Works
St. Michael's Convent
The Beeches
Cemetery
Meredith Lodge
Debney Lodge
South Africa Lodge
Waterloo Sch.
Fitness First
DUKES WALK
Duncan Cooper Ho.
Plant Farm
Frank's Coppice
Stakes Hill Inf. Sch.
Hulbert Jun. Sch.
Waite End Primary School
Playing Field
Hopfield Mews
Hopfield Ho.
Arthur Kille Ho.
Potwell Cl.
Millennium Ct.
Matthews Pl.
Newlease Coppice
Purbrook Inf. & Jun. Sch.
Fielders Park
St. Peter's Catholic Prim. Sch.
Oaklands Catholic School
Johnston's Coppice
Crookhorn College of Technology
Subway
Recreation Ground
Riverside School
South Downs College
Purbrook Park School
Gauntlet Park
Morelands Prim. Sch.
Club House
The Bog
Marrelsmoor Coppice
Woodside
WINCHESTER
HAVANT
Christyne Ct.
Rudolph Ct.
MOUNTBATTEN DR.
ALEXANDER CL.
CORBETT RD.
MONTGOMERY WLK.
MARLBOROUGH CL.
CUNNINGHAM RD.
BOYLE CR.
HAMBLE LA.
KELLY RD.
NOVELLO GS.
WALTON CL.
GILBERT WY.
PURCELL CL.
NEWLEASE RD.
DURHAM GDNS.
LOMBARDY RI.
SULLIVAN WY.
LAMBERT CL.
BRITTEN WY.
KENNEDY CL.
ELGAR WK.
WESTLAND DR.
KHANDALA GS.
CLAREMONT GDS.
CRAIGWELL RD.
MORELANDS ROAD
TIMBERLANE
SANDY ROAD
SHILLINGLEE
ALAMEDA WAY
GREENACRE GDNS.
FRANCES ROAD
SERPENTINE ROAD
VALLEY PARK
BUSHY MEAD
DEVERELL PL.
DOWNSIDE RD.
LONE VALLEY
THE DALE
FIR COPSE ROAD
WIDLEY GDS.
THICKET
PARK AVENUE
ELSTEAD GDS.
PENJAR AV.
BALMORAL DR.
TANGLEWOOD CL.
SOVEREIGN LA.
HA'PENNY DELL
FARTHINGS GATE
PENNY PL.
CROWN CL.
TROJAN
APOLLO DR.
ATHENA
ZEUS LA.
PERSEUS PL.
ORACLE DR.
MERCURY
MINERVA CL.
HECTOR CL.
JASON
ICARUS PL.
ATLANTIS
DELPHI WY.
SCRATCHFACE LA.
Wakefield Ct.
Elsie Fudge Ho.
Comm. Cen.
Purbrook Chase Precinct
Hermitage
STRATFIELD PARK
ASTON ROAD
CORONATION RD.
CHARMINSTER CL.
WINIFRED
BRAMLEY CL.
BROOKLYN DR.
AVONDALE
ROUNDWAY
CAVENDISH DR.
HERMITAGE GDS.
OAKHURST DR.
FERNDALE
STIRLING AV.
HURSTVILLE DR.
HALIFAX RISE
LOWER BERE WOOD
UPPER BERE WOOD
SPRINGWOOD AV.
LANTANA CL.
ORSMOND CL.
ANNE CR.
BEECHWOOD AV.
ELMWOOD AV.
BOXWOOD CL.
MARALYN AV.
HOPFIELD CL.
BROADLANDS AV.
WELLESLEY CL.
HUNTERS RIDE
FOXES CL.
LABURNUM RD.
FARM LANE CL.
WAITLAND CL.
REGENCY GS.
BRIGHTSIDE RD.
GORDON RD.
CHARLES CL.
BERESFORD CL.
WAIT END RD.
CRESCENT
GLOUCESTER RD.
PHILIP RD.
COLTSFOOT DR.
HONEYSUCKLE CL.
ROSEBAY CL.
DOGWOOD DELL
SWEETBRIAR GDS.
FRENDSTAPLE
COVERT GRO.
TAMARISK CL.
BROOM CL.
TREFOIL CL.
SPRUCE AV.
ROBINA CL.
DAISY MEAD
SALVIA CL.
BLUEBELL CL.
MALLOW CL.
HEATHER CL.
CLOVER CL.
Hall
PURBROOK GDNS.
CAMPBELL CR.
POST OFF. RD.
CROFTON CL.
OLD VAN DIEMENS RD.
MARRELSWOOD GS.
ALDERMOOR RD.
QUEENS GRO.
WESTBROOK GRO.
IVY CT.
FARM RD.
PARK GROVE
ALSFORD RD.
NEWLANDS RD.
KENT RD.
IDGE RD.
BURSLEDON PL.
DAYSLONDON RD.
IRELAND WAY
COATES WAY
HOLST WY.
BYRD CL.
ELGAR WK.
ALLMARA DR.
CHILSDOWN WY.
VINE COPPICE
Delius Walk
BLISS CL.
JACQUELINE AV.
ST. JOHN'S RD.
CAPEL LEY
FLORINS
TANNER'S RIDGE
LIDDIARDS WAY
ARDINGTON RISE
THE BOLTONS
MINTER'S LEPE
GUELDERS
GITSHAM GS.
ABBOTS CL.
APPLEWOOD GRO.
THE COPSE
PARKER GS.
UNDER
Playing Field Pav.
Junc.4
LITTLEPARK
Weir

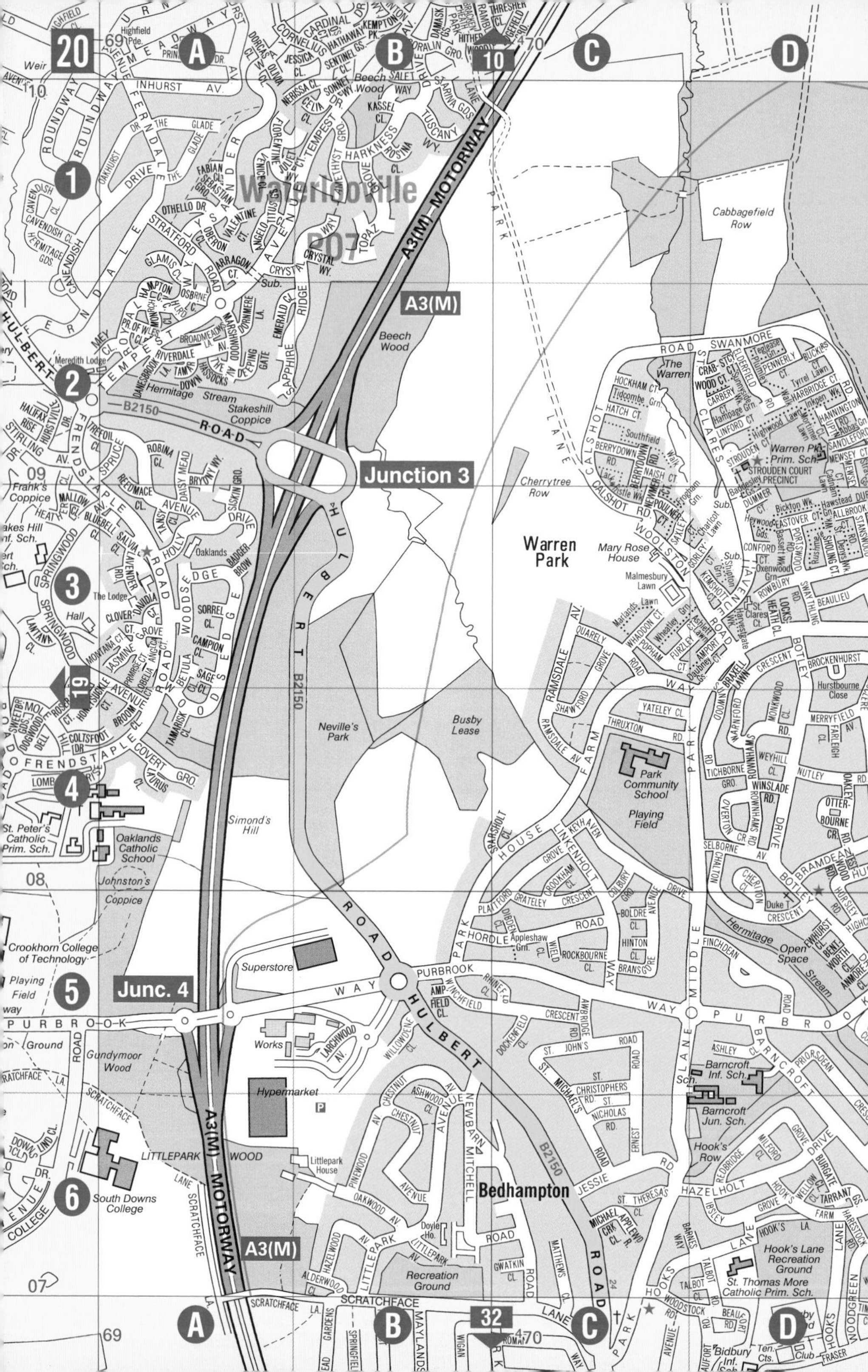

A
B
C
D
10
1
2
3
4
5
6
19
32
Waterlooville
PO7
A3(M) MOTORWAY
A3(M)
Junction 3
Junc. 4
HULBERT ROAD
B2150
Beech Wood
Hermitage Stream
Stakeshill Coppice
Cabbagefield Row
Cherrytree Row
Warren Park
Mary Rose House
Malmesbury Lawn
The Warren
Warren Pk. Prim. Sch.
STROUDEN COURT PRECINCT
Hurstbourne Close
Park Community School
Playing Field
Busby Lease
Neville's Park
Simond's Hill
Superstore
Works
Hypermarket
LITTLEPARK WOOD
Littlepark House
Recreation Ground
Bedhampton
Hermitage Open Space
Barncroft Inf. Sch.
Barncroft Jun. Sch.
Hook's Row
Hook's Lane Recreation Ground
St. Thomas More Catholic Prim. Sch.
Frank's Coppice
The Lodge
Hall
Oaklands
St. Peter's Catholic Prim. Sch.
Oaklands Catholic School
Johnston's Coppice
Crookhorn College of Technology
Playing Field
Gundymoor Wood
South Downs College
Meredith Lodge
Highfield Pde.
Weir
PURBROOK WAY
FRENDSTAPLE ROAD
STRATFORD ROAD
FERNDALE
SCRATCHFACE LANE
MIDDLE PARK WAY
HAZELHOLT
JESSIE RD.
HOOKS LANE
BARNCROFT WAY
69
470
110
09
08
07

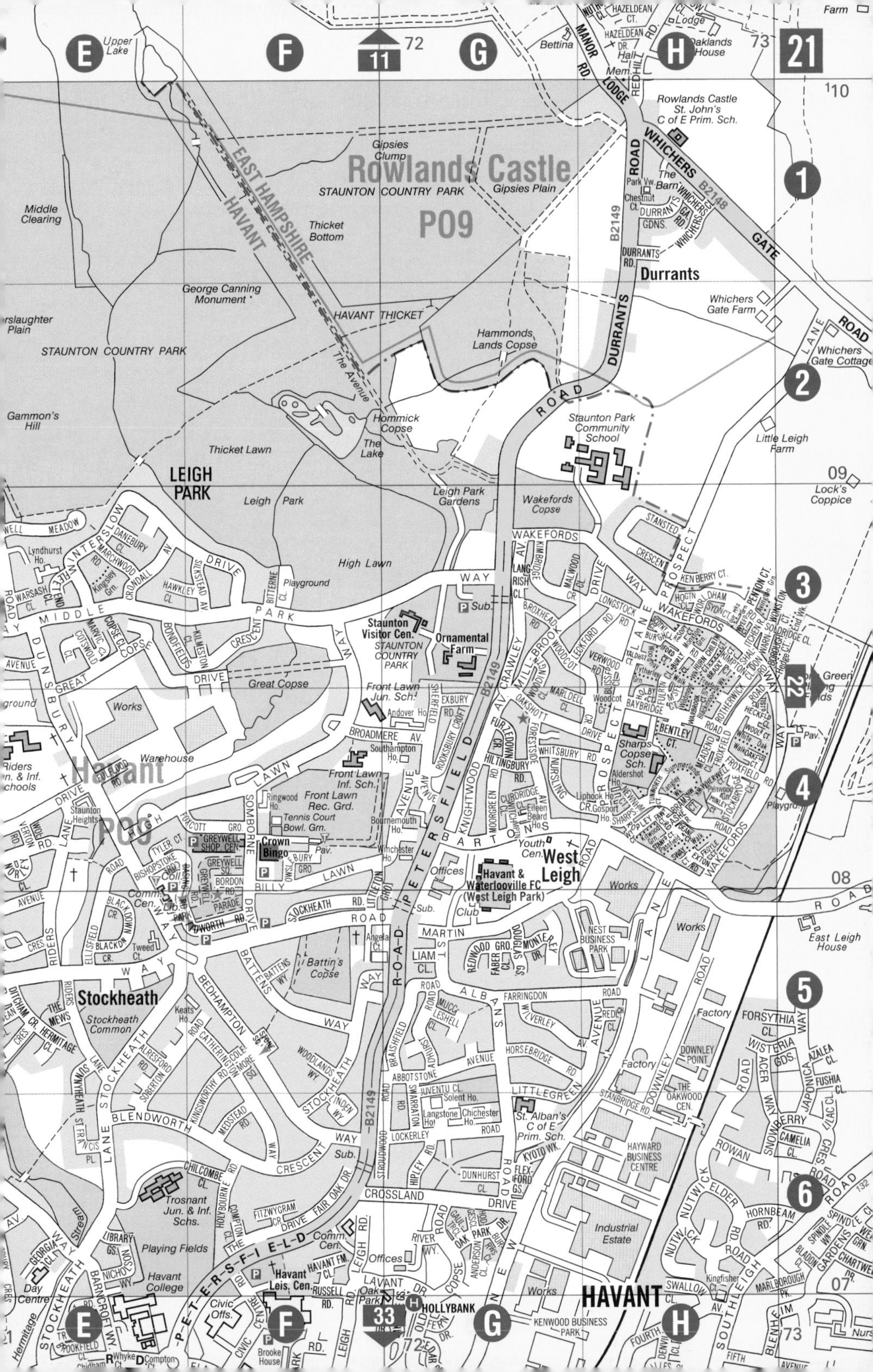

Rowlands Castle
PO9
STAUNTON COUNTRY PARK
EAST HAMPSHIRE
HAVANT
Durrants
LEIGH PARK
West Leigh
Havant
Stockheath
HAVANT
Staunton Visitor Cen.
Ornamental Farm
Staunton Park Community School
Havant & Waterlooville FC (West Leigh Park)
Havant College
Havant Leis. Cen.
Industrial Estate
HOLLYBANK

A
B
C
D
1
2
3
4
5
6
Rowlands Castle
PO9
Havant
PO9
Durrants
Oakland House
Lyels Wood
Woodberry Cottage
Mays Coppice Farm
Whichers Gate Farm
Whichers Gate Cottage
Little Leigh Farm
Lock's Coppice
Comley Bottom
Sandpit
Roundell
Gunters Stone
SOUTHLEIGH FOREST
Blackbush Copse
Blackbush Hanger
Twostone Bottom
Shuffles Plantation
EAST HAMPSHIRE
CHICHESTER
BARTON'S COPSE
Refuse Tip
Bartons Green Playing Fields
The Slip
PORTSMOUTH BUPA HOSPITAL
Gravelpit Cottage
Southleigh Park
Hollybank House
Hollybank Farm
White Lodge
EAST HAMPSHIRE
HAVANT
Helmsley House
East Leigh House
Southleigh Park House
Southleigh Cottage
Parkside Cottages
Woodlands Cottage
Old Stable House
Lock's Farm
The Spinney
Southleigh Farm
Hollybank Grd.
New Brighton
WHICHERS GATE ROAD
B2148
COMLEY ROAD
HILL HORNDEAN ROAD
EMSWORTH COMMON ROAD
EMSWORTH ROAD
BARTONS ROAD
PROSPECT LANE
WOODBERRY LANE
LONG COPSE LANE
HOLLYBANK LANE
SOUTHLEIGH ROAD
EASTLEIGH ROAD
TUDOR AV.
WOODLANDS AVENUE
FORSYTHIA WAY
ROWAN ROAD
SOUTHLEIGH
B2147
21
34
73
74
08
07
09
110

23
E
F
G
H
Saw Mill
The Garden Cottage
Stansted Park
Park Slip
Pennyroyal Wood
Holme Farm Cottages
Stansted
Stubbermere
Lodge
The Groves
Pheasant Court Bungalow
Hams Copse
Furze Belt
Pits Copse
Sindle's Farm
RACTON COMMON
Pond Cottage
Boat House
Brickkiln Ponds
Pond Copse
Redhouse Corner
Watercress Beds
Three Corner Piece
COMMON ROAD
Gunter's Copse
Aldsworth Bridge
Aldsworth House
Aldsworth
Bridge Cottage
Aldsworth Manor Farm
Aldsworth Manor
Valley Farm
Sussex Cottages
Sawmill's Cottages
Westbourne Common
Broadwash Bridge
Sawmill's Farm
Aldsworth Common
Ckt Grd.
Rec. Grd.
Monk's Farm
Fords Copse
Didmans Copse
Venture Farm
Foxbury Dell
Riverside Cottages
Emsworth
PO10
Ractonpark Dell
Var Cottage Wood
CHICHESTER
HAVANT
Hollybank Cottage
Westbourne Prim. Sch.
Hall
River Ems
Resr. (cov.)
Var Cottage
Deepsprings
B2147
FOXBURY LANE
WESTBOURNE CARAVAN PARK
Chapel
Cemetery
CEMETERY LANE
Chantry Farm
The Glen
THE WREN CENTRE
Westbourne Court
WESTBOURNE
Medlars
OLD DAIRY WORKSHOPS
Hampshire Bridge
Willow Barn
The Squirrels
Pine Cottage
Brook Cottages
Lumley Farmhouse
A27
WEST VIEW COTTS.
35

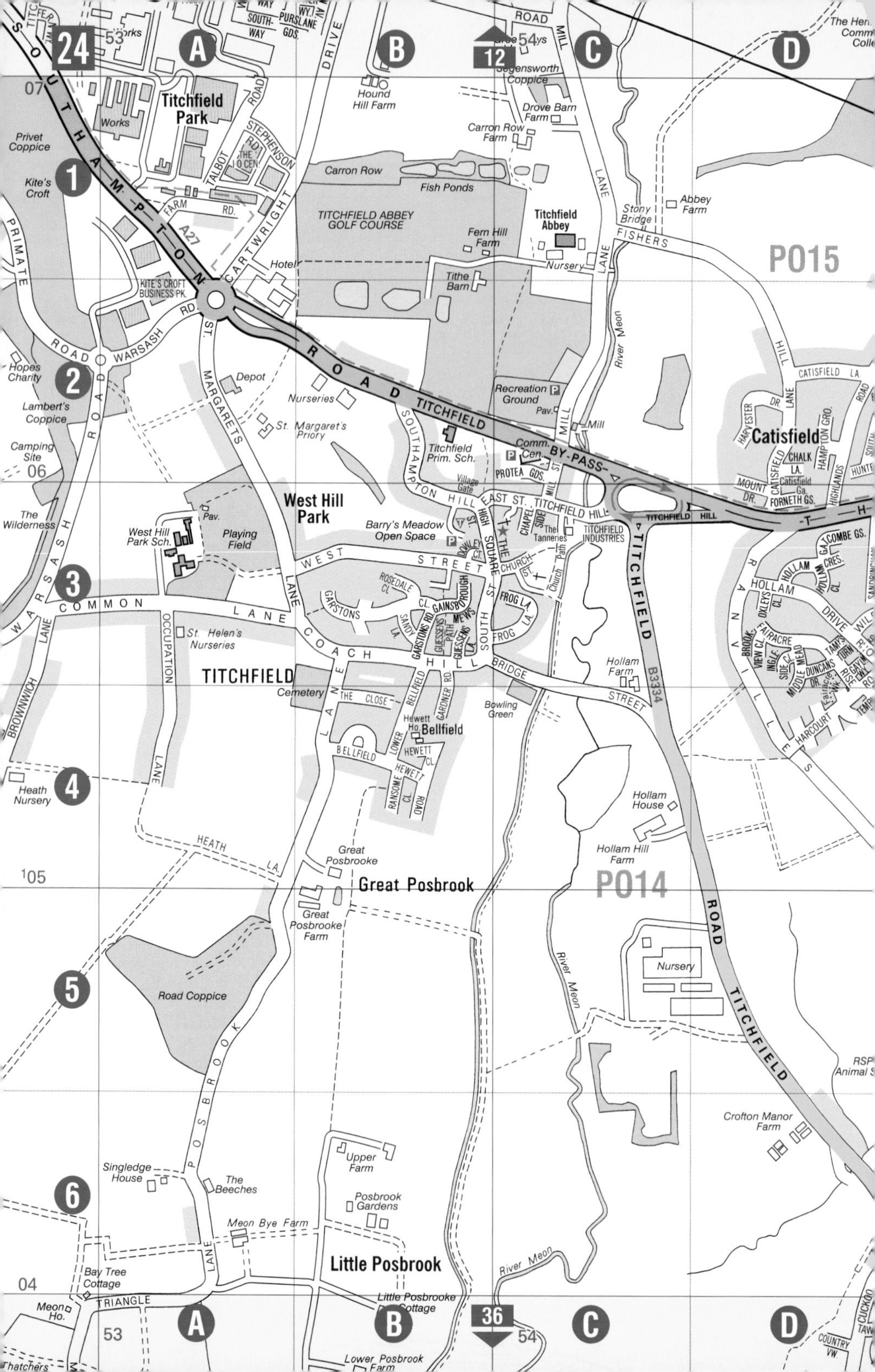

24
12
36
A
B
C
D
1
2
3
4
5
6
07
06
105
04
53
54
Titchfield Park
Works
Privet Coppice
Kite's Croft
SOUTHAMPTON
A27
TALBOT RD.
STEPHENSON RD.
CARTWRIGHT ROAD
FARM RD.
KITE'S CROFT BUSINESS PK.
WARSASH RD.
WARSASH ROAD
PRIMATE ROAD
Hopes Charity
Lambert's Coppice
Camping Site
The Wilderness
Hound Hill Farm
Segensworth Coppice
Drove Barn Farm
Carron Row Farm
Carron Row
Fish Ponds
TITCHFIELD ABBEY GOLF COURSE
Fern Hill Farm
Titchfield Abbey
Nursery
Tithe Barn
Hotel
Stony Bridge
Abbey Farm
FISHERS HILL
MILL LANE
PO15
River Meon
Catisfield
CATISFIELD LA.
HARVESTER DR.
CHALK LA.
MOUNT DR.
FORNETH GS.
HIGHLANDS
HAMPTON GRO.
GASCOMBE GS.
HOLLAM CRES.
HOLLAM DRIVE
OXLEYS CL.
FAIRACRE
BROOK VIEW CL.
INGLE SIDE CL.
MIDDLE MEAD
DUNCANS DR.
TAMYS TURN
RANVILLES
HARCOURT
ROAD TITCHFIELD BY-PASS
TITCHFIELD HILL
ST. MARGARETS LANE
Depot
Nurseries
St. Margaret's Priory
Titchfield Prim. Sch.
Recreation Ground
Pav.
Mill
Comm. Cen.
PROTEA GDS.
MILL ST.
Village Gate
SOUTHAMPTON HILL
EAST ST.
HIGH ST.
THE SQUARE
CHAPEL SIDE
The Tanneries
TITCHFIELD INDUSTRIES
West Hill Park
West Hill Park Sch.
Playing Field
Barry's Meadow Open Space
DOWLEY CT.
WEST STREET
CHURCH ST.
Church Path
ROSEDALE CL.
GARSTONS
GARSTONS RD.
SANDY LA.
GAINSBOROUGH MEWS
GUESSENS PATH
GUESSENS LA.
SOUTH ST.
FROG LA.
COMMON LANE
WARSASH ROAD
BROWNWICH LANE
OCCUPATION LANE
St. Helen's Nurseries
TITCHFIELD
COACH HILL
BRIDGE STREET
Cemetery
THE CLOSE
LOWER BELLFIELD
GARDNER RD.
Hewett Ho.
Bellfield
HEWETT CL.
HEWETT ROAD
RANSOME CL.
BELLFIELD
Bowling Green
Hollam Farm
TITCHFIELD B3334
Heath Nursery
HEATH LA.
Hollam House
Hollam Hill Farm
Great Posbrooke
Great Posbrook
Great Posbrooke Farm
PO14
Road Coppice
Nursery
ROAD TITCHFIELD
POSBROOK LANE
Crofton Manor Farm
Singledge House
The Beeches
Upper Farm
Posbrook Gardens
Meon Bye Farm
Little Posbrook
River Meon
Bay Tree Cottage
Meon Ho.
TRIANGLE
Little Posbrooke Cottage
Lower Posbrook Farm
Thatchers
COUNTRY VW
The Hen... Comm... Coll...
RSP... Animal S...

25
13
37
26
FAREHAM
Fareham
Hill Park
Heathfield
West End
Fareham Junction
Uplands Prim. Sch.
PO16
Depot
Blackbrook Rec. Grd.
BLACKBROOK BUS. PARK
St. Jude's RC Prim. Sch.
Fareham College
Bishopswood
Wallisdean Inf. Sch.
Wallisdean Jun. Sch.
Playing Field
Neville Lovett Comm. Sch.
BROADLAW WALK SHOPPING PRECINCT
St. Francis Special Sch.
Heathfield Sch.
Ranvilles Jun. & Inf. Schs.
Oxleys Coppice
Peak Lodge
Reservoir
Rifle Range
Nursery
Newlands Farm
Cemetery
Recreation Ground
HMS COLLINGWOOD
Fareham Town FC
Cam Alders Sports Centre
A27
AVENUE
LONGFIELD AVENUE
PEAK LANE
STROUD GREEN LANE
TANNER LANE
OAKCROFT LANE
BLACKBROOK ROAD
BLACKBROOK PARK AVENUE
HEATH ROAD
OAK ROAD
ABBEY ROAD
QUEEN ROAD

26
A
B
C
D
1
2
3
4
5
6
57
58
07
06
05
04
14
25
38
FAREHAM
North Wallington
Wallington
Fleetlands
PO16
PO14
Uplands Prim. Sch.
Play. Fld.
SOMERVELL
KILN ACRE (IND. SITE)
THE POTTERIES
ST. CHRISTOPHER
ST. STOPHER'S HOSP.
SERPENTINE
OLD TURNPIKE
WICKHAM RD.
A32
INDUSTRIAL PARK
BRIDGE INDUSTRIES
Works
Depot
Superstore
Fareham Heights
FORT WALLINGTON IND. EST.
MILITARY ROAD
Fareham Leisure Centre
Bowling Green
Park Lane Recreation Ground
Ten. Cts.
Harrison Prim. Sch.
Beechwood Lodge
Elmwood Lodge
Redwood Lodge
Kelly Ct.
NORTHWOOD SQUARE
SOUTHAMPTON ROAD
Old Manor Ho.
Arts Cen.
Civic Cen.
Ferneham Hall
Lib.
FAREHAM SHOP. CEN.
Thackeray Sq.
Delme Sq.
Westbury Sq.
Mall Osborn
Market Quay
Millennium Sq.
Police HQ
Bus Sta.
Mus.
Comm. Cen.
Magistrates Ct.
MALT-HOUSE LA.
Moresby Ct.
Acacia Lodge
Trinity Gdns
Fareham Junction
Fareham
Western Ct.
Riches M.
WEST STREET
EAST STREET
Sub.
Sutton Ct.
WESTERN WAY
A27
EASTERN WAY
BELVOIR CLOSE
The Gillies Open Space
ELMHURST ROAD
COMPASS POINT
Lysses Ct.
Ind. Est.
Wykeham Ho. Sch.
Cedar Ct.
Adelaide Pl.
Madison Ct.
Pav.
Recreation Ground
Swan Quay
Bath Lane Cottages
Upper Wharf
Upper Quay
Town Quay
Play. Fld.
THE BOATYARD IND. EST.
The Rope Wlk.
MAINSAIL DR.
Fareham Lake
Home Office
CARNAC CT.
CAMS HALL ESTATE
Club House
Wilderness
Cunigre Por
CAMS HALL ESTATE GOLF COURSE
Redlands Primary Sch.
Fareham Town FC
Cam Alders Sports Centre
Bowls Club
Solent Ho.
Hamble Ho.
Needles Ho.
Meon Ho.
Spithead Ho.
Medina Ho.
Cams Alder's Ct.
Langstone Ho.
Youngbridge Ct.
PALMERSTON BUSINESS PARK
SALTERNS EST. Works
Eastern Parade Open Space
Salterns Quay
THE MOORINGS
DELTA BUSINESS PARK
FORT FAREHAM INDUSTRIAL SITE
AXIS PK.
FAREHAM ENTERPRISE CENTRE
NEWGATE LANE IND. EST.
PREMIER BUS. PARK
COLLINGWOOD RETAIL PARK
Superstores
NEWGATE LANE IND. EST.
B3385
GOSPORT ROAD
Bus Depot
Factory
Hoeford Lake
Landing Stage
HMS COLLINGWOOD
SPEEDFIELD PARK RETAIL PARK
Superstore
APEX CENTRE
Superstores
Tukes Avenue Playing Field
Factory
REGENTS TRADE PARK
Works
Heli-pads
FAREHAM ROAD
PRIMROSE CL.
BRIDGEMARY GRO.
Hanover Ho.
Cooley Ho. Ho.
Playing Field
NEWGATE LANE

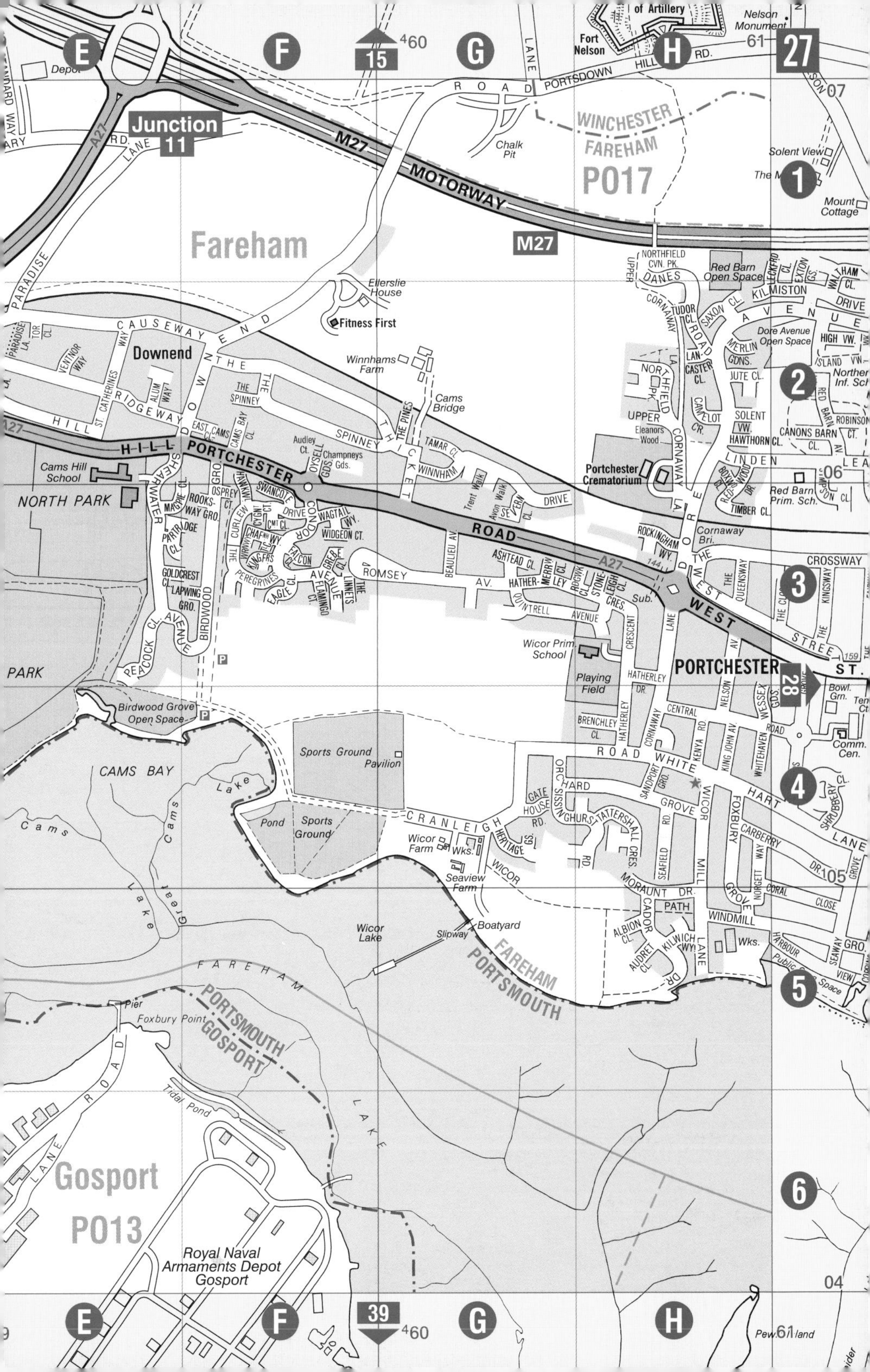
E
F
G
H
15
460
of Artillery
Fort Nelson
Nelson Monument
61
Depot
Junction 11
A27
M27 MOTORWAY
M27
PORTSDOWN HILL RD.
ROAD
LANE
Chalk Pit
WINCHESTER
FAREHAM
PO17
Solent View
Mount Cottage
1
07
Fareham
PARADISE LANE
Ellerslie House
Fitness First
Winnhams Farm
Cams Bridge
CAUSEWAY
Downend
DOWNEND
VENTNOR WAY
ST. CATHERINES WAY
ALUM WAY
THE RIDGEWAY
HILL
THE SPINNEY
SPINNEY
THE PINES
THICKET
Audley Ct.
Champneys Gds.
TAMAR CL.
WINNHAM DRIVE
Trent Walk
Avon Walk
SEVERN CL.
NORTHFIELD CVN. PK.
Red Barn Open Space
DANES
UPPER CORNAWAY
TUDOR CL.
SAXON CL.
KILMISTON
WALTHAM CL.
DRIVE
AVENUE
Dore Avenue Open Space
HIGH VW.
ISLAND VW.
MERLIN GDNS.
LANCASTER CL.
JUTE CL.
NORTHFIELD PK.
CAMELOT CR.
SOLENT VW.
HAWTHORN CL.
2
RED BARN AV.
ROBINSON CT.
CANONS BARN CL.
Eleanors Wood
UPPER CORNAWAY LA.
LINDEN
LEA
06
Portchester Crematorium
BOXWOOD
TIMBER CL.
Red Barn Prim. Sch.
HILL
PORTCHESTER
ROAD
A27
Cams Hill School
NORTH PARK
SHEARWATER
MAGPIE CL.
ROOKSWAY GRO.
OSPREY CT.
SWANCOTE
CONDOR
DRIVE
WAGTAIL WY.
WIDGEON CT.
PARTRIDGE CL.
GOLDCREST CL.
LAPWING GRO.
CURLEW
PEREGRINES
FALCON
GREBE CL.
EAGLE CL.
FLAMINGO CT.
THE LINNETS
AVENUE
ROMSEY AV.
BEAULIEU AV.
ASHTEAD CL.
HATHERLEY
MERRYLEY CL.
STONELEIGH CL.
QUINTRELL AVENUE
CRES.
Cornaway Bri.
ROCKINGHAM WY.
DORE
THE WEST
WEST
STREET
ST.
144
Sub.
THE QUEENSWAY
THE CLOSE
KINGSWAY
CROSSWAY
3
159
BIRDWOOD AVENUE
PEACOCK CL.
PARK
Birdwood Grove Open Space
Wicor Prim. School
Playing Field
CRESCENT
LANE
PORTCHESTER
28
Bowl. Grn.
HATHERLEY DR.
BRENCHLEY CL.
HATHERLEY
CORNAWAY
CENTRAL
NELSON AV.
WESSEX GDS.
ROAD
Comm. Cen.
KENYA RD.
KING JOHN AV.
WHITEHAVEN
ROAD
WHITE HART
LANE
4
SHRUBBERY CL.
Sports Ground Pavilion
CAMS BAY
Lake
ORCHARD
SISSINGHURST
TATTERSHALL CRES.
SANDPORT GRO.
GROVE
WICOR MILL LANE
FOXBURY GROVE
CARBERRY DR.
105
GATE HOUSE RD.
Pond
Sports Ground
CRANLEIGH
HERITAGE GS.
Wicor Farm
Wks.
Seaview Farm
WICOR
SEAFIELD RD.
RD.
NORGETT WAY
CORAL CLOSE
MORAUNT DR.
PATH
WINDMILL
Cams Lake
Great
Cams
Wicor Lake
Boatyard
Slipway
ALBION CL.
CADOR
AUDRET CL.
KILWICH WY.
Wks.
HARBOUR
Public Open Space
SEAWAY GRO.
VIEW
5
FAREHAM
PORTSMOUTH
FAREHAM LAKE
Pier
Foxbury Point
PORTSMOUTH
GOSPORT
ROAD
Tidal Pond
LANE
Gosport
PO13
6
Royal Naval Armaments Depot Gosport
04
39
460
Pewit Island
61

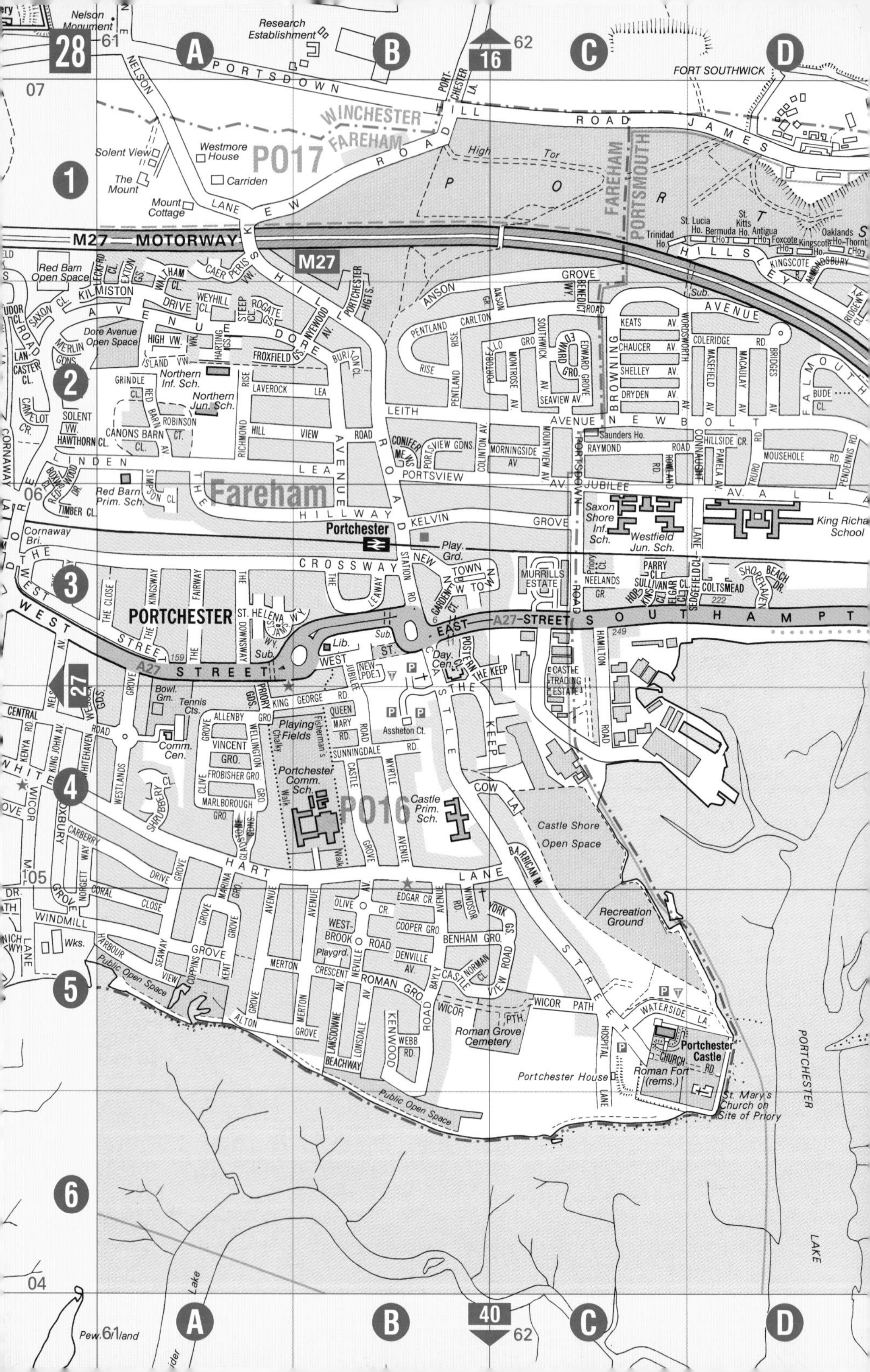

A
B
C
D
1
2
3
4
5
6
16
40
27
61
62
07
06
05
04
Nelson Monument
Research Establishment
FORT SOUTHWICK
PORTSDOWN HILL ROAD
JAMES
WINCHESTER
FAREHAM
PO17
Westmore House
Solent View
The Mount
Carriden
Mount Cottage
NELSON LANE
KEW ROAD
High Tor
PORT
FAREHAM
PORTSMOUTH
M27 MOTORWAY
M27
Fareham
PORTCHESTER
Portchester
Play. Grd.
PO16
Portchester Comm. Sch.
Playing Fields
Castle Prim. Sch.
Castle Shore Open Space
Recreation Ground
Roman Grove Cemetery
Portchester House
Portchester Castle
Roman Fort (rems.)
St. Mary's Church on Site of Priory
Public Open Space
Red Barn Open Space
Dore Avenue Open Space
Northern Inf. Sch.
Northern Jun. Sch.
Red Barn Prim. Sch.
Saxon Shore Inf. Sch.
Westfield Jun. Sch.
King Richard School
MURRILLS ESTATE
CASTLE TRADING ESTATE
A27 WEST STREET
A27 EAST STREET
SOUTHAMPTON ROAD
HART LANE
CASTLE STREET
WICOR PATH
Cornaway Bri.
Lib.
Day. Cen.
Comm. Cen.
Bowl. Grn.
Tennis Cts.
Assheton Ct.
Wks.
PORTCHESTER LAKE
Pewit Island

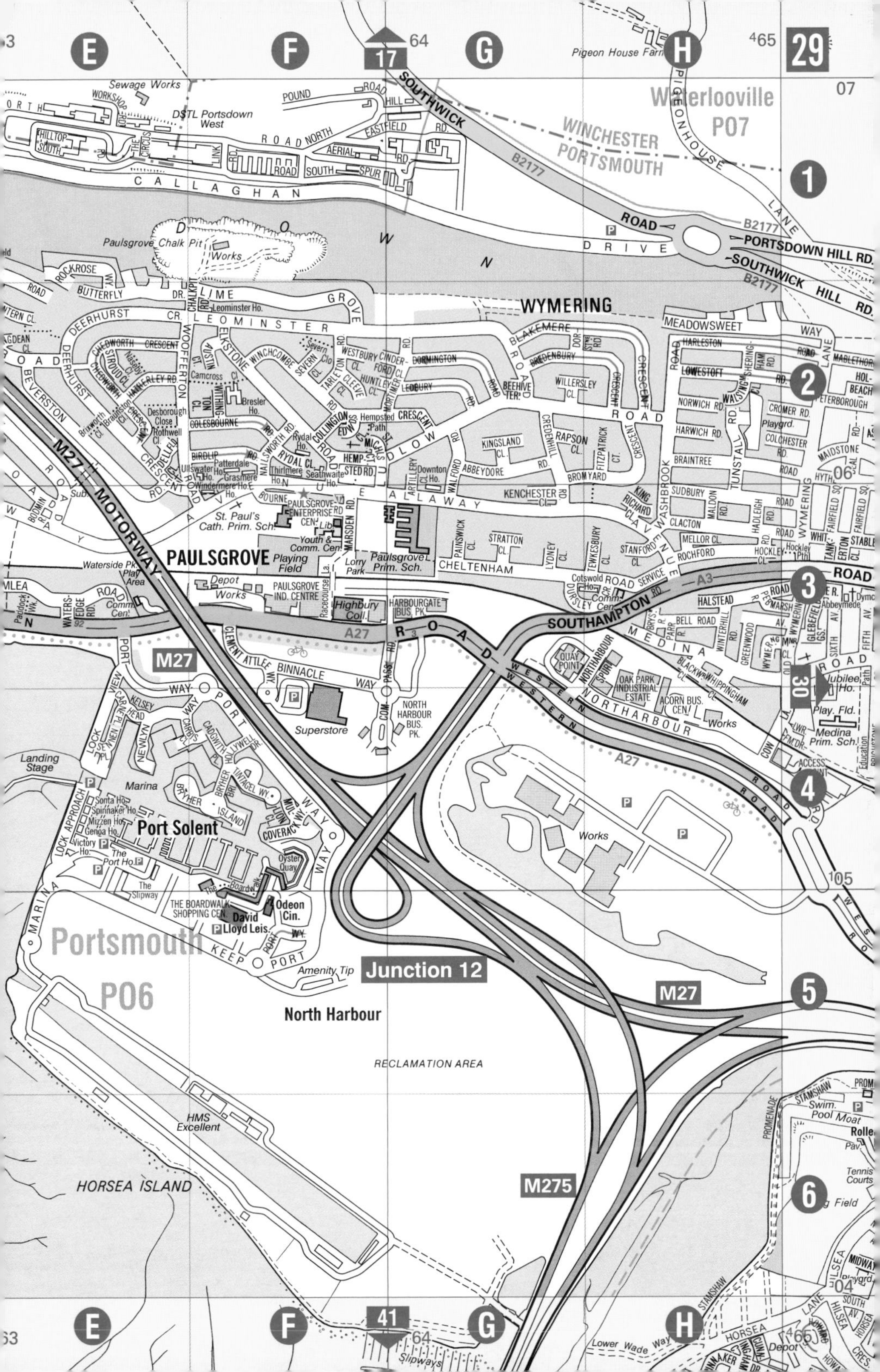

Waterlooville
PO7
WINCHESTER
PORTSMOUTH
WYMERING
PAULSGROVE
Port Solent
Portsmouth
PO6
North Harbour
Junction 12
M27
M275
RECLAMATION AREA
HMS Excellent
HORSEA ISLAND
Paulsgrove Chalk Pit
Sewage Works
DSTL Portsdown West
Pigeon House Farm
SOUTHWICK ROAD
PORTSDOWN HILL RD.
SOUTHWICK HILL RD.
CALLAGHAN DRIVE
SOUTHAMPTON ROAD
WESTERN ROAD
NORTHARBOUR ROAD
Superstore
Paulsgrove Prim. Sch.
St. Paul's Cath. Prim. Sch.
Medina Prim. Sch.
Highbury Coll.
PAULSGROVE IND. CENTRE
OAK PARK INDUSTRIAL ESTATE
NORTH HARBOUR BUS. PK.
THE BOARDWALK SHOPPING CEN.
Odeon Cin.
David Lloyd Leis.
Amenity Tip
Landing Stage
Marina

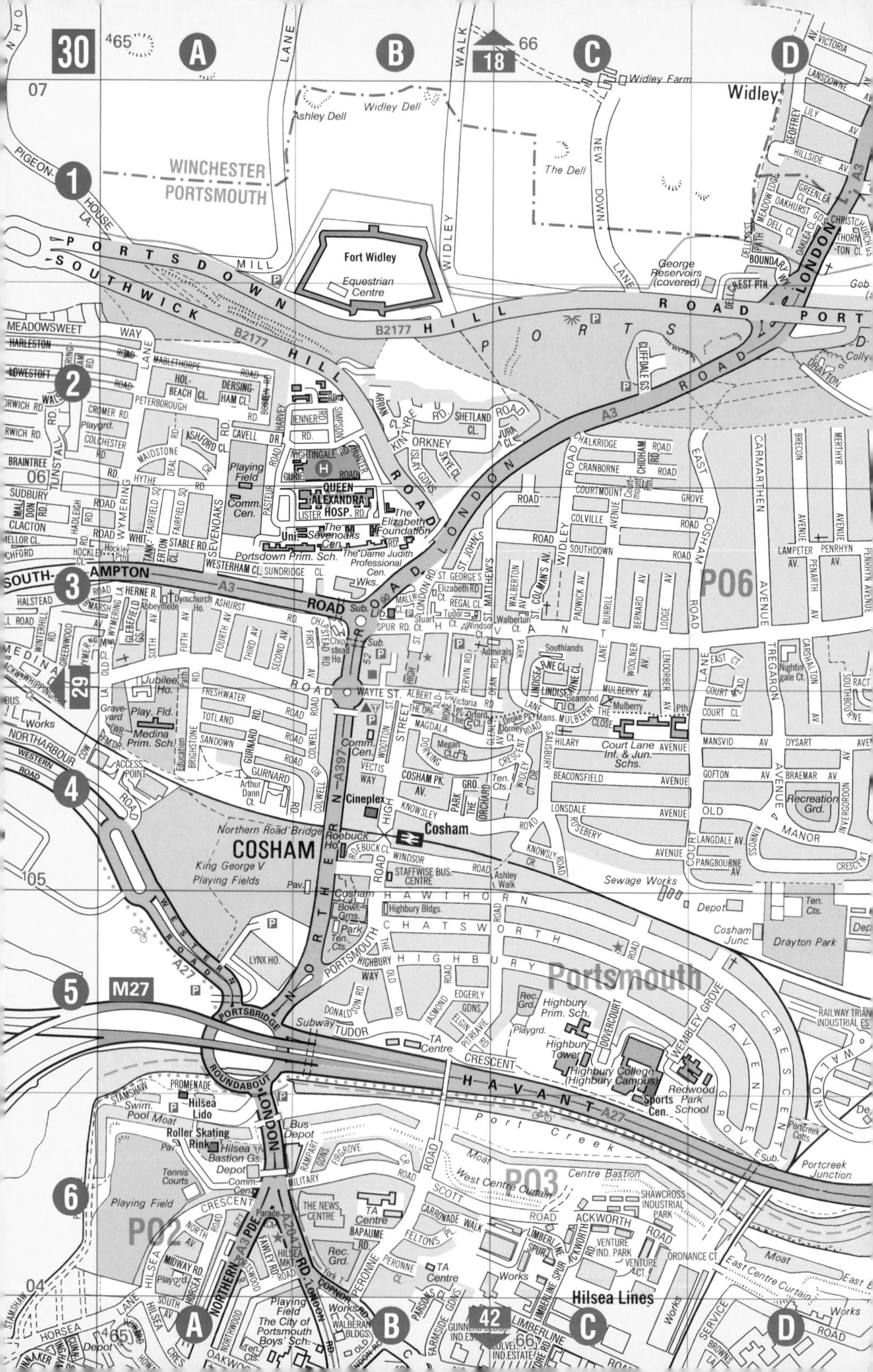
A
B
C
D
18
42
Widley
Widley Farm
Widley Dell
Ashley Dell
The Dell
WINCHESTER
PORTSMOUTH
Fort Widley
Equestrian Centre
PORTSDOWN HILL ROAD
SOUTHWICK HILL ROAD
B2177
LONDON ROAD
A3
George Reservoirs (covered)
PORTSDOWN
QUEEN ALEXANDRA HOSP.
The Elizabeth Foundation
The Dame Judith Professional Cen.
Portsdown Prim. Sch.
SOUTHAMPTON ROAD
Medina Prim. Sch.
Play. Fld.
Playing Field
Comm. Cen.
Cineplex
Cosham
COSHAM
Northern Road Bridge
King George V Playing Fields
NORTHERN ROAD
A397
WESTERN ROAD
A27
M27
PORTSBRIDGE ROUNDABOUT
PO6
PO3
PO2
Portsmouth
Court Lane Inf. & Jun. Schs.
Recreation Grd.
Sewage Works
Cosham Junc.
Drayton Park
Highbury Prim. Sch.
Highbury College (Highbury Campus)
Highbury Tower
Redwood Park School
Sports Cen.
HAVANT ROAD
Port Creek
Portcreek Junction
Hilsea Lido
Roller Skating Rink
Hilsea Bastion Gs.
Playing Field
Tennis Courts
West Centre Curtain
Centre Bastion
East Centre Curtain
Moat
SHAWCROSS INDUSTRIAL PARK
VENTURE IND. PARK
Hilsea Lines
The City of Portsmouth Boys' Sch.
THE NEWS CENTRE
TA Centre
Rec. Grd.
RAILWAY TRIANGLE INDUSTRIAL ESTATE
GUNNERS BLDGS. IND. ESTATE

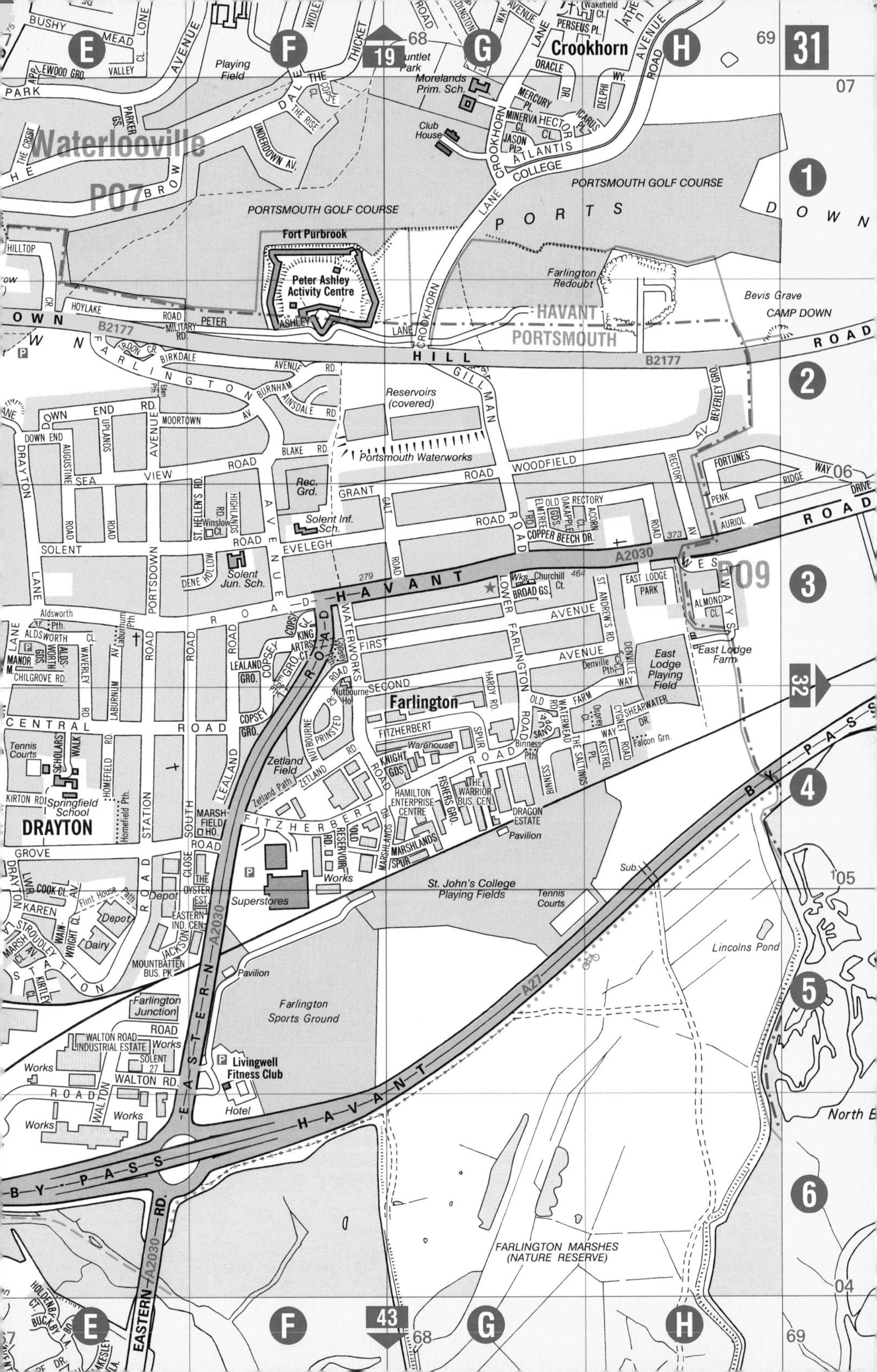
Crookhorn
Waterlooville
PO7
PO9
DRAYTON
Farlington
PORTSMOUTH GOLF COURSE
Fort Purbrook
Peter Ashley Activity Centre
Morelands Prim. Sch.
Club House
Playing Field
Farlington Redoubt
HAVANT
PORTSMOUTH
Bevis Grave
CAMP DOWN
PORTS DOWN
B2177
HILL ROAD
Reservoirs (covered)
Portsmouth Waterworks
Rec. Grd.
Solent Inf. Sch.
Solent Jun. Sch.
HAVANT ROAD
A2030
East Lodge Farm
East Lodge Playing Field
Zetland Field
Springfield School
Tennis Courts
Superstores
Works
Depot
Dairy
St. John's College Playing Fields
Farlington Sports Ground
Farlington Junction
WALTON ROAD INDUSTRIAL ESTATE
Livingwell Fitness Club
Hotel
Pavilion
EASTERN ROAD
A27
HAVANT BY-PASS
Lincolns Pond
FARLINGTON MARSHES (NATURE RESERVE)
North B
HAMILTON ENTERPRISE CENTRE
THE WARRIOR BUS. CEN.
DRAGON ESTATE
MOUNTBATTEN BUS. PK.
EASTERN IND. CEN.
CENTRAL ROAD
SOLENT ROAD
SEA VIEW ROAD
WOODFIELD ROAD
FIRST AVENUE
SECOND AVENUE
FITZHERBERT ROAD
STATION ROAD
DRAYTON LANE
GROVE ROAD
CROOKHORN LANE
COLLEGE ROAD
FARLINGTON AVENUE
LOWER FARLINGTON ROAD
PORTSDOWN AVENUE
19
32
43
E F G H
68 69
07 06 05 04
1 2 3 4 5 6

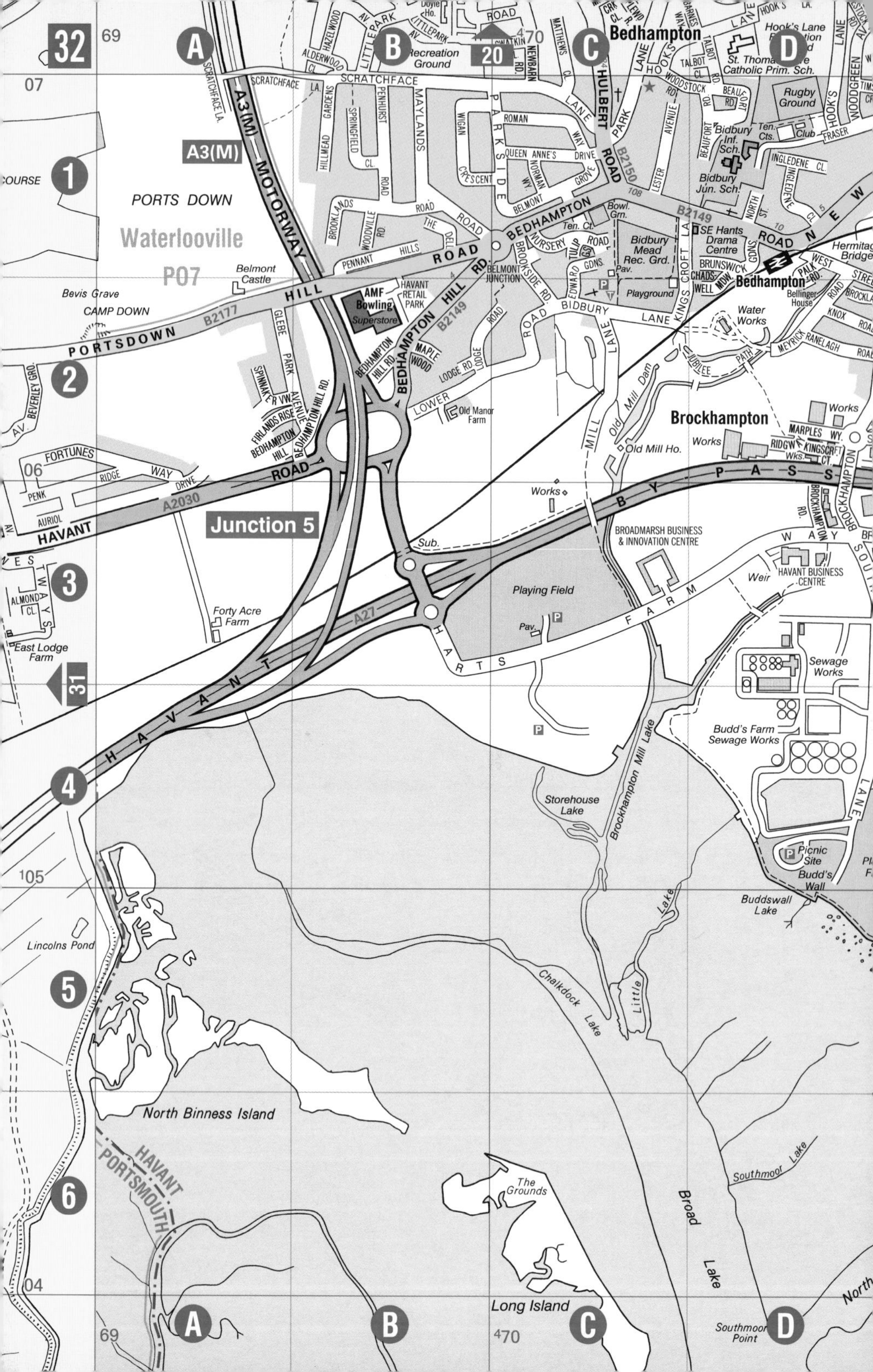

Bedhampton
Hook's Lane
St. Thomas
Catholic Prim. Sch.
Recreation Ground
20
A3(M)
A3(M) MOTORWAY
PORTS DOWN
Waterlooville
PO7
Belmont Castle
Bevis Grave
CAMP DOWN
PORTSDOWN HILL ROAD
B2177
AMF Bowling
Superstore
HAVANT RETAIL PARK
BEDHAMPTON HILL RD.
B2149
B2150
Bidbury Inf. Sch.
Bidbury Jun. Sch.
Rugby Ground
Bidbury Mead Rec. Grd.
Playground
SE Hants Drama Centre
Bedhampton
Hermitage Bridge
Bellinger House
Water Works
Brockhampton
Works
Old Manor Farm
Old Mill Ho.
Old Mill Dam
HAVANT ROAD
A2030
Junction 5
BROADMARSH BUSINESS & INNOVATION CENTRE
HAVANT BUSINESS CENTRE
Weir
Playing Field
Forty Acre Farm
East Lodge Farm
31
HAVANT BY PASS
A27
HARTS FARM WAY
Sewage Works
Budd's Farm Sewage Works
Storehouse Lake
Brockhampton Mill Lake
Picnic Site
Budd's Wall
Buddswall Lake
Lincolns Pond
Chalkdock Lake
Little Lake
North Binness Island
HAVANT PORTSMOUTH
The Grounds
Southmoor Lake
Broad Lake
Long Island
Southmoor Point
Junction
Works
Sub.
Pav.
COURSE

33
21
44
34
HAVANT
Havant
Denvilles
Warblington
Langstone
Hayling Island
PO11
Havant College
Playing Fields
Civic Offs.
Havant Leis. Cen.
HOLLYBANK
Industrial Estate
KENWOOD BUSINESS PARK
Works
Chapel
Cemy.
Havant War Meml. Hosp.
Havant Park
Meridian Centre
Bus Sta.
Lib.
The Pallant
Gazebo Gdn.
Mus. & Arts Cen.
Playing Field
Warblington School
Bowl. Grn.
Superstore
Bosmere Jun. Sch.
Water Works
The Tanneries
Langstone Technology Park
Luxor Park
Pyramid Pk.
Cairo Place
Southmere
Longmead Ct.
Wade Court
Wade Court Farm
Four Winds
The Old Rectory
Warblington Castle
Warblington Castle Farm
Flint House
Langstone Lodge
South Moor
Slipway
Coastguard Cotts.
Quay
Langstone Sailing Club
New Cut
Duckard Point
Northney Marina
North Common
Pontoons
Boat Yard
Boating Lake
Bridge Lake
HAVANT BY PASS
A27
A3023
A259
B2149
LANGSTONE BRIDGE
LANGSTONE ROAD
NORTHNEY
PETERSFIELD RD.
PARK RD. NORTH
PARK RD. SOUTH
EMSWORTH ROAD
EAST STREET
WEST STREET
NEW LANE
PURBROOK
Green Pond Corner
105
06
07
04
72
73
E
F
G
H
1
2
3
4
5
6

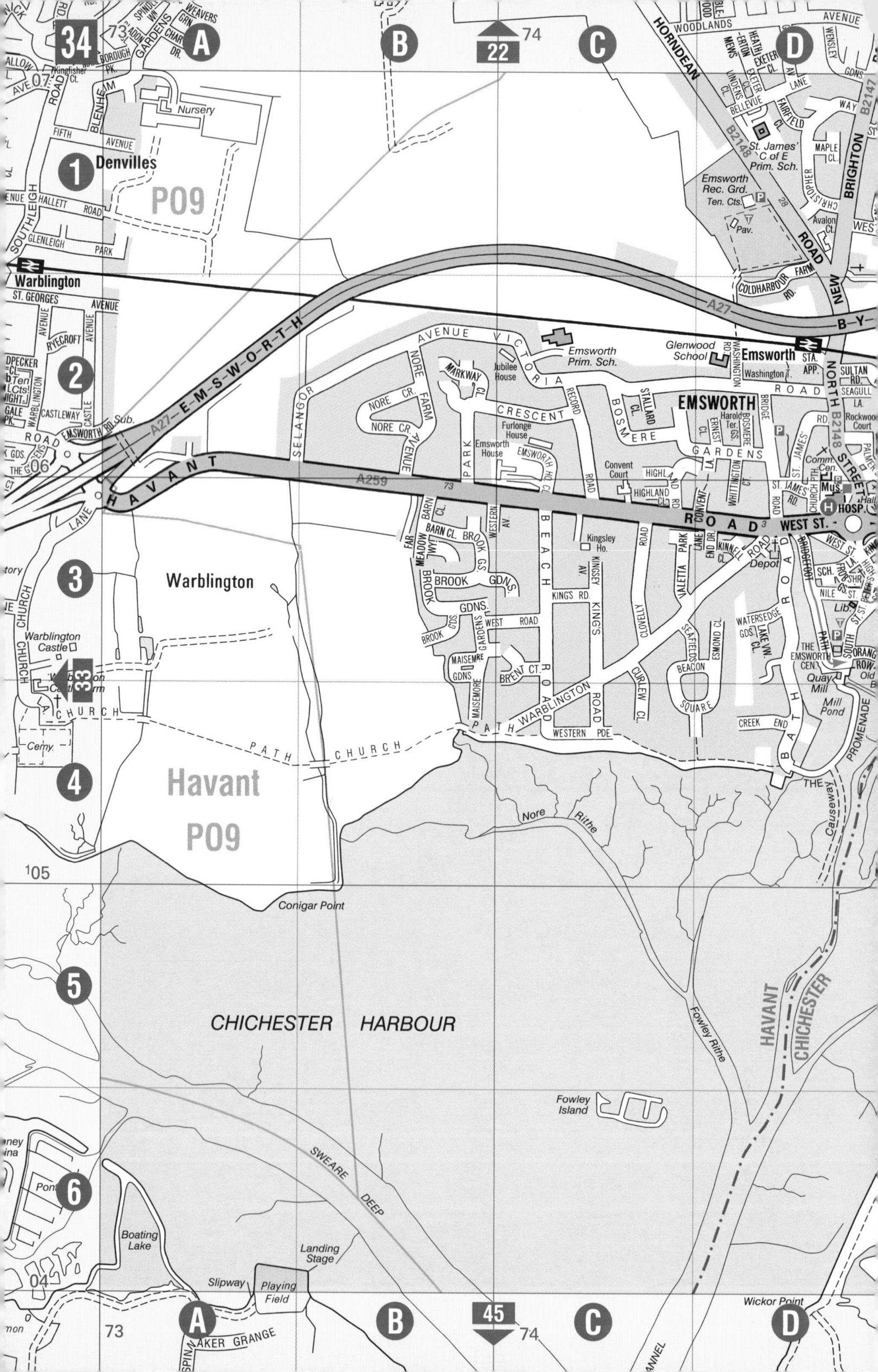

Denvilles
Nursery
PO9
Warblington
Havant
PO9
EMSWORTH
Emsworth
Emsworth Prim. Sch.
Glenwood School
St. James' C of E Prim. Sch.
Emsworth Rec. Grd.
Convent Court
Kingsley Ho.
Jubilee House
Furlonge House
Emsworth House
Warblington Castle
Cemy.
CHICHESTER HARBOUR
Conigar Point
Fowley Island
Fowley Rithe
Nore Rithe
SWEARE DEEP
Landing Stage
Playing Field
Slipway
Boating Lake
Wickor Point
HAVANT
CHICHESTER
A27
A259
B2148
B2147
HAVANT ROAD
EMSWORTH
Quay Mill
Mill Pond
THE EMSWORTH CEN.
HOSP.
Mus.
Lib.
Depot
Pav.
Ten. Cts.

22
33
45

35
23
Lumley
Hermitage
SOUTHBOURNE
Southbourne
Breach
Prinsted
Emsworth
PO10
EMSWORTH HARBOUR
CHICHESTER HARBOUR
THORNEY ISLAND
A27
A259
MAIN ROAD
Lumley Mill
Lumley Mill Farm
Lumley Croft
Brook Cottages
Lumley Farmhouse
Pine Cottage
Playing Fields
Rec. Grd.
The Bourne Community College
Bourne Comm. Leisure Cen.
Works
SOUTHBOURNE IND. EST.
Hall
Library
Southbourne Jun. & Inf. Schs.
Bowl. Grn.
GLEBE HO.
MORCUMB PARK HOMES
Oak Lodge
Gosden Green
Winsley Lodge
Gosden Green Nurseries
Winsley
New Farm
SLIPPER CARAVAN PARK
Claythorn
Mill Pond
Slipway
Hermitage Bridge
John King Shipyard
Hendy's Quay
Emsworth Channel
Pontoon
Boat Yard
Yacht Harbour
Marina Farm
Sewage Wks.
Thornham House
Slipper Hovel
Tanks
Thornham Farm
Dock
Jetty
Thornham Marina
Boat Yard
Nursery
Prinsted Grange
Green Meadows
Swallows
Mayfield
Southlands
Seafields
Playing Field
Little Deep
Eames Farm Cottages
Thornham Point
Printed Point
Airfield Landing Lights
Guardroom
GREAT DEEP
Great Deep
Prinsted Channel
Printsed Point
WEST VIEW COTTS.
THORNEY ROAD
THORNHAM LANE
PRINSTED LANE
STEIN ROAD
MILL LANE
LUMLEY ROAD
WOODFIELD PARK RD.
GORDON ROAD
PENNY LANE
TUPPENNY LANE
SOUTHBOURNE AV.
MANOR ROAD
PARK ROAD
CLOVELLY ROAD
FIRST AVENUE
THE DRIVE
BREACH AVENUE
KELSEY AVENUE
COOKS LA.
EMSWORTH RD.
E F G H
1 2 3 4 5 6
75 76 77
04 05 06 07

A
B
C
D
24
53
54
04
03
02
101
1
2
3
4
5
6
Meon
Little Posbrook
Little Posbrooke Cottage
Lower Posbrook Farm
Churchers Row
Fouracres Nursery
Elmstead
Thatchers Coppice
Meon Ho.
Triangle Lane
Meon Road
River Meon
Fareham
PO14
Crabthorn
Meon View Farm
Titchfield Haven Bird Sanctuary
Titchfield Haven Nature Reserve
Titchfield Haven Nature Reserve Visitor Centre
Titchfield Haven
Hillhead Harbour
Cliff Road
Cliff Cottage
Meon Marsh
Meon Shore Huts
Marsh Lane
Knights Bank Road
Little Gays
Great Gays
Haven Cr.
Old Road
Hill Head Road
Solent Road
Short Rd.
Carisbrooke Road
Plymouth
Cowdray Pk.
Pytchley Cl.
Barlow Cl.
Whaddon Chase
Pembroke Cres.
Corfe Cl.
Berkeley Cl.
Elsfred Rd.
Sanross Cl.
Osborne View Road
Bramble Cl.
Hurst Cl.
Cottes Way
Cottesway East
Ellerslie Cl.
Crofton Avenue
Valsheba Dr.
Seafield Park Rd.
Snows Way
Pilgrims Way
Salterns
Hill Head Sailing Club
Slipway
Crofton
Salterns Park
HILL HEAD
Old Street
Country Vw.
The Oakes
Turtle Cl.
Dolphin Ct.
Finisterre Cl.
Fastnet Wy.
Shannon
Forties Cl.
Hamble Ct.
Cromarty Cl.
Hebrides Cl.
Fair Isle
Dover Cl.
Humber Cl.
Biscay
Viking Cl.
Fury Way
The Scimitars
Forth Cl.
The Gannets
Crabthorn Farm La.
Berry Lane
Vixen Cl.
Sea Kings
Hawk Cl.
Fitzwilliam Av.
Blankney Cl.
Bramham Moor
Good Cl.
Andrew Pl.
Violet Av.
Harriet Cl.
The Grove
Plover Cl.
Moody
Bell
Robinson
Boyd Cl.
Davies
Caspar John Cl.
Invincible Rd.
Illustrious Rd.
Cuckoo Lane
THE SOLENT

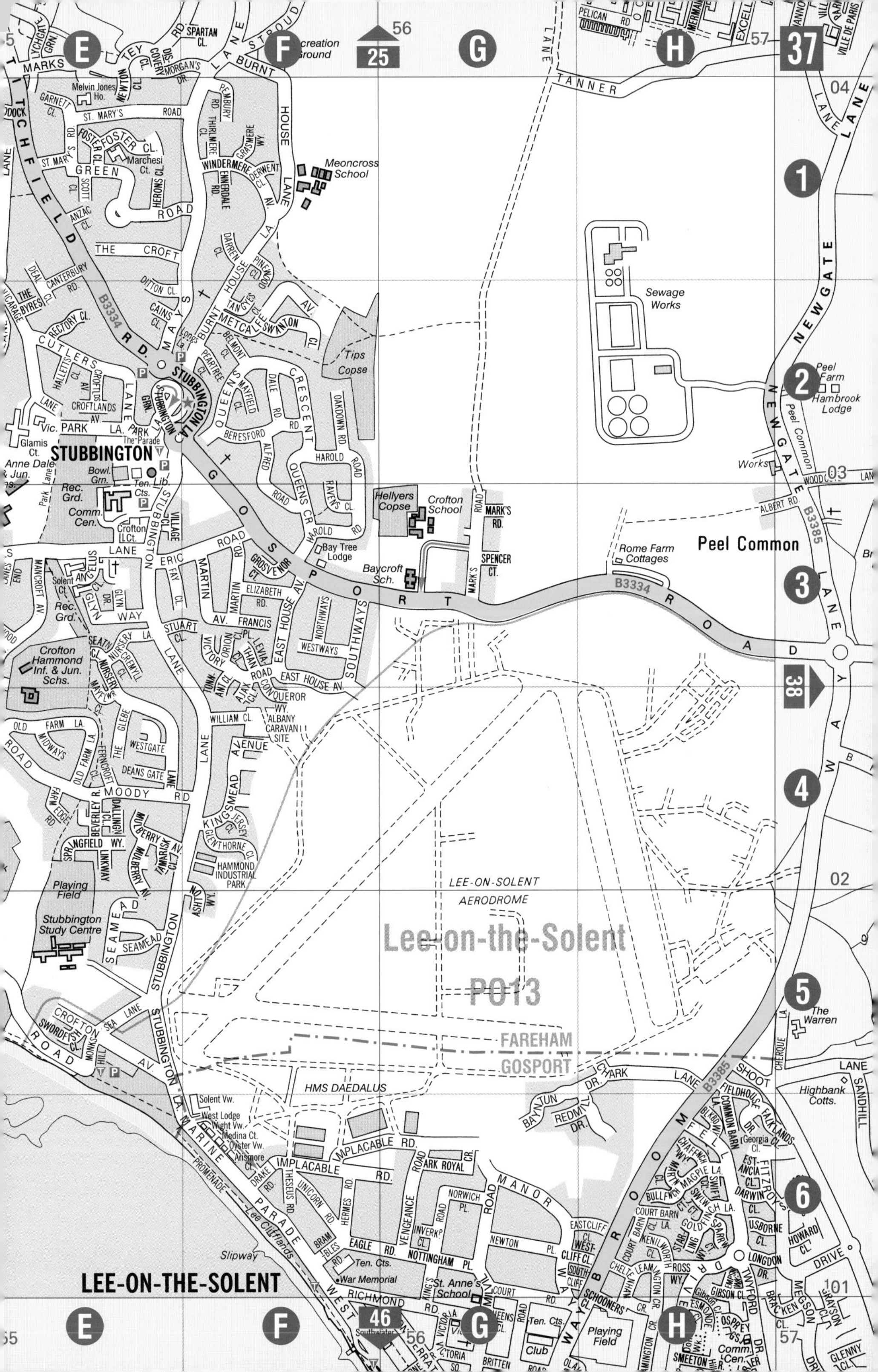

E
F
G
H
25
56
37
57
04
03
02
1
2
3
4
5
6
38
46
01
55
Recreation Ground
Meoncross School
Sewage Works
Tips Copse
Peel Farm
Hambrook Lodge
Peel Common
Works
Rome Farm Cottages
Hellyers Copse
Crofton School
Bay Tree Lodge
Baycroft Sch.
STUBBINGTON
The Parade
Bowl. Grn.
Ten. Cts.
Lib.
Rec. Grd.
Comm. Cen.
Crofton L. Ct.
Anne Dale Inf. & Jun. Schs.
Glamis Ct.
Melvin Jones Ho.
Marchesi Ct.
Crofton Hammond Inf. & Jun. Schs.
Solent Ct.
Albany Caravan Site
Hammond Industrial Park
Playing Field
Stubbington Study Centre
LEE-ON-SOLENT AERODROME
Lee-on-the-Solent
PO13
FAREHAM
GOSPORT
HMS DAEDALUS
The Warren
Highbank Cotts.
Solent Vw.
West Lodge
Wight Vw.
Medina Ct.
Oyster Vw.
Arismore Ct.
Slipway
LEE-ON-THE-SOLENT
Ten. Cts.
War Memorial
St. Anne's School
Club
Playing Field
Comm. Cen.
Southwater
B3334
B3385
GOSPORT ROAD
NEWGATE LANE
PEEL COMMON
TITCHFIELD RD.
STUBBINGTON LA.
STUBBINGTON LANE
BURNT HOUSE LANE
MAYS LA.
TANNER LANE
MARKS RD.
CROFTON LANE
MARINE PARADE WEST
BROOM WAY
CHARK LANE
MANOR WAY
IMPLACABLE RD.
RICHMOND RD.
MOODY RD
OLD FARM LA.
ST. MARY'S ROAD
FOSTER CL.
GREEN ROAD
THE CROFT
CUTLERS LANE
VIC. PARK LA.
ERIC ROAD
GLYN WAY
WILLIAM CL.
AVENUE
KINGSMEAD
SEAMEAD
SPRINGFIELD WY.
NOTTINGHAM PL.
EAGLE RD.
NEWTON PL.
LONGDON DR.
SHOOT LANE
LANE SANDHILL
CHERQUE LA.
PELICAN RD
TANNER
SPARTAN CL.

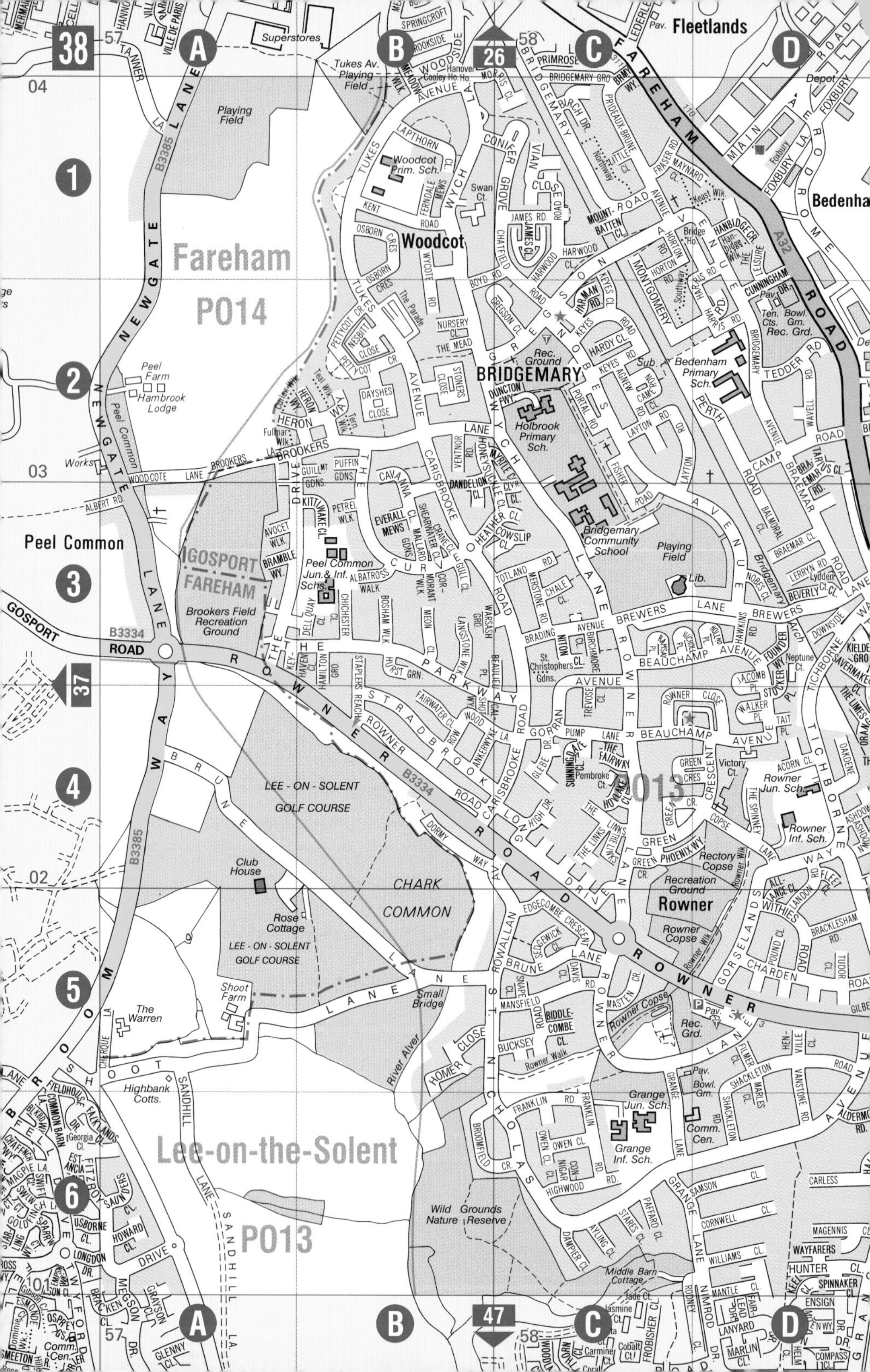

38
A
B
C
D
26
47
37
1
2
3
4
5
6
57
58
04
03
02
01
Fleetlands
Bedenham
Fareham
PO14
Woodcot
BRIDGEMARY
Peel Common
GOSPORT
FAREHAM
PO13
Rowner
Lee-on-the-Solent
Superstores
Tukes Av. Playing Field
Playing Field
Woodcot Prim. Sch.
Swan Ct.
Peel Farm
Hambrook Lodge
Works
Rec. Ground
Holbrook Primary Sch.
Bridgemary Community School
Bedenham Primary Sch.
Ten. Cts.
Bowl. Grn.
Rec. Grd.
Depot
Lib.
Peel Common Jun.& Inf. Schs.
Brookers Field Recreation Ground
LEE - ON - SOLENT GOLF COURSE
Club House
Rose Cottage
CHARK COMMON
Shoot Farm
The Warren
Small Bridge
River Alver
Highbank Cotts.
Wild Grounds Nature Reserve
Middle Barn Cottage
Victory Ct.
Rowner Jun. Sch.
Rowner Inf. Sch.
Rectory Copse
Recreation Ground
Rowner Copse
Rec. Grd.
Grange Jun. Sch.
Grange Inf. Sch.
Comm. Cen.
St. Christophers Gdns.
Pembroke Ct.
Neptune Ct.
NEWGATE LANE
B3385
GOSPORT ROAD
B3334
ROWNER ROAD
BROOM WAY
BRUNE LANE
SHOOT LANE
SANDHILL LANE
FAREHAM ROAD
A32
AERODROME ROAD
MAIN ROAD
FOXBURY LA.
WOODCOTE LANE
BROOKERS LANE
TUKES AVENUE
WYCH LANE
CONIFER GROVE
BRIDGEMARY AVENUE
BRIDGEMARY ROAD
MOUNTBATTEN CL.
GREGSON AVENUE
NOBES AVENUE
BREWERS LANE
BEAUCHAMP AVENUE
CARISBROOKE AVENUE
THE PARKWAY
STRADBROOK
LONGROW
PUMP LANE
THE FAIRWAY
GOSELANDS
ROWNER LANE
ST. NICHOLAS AVENUE
GRANGE LANE
TICHBORNE WAY
HENVILLE CL.
FRANKLIN RD.

Royal Naval Armaments Depot Gosport
Tidal Pond
Frater Lake
Frater Pier
Elson Wood
PORTSMOUTH HARBOUR
FAREHAM LAKE
Pewit Island
PORTSMOUTH
GOSPORT
Normal Tidal Point
FORT ELSON
Frater
Gosport
Don Styler Physical Training Centre
HERITAGE WAY
MONKS WK.
MILITARY RD.
Sports Ground
HERITAGE BUSINESS PK.
SHAMROCK ENTERPRISE CEN.
BROCKHURST IND. ESTATE
Fort Brockhurst
Moat
Holbrook Recreation Centre
Gosport Ice Rink
Rec. Grd.
Factory
FAREHAM ROAD
A32
GUNNERS WAY
ELSON ROAD
PRIORY ROAD
Works
Hardway Sailing Club
Pier
War Mem.
Red Cross HQ
Elson Inf. Sch.
Elson Jun. Sch.
Elson
PO12
Irwin Heights
Vicarage Ter.
B3334
ROAD
Playing Field
Brune Park Community College
Suncourt Villas
BROCKHURST RD.
EASTBOURNE AV.
RYDAL RD.
CHANTRY RD.
Lib.
Comm. Cen.
Prim. Sch.
Hardway
Cygnet Ho.
SEALARK RD.
FORT ROWNER
Moat
Brockhurst Inf. Sch.
Brockhurst
Brockhurst Jun. Sch.
AVERY LANE
Clare Ho.
Bagot Ho.
Russell Churcher Ct.
Grange
HMS
SAN DIEGO
BERYTON ROAD
DUKES
STATION
MILITARY ROAD
Crusader Ct.
BRITANNIA
VANGUARD RD.
SOVEREIGN
Agnew Ho.
Factory

27
40
48

40
PORTSMOUTH HARBOUR
Pewit Island
Spider Lake
BOMBKETCH LAKE
FAREHAM LAKE
PORTCHESTER LAKE
Hardway
Hardway Sailing Club
Gosport
Explosion
Priddy's Hard
Camber Basin
Shell Pier
Reservoir
Jetty
Forton Lake
Rolling Bri.
Burrow Island
North Corner
Middle Slip Jetty
North Railway Jetty
PORTSMOUTH GOSPORT
Portsmouth to:
Bilbao 28hrs.
Caen 5hrs. 45mins. (Seasonal)
Caen 3hrs. 45mins.
(Fast Ferry, Seasonal)
Cherbourg 5hrs. 30mins. (Seasonal)
Cherbourg 3hrs.
(Fast Ferry, Seasonal)
Guernsey 7hrs.
Jersey 10hrs. 30mins.
Le Havre 5hrs 30mins.
St. Malo 10hrs. 45mins. (Seasonal)
28
39
49

41
E
F
G
H
29
50
M275
M275 MOTORWAY
PO6
PO2
PO1
Tipner Lake
Tipner
Tipner Point
Tipner Lake Bridge
Portsmouth Stadium (Greyhound)
ALEXANDRA PARK
Cycling Track
Sports Ground
Tennis Courts
The Mountbatten Centre
Victory Indoor Bowls Club
Alexandra Park
Danger Area
Tipner Range
Brick Kiln Lake
WHALE ISLAND
HMS EXCELLENT
Sports Ground
Football Ground
Stamshaw
Stamshaw Park
Stamshaw Junior Sch.
Leisure Cen.
CONTINENTAL FERRY PORT
Fountain Lake
Fountain Lake Jetty
North West Wall
Albert Johnson Quay
Floating Dock
Landing Stage
Basin No. 3
Tidal Basin
Lock
Portsmouth
Landport
Dickens Mus.
Odeon Cinema
Buckland Park
Rudmore Roundabout
NORTHERN
KINGSTON CR.
LONDON RD.
KINGSTON RD.
MILE END RD.
TWYFORD AV.
Slipways
Slipway
Pier
Pontoons
VICTORY RETAIL PARK

42
30
41
51
A
B
C
D
1
2
3
4
5
6
Hilsea Lines
HILSEA
Hilsea
NORTH END
Copnor
Buckland
Kingston
Landport
Baffins
Portsmouth
PO2
PO3
PORTSEA ISLAND
NORTHERN PARADE
LONDON ROAD
COPNOR ROAD
KINGSTON ROAD
FRATTON ROAD
MILTON ROAD
A3
A2047
A288
ALEXANDRA PARK
Cycling Track
Tennis Courts
Victoria Indoor Bowls Club
The City of Portsmouth Boys' Sch.
Playing Field
Hilsea Mkt.
Rec. Grd.
TA Centre
Gunners Bldgs. Ind. Estate
Culverin Sq. Ind. Estate
Broad Oak Works
Rugby Camp Playing Field
Roko Health & Fitness
Sports Ground
Football Pitches
Bowling Green
Tennis Courts
Gatcombe Gardens
Hilsea Lodge
Northern Pde. Inf. & Jun. Schs.
Coronation Eventide Homes
Alexandra Lodge
The Admiral Pk.
The Challenge Ent. Cen.
Airport Ind. Estate
Quadra Point
Portfield Ind. Est.
Highgrove Ind. Pk.
Portsmouth Enterprise Cen.
Pyramid Centre
The Nelson Centre
Quartremaine Road Ind. Estate
O'Jays Ind. Park
Victory Trading Estate
Phoenix Bldgs.
Ocean Park
Burrfields Retail Park
Dundas Recreation
The Willows Sch.
Cliffdale Prim. Sch.
Mayfield Sch.
Play. Flds.
College Park
College Pk. Inf. Sch.
Odeon Cin.
The Mall
Bowling Green
Copnor Inf. & Jun. Schs.
Sports Ground
GREAT SALT RECREAT GROUN
Playground
Fire Brig. Div. HQ
Isambard Brunel Jun. Sch.
Meredith Inf. Sch.
Comm. Cen.
Newbridge Jun. Sch.
Copnor Bridge
War Mem.
War Memorial
KINGSTON CEMETERY
Manor Inf. Sch.
Westover Prim. Sch.
Baffins Pond
Play Area
Langstone Jun. Sch.
Langstone Inf. Sch.
Playing Field
HMP KINGSTON
Girls' Sch.
Sargent Cres.

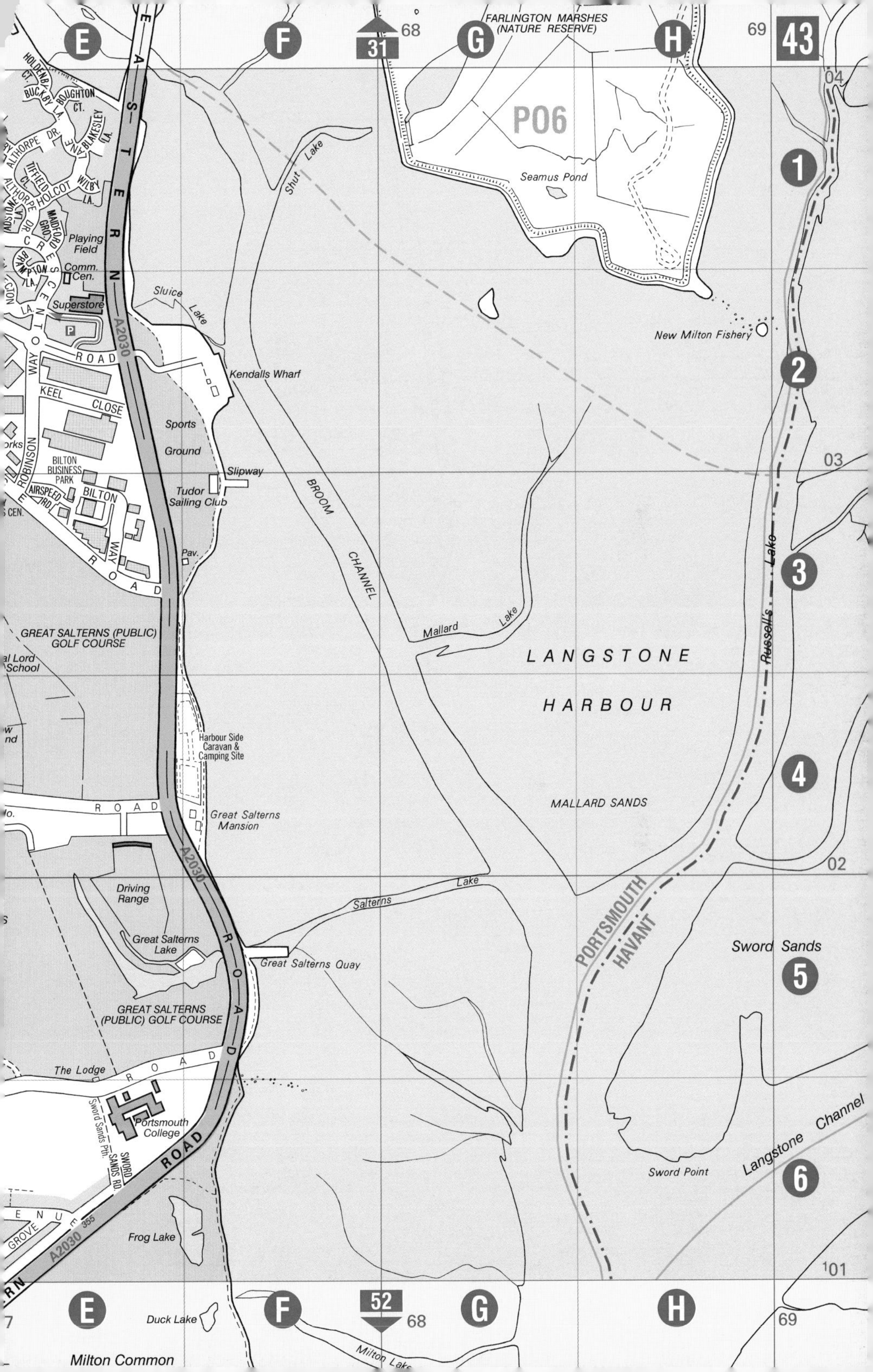

FARLINGTON MARSHES (NATURE RESERVE)
PO6
Seamus Pond
New Milton Fishery
Shut Lake
Sluice Lake
Kendalls Wharf
Sports Ground
Slipway
Tudor Sailing Club
Pav.
BROOM CHANNEL
Mallard Lake
LANGSTONE HARBOUR
Russell's Lake
MALLARD SANDS
PORTSMOUTH
HAVANT
Sword Sands
Sword Point
Langstone Channel
Salterns Lake
Great Salterns Quay
Great Salterns Mansion
Harbour Side Caravan & Camping Site
GREAT SALTERNS (PUBLIC) GOLF COURSE
Driving Range
Great Salterns Lake
The Lodge
Portsmouth College
Sword Sands Pth.
SWORD SANDS RD.
Frog Lake
Duck Lake
Milton Common
Milton Lake
EASTERN ROAD
A2030
HOLDENBY CT.
BUCKBY LA.
BOUGHTON CT.
BLAKESLEY LA.
ALTHORPE DR.
TIFFIELD CL.
HOLCOT LA.
WILBY LA.
MAIDFORD GRO.
CRESCENT
Playing Field
Comm. Cen.
Superstore
WAY
ROAD
KEEL CLOSE
ROBINSON
BILTON BUSINESS PARK
AIRSPEED RD.
BILTON WAY
ROAD
GROVE
AVENUE
E F G H
31
52
68
69
04
03
02
101
355
1 2 3 4 5 6

33
54
A
B
C
D
1
2
3
4
5
6
71
72
04
03
02
01
North Lake
Penner
Penner South Point
South Lake
NORTHNEY ROAD
Bridge House Farm
North Common
Homestead
Rec. Grd.
HAVANT ROAD
A3023
NEW CUT
ISLAND CL.
KINGSWAY
QUEENSWAY
ISLAND
CL.
Stoke Common
AVENUE
ROAD
MEADOW CL.
MEAD
ROGERS
VICTORIA ROAD
Hayling Island
PO11
HAYLING ISLAND
Stoke Common Lake
MILL CL.
Cockle Rithe
Knott's Marsh
Westcroft Riding School
Old Oyster Beds
CROFT LA.
NORTHWOOD LANE
Stoke Farm
Northwood Farm
STOKE
LANE
CASTLEMANS LANE
Upper Rithe
FINCHWOOD FARM INDUSTRIAL UNITS
North Copse
Finchwood Farmhouse
Copsewood House
Stoke Fruit Farm
WEST LANE
COPSE
Fleet
YEW TREE ROAD
Fleet Fm
Aston House
DAW LANE
FLEET FARM CAMPING & CARAVAN SITE
VERNER COMM
Quay
MILL RYTHE LA
Slipways
Jetties
Yachtbuilding Yard
Manor Farm
Manor House
Boating

Boating Lake

Slipway

Landing Stage

Playing Field

SPINNAKER GRANGE

NORTHNEY LA.

Northney

Northney Farm

CLOVELLY RD.

SPYCROFT CL.

CHURCH LANE

Church Farm

NORTH HAYLING

Hall

St PETER'S AV.

Thorney View

L I N G

A N D

ROAD

GUNNER LANE

CHICHESTER ROAD

Upper Tye Farm

Tye

rm

A

WOODGASTON LA.

Lower Tye Farm

Gutner Farm

WOODGASTON LA.

YE CARAVAN NG CENTRE

WOODGASTON LA.

Point Ho.

Marshlands

Slipway

Slipway

White Lodge

Meadow Farm Nursery

Shallows

Slipways

73

MILL RYTHE HOLIDAY VILLAGE

Wickor Point

GREAT DEEP

04

THORNEY ISLAND

1

2

Emsworth 03

PO10

3

Marker Point

4

02

EMSWORTH CHANNEL

CHICHESTER HAVANT

5

6

101

MILL RYTHE

455
A
B
C
D
56
37
01
1
2
3
4
5
6
100
99
098
LEE-ON-THE-SOLENT
THE SOLENT
Slipway
MARINE
EAGLE RD.
NEWTON PL.
CLIFF CL.
BROOM WY.
St. Aidan's School
RICHMOND RD.
COURT RD.
SCHOONERS
Playing Field
Ten. Cts.
Club
South water
MONTSERRAT RD.
PARADE
VICTORIA SQ.
QUEENS CL.
BRITTEN ROAD
Swimming Bath
Freshwater Ct.
Promenade Ct.
SWANAGE
GROVE
MANOR WAY
B3385
RUSSELL CL.
PETRIE RD.
ROAD
LEAMINGTON CR.
Hove Ct.
Milvil Ct.
CLANWILLIAM RD.
Solent Gdns.
War Mem.
PIER S.
East Lodge
Bembridge Lodge
Nicholas Ct.
William George Ct.
Homeryde Ho.
MARINE PARADE
B3333
ESPLANADE
PROMENADE
BEACH RD.
Hornetide Ho.
Solent Heights
HIGH STREET
RUSSELL
Lee-Clifflands
Tennis Cts.
Recreation Ground
Pav.
Lib.
Lee-on-the-Solent Inf. Sch.
Lee-on-the-Solent Jun. Sch.
Rogers Ho.
Berkeley Ct.
HOLLYBANK
CAMBRIDGE
Seaview Ct.
GOSPORT RD.
Water's Edge
Castle Marina
PORTSMOUTH RD.
ELMORE
Woburn Ct.
QUEENS RD.
LAKESIDE
Lee-on-the-Solent Sailing Club
EAST
SPENCER
SPRING CT.
AVON CL.
DERWENT ROAD
TRENT WAY
SEA CREST
SKIPPER WAY
DRIVE
WAVENEY CL.
SMEETON RD.
Comm. Cen.
Gibson CL.
TWYFORD

47
38
E
F
G
H
1
2
3
4
5
6
58
59
57
01
100
99
098
Lee-on-the-Solent
PO13
Gosport
Grange
HMS SULTAN
Middle Barn Cottage
Jade Ct.
Jasmine Ct.
Magenta Ct.
Carmine Ct.
Cobalt Ct.
Coral Ct.
FROBISHER CL.
WOODLANDS CL.
OAKTHORN CL.
St. Davids Ct.
Exeter Ct.
RAMBLER DR.
Bath & Wells Ct.
Derby Ct.
Bradford Ct.
RAVEN
Hereford Ct.
Worcester Ct.
Truro Ct.
Sheffield Ct.
DAVENPORT CL.
Bristol Ct.
HOWE ROAD
MANDARIN
GRIFFIN WK.
Siskin Inf. Sch.
Siskin Jun. Sch.
Rowner Swimming Centre
Comm. Cen.
NIMROD DR.
RODNEY CL.
WILLIAMS CL.
WAYFARERS
SPINNAKER CL.
MANTLE CL.
LANYARD DR.
MARLIN CL.
ENSIGN DR.
COMPASS CL.
Lawrence Wk.
DARWIN WY.
COCHRANE CL.
PEGASUS CL.
GAZELLE CL.
OTTER CL.
NAPIER CL.
LINDBERGH
BALFOUR
Coventry Cl.
CLOSE
Rochester Ct.
Blackburn Ct.
Liverpool Ct.
Birmingham Ct.
Ripon Ct.
Ely Ct.
Leicester Ct.
Lincoln Ct.
Manchester Ct.
Winchester Ct.
St. Albans Ct.
Guildford Ct.
RANSON CL.
Grange Farm
The 1664 Living History Village
HMS DAEDALUS CARAVAN PARK
LITTLE WOODHAM LA.
ROAD
Motte & Bailey
Alder Moor
Apple Dumpling Bridge
Civic Amenity Tip
Grange Open Space
River Alver
Sports Field
GRANGE ROAD
ALDER LANE
Ten. Cts.
Pav.
FORT GRANGE
Tennis Courts
Sultan House
MILITARY
Fairview Ct.
SANDHILL
LANE
Works
Gravel Pit
MEGSON DRIVE
GRAYSON CL.
GLENNY CL.
DAVID
BRYSON CL.
HOLT CL.
LANGTON CL.
SHERBROOKE CL.
WESSEX CL.
TIGER
MOTH
BEAUFORT CL.
FIREFLY CL.
NEWBERRY
MARTLET CL.
WELLINGTON DR.
HOVERFLY CL.
HARVARD CL.
ALBACORE CL.
MAGISTER
DRIVE
CORSAIR CL.
PERCIVAL CL.
WESTLAND
SEAFIRE RD.
MARTINET DR.
SKIPPER WAY
AVENUE
ELMORE AV.
ROAD
WOOTTON ROAD
ANGLESEA RD.
THE SEAGULLS
ROAD
CLIFTON RD.
RYDE PLACE
SOUTH PLACE
WOOTTON RD.
WARWICK CL.
PENNINE WY.
LANCASTER CL.
YORK CRESCENT
CHESTER CRESCENT
CANTERBURY CL.
PORTSMOUTH ROAD
PRIVETT ROAD
B3333
Browndown Training Camp
MILITARY ROAD
BROWNDOWN ROAD
KINGFISHER CARAVAN PARK
Rifle Ranges
BROWNDOWN
Browndown Battery
Bay House Sch. Playing Fld.
Ten. Cts.
Bay House Sports Hall
Shirrel Ct.
Ashurst Ct.
Cadnam Ct.
Fair Oak Ct.
Tower Ct.
PORTLAND DR.
BROADSANDS DR.
SANDOWN CL.
Woolston Ct.
Seaview Ct.
GOMER ROAD
GOMER LANE
Wickham Ct.
MARTELLO CL.
GALE MOOR AV.
Whitecliffe Ct.
Milford Ct.
Moat Ct.
SANDFORD AV.
CHURCHER WK.
STOKES BAY MOBILE HOME PK.
Bay House School
STOKES BAY ROAD
STOKES BAY
REPTON
HELSTED
AMERSHAM
MONROE
Waverley Path
ST. GRAYS
STANLEY PARK

48
59
A
B
C
D
460
39
47
1
2
3
4
5
6
098
99
100
ROWNER
Inf. Sch.
Brockhurst Jun. Sch.
AVERY
TEIGNMOUTH RD.
BROCKHURST ROAD
Brockhurst
A32
FORTON ROAD
Grange
HMS SULTAN
HMS Sultan
CAMBRIDGE ROAD
FORT GRANGE
Tennis Courts
Sultan House
Sports Ground
Playing Field
Sports Field
MILITARY ROAD
ALDER LANE
SOUTHCROFT ROAD
MIDDLECROFT LANE
Ann's Hill Cemetery
War Mem.
Ann's Hill
WILMOTT LANE
Camdentown
St. Mary's Catholic Prim. Sch.
LEESLAND ROAD
Leesland Play Area
Cemetery
Forton
Leesland Park
Privett Park (Recreation Ground)
Tennis Courts
Gosport Borough FC
Depot
HOUSE FARM RD.
PRIVETT ROAD
B3333
Privett
Queen's Pde.
Gomer Jun. & Inf. Schs.
Privett Gdns.
BURY HALL LANE
BURY ROAD
GOSPORT WAR MEML. HOSP.
Thorngate Hall
Leesland C of E Jun. Sch.
FOSTER ROAD
SOUTH ROAD
Dolphin Ho.
Foster Gdns.
BEECH GROVE
Anglesey Gdns.
TESTCOMBE RD.
BEECHCROFT RD.
ST. MARY'S AVENUE
Gosport
PO12
Ewer Common
Alverstoke Jun. Sch.
Alverstoke Tennis & Squash Club
Northcott House
ALVERSTOKE
VECTIS ROAD
WESTERN WAY
SOLENT WAY
STANLEY PARK
Bay House School
STOKES BAY MOBILE HOME PK.
Alverbank House
CRESCENT
PALMERSTON WAY
Open Space
Tennis Courts
VILLAGE ROAD
LITTLE ANGLESEY ROAD
Little Anglesey Viaduct
Bodrick Meml. Hall
Play. Fld.
CLAYHALL ROAD
St. Mark's Place
Alverstoke Inf. Sch.
STOKES BAY ROAD
PROMENADE
Stokes Bay Sailing Club
STOKES BAY
Stokes Bay Open Space
FORT ROAD
Anglesey
Moncton House
Royal Naval Physiological Laboratory
GOSPORT & STOKES BAY GOLF COURSE
Sports Ground
Quayside Education Centre
MILL POND RD.
Bowling Green
Alver Quay Viaduct
Bowl. Grns.
Ten. Cts.

GOSPORT
Forton Lake
Rolling Bri.
Burrow Island
(site of Fort James)
Galleon Pl.
Ledwell Ct.
Royal Clarence Yard
Weevil Lake
Pier
Slipway
Jetty
Depot
Vincent Leisure Centre
The Officers Quarters
Harlequin Ct.
Sanderling Lodge
ROPE QUAYS
Jacana Ct.
CLARENCE WHARF
Gosport Marina
MUMBY ROAD
A32
Playing Field
The Quarterdeck
Charles Ho.
King Charles's Fort
Falklands Gds.
Gosport to Portsea 8mins. (Foot Ferry)
Superstore
Martin Snape Ho.
Gosport Gallery
HIGH STREET
SOUTH STREET
B3333
WALPOLE ROAD
Walpole Park
Boating Pond
Cockle Pond
Bus Sta.
South Wharf
Landing Stage
Slipways
THE ESPLANADE
PORTSMOUTH
GOSPORT
Newtown
Seafield
Workhouse Lake
Gas Works
Boat Yard
Watergate
Moat
Rampart Row
HASLAR
Haslar Bridge
HMS Alliance
Haslar Jetty
Royal Navy Submarine Mus.
HM Sub. Holland 1
Sail Train. Cen.
Defence Research Agency
Recreation Ground
Tennis Cts.
ROYAL HOSPITAL HASLAR
Foremans Cotts.
Cemy.
Haslar Ter.
HASLAR SEA WALL
ADMIRALTY ROAD
HMS DOLPHIN
Fort Blockhouse
GOSPORT PARK
Tennis Courts
Pond
Lake
Clayhall
DOLPHIN WAY
HMP HASLAR
Club House
GOSPORT & STOKES BAY GOLF COURSE
FORT MONCKTON
MILITARY ROAD
SPITHEAD
Spit Sand
Portsmouth to Ryde 18mins. (Foot Ferry,Fast Ferry)
Portsmouth to Fishbourne 35mins.
PORTSMOUTH HARBOUR
HM NAVAL BASE
VICTORIA ROAD
Middle Slip Jetty
North Railway Jetty
Sheer Jetty
Pitch Ho. Jetty
Boat Ho. Jetty
Kings Stairs Jetty
South Railway Jetty
Mary Rose Ship Hall
HMS Victory
Royal Naval Mus.
Mary Rose Mus.
Lion Gate
Visitor Cen.
South Camber
Portsea
HMS Warrior
Common Hard
PORTSMOUTH HARBOUR
GUNWHARF QUAYS
Spinnaker Tower
New Hampshire Boulevard
Canalside
THE POINT
Old Portsmouth
The Round Tower
Point Battery
Sally Port
The Square Tower
Victoria Pier
North Bastion
West Demi Bastion
East Demi Bastion
I.O.W. Ferry Terminal (Vehicular)
Outer Camber
Inner Camber
BROAD ST.
HIGH ST.
E
F
G
H
1
2
3
4
5
6
40
50
62
63
98
99
100

A
B
C
D
41
1
2
3
4
5
6
4
5
49
63
64
100
99
98
PORTSMOUTH
Portsea
SOUTHSEA
Somers Town
Landport
SPITHEAD
HM NAVAL BASE
HMS Victory
Mary Rose Mus.
PORTSMOUTH HARBOUR
GUNWHARF QUAYS
Spinnaker Tower
HMS NELSON
HMS Temeraire
University of Portsmouth (University Quarter)
University of Portsmouth
PORTSMOUTH & SOUTHSEA
Victoria Park
Victoria Swim. Cen.
Guildhall
CASCADES CENTRE
Cathedral
City Mus. & Art Gall.
Royal Garrison Church
King's Bastion
The Round Tower
The Sq. Tower
Victoria Pier
Clarence Pier Amusement Park
Clarence Pier Pavilion
I.O.W. Hovercraft Terminal
I.O.W. Ferry Terminal (Vehicular)
Clarence Ground
Nelson's Statue
SOUTHSEA COMMON
Royal Naval War Meml.
Blue Reef Aquarium
D-Day Mus.
Southsea Castle & Mus.
The Pyramids Leisure Cen.
The Rock Gardens
The Castle Field
Skatepark
Putting Green
Floral Clock
Ornamental Lake
Sea Wall
Portsmouth to Fishbourne 35mins.
Portsmouth to Ryde 18mins. (Foot Ferry,Fast Ferry)
Portsmouth to Ryde 10mins. (Foot Ferry, Hovercraft)
QUEEN STREET
ST. GEORGE'S RD.
CAMBRIDGE RD.
HIGH STREET
BROAD STREET
PEMBROKE RD.
PIER ROAD
CLARENCE PDE.
WESTERN PDE.
SOUTH PARADE
CLARENCE ESPLANADE
ANGLESEA RD.
HAMPSHIRE TER.
MARKETWAY
COMMERCIAL RD.
WINSTON CHURCHILL AV.
KINGS ROAD
ELM GROVE
VICTORIA ROAD SOUTH
MUSEUM RD.
GREETHAM ST.
ARUNDEL ST.
LAKE RD.
A3
A288
A2030
B2154
B2151
B2152

51
42
52
Kingston
Portsmouth
Fratton
Southsea
MILTON
PO3
PO4
ST. MARY'S HOSPITAL (East Wing)
ST. MARY'S HOSPITAL (West Wing)
ST. JAMES' HOSPITAL
HMP KINGSTON
Kingston Cemetery
Milton Cemetery
Highland Road Cemetery
Portsmouth FC (Fratton Park)
Fitness First
The Pompey Centre
Kingston Park
Milton Park
Canoe Lake
Natural History Mus.
Southsea Model Village
Royal Marines Mus.
South Parade Pier
Landing Stage
Eastney Fort East
Eastney Fort West
Miniature Golf Course
St. Helen's Playing Field
Cricket Ground
Playing Fields
Miniature Railway
GOLDSMITH AVENUE
MILTON ROAD
EASTNEY ROAD
HIGHLAND ROAD
EASTERN PARADE
SOUTH PARADE
EASTERN AV.
VELDER AV.
LANGSTONE ROAD
FRATTON ROAD
A2030
A288
A2047
B2154
B2155
E
F
G
H
1
2
3
4
5
6
65
66
67
01
99
98
100

A
B
C
D
1
2
3
4
5
6
67
68
43
51
Frog Lake
Portsmouth
PO3
Milton Common
Duck Lake
Milton Lake
Swan Lake
EASTERN ROAD
A2030
MOORINGS
Ind. Est.
THE HAVEN
MARINERS WLK.
WARREN
EDENBRIDGE
MAYLES
SHELFORD
ST. JAMES HOSPITAL
LANGSTONE
CHAPEL WK.
NELSON
King Villa
Light Villa
Devine Villa
Hamble Ho.
WOODLANDS WK.
The Orchards
The Beeches
Yew Ho.
Fair Oak Ho.
FAIR OAK
CHERITON
OAKDENE RD.
Inf. Sch.
LONGFIELD
SISKIN
LAPWING RD.
SANDERLING RD.
Queen Elizabeth The Queen Mother Hall (Halls of Residence)
University of Portsmouth (Langstone Campus)
(BUSES ONLY)
FURZE LA
BROOM
BROOM CL.
BROOM SQUARE
LONGSHORE WAY
Locks Sailing Club
Milton Locks
Tennis Courts
Southsea
PO4
Cricket Ground
Pav.
THE DRIVEWAY
SOLENT
DRIVE
LOCKS WAY
ROAD
Comm. Cen.
Inf. Sch.
100
MORGAN RD.
IRONBRIDGE
TREVIS RD.
MERYL
Towpath Mead
WATERLOCK GDNS.
SEAWAY CR.
SEAWAY
Milton Piece
REDLANDS GRO.
SHIRLEY
BERNEY
TIDEWAY GDNS.
MAURICE RD.
MELROSE CL.
DUNBAR
OLD CANAL
Milford Ct.
Coach Ho. M.
AMYAS CT.
KINGSLEY
Societies
BRANSBURY PARK
Playing Fields
Miniature Railway
Play-grd.
Ten. Cts.
Comm. Cen.
BRANSBURY
Pav.
Eastney Pumping Station Mus.
Henderson Park Mobile Homes
Eastney Lake
Langstone Harbour
Lock Lake
Lock Gates
Langstone Marina
Works
Eastlake Heights
Langstone Marina Heights
Spithead Hts.
Solent Hts.
HORSE SANDS CL.
FERRY ROAD
FERRY RD.
LUMSDEN RD.
FINCH
GIBRALTAR
CUMBERLAND ROAD
FORT CUMBERLAND
FORT
Fraser Range
EASTNEY
FARM RD.
MINSTEAD
FORDINGBRIDGE
CADNAM
Grand Division Rw.
HENDERSON
TAMARISK CL.
COCKLESHELL GS.
HALLIDAY CRESCENT
Eastney Sports Ground
Pav.
Comm. Cen.
CENTURION GA.
VANGUARD CT.
MELVILLE
Southsea Caravan Activity Park
Danger Area
99
DAYSDALE M.
PITCAIRN
Pavilion
Royal Marines Mus.
BATTEN
Tennis Court
DRIFTWOOD GDNS.
ESPLANADE GDNS.
ESPLANADE
GATE
BARRACKS
Eastney Swimming Pool
Eastney Fort East
EASTNEY
University of Portsmouth (Marine Sciences)
Inshore Rescue Boat Station
Landing Stage
Ferry (Foot)
Landing Stages
Slipway
Sewage Works
Pipes
Sewage Outfall
Pipe Lines
PORTSMOUTH
HAVANT
Langstone Channel
West Winner
098

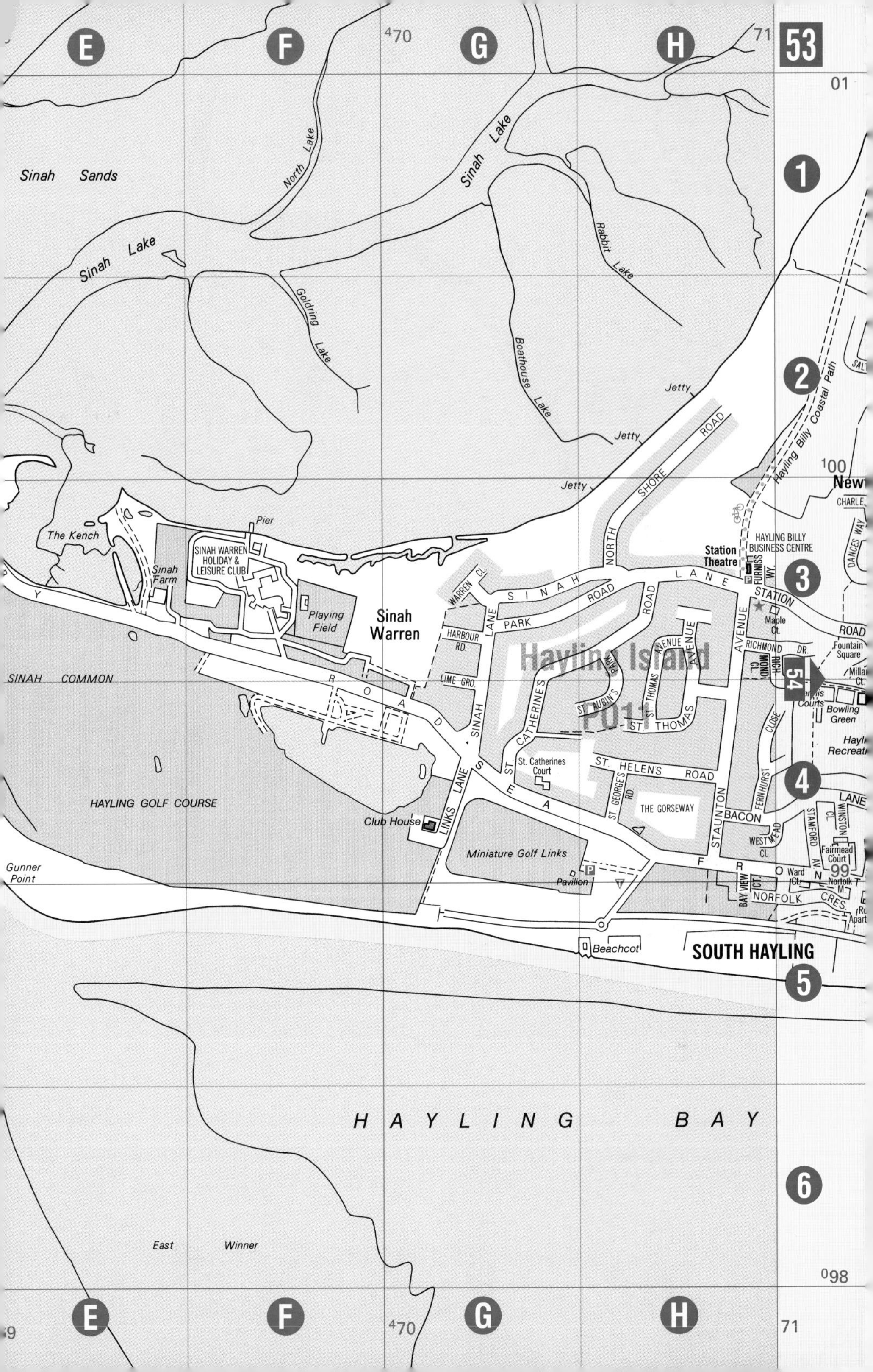

E
F
470
G
H
71
01
1
Sinah Sands
North Lake
Sinah Lake
Sinah Lake
Rabbit Lake
Goldring Lake
Boathouse Lake
2
Hayling Billy Coastal Path
Jetty
Jetty
Jetty
SHORE ROAD
100
Newt
CHARLES
DANCES WAY
Pier
The Kench
SINAH WARREN HOLIDAY & LEISURE CLUB
Sinah Farm
Playing Field
Sinah Warren
Station Theatre
HAYLING BILLY BUSINESS CENTRE
FURNISS WY.
3
NORTH
WARREN CL.
SINAH LANE
STATION ROAD
PARK ROAD
ROAD
Maple Ct.
HARBOUR RD.
LIME GRO.
LANE
Hayling Island
PO11
AVENUE
RICHMOND DR.
Fountain Square
SINAH COMMON
ROAD
SINAH
ST. CATHERINES
ST. AUBIN'S PARK
ST. THOMAS AVENUE
ST. THOMAS
54
Tennis Courts
Bowling Green
Millard Ct.
Hayling Recreation
CLOSE
4
ST. HELENS ROAD
St. Catherines Court
FERNHURST
LANE
HAYLING GOLF COURSE
LINKS LANE
SEA
ST. GEORGE'S RD.
THE GORSEWAY
STAUNTON
BACON
WEST MEAD CL.
STAMFORD AV.
WINSTON CL.
Fairmead Court
Club House
Miniature Golf Links
FRONT
Ward Ct.
99
Norfolk M.
Gunner Point
Pavilion
BAY VIEW CT.
NORFOLK CRES.
Beachcot
SOUTH HAYLING
5
HAYLING BAY
6
East Winner
098
E
F
470
G
H
71

44
53
A
B
C
D
1
2
3
4
5
6
71
72
01
100
99
098
HAYLING ISLAND
Hayling Island
PO11
HAYLING BAY
Newtown
Gable Head
West Town
Westfield
Mengham
Sea View
SOUTH HAYLING
HAVANT ROAD
A3023
CHURCH RBT.
CHURCH ROAD
MANOR ROAD
BEACH ROAD
MILL RYTHE LANE
WEST LANE
BRIGHTS LA.
WOODLANDS LA.
SALTMARSH LANE
DENHILL CL.
HIGWORTH LA.
STATION RD.
ST. MARY'S RD.
SOUTH ROAD
ELM GROVE
ELM ST.
TOURNERBURY LANE
KINGS ROAD
KINGS AVENUE
MENGHAM LANE
MENGHAM RD.
SELSMORE ROAD
LEONARDS AVENUE
BACON LANE
HOLLOW LANE
VICTORIA AVE.
WESTFIELD AV.
SEA FRONT
STAUNTON AVENUE
NORFOLK CRES.
Manor Farm
Manor House
Yachtbuilding Yard
Slipways
Jetties
Mill Rythe Jun. & Inf. Schools
Boating Lake
Pound Marsh
Pound Copse
Honeyrings Copse
Nursery
THE OVEN CAMP SITE
Higworth Farm
HIGWORTH CARAVAN PARK
The Hayling School
Driving Range
Club Ho.
War Meml.
Olive Leaf Court
Hayling Billy Coastal Path
Station Theatre
HAYLING BILLY BUSINESS CENTRE
Fountain Square
Kensington Ho.
Lynden Ct.
Maple Ct.
Millam Ct.
Tennis Courts
Bowling Green
Comm. Cen.
Hayling Park Recreation Ground
Rec. Grd.
Bowl. Grn.
Mengham Junior School
Mengham Inf. Sch.
Lib.
Mengham Court
Mengham House
Jetty
Pond Head Ho.
Mary Coombs Ct.
The Pct.
Seacourt Tennis Club
Funlands Amusements
Royal Apartments
Reading Holm-Ho. Ct.
East Hayling Light Railway
The Beach
Coastguard Lookout
Roundhouse Ct.
Scarff Ct.
Mengham Pk. Rec. Grd.
NORTH CRESCENT

1

MILL RYTHE
HOLIDAY VILLAGE

Middle Marsh

MILL RITHE

2

W

G

100

GOLF COURSE

D

3

Tourner Bury Marsh

Dip Rithe

Tourner Bury

Tourner Bury Wood

Mengham Rithe

Tourner Bury Plantations

CHICHESTER

HAVANT

EMSWORTH

CHANNEL

4

Slipway

Mengham Rythe Sailing Club

Mengham Salterns

Landing Stage

Black Point

My Lord's Pond

Salterns Quay

99

SALTERNS CL.

MARINE WALK

Jetty

Boat Yard

Hayling Island Sailing Club

SIMMONS GRN.

LANE

ROAD

Cockle Point

Yacht Harbour

SANDY

Selsmore

SEAVIEW

ASTRID

BURDA DR.

Slipway

SELSMORE AV.

BLACKTHORN DRIVE

CHAND-LERS CL.

WOODCOT CVN. PK)

North's Salterns

Jetty

WITTERING RD.

EARNLEY

SELSEY CL.

5

BLACKTHORN RD.

ILEX WALK

KINGFISHER CL.

FISHERS CVN. PK.

LAKESIDE HOLIDAY VILLAGE

THE TRIANGLE

CAMAROW CVN. PK.

THE HOLLIES CARAVAN PK.

RD.

TYDLESHAM CL.

SANDY POINT

RD.

99

FISHERY

LANE

Boating Lake

WATERS EDGE CVN. PK.

BEVERLEY CVN. PK.

FISHERMAN'S

HASLEMERE GARDENS

ITCHENOR ROAD

FORELAND CT.

ST. HERMAN'S CARAVAN ESTATE

FISHERY CREEK CARAVAN & CAMPING PK.

Quay

TWO ACRES CVN. PK.

THE RETREAT HOLIDAY CVN. PK.

THE GLADE HOLIDAY HOME PK.

AVENUE

BOSMERE

ROAD

BRACKLESHAM

TRELOAR RD.

Hayling Island Lifeboat Station & Museum

ST. HERMAN'S

Slipway

Jetty

THE BINNACLE CVN. PK.

CHERRY TREE HOLIDAY CVN. PK.

ELLIOTS CVN. EST.

HAVEN ROAD

WALK SANDY POINT RD.

Eastoke

ROWIN CLOSE

GOOSE GRN. CVN. PK.

BRIXHAM RD.

NUTBOURNE

CORONATION RD.

ROAD

SEAFARERS

SOUTH

BURGESS

HAVEN ROAD

TRELR RD.

Sandy Point Nature Reserve

6

SEMBRIDGE

THE GLADE

NEATH CT.

SOUTHWOOD RD.

WEST HAYE RD.

GREENHAVEN CARAVAN PARK

Sandy

WHEATLANDS CRES.

SACH ADNS

EASTOKE

WOOD

ROAD

Silhouette Ct.

Miles Ct.

Sheerwater Ct.

Belmont Gdns.

P Comm. Cen.

POINT

AVENUE

CHICHDR DR.

THE STRAND W.

WINDSOR CL.

Anchor Ct.

Pebble Ct.

Maloney M.

WHEATLANDS

ROAD

NUTBOURNE

ROAD

098

Beach Ct.

P

Tidal Pond

Eastoke Point

475

Steep
Bedales School
Ridge Common
Stonerwood Park
Patrick's Copse
Sole Copse
Soal Farm Cotts.
Soal Farm
Poultry House
Collyers
Collier's Copse
Melstock Farm Cottage
SANDSBURY LANE
Cooks Cottages
Aldersnapp Farm
The Lodge
Playing Field
Swim. Bath
Fairhaven
Dunhurst (Bedales Jun. School)
Oakley Cottage
Warren Copse
Vicarage
Little Shackles
Windward
Tilmore Farm
Steep House
Lower Tilmore
Tilmore Brook
Bell Hill
Buckmore Cottage
Buckmore
GU32
Tilmore Gardens
Buckmore Farm
Stroud Farm
Red House
WINCHESTER ROAD
A272
Works
Petersfield
New Buildings Farm
Depot
PETERSFIELD BUSINESS PARK
PETERSFIELD COMM. HOSP.
AMEY IND. EST.
Superstore
The Petersfield School
ROTHERBROOK COURT
RIDGEWAY OFFICE PARK
Causeway
Depository
Fairfield Farm
Causeway Farm
BROADWAY PARK
Landpits
Weston Farm
Weston
Trinity Barns
WYLDS LANE
THE CAUSEWAY
B2070
A3
Galleries
Gall.
Mus.
The Mint
Heath Ct.
Cemet.
Britnell House

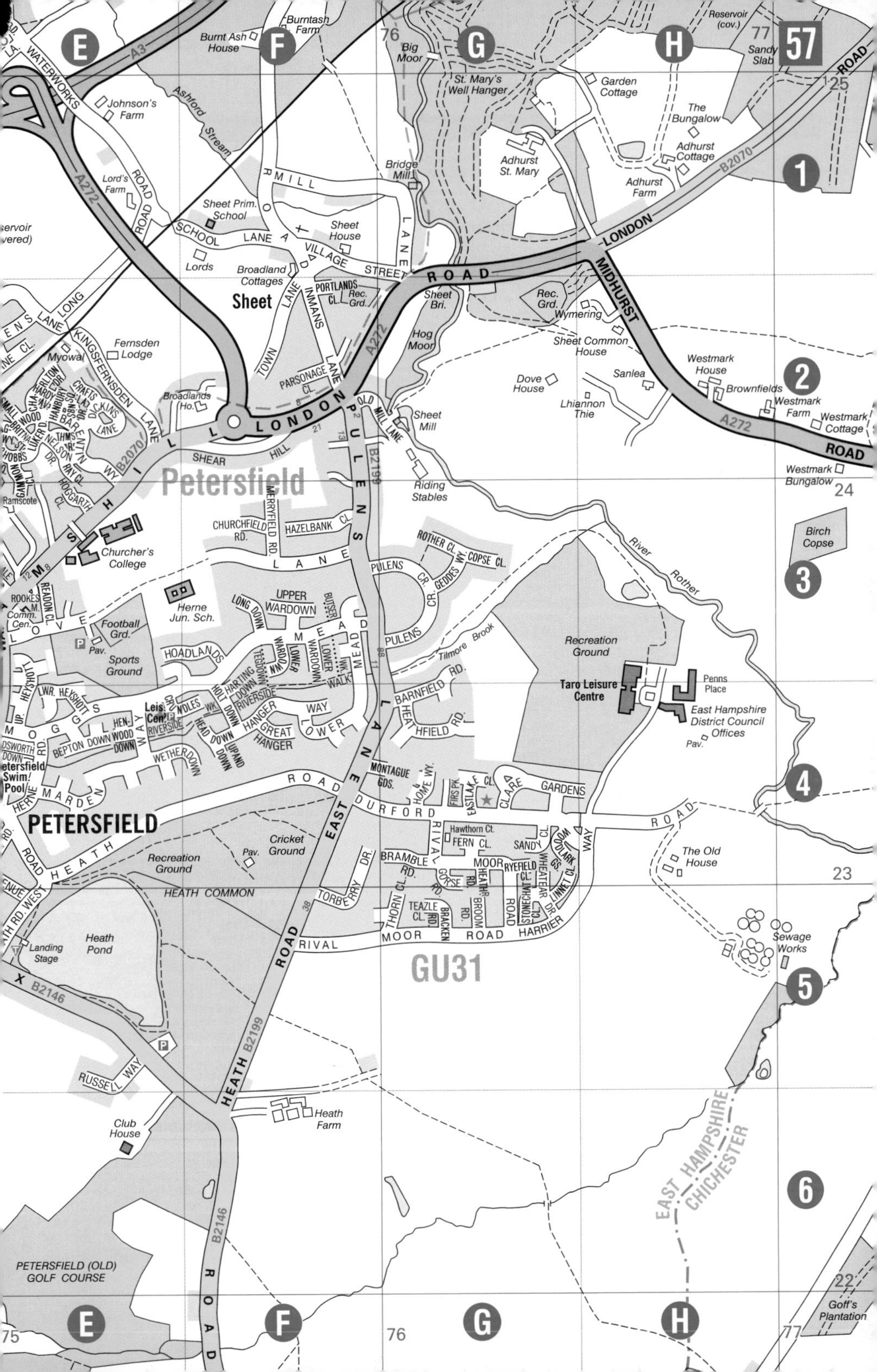
E
F
G
H
E
F
G
H
1
2
3
4
5
6
76
77
75
76
77
125
24
23
22
Reservoir (cov.)
Sandy Slab
Burntash Farm
Burnt Ash House
Big Moor
St. Mary's Well Hanger
Garden Cottage
The Bungalow
Adhurst Cottage
Adhurst St. Mary
Adhurst Farm
Johnson's Farm
Ashford Stream
Lord's Farm
WATERWORKS
A3
A272
B2070
ROAD
LONDON
ROAD
MILL LANE
Bridge Mill
Sheet Prim. School
Sheet House
SCHOOL LANE
VILLAGE STREET
Lords
Broadland Cottages
Sheet
TOWN LANE
INMANS
PORTLANDS CL.
Rec. Grd.
Sheet Bri.
Hog Moor
Rec. Grd.
Wymering
MIDHURST
Sheet Common House
Westmark House
Brownfields
Westmark Farm
Westmark Cottage
Dove House
Lhiannon Thie
Sanlea
ROAD
Westmark Bungalow
LONG LANE
KINGSFERNSDEN LANE
Fernsden Lodge
Myowal
PARSONAGE CL.
Broadlands Ho.
LONDON
OLD MILL LANE
Sheet Mill
Riding Stables
SHEAR HILL
Petersfield
HOGARTH CL.
Ramscote
Churcher's College
CHURCHFIELD RD.
MERRYFIELD RD.
HAZELBANK CL.
PULENS
B2199
LANE
ROTHER CL.
COPSE CL.
GEDDES WY.
PULENS CR.
Birch Copse
River Rother
Herne Jun. Sch.
UPPER WARDOWN
LONG DOWN
BUTSER
MEAD
LOVE
READON CL.
Comm. Cen.
Football Grd.
Pav.
Sports Ground
HOADLANDS
Tilmore Brook
Recreation Ground
Taro Leisure Centre
Penns Place
East Hampshire District Council Offices
Pav.
LWR. HEYSHOTT
HEYSHOTT
Leis. Cen.
RIVERSIDE
HARTING DOWN
HOLT DOWN
HEAD DOWN
UPAND DOWN
HANGER
GREAT HANGER
LOWER WAY
BARNFIELD RD.
HEATHFIELD RD.
MOGGS
BEPTON DOWN
HENWOOD DOWN
WETHERDOWN
Petersfield Swim. Pool
HERNE
MARDEN
ROAD
MONTAGUE GDS.
HOME WY.
FIRS PK.
EASTLAKE CL.
CLARE GARDENS
DURFORD ROAD
EAST
PETERSFIELD
HEATH
Recreation Ground
Pav.
Cricket Ground
HEATH COMMON
Hawthorn Ct.
FERN CL.
SANDY CL.
BRAMBLE RD.
GORSE RD.
HEATHER RD.
RYEFIELD CL.
WHEATEAR DR.
LARK GS.
LINNET CL.
WAY
ROAD
The Old House
TORBERRY DR.
THORN CL.
TEAZLE CL.
BRACKEN RD.
BROOM RD.
STONECHAT CL.
RIVAL MOOR ROAD
HARRIER
GU31
Sewage Works
HEATH RD. WEST
Landing Stage
Heath Pond
B2146
RUSSELL WAY
HEATH ROAD
B2199
Heath Farm
Club House
EAST HAMPSHIRE
CHICHESTER
B2146
ROAD
PETERSFIELD (OLD) GOLF COURSE
Goff's Plantation

INDEX

Including Streets, Places & Areas, Hospitals & Hospices,
Industrial Estates, Selected Flats & Walkways, Stations and Selected Places of Interest.

HOW TO USE THIS INDEX

1. Each street name is followed by its Postcode District, then by its Locality abbreviation(s) and then by its map reference;
e.g. **Abbeyfield Dr.** PO15: Fare . . . .1E **25** is in the PO15 Postcode District and the Fareham Locality and is to be found in square 1E on page **25**. The page number is shown in bold type.

2. A strict alphabetical order is followed in which Av., Rd., St., etc. (though abbreviated) are read in full and as part of the street name; e.g. **Apple Gro.** appears after **Applegate Pl.** but before **Appleshaw Grn.**

3. Streets and a selection of flats and walkways too small to be shown on the maps, appear in the index with the thoroughfare to which it is connected shown in brackets; e.g. **Admiral's Cnr.** PO5: S'sea . . . .5D **50** (off Clarence Pde.)

4. Addresses that are in more than one part are referred to as not continuous.

5. Places and areas are shown in the index in BLUE TYPE and the map reference is to the actual map square in which the town centre or area is located and not to the place name shown on the map; e.g. **ALVERSTOKE** 5C **48**

6. An example of a selected place of interest is **Bear Mus., The** 4D **56**

7. An example of a station is **Bedhampton Station (Rail)** 1D **32**

8. An example of a hospital or hospice is **GOSPORT WAR MEMORIAL HOSPITAL.** . . .3C **48**

9. Map references for entries that appear on large scale pages **4** & **5** are shown first, with small scale map references shown in brackets; e.g. **A'Becket Ct.** PO1: Ports 5C **4** (3A **50**)

GENERAL ABBREVIATIONS

All. : Alley	**Gdns.** : Gardens	**Pas.** : Passage
App. : Approach	**Ga.** : Gate	**Pl.** : Place
Arc. : Arcade	**Gt.** : Great	**Pct.** : Precinct
Av. : Avenue	**Grn.** : Green	**Prom.** : Promenade
Blvd. : Boulevard	**Gro.** : Grove	**Ri.** : Rise
Bri. : Bridge	**Hgts.** : Heights	**Rd.** : Road
Bldgs. : Buildings	**Ho.** : House	**Rdbt.** : Roundabout
Bus. : Business	**Ind.** : Industrial	**Shop.** : Shopping
Cvn. : Caravan	**Info.** : Information	**Sth.** : South
Cen. : Centre	**Junc.** : Junction	**Sq.** : Square
Cl. : Close	**La.** : Lane	**St.** : Street
Comn. : Common	**Lit.** : Little	**Ter.** : Terrace
Cnr. : Corner	**Lwr.** : Lower	**Twr.** : Tower
Cotts. : Cottages	**Mnr.** : Manor	**Trad.** : Trading
Ct. : Court	**Mans.** : Mansions	**Up.** : Upper
Cres. : Crescent	**Mkt.** : Market	**Va.** : Vale
Cft. : Croft	**Mdw.** : Meadow	**Vw.** : View
Dr. : Drive	**Mdws.** : Meadows	**Vs.** : Villas
E. : East	**M.** : Mews	**Vis.** : Visitors
Ent. : Enterprise	**Mt.** : Mount	**Wlk.** : Walk
Est. : Estate	**Mus.** : Museum	**W.** : West
Fld. : Field	**Nth.** : North	**Yd.** : Yard
Flds. : Fields	**Pde.** : Parade	
Gdn. : Garden	**Pk.** : Park	

LOCALITY ABBREVIATIONS

Bed : **Bedhampton**	H Isl : **Hayling Island**	S'sea : **Southsea**
Blen : **Blendworth**	Horn : **Horndean**	S'wick : **Southwick**
Boar : **Boarhunt**	Ids : **Idsworth**	Ste : **Steep**
Cath : **Catherington**	K Vil : **Knowle Village**	Stro : **Stroud**
Chal : **Chalton**	Lang : **Langstone**	Stub : **Stubbington**
Clan : **Clanfield**	Lee S : **Lee-on-the-Solent**	T Isl : **Thorney Island**
Cosh : **Cosham**	Love : **Lovedean**	Titch : **Titchfield**
Cowp : **Cowplain**	N Boa : **North Boarhunt**	T Cmn : **Titchfield Common**
Den : **Denmead**	Pet : **Petersfield**	Warb : **Warblington**
Dray : **Drayton**	Portc : **Portchester**	W'lle : **Waterlooville**
Ems : **Emsworth**	Ports : **Portsmouth**	Westb : **Westbourne**
Fare : **Fareham**	P Sol : **Port Solent**	W'ton : **Weston**
Farl : **Farlington**	Purb : **Purbrook**	White : **Whiteley**
Fun : **Funtley**	R Cas : **Rowlands Castle**	Wick : **Wickham**
Gos : **Gosport**	Seg : **Segensworth**	Wid : **Widley**
Hav : **Havant**	S'urne : **Southbourne**	Wood : **Woodmancote**

I O Cen., The PO15: Titch 1A **24**
1664 Living History Village, The 2G **47**

A

Abbas Grn. PO9: Hav 2D **20**
Abbeydore Rd. PO6: Cosh 2G **29**
Abbeyfield Dr. PO15: Fare 1E **25**

Abbeymede PO6: Cosh 3A **30**
Abbey Rd. PO15: Fare 1F **25**
Abbots Cl. PO7: Purb 5E **19**
Abbotstone Av. PO9: Hav 5G **21**
Abbots Way PO15: Fare 2F **25**
A'Becket Ct. PO1: Ports 5C **4** (3A **50**)
Aberdare Av. PO6: Dray 2D **30**
Aberdeen Cl. PO15: Fare 6G **13**
Abingdon Cl. PO12: Gos 3D **48**
Acacia Gdns. PO8: Horn 2B **10**
Acacia Lodge PO16: Fare 2B **26**
Acanthas Ct. PO15: White 1A **12**

Access Point PO6: Cosh 4A **30**
Acer Way PO9: Hav 5H **21**
Ackworth Rd. PO3: Ports 6C **30**
Acorn Bus. Cen. PO6: Cosh 4H **29**
Acorn Cl. PO6: Farl 3H **31**
      PO13: Gos 4D **38**
Acorn Gdns. PO8: Horn 1B **10**
Acre La. PO7: W'lle 6C **10**
Action Stations Exhibition Mus. . . .2B **4** (2A **50**)
Adair Rd. PO4: S'sea 5G **51**
Adames Rd. PO1: Ports 1E **51**
Addenbroke PO12: Gos 3E **49**

Adderbury Av.—Astra Wlk.

Adderbury Av. PO10: Ems 6D **22**
Addison Rd. PO4: S'sea 4E **51**
Adelaide Pl. PO16: Fare 2C **26**
Adhurst Rd. PO9: Hav 5G **21**
Admiral Pk., The PO3: Ports 2C **42**
Admiral's Cnr. *PO5: S'sea* *5D 50*
(off Clarence Pde.)
Admirals Ct. PO5: S'sea 5C **50**
Admirals Ho. PO4: S'sea 3H **51**
Admirals Pl. PO6: Cosh 3B **30**
Admirals Wlk. PO1: Ports 1A **4** (1H **49**)
PO12: Gos 4B **48**
Admiralty Cl. PO12: Gos 6A **40**
Admiralty Rd. PO1: Ports 2B **4** (2A **50**)
PO12: Gos 5G **49**
Adsdean Cl. PO9: Hav 5E **21**
Adstone La. PO3: Ports 1E **43**
Adur Cl. PO12: Gos 6F **39**
Aerial Rd. PO17: S'wick 1F **29**
Aerodrome Rd. PO13: Gos 1D **38**
Agincourt Rd. PO2: Ports 6H **41**
Agnew Ho. PO12: Gos 1D **48**
Agnew Rd. PO13: Gos 2C **38**
Ainsdale Rd. PO6: Dray 2F **31**
Aintree Dr. PO7: W'lle 6B **10**
Airport Ind. Est. PO3: Ports 2D **42**
Airport Service Rd. PO3: Ports 1C **42**
Airspeed Rd. PO3: Ports 3E **43**
Ajax Cl. PO14: Stub 4F **37**
Alameda Rd. PO7: Purb 5F **19**
Alameda Way PO7: Purb 5F **19**
Alan Gro. PO15: Fare 1G **25**
Albacore Cl. PO13: Lee S 2E **47**
Albany Cvn. Site PO14: Stub 4F **37**
Albany Ct. PO12: Gos 3D **48**
Albany Rd. PO5: S'sea 6H **5** (4D **50**)
Albatross Wlk. PO13: Gos 3B **38**
Albemarle Av. PO12: Gos 6H **39**
Albert Gro. PO5: S'sea 4D **50**
Albert Rd. PO4: S'sea 4D **50**
PO5: S'sea 4D **50**
PO6: Cosh 4B **30**
PO7: W'lle 2G **19**
PO14: Fare 3H **37**
Albert St. PO12: Gos 2E **49**
Albion Cl. PO16: Portc 5H **27**
Albretia Av. PO8: Cowp 4F **9**
Alchorne Pl. PO3: Ports 2D **42**
Alderfield GU32: Pet 4C **56**
Alder La. PO12: Gos 2H **47**
Aldermoor Rd. PO7: Purb 5F **19**
PO13: Gos 6D **38**
Aldermoor Rd. E. PO7: Purb 4F **19**
Aldershot Ho. PO9: Hav 4H **21**
Alders Rd. PO16: Fare 4B **26**
Alderwood Cl. PO9: Bed 6B **20**
Aldrich Rd. PO1: Ports 1A **50**
Aldridge Cl. PO8: Clan 2G **7**
Aldroke St. PO6: Cosh 4B **30**
ALDSWORTH **3G 23**
Aldsworth Cl. PO6: Dray 3E **31**
Aldsworth Comn. Rd. PO10: Westb 4G **23**
Aldsworth Gdns. PO6: Dray 3E **31**
Aldsworth Path PO6: Dray 3E **31**
Aldwell St. PO5: S'sea 4H **5** (3D **50**)
Alec Rose Ho. PO12: Gos 3E **49**
Alec Rose La.
PO1: Ports 3F **5** (2C **50**)
Alecto Rd. PO12: Gos 4D **48**
Alencon Cl. PO12: Gos 5A **40**
Alexander Cl. PO7: W'lle 3F **19**
Alexander Gro. PO16: Fare 3A **26**
Alexandra Av. PO11: H Isl 5B **54**
Alexandra Pk. PO9: Hav 4E **33**
Alexandra Rd. PO1: Ports 1H **5** (1D **50**)
Alexandra St. PO12: Gos 1C **48**
Alfred Rd. PO1: Ports 2E **5** (2B **50**)
PO14: Stub 2F **37**
Alfrey Cl. PO10: S'urne 3G **35**
Algiers Rd. PO3: Ports 3D **42**
Alhambra Rd. PO4: S'sea 6E **51**
Allaway Av. PO6: Cosh 3D **28**
Allbrook Ct. PO9: Hav 3D **20**
Allcot Rd. PO3: Ports 3B **42**
Allenby Gro. PO16: Portc 4A **28**
Allenby Rd. PO12: Gos 1A **48**
Allendale Av. PO10: Ems 6C **22**
Allen's Rd. PO4: S'sea 5E **51**
Alliance Cl. PO13: Gos 4D **38**
Alliance Ho. PO1: Ports 1E **51**
Allmara Dr. PO7: W'lle 5H **19**
All Saint's Rd. PO1: Ports 6H **41**
All Saints St. PO1: Ports 1C **50**
Alma St. PO12: Gos 1C **48**
Alma Ter. PO4: S'sea 4G **51**
Almond Cl. PO8: Horn 3C **10**
PO9: Bed 3H **31**
Almondsbury Rd. PO6: Cosh 1D **28**
Almondside PO13: Gos 4E **39**
Alphage Rd. PO12: Gos 4F **39**
Alresford Rd. PO9: Hav 5E **21**
Alsford Rd. PO7: Purb 4F **19**
Alten Rd. PO7: W'lle 5E **9**
Althorpe Dr. PO3: Ports 1E **43**
Alton Gro. PO16: Portc 5A **28**
Alum Way PO16: Fare 2E **27**
Alvara Rd. PO12: Gos 5C **48**
Alver Bri. Vw. PO12: Gos 4D **48**
Alvercliffe Dr. PO12: Gos 5B **48**
Alver Quay PO12: Gos 4D **48**
Alver Rd. PO1: Ports 1E **51**
PO12: Gos 3D **48**
(not continuous)
ALVERSTOKE **5C 48**
Alverstoke Ct. PO12: Gos 5C **48**
Alverstoke Tennis & Squash Club **4C 48**
Alverstone Rd. PO4: S'sea 2G **51**
Alveston Av. PO14: Fare 3F **25**
Amarylis Cl. PO15: Seg 5A **12**
Amberley Ct. *PO17: K Vil* *2G 13*
(off Knowle Av.)
Amberley Rd. PO2: Ports 2B **42**
PO8: Clan 2H **7**
PO12: Gos 5G **39**
Ambleside Ct. PO12: Gos 6C **48**
Amersham Cl. PO12: Gos 3A **48**
Amethyst Gro. PO7: W'lle 1B **20**
Amey Ind. Est. GU32: Pet 4C **56**
AMF Bowling
Bedhampton **2B 32**
Portsmouth **2G 5 (2C 50)**
Ampfield Cl. PO9: Hav 5B **20**
Amport Ct. PO9: Hav 3D **20**
Amyas Ct. PO4: S'sea 3A **52**
Anchorage, The PO12: Gos 3E **49**
Anchorage Rd. PO3: Ports 1D **42**
Anchor Ct. PO11: H Isl 6F **55**
Anchor Ga. PO1: Ports 1D **4** (1B **50**)
Anchor Ga. Rd. PO1: Ports 1C **4** (1A **50**)
Anchor La. PO1: Ports 2A **4** (2H **49**)
Anderson Cl. PO9: Hav 6G **21**
Andover Ho. PO9: Hav 4G **21**
Andover Rd. PO4: S'sea 5F **51**
Andrew Bell St. PO1: Ports 1C **50**
Andrew Cl. PO3: Ports 1F **51**
Andrew Cres. PO7: W'lle 5F **9**
Andrew Pl. PO14: Stub 3D **36**
Angela Ct. PO9: Hav 5F **21**
Angelica Ct. PO7: W'lle 3A **20**
Angelica Way PO15: White 1A **12**
Angelo Cl. PO7: W'lle 1A **20**
Angelus Cl. PO14: Stub 3E **37**
Angerstein Rd. PO2: Ports 4H **41**
Anglesea Rd. PO1: Ports 2E **5** (2B **50**)
PO13: Lee S 3E **47**
ANGLESEY **6D 48**
Anglesey Arms Rd. PO12: Gos 5C **48**
Anglesey Rd. PO12: Gos 6C **48**
Anglesey Vw. PO12: Gos 4D **48**
Angmering Ho. PO1: Ports 2G **5** (2C **50**)
Angus Cl. PO15: Fare 6G **13**
Anjou Cres. PO15: Fare 1F **25**
Anker La. PO14: Stub 1E **37**
Ankerwyke PO13: Gos 4B **38**
ANMORE **3D 8**
Anmore Cl. PO9: Hav 5D **20**
Anmore Dr. PO7: W'lle 5F **9**
Anmore La. PO7: Den 3D **8**
Anmore Rd. PO7: Den 3C **8**
Anne Cres. PO7: W'lle 3G **19**
Annes Ct. PO11: H Isl 5A **54**
ANN'S HILL **3C 48**
Ann's Hill Rd. PO12: Gos 1C **48**
Anson Cl. PO13: Gos 2H **47**
Anson Ct. PO1: Ports 4B **4** (3A **50**)
Anson Gro. PO16: Portc 2B **28**
Anson Rd. PO4: S'sea 2G **51**
ANTHILL COMMON **2A 8**
Anthony Gro. PO12: Gos 4F **39**
Anthony Way PO10: Ems 6D **22**
Antigua Ho. PO6: Cosh 1D **28**
Anvil Cl. PO7: W'lle 6C **10**
Anvil Ct. PO4: S'sea 3H **51**
Anzac Cl. PO14: Stub 1E **37**
Apex Cen. PO14: Fare 6A **26**
Apollo Cinema
Fareham *2B 26*
(off Market Quay)
Apollo Ct. PO5: S'sea 5G **5** (3D **50**)
Apollo Dr. PO7: Purb 6H **19**
Applegate Pl. PO8: Horn 1A **10**
Apple Gro. PO10: S'urne 3F **35**
Appleshaw Grn. PO9: Hav 5C **20**
Appleton Rd. PO15: Fare 2E **25**
Applewood Gro. PO7: Wid 6E **19**
Applewood Rd. PO9: Bed 6C **20**
Approach, The PO3: Ports 4C **42**
April Sq. PO1: Ports 1H **5** (1D **50**)
Apsley Rd. PO4: S'sea 3G **51**
Archer Ho. PO12: Gos 6E **49**
Archery La. PO16: Fare 1C **26**
Arden Cl. PO12: Gos 3B **48**
Ardington Ri. PO7: Purb 6G **19**
Arenthusa Ho. PO1: Ports 5B **4** (3A **50**)
Argyle Cres. PO15: Fare 1G **25**
Ariel Rd. PO1: Ports 2E **51**
Arismore Ct. PO13: Lee S 6F **37**
Ark Royal Cres. PO13: Lee S 6G **37**
Arle Cl. PO8: Clan 1C **6**
Arminers Cl. PO12: Gos 6D **48**
Armory La. PO1: Ports 5C **4** (3A **50**)
Armstrong Cl. PO7: W'lle 5F **9**
PO12: Gos 2E **49**
Arnaud Cl. PO2: Ports 6H **41**
Arnside Rd. PO7: W'lle 1G **19**
Arragon Ct. PO7: W'lle 1A **20**
Arran Cl. PO6: Cosh 2B **30**
Arras Ho. PO15: Fare 1E **25**
Arreton Ct. PO12: Gos 2C **48**
Arthur Dann Ct. PO6: Cosh 4A **30**
Arthur Kille Ho. PO7: W'lle 3F **19**
Arthur Pope Ho. PO5: S'sea 4H **5** (3D **50**)
Arthur St. PO2: Ports 6A **42**
Artillery Cl. PO6: Cosh 2G **29**
Arun Cl. GU31: Pet 5C **56**
Arundel Dr. PO16: Fare 1A **26**
Arundel Rd. PO12: Gos 2B **48**
Arundel St. PO1: Ports 2F **5** (2C **50**)
Arundel Way PO1: Ports 2G **5** (2C **50**)
Ascot Rd. PO3: Ports 6C **42**
Ashburton Ct. *PO5: S'sea* *5C 50*
(off Ashburton Rd.)
Ashburton Rd. PO5: S'sea 5C **50**
PO12: Gos 5B **48**
Ashby Pl. PO5: S'sea 5C **50**
PO12: Gos 3F **49**
Ash Cl. PO8: Cowp 4G **9**
PO12: Gos 3D **48**
PO14: Fare 3G **25**
Ash Copse PO8: Cowp 2H **9**
Ashcroft Arts Cen. **1C 26**
Ashcroft Ct. GU32: Pet 3D **56**
Ashdown PO13: Gos 4D **38**
Ashe Rd. PO9: Hav 4H **21**
Ashford Cl. PO6: Cosh 2A **30**
Ashington Cl. PO8: Cowp 3A **10**
Ashlett Lawn PO9: Hav 3D **20**
Ashley Cl. PO8: Love 2H **9**
PO9: Hav 5D **20**
Ashley Ct. PO12: Gos 2C **48**
Ashley Wlk. PO6: Cosh 4C **30**
Ashling Cl. PO7: Den 3B **8**
Ashling Gdns. PO7: Den 3B **8**
Ashling La. PO2: Ports 4H **41**
Ashling Pk. Rd. PO7: Den 3B **8**
Ashlyn Cl. PO15: Fare 2E **25**
Ashtead Cl. PO16: Portc 3G **27**
Ashton Way PO14: Stub 5F **37**
Ashurst Ct. PO12: Gos 4H **47**
Ashurst Rd. PO6: Cosh 3A **30**
Ashwood PO15: White 4A **12**
Ashwood Cl. PO9: Bed 5B **20**
PO11: H Isl 4C **54**
Ashwood Lodge *PO16: Fare* *1B 26*
(off Northwood Sq.)
Aspengrove PO13: Gos 4E **39**
Aspen Way PO8: Horn 2A **10**
Aspex Art Gallery **5G 5 (3C 50)**
Assheton Ct. PO16: Portc 4B **28**
Astley St. PO5: S'sea 5E **5** (3C **50**)
Aston Rd. PO4: S'sea 4F **51**
PO7: W'lle 6F **9**
Astra Wlk. PO12: Gos 3F **49**

A-Z Portsmouth 59

Astrid Cl. PO11: H Isl .4E **55**
Atalanta Cl. PO4: S'sea .2A **52**
Athena Av. PO7: Purb .6H **19**
Atherley Rd. PO11: H Isl .2A **54**
Atherstone Wlk. PO5: S'sea .5F **5** (3C **50**)
Atkinson Cl. PO12: Gos .5C **48**
Atkins Pl. PO15: Fare .6E **13**
Atlantis Av. PO7: Purb .1G **31**
Aubrey Cl. PO11: H Isl .3A **54**
Auckland Rd. E. PO5: S'sea .5C **50**
Auckland Rd. W. PO5: S'sea .5C **50**
Audley Ct. PO16: Fare .2F **27**
Audret Cl. PO16: Portc .5H **27**
Augustine Rd. PO6: Dray .2E **31**
Auriol Dr. PO9: Bed .3H **31**
Austerberry Way PO13: Gos .5E **39**
Austin Ct. PO6: Cosh .2F **29**
Australia Cl. PO1: Ports .2H **5** (2D **50**)
Aust Rd. PO14: Fare .3F **25**
Avalon Ct. PO10: Ems .1D **34**
Avenue, The GU31: Pet .4D **56**
PO12: Gos .5C **48**
PO14: Fare .3D **24**
Avenue Ct. PO12: Gos .5C **48**
Avenue De Caen PO5: S'sea .6C **50**
Avenue Lawn Tennis & Squash Club .2H 33
Avenue Rd. PO11: H Isl .2B **44**
PO12: Gos .2E **49**
PO14: Fare .2H **25**
Avery La. PO12: Gos .6F **39**
Avington Grn. PO9: Hav .3H **21**
Avocet Cl. PO4: S'sea .2H **51**
Avocet Ho. PO4: S'sea .2H **51**
Avocet Quay PO10: S'urne .4E **35**
Avocet Wlk. PO13: Gos .3A **38**
Avocet Way PO8: Horn .6A **6**
Avon Cl. GU31: Pet .6C **56**
PO13: Lee S .2D **46**
Avon Ct. PO8: Cowp .3H **9**
Avondale Rd. PO1: Ports .1F **51**
PO7: W'lle .1H **19**
Avon Wlk. PO16: Portc .3G **27**
Awbridge Rd. PO9: Hav .5C **20**
Axis Pk. PO14: Fare .5A **26**
Aylen Rd. PO3: Ports .3C **42**
Aylesbury Rd. PO2: Ports .5B **42**
Ayling Cl. PO13: Gos .6C **38**
Aylward St. PO1: Ports .2C **4** (2A **50**)
Aysgarth Rd. PO7: W'lle .1G **19**
Azalea Cl. PO9: Hav .5A **22**

B

Back La. PO17: S'wick .3C **16**
Bacon La. PO11: H Isl .4H **53**
Baddesley Gdns. PO9: Hav .2D **20**
Bader Way PO15: White .4A **12**
Badger Brow PO7: W'lle .3A **20**
Badger Cl. PO15: Fare .1F **25**
Badger Rd. PO14: Fare .6H **25**
BAFFINS .6C 42
Baffins Rd. PO3: Ports .1G **51**
Bagot Ho. PO12: Gos .6F **39**
Bailey's Rd. PO5: S'sea .4H **5** (3D **50**)
Baker St. PO1: Ports .6H **41**
Balchin Ho. PO1: Ports .2C **4**
Balderton Cl. PO2: Ports .1B **42**
Balfour Cl. PO13: Gos .1H **47**
Balfour Rd. PO2: Ports .4A **42**
Ballard Ct. PO12: Gos .3D **48**
Balliol Rd. PO2: Ports .5A **42**
Balmoral Cl. PO13: Gos .3D **38**
Balmoral Dr. PO7: Purb .5E **19**
Balmoral Rd. PO15: Fare .6G **13**
Balmoral Way GU32: Pet .3D **56**
Bankside PO12: Gos .5B **48**
Bannerman Rd. GU32: Pet .3D **56**
Bapaume Rd. PO3: Ports .6B **30**
Barbican M. PO16: Portc .4C **28**
Barclay Ho. *PO12: Gos .3G 49*
(off Trinity Grn., not continuous)
Bardon Way PO14: Fare .3F **25**
Barentin Way GU31: Pet .2E **57**
Barfleur Cl. PO15: Fare .1F **25**
Barfleur Rd. PO14: Fare .6A **26**
Barham Cl. PO12: Gos .1D **48**
Barham Rd. GU32: Pet .4D **56**
Barham Way PO2: Ports .1H **41**
Barkis Ho. PO1: Ports .6H **41**
Barlow Cl. PO14: Stub .3D **36**
Barn Cl. PO10: Ems .3B **34**
Barncroft Way PO9: Hav .5D **20**
Barnes Rd. PO1: Ports .1E **51**
Barnes Wallis Rd. PO15: Seg .5A **12**
Barnes Way PO9: Bed .6D **20**
Barney Evans Cres. PO8: Cowp .4F **9**
Barnfield Cl. PO10: S'urne .2H **35**
Barnfield Ct. PO14: Fare .3G **25**
Barnfield Rd. GU31: Pet .4G **57**
Barn Fold PO7: W'lle .6B **10**
Barn Grn. Cl. PO7: Den .3B **8**
Barnwood Rd. PO15: Fare .2F **25**
Baroda Ct. PO2: Ports .5A **42**
Baronsmere Ct. PO12: Gos .3C **48**
Barracks Rd. PO4: S'sea .5A **52**
Barrington Ho. PO2: Ports .6H **41**
Barrington Ter. PO5: S'sea .6F **5**
Bartlett Cl. PO15: Fare .6G **13**
Barton Cross PO8: Horn .6B **6**
Barton Gro. PO3: Ports .2D **42**
Bartons Rd. PO9: Hav .4G **21**
Barwell Gro. PO10: Ems .6C **22**
Barwell La. PO13: Gos .6C **26**
Basing Rd. PO9: Hav .4E **21**
Basin St. PO2: Ports .5H **41**
Bassett Wlk. PO9: Hav .3D **20**
Bateson Hall PO1: Ports .3F **5**
Bath & Wells Ct. PO13: Gos .1G **47**
Bathing La. PO1: Ports .5A **4** (4H **49**)
Bath La. PO16: Fare .2C **26**
Bath La. Cotts. PO16: Fare .3C **26**
Bath La. Lwr. PO16: Fare .2C **26**
Bath Rd. PO4: S'sea .4F **51**
PO10: Ems .4D **34**
Bath Sq. PO1: Ports .5A **4** (3H **49**)
Bathurst Cl. PO11: H Isl .4A **54**
Bathurst Way PO2: Ports .3F **41**
Battenburg Av. PO2: Ports .3A **42**
Battenburg Rd. PO12: Gos .2E **49**
Battens Way PO9: Hav .5F **21**
Battery Cl. PO12: Gos .5F **39**
Battery Prom. PO1: Ports .6A **4** (4H **49**)
Battery Row PO1: Ports .6B **4** (4A **50**)
Baybridge Rd. PO9: Hav .4H **21**
Bayfields *PO5: S'sea .5C 50*
(off Shaftesbury Rd.)
Bayly Av. PO16: Portc .5B **28**
Bayntun Dr. PO13: Lee S .6G **37**
Bay Rd. PO12: Gos .4B **48**
Bayswater Ho. PO5: S'sea .4D **50**
Baythorn Cl. PO2: Ports .6H **41**
Bay Tree Lodge PO14: Stub .3F **37**
Bayview Ct. PO11: H Isl .5H **53**
Beach Ct. PO11: H Isl .6F **55**
Beach Dr. PO6: Cosh .3D **28**
Beach Rd. PO5: S'sea .6D **50**
PO10: Ems .3C **34**
PO11: H Isl .5A **54**
(not continuous)
PO13: Lee S .2C **46**
Beachway PO16: Portc .5B **28**
Beaconsfield Av. PO6: Cosh .4C **30**
Beaconsfield Rd. PO7: W'lle .1G **19**
PO16: Fare .3B **26**
Beacon Sq. PO10: Ems .3C **34**
Beamond Ct. PO6: Cosh .4C **30**
Bear Mus., The .4D 56
Beasant Cl. PO3: Ports .1H **51**
Beatrice Rd. PO4: S'sea .5E **51**
Beatty Dr. PO12: Gos .5B **48**
Beatty Ho. PO1: Ports .1H **5**
Beauchamp Av. PO13: Gos .3C **38**
Beaufort Av. PO16: Fare .6H **13**
Beaufort Cl. PO13: Lee S .1E **47**
Beaufort Rd. PO5: S'sea .6D **50**
PO9: Bed .1D **32**
Beaulieu Av. PO9: Hav .3D **20**
PO16: Portc .3G **27**
Beaulieu Ct. *PO8: Cowp .3H 9*
(off Crombie Cl.)
Beaulieu Pl. PO13: Gos .3C **38**
Beaulieu Rd. PO2: Ports .4A **42**
Beaumont Cl. PO15: Fare .6F **13**
Beaumont Ct. PO12: Gos .5G **39**
Beaumont Ri. PO15: Fare .5F **13**
Beckham La. GU32: Pet .3B **56**
Beck St. PO1: Ports .2D **4** (2B **50**)
BEDENHAM .1D 38
Bedenham La. PO13: Gos .2D **38**
(not continuous)
Bedford Cl. PO9: Warb .3H **33**
Bedford Rd. GU32: Pet .3B **56**
Bedford St. PO5: S'sea .4F **5** (3C **50**)
PO12: Gos .1C **48**
BEDHAMPTON .1C 32
Bedhampton Hill PO9: Bed .2A **32**
Bedhampton Hill Rd. PO9: Bed .2B **32**
(not continuous)
Bedhampton Ho. PO1: Ports .1H **5**
Bedhampton Rd. PO2: Ports .5B **42**
PO9: Bed .1C **32**
Bedhampton Station (Rail) .1D 32
Bedhampton Way PO9: Hav .5F **21**
Beecham Rd. PO1: Ports .6A **42**
Beech Cl. PO8: Cowp .5H **9**
Beechcroft Cl. PO15: Fare .2D **24**
Beechcroft Rd. PO12: Gos .4C **48**
Beeches, The PO7: W'lle .1H **19**
Beech Gro. PO11: H Isl .3D **54**
PO12: Gos .4C **48**
Beech Rd. PO8: Clan .2G **7**
PO15: Fare .1G **25**
Beech Way PO8: Horn .2B **10**
Beechwood Av. PO7: W'lle .3G **19**
Beechwood Lodge PO16: Fare .1B **26**
Beechwood Rd. PO2: Ports .1A **42**
Beechworth Rd. PO9: Hav .2F **33**
Beehive Ter. PO6: Cosh .2G **29**
Beehive Wlk.
PO1: Ports .5C **4** (3A **50**)
Beeston Ct. PO1: Ports .6A **42**
Behrendt Cl. PO12: Gos .1C **48**
Belgravia Rd. PO2: Ports .4B **42**
Belham Apartments PO2: Ports .4A **42**
Bellair Ho. PO9: Hav .2G **33**
Bellair Rd. PO9: Hav .2G **33**
Bell Cres. PO7: W'lle .3G **19**
Bell Davies Rd. PO14: Stub .4D **36**
Bellevue La. PO10: Ems .1D **34**
Bellevue Ter. PO5: S'sea .6E **5** (4B **50**)
BELLFIELD .4B 24
Bellfield PO14: Titch .4B **24**
Bellflower Way PO15: Titch .6B **12**
BELL HILL .2C 56
Bell Hill GU32: Pet .1C **56**
Bell Hill Ridge GU32: Pet .2C **56**
Bellinger Ho. PO9: Bed .2D **32**
Bell Rd. PO6: Cosh .3H **29**
Bells La. PO14: Stub .3E **37**
Belmont Cl. PO8: Horn .2C **6**
PO14: Stub .2F **37**
Belmont Gdns. PO11: H Isl .6F **55**
Belmont Gro. PO9: Bed .1C **32**
Belmont Junc. PO9: Bed .1C **32**
Belmont Pl. PO5: S'sea .6G **5** (4C **50**)
Belmont St. PO5: S'sea .6G **5** (4C **50**)
Belmore Cl. PO1: Ports .6A **42**
Belney La. PO7: S'wick .2H **17**
PO17: S'wick .2H **17**
Belvedere Pl. GU32: Pet .3D **56**
Belvoir Cl. PO16: Fare .2A **26**
Bembridge Ct. PO11: H Isl .6E **55**
Bembridge Cres. PO4: S'sea .6E **51**
Bembridge Dr. PO11: H Isl .6E **55**
Bembridge Ho. PO11: H Isl .5D **54**
Bembridge Lodge PO13: Lee S .2C **46**
Bemister's La. PO12: Gos .3G **49**
Benbow Cl. PO8: Horn .6C **6**
Benbow Ho. PO1: Ports .2B **4**
Benbow Pl. PO1: Ports .2B **4** (2A **50**)
Benedict Way PO16: Portc .2C **28**
Beneficial St. PO1: Ports .2B **4** (2A **50**)
Benham Dr. PO3: Ports .1B **42**
Benham Gro. PO16: Portc .5B **28**
Bentham Rd. PO12: Gos .4D **48**
Bentley Cl. PO8: Horn .5C **6**
Bentley Ct. PO9: Hav .4H **21**
Bentley Cres. PO16: Fare .1H **25**
Bentworth Cl. PO9: Hav .5D **20**
Bepton Down GU31: Pet .4E **57**
Bere Farm La. PO17: N Boa .2F **15**
Bere Rd. PO7: Den .3B **8**
Beresford Cl. PO7: W'lle .3G **19**
Beresford Rd. PO2: Ports .4A **42**
PO14: Stub .2F **37**
Berkeley Cl. PO14: Stub .3D **36**
Berkeley Ct. PO13: Lee S .2D **46**
Berkeley Sq. PO9: Warb .2H **33**
Berkshire Cl. PO1: Ports .2D **50**
Bermuda Ho. PO6: Cosh .1D **28**
Bernard Av. PO6: Cosh .3C **30**
Bernard Powell Ho. PO9: Hav .2G **33**

Berney Rd.—Britannia Rd.

Berney Rd. PO4: S'sea 3A **52**
Bernina Av. PO7: W'lle 5E **9**
Bernina Cl. PO7: W'lle 5E **9**
Berrydown Rd. PO9: Hav 2C **20**
Berry La. PO14: Stub 3C **36**
Berry Mdw. Cotts. PO17: S'wick 3C **16**
Bertie Rd. PO4: S'sea 3H **51**
Berwyn Wlk. PO14: Fare 3G **25**
Beryl Av. PO12: Gos 5F **39**
Beryton Cl. PO12: Gos 1C **48**
Beryton Rd. PO12: Gos 1C **48**
Bettesworth Rd. PO1: Ports 6A **42**
Betula Cl. PO7: W'lle 3A **20**
Bevan Rd. PO8: Cowp 2H **9**
Beverley Cvn. Pk. PO11: H Isl 5G **55**
Beverley Gro. PO6: Farl 2H **31**
Beverley Rd. PO14: Stub 4E **37**
Beverly Cl. PO13: Gos 3D **38**
Beverston Rd. PO6: Cosh 2E **29**
Bevis Rd. PO2: Ports 4H **41**
PO12: Gos 2D **48**
Bevis Rd. Nth. PO2: Ports 4H **41**
Bickton Wlk. PO9: Hav 3D **20**
Bidbury La. PO9: Bed 2C **32**
Biddlecombe Cl. PO13: Gos 5C **38**
Biggin Wlk. PO14: Fare 3G **25**
Billett Av. PO7: W'lle 6H **9**
Billing Cl. PO4: S'sea 4H **51**
Bill Sargent Cres. PO1: Ports 1E **51**
Bill Stillwell Ct. PO2: Ports 3G **41**
Billy Lawn Av. PO9: Hav 4F **21**
Bilton Bus. Pk. PO3: Ports 2E **43**
Bilton Way PO3: Ports 3E **43**
Binnacle Cvn. Pk., The PO11: H Isl 5G **55**
Binnacle Way PO6: Cosh 3F **29**
Binness Path PO6: Farl 4G **31**
Binness Way PO6: Farl 4G **31**
Binsteed Rd. PO2: Ports 5A **42**
Birch Cl. PO8: Cowp 4G **9**
Birch Dr. PO13: Gos 1C **38**
Birchmore Cl. PO13: Gos 3C **38**
Birch Tree Cl. PO10: Ems 5D **22**
Birch Tree Dr. PO10: Ems 5D **22**
Birchwood Lodge *PO16: Fare* *1B 26*
(off Northwood Sq.)
Birdham Rd. PO11: H Isl 5G **55**
Birdlip Cl. PO8: Horn 1A **10**
Birdlip Rd. PO6: Cosh 2F **29**
Birdwood Gro. PO16: Portc 3F **27**
Birkdale Av. PO6: Dray 2E **31**
Birmingham Ct. PO13: Gos 2H **47**
Biscay Cl. PO14: Stub 2D **36**
Bishopsfield Rd. PO14: Fare 4G **25**
Bishopstoke Rd. PO9: Hav 4E **21**
Bishop St. PO1: Ports 2C **4** (2A **50**)
Bittern Cl. PO12: Gos 6H **39**
Bitterne Cl. PO9: Hav 3F **21**
Blackberry Cl. PO8: Clan 1D **6**
Blackbird Cl. PO8: Cowp 3H **9**
Blackbird Way PO13: Lee S 6H **37**
Blackbrook Bus. Pk. PO15: Fare 2G **25**
Blackbrook Ho. Dr. PO14: Fare 2G **25**
Blackbrook Pk. Av. PO15: Fare 2G **25**
Blackbrook Rd. PO15: Fare 1E **25**
Blackburn Ct. PO13: Gos 2H **47**
Blackcap Cl. PO9: R Cas 6G **11**
Blackdown Cres. PO9: Hav 5E **21**
Blackfriars Cl. PO5: S'sea 4H **5** (3D **50**)
Blackfriars Rd. PO5: S'sea 3H **5** (2D **50**)
Blackhouse La. PO17: N Boa 1G **15**
Blackmoor Wlk. PO9: Hav 4H **21**
Blackthorn Dr. PO11: H Isl 4E **55**
PO12: Gos 4G **39**
Blackthorn Rd. PO8: Horn 3C **6**
PO11: H Isl 4E **55**
Blackthorn Ter. PO1: Ports 1C **4** (1B **50**)
Blackthorn Wlk. *PO7: W'lle* *6B 10*
(off Barn Fold)
Blackwater Cl. PO6: Cosh 3H **29**
Blackwood Ho. PO1: Ports 6H **41**
Bladon Cl. PO9: Hav 6A **22**
Blair Atholl Ri. PO15: Fare 1H **25**
Blake Ct. PO12: Gos 3G **49**
Blake Ho. PO1: Ports 4A **4** (3H **49**)
Blakemere Cres. PO6: Cosh 2G **29**
Blake Rd. PO1: Ports 6D **40**
PO6: Farl 2F **31**
PO12: Gos 2E **49**
Blakesley La. PO3: Ports 1E **43**
Blankney Cl. PO14: Stub 3D **36**
Blaven Wlk. PO14: Fare 3G **25**
BLENDWORTH 6D **6**
Blendworth Cres. PO9: Hav 6E **21**
Blendworth Ho. PO1: Ports 1H **5**
Blendworth La. PO8: Blen 6D **6**
Blendworth Rd. PO4: S'sea 2H **51**
Blenheim Ct. PO4: S'sea 4G **51**
Blenheim Gdns. PO9: Hav 1H **33**
PO12: Gos 5H **39**
Blenheim Rd. PO8: Horn 2A **10**
Bleriot Cres. PO15: White 4A **12**
Bliss Cl. PO7: W'lle 4G **19**
Blissford Cl. PO9: Hav 3H **21**
Blossom Sq. PO1: Ports 1C **4** (1A **50**)
Blount Rd. PO1: Ports 6D **4** (4B **50**)
Bluebell Cl. PO7: W'lle 3H **19**
Bluebell Way PO15: White 1A **12**
Blueprint Portfield Rd. PO3: Ports 3C **42**
Blue Reef Aquarium 6C **50**
Boardwalk, The PO6: P Sol 4F **29**
Boardwalk Shop. Cen., The
PO6: P Sol 5E **29**
BOARHUNT 4H **15**
Boarhunt Cl. PO1: Ports 2H **5** (2D **50**)
Boarhunt Rd. PO17: Boar, Fare 6E **15**
Boatyard Ind. Est., The
PO16: Fare 3B **26**
Bodmin Rd. PO6: Cosh 3E **29**
Boiler Rd. PO1: Ports 6D **40**
Bolde Cl. PO3: Ports 2D **42**
Boldens Rd. PO12: Gos 6D **48**
Boldre Cl. PO9: Hav 5C **20**
Bolton Dr. PO12: Gos 6A **40**
Boltons, The PO7: Purb 6G **19**
Bonchurch Rd. PO4: S'sea 2G **51**
Bondfields Cres. PO9: Hav 3E **21**
Bonfire Cnr. PO1: Ports 1B **4** (1A **50**)
Bordon Rd. PO9: Hav 4F **21**
Borough, The *GU32: Pet* *4C 56*
(off Borough Hill)
Borough Gro. GU32: Pet 5C **56**
Borough Hill GU32: Pet 4C **56**
Borough Rd. GU32: Pet 5B **56**
Bosham Rd. PO2: Ports 5B **42**
Bosham Wlk. PO13: Gos 3B **38**
Bosmere Gdns. PO10: Ems 2C **34**
Bosmere Rd. PO11: H Isl 5G **55**
Boston Rd. PO6: Cosh 2A **30**
Bosuns Cl. PO16: Fare 5B **26**
Botley Dr. PO9: Hav 3D **20**
Boughton Ct. PO3: Ports 1E **43**
Boulter La. PO17: S'wick 2E **17**
Boulton Rd. PO5: S'sea 4E **51**
Boundary Wlk. PO17: K Vil 2G **13**
Boundary Way PO6: Cosh 1D **30**
PO9: Hav 2E **33**
Bound La. PO11: H Isl 5C **54**
Bourne Cl. PO8: Horn 1B **10**
Bourne Community Leisure Cen. 2G **35**
Bournemouth Av. PO12: Gos 6G **39**
Bournemouth Ho. PO9: Hav 4G **21**
Bourne Rd. PO6: Cosh 3F **29**
Bourne Vw. Cl. PO10: S'urne 1H **35**
Bowen La. GU31: Pet 4D **56**
Bowers Cl. PO8: Cowp 3A **10**
Bowes Hill PO9: R Cas 4H **11**
Bowes-Lyon Ct. PO8: Horn 6B **6**
Bowler Av. PO3: Ports 1F **51**
Bowler Ct. PO3: Ports 1F **51**
Bowlplex
Portsmouth 4B **4**
Boxgrove Ho. PO1: Ports 1H **5** (1D **50**)
Boxwood Cl. PO7: W'lle 3G **19**
PO16: Portc 2H **27**
Boyd Cl. PO14: Stub 4D **36**
Boyd Rd. PO13: Gos 2B **38**
Boyes La. PO8: Blen, Ids 5F **7**
Boyle Cres. PO7: W'lle 4F **19**
Brabazon Rd. PO15: Seg 4A **12**
Bracken Cl. PO13: Lee S 1D **46**
Bracken Heath PO7: W'lle 6B **10**
Bracken Rd. GU31: Pet 5G **57**
Bracklesham Rd. PO11: H Isl 6H **55**
PO13: Gos 5D **38**
Bradford Ct. PO13: Gos 1G **47**
Bradford Junc. PO5: S'sea 3E **51**
Bradford Rd. PO5: S'sea 4H **5** (3D **50**)
Brading Av. PO4: S'sea 5G **51**
PO13: Gos 3C **38**
Bradley Ct. PO9: Hav 3H **21**
Bradly Rd. PO15: Fare 1E **25**
Braemar Av. PO6: Cosh 4D **30**
Braemar Cl. PO13: Gos 3D **38**
PO15: Fare 6G **13**
Braemar Rd. PO13: Gos 2D **38**
Braganza Ho. PO1: Ports 5C **4**
Braintree Rd. PO6: Cosh 2H **29**
Braishfield Rd. PO9: Hav 5G **21**
Bramber Rd. PO12: Gos 6G **39**
Bramble Cl. PO9: Hav 6A **22**
PO14: Stub 4C **36**
Bramble Ct. *GU31: Pet* *4G 57*
(off Rival Moor Rd.)
Bramble La. PO8: Clan 1F **7**
Bramble Rd. GU31: Pet 4G **57**
PO4: S'sea 3E **51**
Brambles Bus. Cen., The PO7: W'lle 1E **19**
Brambles Ent. Cen., The PO7: W'lle 6E **9**
Brambles Farm Ind. Est. PO7: W'lle 1F **19**
Brambles Rd. PO13: Lee S 6F **37**
Bramble Way PO13: Gos 3A **38**
Brambling Rd. PO9: R Cas 6H **11**
Bramdean Dr. PO9: Hav 4D **20**
Bramham Moor PO14: Stub 3D **36**
Bramley Cl. PO7: W'lle 1H **19**
Bramley Gdns. PO10: S'urne 3F **35**
PO12: Gos 6C **48**
Bramley Ho. PO5: S'sea 5G **5** (3C **50**)
Brampton La. PO3: Ports 1E **43**
Bramshaw Ct. PO9: Hav 4H **21**
Bramshott Rd. PO4: S'sea 3F **51**
Brandon Ct. PO5: S'sea 4E **51**
Brandon Ho. PO5: S'sea 5E **51**
Brandon Rd. PO5: S'sea 5D **50**
Branewick Cl. PO15: Seg 6A **12**
Bransbury Rd. PO4: S'sea 4H **51**
Bransgore Av. PO9: Hav 5C **20**
Brasted Ct. PO4: S'sea 2A **52**
Braunston Cl. PO6: Cosh 2E **29**
Braxell Lawn PO9: Hav 3D **20**
BREACH 1H **35**
Breach Av. PO10: S'urne 1H **35**
Brecon Av. PO6: Dray 2D **30**
Brecon Cl. PO14: Fare 3G **25**
Brecon Ho. PO1: Ports 3A **50**
Bredenbury Cres. PO6: Cosh 2G **29**
Bredon Wlk. PO14: Fare 3G **25**
Breech Cl. PO3: Ports 1B **42**
Brenchley Cl. PO16: Portc 4H **27**
Brendon Rd. PO14: Fare 3F **25**
Brent Ct. PO10: Ems 3C **34**
Bresler Ho. PO6: Cosh 2F **29**
Brewers La. PO13: Gos 3C **38**
Brewer St. PO1: Ports 1G **5** (1C **50**)
Brewster Cl. PO8: Cowp 4A **10**
Briar Cl. PO8: Horn 2B **10**
PO12: Gos 4A **48**
Briarfield Gdns. PO8: Horn 1B **10**
Briars, The PO7: W'lle 1E **19**
Briarwood Cl. PO16: Fare 3B **26**
Briarwood Gdns. PO11: H Isl 4B **54**
Bridefield Cl. PO8: Cowp 4F **9**
Bridefield Cres. PO8: Cowp 4F **9**
Bridgefoot Dr. PO16: Fare 2C **26**
Bridgefoot Hill PO16: Fare 2D **26**
Bridgefoot Path PO10: Ems 3D **34**
Bridge Ho. PO13: Gos 1C **38**
Bridge Industries PO16: Fare 6C **14**
BRIDGEMARY 2C **38**
Bridgemary Av. PO13: Gos 2D **38**
Bridgemary Gro. PO13: Gos 6C **26**
Bridgemary Rd. PO13: Gos 6C **26**
Bridgemary Way PO13: Gos 6C **26**
Bridge Rd. PO10: Ems 2D **34**
Bridges Av. PO6: Cosh 2D **28**
Bridge Shop. Cen., The PO1: Ports 2E **51**
Bridgeside Cl. PO1: Ports 2H **5**
Bridge St. PO14: Titch 3C **24**
PO17: S'wick 3B **16**
PO17: Wick 1A **14**
Bridget Cl. PO8: Horn 6C **6**
Bridle Path PO8: Horn 5B **6**
Bridport St. PO1: Ports 2G **5** (2C **50**)
Brigham Cl. PO2: Ports 2A **42**
Brighstone Rd. PO6: Cosh 4A **30**
Brighton Av. PO12: Gos 5F **39**
Brightside PO7: W'lle 3F **19**
Brights La. PO11: H Isl 2B **54**
Brisbane Ho. PO1: Ports 6H **41**
Bristol Ct. PO13: Gos 2G **47**
Bristol Rd. PO4: S'sea 5F **51**
Britain St. PO1: Ports 3C **4** (2A **50**)
Britannia Rd. PO5: S'sea 3D **50**

A-Z Portsmouth 61

Britannia Rd. Nth. PO5: S'sea 3D 50
Britannia St. GU31: Pet 2E 57
Britannia Way PO12: Gos 6A 40
Britnell Ho. GU31: Pet 3D 56
Britten Rd. PO13: Lee S 1C 46
Britten Way PO7: W'lle 5G 19
Brixworth Cl. PO6: Cosh 2E 29
Broadcut PO16: Fare 1C 26
Broad Gdns. PO6: Farl 3G 31
Broadlands Av. PO7: W'lle 3G 19
Broadlaw Wlk. Shop. Pct.
    PO14: Fare 4G 25
Broadmarsh Bus. & Innovation Cen.
    PO9: Hav 3C 32
Broadmeadows La. PO7: W'lle 2A 20
Broadmere Av. PO9: Hav 4F 21
Broad Oak Works PO3: Ports 1D 42
Broadsands Dr. PO12: Gos 4H 47
Broadsands Wlk. PO12: Gos 4H 47
Broad St. PO1: Ports 5A 4 (3H 49)
Broad Wlk. PO8: Horn 2E 11
Broadway La. PO8: Love 1F 9
Broadway Pk. GU31: Pet 6D 56
Brockenhurst Av. PO9: Hav 3D 20
BROCKHAMPTON 2D 32
Brockhampton La. PO9: Hav 2E 33
Brockhampton Rd. PO9: Hav 3D 32
    (not continuous)
BROCKHURST 1C 48
Brockhurst Ind. Est. PO12: Gos 4F 39
Brockhurst Rd. PO12: Gos 5F 39
Brocklands PO9: Hav 2D 32
Brodrick Av. PO12: Gos 4C 48
Brompton Pas. PO2: Ports 6H 41
Brompton Rd. PO4: S'sea 5F 51
Bromyard Cres. PO6: Cosh 2G 29
Brookdale Cl. PO7: W'lle 1H 19
Brooke Ho. PO9: Hav 1F 33
Brookers La. PO13: Gos 2A 38
    (not continuous)
Brook Farm Av. PO15: Fare 2H 25
Brookfield Cl. PO9: Hav 1E 33
Brookfield Rd. PO1: Ports 1E 51
Brook Gdns. PO10: Ems 3B 34
Brooklands Ct. PO7: W'lle 6H 9
Brooklands Rd. PO9: Bed 1B 32
Brooklyn Dr. PO7: W'lle 1H 19
Brookmeadow PO15: Fare 2H 25
Brookmead Way PO9: Lang 3F 33
Brookside PO13: Gos 6B 26
Brookside Cl. PO7: Den 3B 8
Brookside Rd. PO9: Bed 1C 32
    PO9: Hav 3D 32
Brookview Cl. PO14: Fare 3D 24
Broom Cl. PO4: S'sea 2B 52
    PO7: W'lle 4A 20
Broomfield Cres. PO13: Gos 6B 38
Broom Rd. PO13: Gos 5G 57
Broom Sq. PO4: S'sea 2B 52
Broom Way PO13: Lee S 6H 37
Brougham La. PO12: Gos 1C 48
Brougham Rd. PO5: S'sea 5F 5 (3C 50)
Brougham St. PO12: Gos 1C 48
Brow, The PO7: Wid 1D 30
    PO12: Gos 3G 49
Browndown Rd. PO12: Gos 4G 47
    PO13: Lee S 4G 47
Brownfield Ho. GU32: Pet 3D 56
Browning Av. PO6: Cosh 2C 28
Brownlow Cl. PO1: Ports 6H 41
Browns La. PO3: Ports 1D 42
Brownwich La. PO14: Titch 4A 24
Brow Path PO7: Wid 1E 31
Broxhead Rd. PO9: Hav 3G 21
Bruce Cl. PO16: Fare 4A 26
Bruce Rd. PO4: S'sea 5F 51
Brune La. PO13: Gos 4A 38
    PO13: Lee S 4A 38
    (not continuous)
Brunel Rd. PO2: Ports 2A 42
Brunel Way PO15: Seg 4A 12
Brunswick Gdns. PO9: Bed 1D 32
Brunswick St. PO5: S'sea 5F 5 (3C 50)
Bryher Bri. PO6: P Sol 4F 29
Bryher Island PO6: P Sol 4E 29
Bryony Way PO7: W'lle 2A 20
Bryson Cl. PO13: Lee S 1E 47
Bryson Rd. PO6: Cosh 3H 29
Buckby La. PO1: Ports 1E 43
Buckingham Ct. PO15: Fare 6F 13
Buckingham Grn. PO1: Ports 6A 42

Buckingham Rd. GU32: Pet 4B 56
Buckingham St. PO1: Ports 1G 5 (1C 50)
BUCKLAND .5H 41
Buckland Cl. PO7: W'lle 4F 9
Buckland Path PO2: Ports 6H 41
Buckland St. PO2: Ports 6A 42
    (not continuous)
Bucklers Ct. PO2: Ports 4H 41
    PO9: Hav 2D 20
Bucklers Rd. PO12: Gos 5A 40
Buckmore Av. GU32: Pet 2B 56
Bucksey Rd. PO13: Gos 5C 38
Buddens Rd. PO17: Wick 1A 14
Bude Cl. PO6: Cosh 2D 28
Bulbarrow Wlk. PO14: Fare 3G 25
Bulbeck Rd. PO9: Hav 2F 33
Bullfinch Ct. PO13: Lee S 6H 37
Bulwark Rd. PO14: Stub 4D 36
BUNKERS HILL 3A 8
Bunkers Hill PO7: Den 4A 8
Bunting Gdns. PO7: Den 3H 9
Burbidge Gro. PO4: S'sea 5G 51
Burcote Dr. PO3: Ports 1D 42
Burdale Dr. PO11: H Isl 4F 55
Burgate Cl. PO9: Bed 6D 20
Burgesmede Ho. GU31: Pet 4D 56
Burgess Cl. PO11: H Isl 6F 55
Burghclere Rd. PO9: Hav 3H 21
Burgoyne Rd. PO5: S'sea 6D 50
Burgundy Ter. PO2: Ports 2A 42
Buriton Cl. PO16: Portc 2B 28
Buriton Ho. PO1: Ports 2H 5
    (off Buriton St.)
Buriton St. PO1: Ports 1H 5 (1D 50)
Burleigh Rd. PO1: Ports 6B 42
Burley Cl. PO9: Hav 3H 21
Burlington Rd. PO2: Ports 4A 42
Burnaby Rd. PO1: Ports 3D 4 (2B 50)
Burnett Rd. PO12: Gos 1B 48
Burney Ho. PO12: Gos 3F 49
    (off South St.)
Burney Rd. PO12: Gos 4A 48
Burnham Rd. PO6: Dray 2F 31
Burnham's Wlk. PO12: Gos 3F 49
Burnham Wood PO16: Fare 6A 14
Burnside PO7: W'lle 6A 10
    PO13: Gos 6B 26
Burnt Ho. La. PO14: Stub 6F 25
Burrell Ho. PO5: S'sea 6E 5
Burrfields Retail Pk. PO3: Ports 4D 42
Burrfields Rd. PO3: Ports 4C 42
Burrill Av. PO6: Cosh 3C 30
Burrows Cl. PO9: Hav 6G 21
Bursledon Pl. PO7: Purb 4F 19
Bursledon Rd. PO7: Purb 4F 19
Burwood Gro. PO11: H Isl 2C 54
Bury Cl. PO12: Gos 3D 48
Bury Cres. PO12: Gos 3D 48
Bury Cross PO12: Gos 3C 48
Bury Hall La. PO12: Gos 4A 48
Bury Rd. PO12: Gos 3C 48
Bush Ho. PO5: S'sea 6F 5 (4C 50)
Bush St. E. PO5: S'sea 6F 5 (4C 50)
Bush St. W. PO5: S'sea 6F 5 (4C 50)
Bushy Mead PO7: Wid 6E 19
Butcher St. PO1: Ports 3B 4 (2A 50)
Butser Ct. PO8: Horn 2D 6
Butser Wlk. GU31: Pet 3F 57
    PO14: Fare 3G 25
Butterfly Dr. PO6: Cosh 2E 29
Byerley Cl. PO10: Westb 4F 23
Byerley Rd. PO1: Ports 2F 51
    (not continuous)
Byngs Bus. Pk. PO7: Den 5D 8
Byrd Cl. PO7: W'lle 4G 19
Byres, The PO14: Stub 2E 37
Byron Cl. PO16: Fare 1A 26
Byron Rd. PO2: Ports 5B 42

C

Cadgwith Pl. PO6: P Sol 4F 29
Cadnam Ct. PO12: Gos 4H 47
Cadnam Lawn PO9: Hav 2D 20
Cadnam Rd. PO4: S'sea 4H 51
Cador Dr. PO16: Portc 5H 27
Caen Ho. PO14: Fare 3G 25
Caer Peris Vw. PO16: Portc 1A 28
Cains Cl. PO14: Stub 2E 37
Cairo Pl. PO9: Hav 4E 33

Cairo Ter. PO2: Ports 6H 41
Caldecote Wlk. PO5: S'sea 4E 5 (3C 50)
Calder Ho. PO1: Ports 2B 4
Calshot Rd. PO9: Hav 2C 20
Calshot Way PO13: Gos 4B 38
Cam Alders Sports Cen. 4A 26
Camaron Cvn. Pk. PO11: H Isl 5G 55
Camber Pl. PO1: Ports 6B 4 (4A 50)
Cambrian Ter. PO5: S'sea 6H 5
Cambrian Wlk. PO14: Fare 4H 25
Cambridge Junc. PO1: Ports 5D 4 (3B 50)
Cambridge Rd. PO1: Ports 5D 4 (3B 50)
    PO12: Gos 1A 48
    PO13: Lee S 2D 46
Camcross Cl. PO6: Cosh 2F 29
Camden St. PO12: Gos 1C 48
CAMDENTOWN 1C 48
Camelia Cl. PO9: Hav 6A 22
Camelot Cres. PO16: Portc 2H 27
Cameron Cl. PO13: Gos 2C 38
Campbell Cres. PO7: Purb 4E 19
Campbell Mans. PO5: S'sea 4E 51
Campbell Rd. PO5: S'sea 4D 50
Campion Cl. PO7: W'lle 3A 20
Camp Rd. PO13: Gos 2D 38
Cams Bay Cl. PO16: Portc 2F 27
Cams Hall Est. PO16: Fare 3D 26
Cams Hill PO16: Fare 2D 26
    (not continuous)
Canada Ct. PO12: Gos 5A 40
    (off Hayling Cl.)
Canalside, The PO1: Ports 4A 4 (3A 50)
Canal Wlk. PO1: Ports 3H 5 (2D 50)
Canberra Cl. PO12: Gos 3B 48
Canberra Ct. PO12: Gos 3B 48
Canberra Ho. PO1: Ports 2G 5 (2C 50)
Cannock Wlk. PO14: Fare 4G 25
Canons Barn Cl. PO16: Portc 2A 28
Canterbury Cl. PO13: Lee S 3F 47
Canterbury Rd. PO4: S'sea 4F 51
    PO14: Stub 2E 37
Capel Ley PO7: Purb 5G 19
Captains Cl. PO12: Gos 5F 39
Captains Row PO1: Ports 6B 4 (4A 50)
Caraway PO7: W'lle 2A 12
Carberry Dr. PO16: Portc 4H 27
Carbery Ct. PO9: Hav 2D 20
Carbis Cl. PO6: P Sol 4E 29
Cardiff Rd. PO2: Ports 3H 41
Cardinal Dr. PO7: W'lle 6B 10
Carisbrooke Av. PO14: Stub 3C 36
Carisbrooke Ct. PO9: Hav 1H 33
Carisbrooke Ct. PO17: K Vil 2G 13
    (off Knowle Av.)
Carisbrooke Rd. PO4: S'sea 3G 51
    PO13: Gos 2B 38
Carless Cl. PO12: Gos 6D 38
Carlisle Rd. PO5: S'sea 3H 5 (2D 50)
Carlton Rd. PO12: Gos 2E 49
    PO16: Portc 2B 28
Carlton Way PO12: Gos 2E 49
Carlyle Rd. PO12: Gos 2D 48
Carmarthen Av. PO6: Dray 2D 30
Carmine Ct. PO13: Gos 1G 47
Carnac Ct. PO16: Fare 3D 26
Carnarvon Rd. PO2: Ports 5B 42
    PO12: Gos 3C 48
Carne Pl. PO6: P Sol 4E 29
Caroline Gdns. PO15: Fare 1E 25
Caroline Lodge PO1: Ports 1C 4
Caroline Pl. PO12: Gos 1D 48
Carpenter Cl. PO4: S'sea 4G 51
Carran Wlk. PO14: Fare 4G 25
Carrick Ho. PO7: W'lle 2G 19
Carronade Wlk. PO3: Ports 6B 30
Carshalton Av. PO6: Cosh 3D 30
Carter Ho. PO1: Ports 2C 4 (2A 50)
    PO13: Gos 6B 26
    (off Woodside)
Cartwright Dr. PO15: Titch 1A 24
Cascades App. PO1: Ports 1F 5 (1C 50)
Cascades Cen. PO1: Ports 1F 5 (1C 50)
Cases Bakery Ct. PO17: Wick 1A 14
Caspar John Cl. PO14: Stub 4D 36
Castle Av. PO9: Warb 4H 21
Castle Cl. PO5: S'sea 6F 5 (4C 50)
Castle Esplanade PO5: S'sea 6C 50
Castle Gdn. GU32: Pet 4C 56
Castle Gro. PO16: Portc 4B 28
Castlemans La. PO11: H Isl 4C 44
Castle Marina PO13: Lee S 3D 46

Castle Rd.—Clanwilliam Rd.

Castle Rd. PO5: S'sea 6E 5 (4B 50)
PO9: R Cas 5G 11
PO17: S'wick 3D 16
Castle St. PO16: Portc 3B 28
Castleton Ct. *PO5: S'sea 4B 50*
(off Southsea Ter.)
Castle Trad. Est. PO16: Portc 3C 28
Castle Vw. PO12: Gos 5H 39
Castle Vw. Rd. PO16: Portc 5B 28
Castleway PO9: Warb 2H 33
Cathedral Ho. PO1: Ports 6B 4
CATHERINGTON 4A 6
Catherington Bus. Pk. PO8: Cath 5A 6
Catherington Down Nature Reserve 4A 6
Catherington Hill PO8: Cath 2B 6
Catherington La. PO8: Cath, Horn 5A 6
Catherington Way PO9: Hav 5F 21
CATISFIELD 2E 25
Catisfield Gate PO15: Fare 2D 24
Catisfield Ho. PO1: Ports 1H 5
Catisfield La. PO15: Fare 2D 24
Catisfield Rd. PO4: S'sea 2H 51
PO15: Fare 2E 25
CAUSEWAY 5D 56
Causeway, The GU31: Pet 6B 56
PO16: Fare 2E 27
Causeway Farm PO8: Horn 1B 10
Cavanna Cl. PO13: Gos 2B 38
Cavell Dr. PO6: Cosh 2A 30
Cavendish Cl. PO7: W'lle 1H 19
Cavendish Dr. PO7: W'lle 2H 19
Cavendish Rd. PO5: S'sea 4D 50
Cawte's Pl. PO16: Fare 2C 26
Cecil Gro. PO5: S'sea 6E 5 (4B 50)
Cecil Pl. PO5: S'sea 6E 5 (4B 50)
Cedar Cl. PO7: W'lle 3G 19
PO12: Gos 4G 39
Cedar Ct. PO5: S'sea 6H 5 (4D 50)
PO16: Fare 2C 26
Cedar Cres. PO8: Horn 2C 10
Cedar Gdns. PO9: Hav 1G 33
Cedar Gro. PO3: Ports 6D 42
Cedars, The PO16: Fare 5H 13
Cedar Way PO14: Fare 3G 25
Cedarwood Lodge *PO16: Fare 1B 26*
(off Northwood Sq.)
Celandine Av. PO8: Cowp 4B 10
Celia Cl. PO7: W'lle 1B 20
Cemetery La. PO7: Den 2B 8
PO10: Westb, Wood 5G 23
Centaur St. PO2: Ports 5H 41
Centenary Gdns. PO9: Hav 1F 33
Central Rd. PO6: Dray 4E 31
PO16: Portc 4H 27
Central St. PO1: Ports 1H 5 (1D 50)
Centurion Ct. PO1: Ports 4B 4 (3A 50)
Centurion Ga. PO4: S'sea 4B 52
Cessac Ho. PO12: Gos 6E 49
Chadderton Gdns. PO1: Ports 6D 4 (4B 50)
Chadswell Mdw. PO9: Bed 2D 32
Chaffinch Grn. PO8: Cowp 3G 9
Chaffinch Way PO13: Lee S 6H 37
PO16: Portc 3F 27
Chale Cl. PO13: Gos 3C 38
Chalford Grange PO15: Fare 2F 25
Chalk Hill Rd. PO8: Horn 5C 6
Chalk La. PO15: Fare 2D 24
Chalkpit Rd. PO6: Cosh 2F 29
Chalk Ridge PO8: Cath 2D 6
Chalkridge Rd. PO6: Cosh 2C 30
Chalky Wlk. PO16: Portc 4A 28
Challenge Ent. Cen., The
PO3: Ports 2D 42
Challenger Dr. PO12: Gos 6A 40
Chalton Cres. PO9: Hav 4D 20
Chalton Ho. PO1: Ports 1G 5 (1C 50)
Chalton La. PO8: Clan 1F 7
(not continuous)
Chamberlain Gro. PO14: Fare 3A 26
Champneys Gdns. PO16: Fare 2F 27
Chanctonbury Ho. PO5: S'sea 6G 5 (4C 50)
Chandlers Cl. PO11: H Isl 5E 55
Chandos Ri. PO1: Ports 1G 5
Chantrell Wlk. PO15: Fare 6F 13
Chantry Rd. PO8: Horn 5B 6
PO12: Gos 6F 39
Chapel Ct. *PO1: Ports 6H 41*
(off Victoria St.)
Chapel La. PO7: W'lle 2G 19
Chapelside PO14: Titch 3C 24
Chapel Sq. PO12: Gos 6F 39
Chapel St. GU32: Pet 3D 56
PO2: Ports 5A 42
PO5: S'sea 6E 5 (4C 50)
PO12: Gos 5H 39
Chapel Vw. PO4: S'sea 2A 52
Chaplains Av. PO8: Cowp 4F 9
Chaplains Cl. PO8: Cowp 4F 9
Charden Rd. PO13: Gos 5D 38
Charfield Cl. PO14: Fare 3F 25
Charity Vw. PO17: K Vil 2G 13
Chark La. PO13: Lee S 5H 37
Charlcot Lawn PO9: Hav 3D 20
Charlemont Dr. PO16: Fare 2D 26
Charlesbury Av. PO12: Gos 3B 48
Charles Clark Ho. PO4: S'sea 3G 51
Charles Cl. PO7: W'lle 3F 19
Charles Dickens Birthplace Mus. 6G 41
Charles Dickens St. PO1: Ports 3F 5 (2C 50)
Charles Ho. PO12: Gos 2G 49
Charles Norton-Thomas Ct. *PO1: Ports 3C 4*
(off St George's Way)
Charles St. GU32: Pet 4C 56
PO1: Ports 1H 5 (1D 50)
Charleston Cl. PO11: H Isl 3A 54
Charlesworth Dr. PO7: W'lle 6E 9
Charlesworth Gdns. PO7: W'lle 6F 9
Charlotte Ct. PO5: S'sea 6F 5 (4C 50)
Charlotte Dr. PO12: Gos 6A 40
Charlotte M. PO12: Gos 5C 48
Charlotte St. PO1: Ports 1F 5 (1C 50)
Charlton Dr. GU31: Pet 2E 57
Charminster *PO4: S'sea 5E 51*
(off Craneswater Pk.)
Charminster Cl. PO7: W'lle 1G 19
Charnwood PO13: Gos 3E 39
Charter Ho. PO1: S'sea 4E 5
Chartwell Dr. PO9: Hav 6A 22
Chase, The PO12: Gos 3B 48
Chasewater Av. PO3: Ports 6C 42
Chatburn Av. PO8: Cowp 4G 9
Chatfield Av. PO2: Ports 4E 41
Chatfield Ho. PO1: Ports 1H 5
Chatfield Rd. PO13: Gos 1C 38
Chatham Cl. PO12: Gos 6A 40
Chatham Dr. PO1: Ports 6D 4 (4B 50)
Chatsworth Av. PO6: Cosh 5B 30
Chatsworth Cl. PO15: Fare 2E 25
Chatsworth Ct. PO5: S'sea 4D 50
Chaucer Av. PO6: Cosh 2C 28
Chaucer Cl. PO7: W'lle 5G 9
PO16: Fare 1H 25
Chayofa Pl. PO12: Gos 1C 48
Chedworth Cres. PO6: Cosh 2E 29
Cheeryble Ho. PO1: Ports 6H 41
Chelmsford Rd. PO2: Ports 3B 42
Chelsea Rd. PO5: S'sea 4D 50
Cheltenham Cres. PO13: Lee S 6H 37
Cheltenham Rd. PO6: Cosh 3G 29
Chepstow Ct. PO7: W'lle 6B 10
Chequers Quay *PO10: Ems 3E 35*
(off Queen St.)
Cheriton Cl. PO8: Horn 6B 6
PO9: Hav 4D 20
Cheriton Rd. PO4: S'sea 3A 52
PO12: Gos 3B 48
Cherque La. PO13: Lee S 5A 38
Cherry Blossom Ct. PO2: Ports 6H 41
Cherry Cl. PO13: Lee S 2E 47
Cherrygarth Rd. PO15: Fare 2E 25
Cherry Tree Apartments PO7: W'lle 6F 9
Cherry Tree Av. PO8: Cowp 4B 10
PO14: Fare 3F 25
Cherry Tree Holiday Cvn. Pk.
PO11: H Isl 5G 55
Cherrywood Gdns. PO11: H Isl 3C 54
Chervil Cl. PO8: Horn 4C 6
Cheshire Cl. PO15: White 4B 12
Cheshire Way PO10: S'urne 1H 35
Cheslyn Rd. PO3: Ports 1H 51
Chester Courts PO12: Gos 3E 49
Chester Cres. PO13: Lee S 3F 47
Chesterfield Rd. PO3: Ports 5C 42
Chester Pl. PO5: S'sea 5D 50
Chesterton Gdns. PO8: Cowp 4G 9
Chestnut Av. PO4: S'sea 3F 51
PO8: Horn 2C 10
PO9: Bed 6B 20
Chestnut Cl. PO7: Den 3B 8
Chestnut Ct. PO9: R Cas 1H 21
Chestnut Dr. GU31: Pet 6D 56
Chestnut Wlk. PO12: Gos 4G 39
Chetwynd Rd. PO4: S'sea 4E 51
Chevening Ct. PO4: S'sea 2H 51
Cheviot Wlk. PO14: Fare 4H 25
Chewter Cl. PO4: S'sea 6E 51
Cheyne Way PO13: Lee S 2D 46
Chichester Av. PO11: H Isl 5B 54
Chichester Cl. PO13: Gos 3B 38
Chichester Ho. PO9: Hav 6G 21
Chichester Rd. PO2: Ports 5H 41
PO11: H Isl 4E 45
Chidham Cl. PO9: Hav 1E 33
Chidham Dr. PO9: Hav 1E 33
Chidham Rd. PO6: Cosh 2C 30
Chidham Sq. PO9: Hav 1E 33
Chidham Wlk. PO9: Hav 1E 33
Chilbolton Ct. PO9: Hav 3H 21
Chilcomb Cl. PO13: Lee S 1D 46
Chilcombe Cl. PO9: Hav 6F 21
Chilcote Rd. PO3: Ports 6C 42
Childe Sq. PO2: Ports 3G 41
Chilgrove Rd. PO6: Dray 3E 31
Chilsdown Way PO7: W'lle 5G 19
Chiltern Ct. PO5: S'sea 6D 50
PO12: Gos 2D 48
Chiltern Wlk. PO14: Fare 4H 25
Chilworth Gdns. PO8: Clan 1C 6
Chilworth Gro. PO12: Gos 2C 48
Chine, The PO13: Gos 4E 39
Chipstead Ho. PO6: Cosh 3B 30
Chipstead Rd. PO6: Cosh 3B 30
Chitty Rd. PO4: S'sea 5G 51
Chivers Cl. PO5: S'sea 6G 5 (4C 50)
Christchurch Gdns. PO7: Wid 1D 30
Christopher Way PO10: Ems 1D 34
Christyne Ct. PO7: Purb 4F 19
Church Cl. PO8: Clan 1F 7
Churcher Cl. PO12: Gos 4H 47
Churcher Rd. PO10: Westb 5F 23
Churcher Wlk. PO12: Gos 4H 47
Churchfield Rd. GU31: Pet 3F 57
Churchill Ct. PO6: Farl 3G 31
PO8: Horn 1A 10
Churchill Dr. PO10: Ems 5D 22
Churchill M. *PO12: Gos 1C 48*
(off Forton Rd.)
Churchill Sq. PO4: S'sea 5H 51
Churchill Yd. Ind. Est.
PO7: W'lle 6F 9
Church La. PO9: Warb 3H 33
PO11: H Isl 2E 45
Church M. *PO4: S'sea 5G 51*
(off Priory Rd.)
Church Path PO8: Horn 1D 10
PO9: Warb 4H 33
PO10: Ems 4B 34
(Maisemore Gdns.)
PO10: Ems 3D 34
(St James's Rd.)
PO12: Gos 3F 49
PO14: Titch 3C 24
PO16: Fare 2C 26
Church Path Nth. PO1: Ports 1G 5 (1D 50)
Church Pl. PO16: Fare 1C 26
Church Rd. GU32: Ste 1D 56
PO1: Ports 1H 5 (1D 50)
(not continuous)
PO10: S'urne 3H 35
PO10: Westb 6F 23
PO11: H Isl 3C 54
PO12: Gos 5C 48
PO16: Portc 5C 28
Church Rd. Rdbt. PO11: H Isl 1C 54
Church St. PO1: Ports 6G 41
PO14: Titch 3C 24
Church Vw. PO4: S'sea 3G 51
PO10: Westb 6F 23
Cinderford Cl. PO6: Cosh 2G 29
Cineplex 4B 30
Circle, The PO5: S'sea 5D 50
PO17: Wick 1A 14
Circular Rd. PO1: Ports 1D 4 (6F 41)
Circus, The *PO17: S'wick 1E 29*
(off North Rd.)
City Mus. & Art Gallery 6D 4 (4B 50)
Civic Cen. Rd. PO9: Hav 1F 33
Civic Way PO16: Fare 2C 26
Clacton Rd. PO6: Cosh 3H 29
Claire Gdns. PO8: Horn 3C 6
CLANFIELD 1F 7
Clanfield Ho. PO1: Ports 1H 5 (1D 50)
Clanwilliam Rd. PO13: Lee S 1D 46

Clare Gdns. GU31: Pet 4G 57
Clare Ho. PO12: Gos 6F 39
Claremont Gdns. PO7: Purb 5G 19
Claremont Rd. PO1: Ports 2E 51
Clarence Esplanade PO5: S'sea 5B 50
Clarence Pde. PO5: S'sea 5B 50
Clarence Pier Amusement Pk. 5A 50
Clarence Rd. PO5: S'sea 5D 50
   PO12: Gos 2F 49
Clarence St. PO1: Ports 1C 50
Clarence Wharf PO12: Gos 2F 49
Clarendon Cl. PO7: Den 2B 8
Clarendon Ct. PO5: S'sea 6D 50
                        (off Clarendon Rd.)
Clarendon Pl. PO1: Ports 2G 5 (2C 50)
                        (Arundel Way)
   PO1: Ports 1D 50
                        (Clarendon St.)
Clarendon Rd. PO4: S'sea 6E 51
   PO5: S'sea 5C 50
   PO9: Hav 2E 33
Clarendon St. PO1: Ports 1D 50
Clarke's Rd. PO1: Ports 1F 51
Claudia Ct. PO12: Gos 1B 48
Claxton St. PO1: Ports 2H 5 (2D 50)
Claybank Rd. PO3: Ports 4C 42
Claybank Spur PO3: Ports 4C 42
Claydon Av. PO4: S'sea 3G 51
CLAYHALL 5E 49
Clayhall Rd. PO12: Gos 5C 48
Clearwater Apartments
   PO4: S'sea 6E 51
Clee Av. PO14: Fare 3F 25
Cleeve Cl. PO6: Cosh 2F 29
Clegg Rd. PO4: S'sea 4G 51
Clement Attlee Way PO6: Cosh 3F 29
Cleveland Dr. PO14: Fare 3F 25
Cleveland Rd. PO5: S'sea 3E 51
   PO12: Gos 4D 48
Cleverley Ho. PO1: Ports 3B 4
Cliffdale Gdns. PO6: Cosh 2C 30
Cliff Rd. PO14: Stub 4A 36
Clifton Cres. PO7: Den 3D 8
Clifton Rd. PO5: S'sea 5C 50
   PO13: Lee S .3E 47
Clifton St. PO1: Ports 1E 51
   PO12: Gos 1B 48
Clifton Ter. PO5: S'sea 5C 50
Climaur Ct. PO5: S'sea 5D 50
Clinton Rd. PO7: W'lle 4E 9
Clive Gro. PO16: Portc 4A 28
Clive Rd. PO1: Ports 1E 51
Clock Ho. PO7: W'lle 2G 19
Clock St. PO1: Ports 3B 4 (2A 50)
Clocktower Dr. PO4: S'sea 5H 51
Cloisters, The PO15: Fare 1E 25
Close, The PO6: Cosh 4C 30
   PO14: Titch 4B 24
   PO16: Portc 3A 28
Closewood Rd. PO7: Den 6C 8
Clovelly Rd. PO4: S'sea 3G 51
   PO10: Ems 3C 34
   PO10: S'urne .2H 35
   PO11: H Isl 1E 45
Clover Cl. PO13: Gos 3C 38
Clover Ct. PO7: W'lle 3A 20
Cluster Ind. Est. PO4: S'sea 2F 51
Clydebank Rd. PO2: Ports 5H 41
Clyde Ct. PO12: Gos 1B 48
Clyde Rd. PO12: Gos 1B 48
Coach Hill PO14: Titch 3B 24
Coach Ho. PO4: S'sea 3A 52
Coal Yd. Rd. PO4: S'sea 2F 51
Coastguard Cl. PO12: Gos 5B 48
Coastguard Cotts. PO9: Lang 5F 33
Coates Way PO7: W'lle 4G 19
Cobalt Ct. PO13: Gos 1G 47
Cobblewood PO10: Ems 6D 22
Cobden Av. PO3: Ports 5C 42
Cobden St. PO12: Gos 2D 48
Cobham Gro. PO15: White 4A 12
Coburg St. PO1: Ports 2D 50
Cochrane Cl. PO13: Gos 1H 47
Cochrane Ho. PO1: Ports 3B 4 (2A 50)
Cockleshell Gdns. PO4: S'sea 4A 52
Cockleshell Sq. PO12: Gos 2F 49
Codrington Ho. PO1: Ports 2B 4
Coghlan Cl. PO16: Fare 1B 26
Colbury Rd. PO9: Hav 4C 20
Colchester Rd. PO6: Cosh 2H 29
Cold Harbour Cl. PO17: Wick 1A 14

Coldharbour Farm Rd. PO10: Ems 2D 34
Coldhill La. PO8: Love 6A 6
Colebrook Av. PO3: Ports 5D 42
Colemore Sq. PO9: Hav 5F 21
Colenso Rd. PO16: Fare 2A 26
Coleridge Gdns. PO8: Cowp 3H 9
Coleridge Rd. PO6: Cosh 2D 28
Colesbourne Rd. PO6: Cosh 2F 29
Colinton Av. PO16: Portc 2B 28
College Cl. PO9: R Cas 5H 11
College La. PO1: Ports 3B 4 (2A 50)
College St. GU31: Pet 4D 56
   GU32: Pet 4D 56
   PO1: Ports 3B 4 (2A 50)
Collingwood Cres. PO6: Cosh 2F 29
Collingwood Ho. PO15: Fare 1F 25
Collingwood Retail Pk. PO14: Fare 5A 26
Collingwood Rd. PO5: S'sea 5D 50
Collingwood Way GU31: Pet 2E 57
Collins Rd. PO4: S'sea 5G 51
Collis Rd. PO3: Ports 5C 42
Colpoy St. PO5: S'sea 5E 5 (3B 50)
Coltsfoot Dr. PO7: W'lle 4H 19
Coltsmead PO6: Cosh 3D 28
Colville Rd. PO6: Cosh 3C 30
Colwell Rd. PO6: Cosh 4B 30
Comfrey Cl. PO8: Horn 4C 6
Comley Hill PO9: Ems, R Cas 3A 22
Commercial Pl. PO1: Ports 1G 5 (1C 50)
Commercial Rd. PO1: Ports 2F 5 (2C 50)
                        (not continuous)
Commodore Pl. PO12: Gos 1F 49
Common Barn La. PO13: Lee S 6H 37
                        (Broom Way, not continuous)
   PO13: Lee S .1E 47
                        (Megson Dr.)
Common La. PO14: Titch 3A 24
   PO17: S'wick .1C 16
Commonside PO10: Westb 4F 23
Common St. PO1: Ports 1H 5 (1D 50)
Compass Ct. PO13: Gos 1H 47
Compass Point PO16: Fare 3B 26
Compass Rd. PO6: Cosh 4F 29
Compton Cl. PO9: Hav 6F 21
   PO13: Lee S .1D 46
Compton Ct. PO9: Hav 1E 33
Compton Rd. PO2: Ports 2A 42
Conan Rd. PO2: Ports 1A 42
Concorde Cl. PO15: Seg 4A 12
Concorde Way PO15: Seg 4A 12
Condor Av. PO16: Portc 3F 27
Conford Ct. PO9: Hav 3D 20
Conifer Cl. PO8: Cowp 5A 10
Conifer Gro. PO13: Gos 1B 38
Conifer M. PO16: Portc 2B 28
Conigar Rd. PO10: Ems 6D 22
Coniston Av. PO3: Ports 5C 42
Coniston Wlk. PO14: Fare 4G 25
Connaught La. PO6: Cosh 2D 28
Connaught Pl. PO9: Hav 2G 33
                        (off Oaklands Rd.)
Connaught Rd. PO2: Ports 3H 41
   PO9: Hav 2G 33
Connigar Cl. PO13: Gos 6C 38
Connors Keep PO8: Cowp 3F 9
Conqueror Way PO14: Stub 4F 37
Consort Ct. PO16: Fare 2C 26
Consort Ho. PO1: Ports 6H 41
                        (off Princes St.)
Consort M. PO17: K Vil 2F 13
Constable Cl. PO12: Gos 6E 49
Convent Ct. PO10: Ems 2C 34
Convent La. PO10: Ems 3D 34
                        (not continuous)
Cooks La. PO10: S'urne 2H 35
   PO18: S'urne .2H 35
Cooley Ho. PO13: Gos 6B 26
Coombe Farm Av. PO16: Fare 3A 26
Coombe Rd. PO12: Gos 6H 39
Coombs Cl. PO8: Horn 4C 6
Cooper Gro. PO16: Portc 5B 28
Cooper Rd. PO3: Ports 5D 42
COPNOR 4C 42
Copnor Bri. Bus. Pk.
   PO3: Ports 6C 42
Copnor Rd. PO3: Ports 6B 30
Copper Beech Dr. PO6: Farl 3G 31
Copperfield Ho. PO1: Ports 6H 41
Copper St. PO5: S'sea 6E 5 (4B 50)

Coppice, The PO8: Horn 1A 10
   PO13: Gos 3D 38
Coppice Way PO15: Fare 6F 13
Coppins Gro. PO16: Portc 5A 28
Copse, The PO15: Fare 5F 13
Copse Cl. GU31: Pet 3G 57
   PO7: Wid 1F 31
Copse La. PO11: H Isl 5C 44
   PO13: Gos 4D 38
Copsey Cl. PO6: Dray 3F 31
Copsey Gro. PO6: Dray 4F 31
Copsey Path PO6: Farl 3F 31
Copythorn Rd. PO2: Ports 4B 42
Coral Cl. PO16: Portc 5A 28
Coral Ct. PO13: Gos 1G 47
Coralin Gro. PO7: W'lle 6B 10
Corbett Rd. PO7: W'lle 3F 19
Corby Cres. PO3: Ports 1D 42
Corfe Cl. PO14: Stub 3C 36
Corhampton Cres. PO9: Hav 5D 20
Corhampton Ho. PO1: Ports 1H 5
Coriander Way PO15: White 1A 12
Cormorant Cl. PO16: Portc 3F 27
Cormorant Wlk. PO13: Gos 3B 38
Cornaway La. PO16: Portc 4H 27
Cornbrook Gro. PO7: W'lle 6C 10
Cornelius Dr. PO7: W'lle 6A 10
Corner Mead PO7: Den 3B 8
Cornfield PO16: Fare 5B 14
Cornfield Rd. PO13: Lee S 1D 46
Cornwallis Cres. PO1: Ports 1D 50
Cornwallis Ho. PO1: Ports 1H 5
Cornwall Rd. PO1: Ports 2E 51
Cornwell Cl. PO2: Ports 3F 41
   PO13: Gos 6D 38
Coronado Rd. PO12: Gos 6H 39
Coronation Eventide Homes PO2: Ports . . .1A 42
Coronation Rd. PO7: W'lle 1G 19
   PO11: H Isl 6G 55
Corsair Cl. PO13: Lee S 2E 47
Cort Way PO15: Fare 5E 13
COSHAM 5B 30
Cosham Pk. Av. PO6: Cosh 4B 30
Cosham Station (Rail) 4B 30
Cotswold Cl. PO9: Hav 3E 21
Cotswold Ho. PO6: Cosh 3H 29
Cotswold Wlk. PO14: Fare 4H 25
Cottage Cl. PO7: Den 4B 8
Cottage Gro. PO5: S'sea 5G 5 (3C 50)
   PO12: Gos 2D 48
Cottage Vw. PO1: Ports 2H 5 (2D 50)
Cotteridge Ho. PO5: S'sea 4H 5 (2D 50)
Cottesloe Ct. PO5: S'sea 5C 50
Cottes Way PO14: Stub 4C 36
Cottesway E. PO14: Stub 4D 36
Cotton Dr. PO10: Ems 5C 22
                        (Diana Cl.)
   PO10: Ems 6C 22
                        (Neville Gdns.)
Cotwell Av. PO8: Cowp 3B 10
Coulmere Rd. PO12: Gos 1C 48
Country Vw. PO14: Stub 1D 36
County Gdns. PO14: Fare 3E 25
Court Barn Cl. PO13: Lee S 6H 37
Court Barn La. PO13: Lee S 6H 37
Court Cl. PO6: Cosh 4D 30
Courtenay Cl. PO15: Seg 6A 12
Courtlands Ter. PO8: Cowp 3A 10
Court La. PO6: Cosh 4D 30
Court Mead PO6: Cosh 3D 30
Courtmount Gro. PO6: Cosh 3C 30
Courtmount Path PO6: Cosh 2C 30
Court Rd. PO13: Lee S 6G 37
Court Yd., The GU31: Pet 4D 56
Cousins Gro. PO4: S'sea 5G 51
Coventry Ct. PO13: Gos 1H 47
Coverack Way PO6: P Sol 4F 29
Covert Gro. PO7: W'lle 4A 20
Covindale Ho. PO4: S'sea 4G 51
Covington Rd. PO10: Westb 4D 22
Cowan Rd. PO7: W'lle 4F 19
Coward Rd. PO12: Gos 5B 48
Cowdray Ho. PO1: Ports 2H 5
Cowdray Pk. PO14: Stub 3C 36
Cowes Ct. PO14: Fare 3E 25
Cow La. PO6: Cosh 4H 29
   PO16: Portc 4B 28
Cowper Rd. PO1: Ports 1E 51
COWPLAIN 4A 10
Cowplain Activity Cen. 5B 10
Cowslip Cl. PO13: Gos 3C 38

Coxes Mdw.—Discovery Cl.

Coxes Mdw. GU32: Pet . . . 2C **56**
Crabbe Ct. PO5: S'sea . . . 5G **5** (3C **50**)
CRABTHORN . . . 3D **36**
Crabthorn Farm La. PO14: Stub . . . 2D **36**
Crabwood Ct. PO9: Hav . . . 2D **20**
Craddock Ho. PO1: Ports . . . 2B **4**
Crafts La. GU31: Pet . . . 2E **57**
Craig Ho. *PO5: S'sea . . . 5D 50*
(off Marmion Av.)
Craigwell Rd. PO7: Purb . . . 5G **19**
Cranborne Rd. PO6: Cosh . . . 2C **30**
Cranborne Wlk. PO14: Fare . . . 4G **25**
Cranbourne Rd. PO12: Gos . . . 4E **49**
Crane Cl. PO13: Gos . . . 3B **38**
Craneswater Av. PO4: S'sea . . . 6E **51**
Craneswater Ga. PO4: S'sea . . . 6E **51**
Craneswater M. *PO4: S'sea . . . 5E 51*
(off Craneswater Pk.)
Craneswater Pk. PO4: S'sea . . . 5E **51**
Cranford Rd. GU32: Pet . . . 5B **56**
Cranleigh Av. PO1: Ports . . . 1E **51**
Cranleigh Rd. PO1: Ports . . . 1E **51**
PO16: Portc . . . 4G **27**
Crasswell St. PO1: Ports . . . 1G **5** (1C **50**)
(not continuous)
Craven Ct. PO15: Fare . . . 6G **13**
Crawford Dr. PO16: Fare . . . 6H **13**
Crawley Av. PO9: Hav . . . 3G **21**
Crawters La. *GU31: Pet . . . 4D 56*
(off Bowen La.)
Credenhill Rd. PO6: Cosh . . . 2G **29**
Creech Vw. PO7: Den . . . 3A **8**
Creek End PO10: Ems . . . 4D **34**
Creek Rd. PO11: H Isl . . . 5F **55**
PO12: Gos . . . 3F **49**
Cremorne Pl. GU32: Pet . . . 3D **56**
Cremyll Cl. PO14: Stub . . . 3E **37**
Crescent, The PO7: Purb . . . 5E **19**
PO10: S'urne . . . 3H **35**
Crescent Gdns. PO16: Fare . . . 2A **26**
Crescent Rd. PO12: Gos . . . 6C **48**
PO16: Fare . . . 2A **26**
Cressy Rd. PO2: Ports . . . 6H **41**
Crest, The PO7: Wid . . . 1E **31**
Cresta Ct. PO4: S'sea . . . 5F **51**
Crest Cl. PO16: Fare . . . 2D **26**
Crestland Cl. PO8: Cowp . . . 4A **10**
Cricket Dr. PO8: Cowp . . . 2A **10**
Crinoline Gdns. PO4: S'sea . . . 5G **51**
Crisspyn Cl. PO8: Horn . . . 1B **10**
Croad Ct. PO16: Fare . . . 2C **26**
Crockford Rd. PO10: Westb . . . 5F **23**
Croft, The PO14: Stub . . . 1E **37**
Croftlands Av. PO14: Stub . . . 2E **37**
Croft La. PO11: H Isl . . . 4C **44**
Crofton Av. PO13: Lee S . . . 5E **37**
Crofton Cl. PO7: Purb . . . 4E **19**
Crofton Ct. PO14: Stub . . . 3E **37**
Crofton La. PO14: Stub . . . 4D **36**
Crofton Rd. PO2: Ports . . . 3A **42**
PO4: S'sea . . . 2H **51**
Croft Rd. PO2: Ports . . . 4H **41**
(not continuous)
Cromarty Av. PO4: S'sea . . . 3H **51**
Cromarty Cl. PO14: Stub . . . 2D **36**
Crombie Cl. PO8: Cowp . . . 3H **9**
(not continuous)
Cromer Rd. PO6: Cosh . . . 2A **30**
Cromhall Cl. PO14: Fare . . . 3E **25**
Cromwell Rd. PO4: S'sea . . . 5H **51**
Crondall Av. PO9: Hav . . . 3E **21**
Crooked Wlk. La. PO17: S'wick . . . 6C **16**
Crookham Cl. PO9: Hav . . . 4C **20**
CROOKHORN . . . 6G **19**
Crookhorn La. PO7: Purb . . . 2G **31**
Crossbill Cl. PO8: Horn . . . 6A **6**
Crossfell Wlk. PO14: Fare . . . 4G **25**
Crossland Cl. PO12: Gos . . . 4E **49**
Crossland Dr. PO9: Hav . . . 6F **21**
Cross La. PO8: Horn . . . 2A **10**
Cross Rd. PO13: Lee S . . . 3E **47**
Cross St. PO1: Ports . . . 2C **4** (2A **50**)
PO5: S'sea . . . 4H **5** (3D **50**)
Cross Way PO9: Hav . . . 1E **33**
Crossway, The PO16: Portc . . . 3H **27**
Crossways, The PO12: Gos . . . 1D **48**
Crouch La. PO8: Horn . . . 6A **6**
Crown Bingo . . . 4F **21**
Crown Cl. PO7: Purb . . . 6G **19**
Crown Ct. PO1: Ports . . . 1D **50**
(Common St.)
Crown Ct. PO1: Ports . . . 6C **4**
(High St.)
Crown M. PO12: Gos . . . 3F **49**
Crown St. PO1: Ports . . . 1D **50**
Crowsbury Cl. PO10: Ems . . . 6C **22**
Crundles GU31: Pet . . . 4E **57**
Crusader Ct. PO12: Gos . . . 6A **40**
Crystal Way PO7: W'lle . . . 1A **20**
Cuckoo La. PO14: Stub . . . 2D **36**
Culloden Cl. PO15: Fare . . . 1G **25**
Culloden Rd. PO14: Fare . . . 5H **25**
Culver Dr. PO11: H Isl . . . 6E **55**
Culverin Sq. Ind. Est. PO3: Ports . . . 1C **42**
Culver Rd. PO4: S'sea . . . 5G **51**
Cumberland Av. PO10: Ems . . . 5C **22**
Cumberland Bus. Cen. PO5: S'sea . . . 2D **50**
Cumberland Ct. PO4: S'sea . . . 5F **51**
Cumberland Ho. PO1: Ports . . . 1C **4** (1A **50**)
Cumberland House Natural History Mus. . . . 6F **51**
Cumberland Rd. PO5: S'sea . . . 2D **50**
Cumberland St. PO1: Ports . . . 1C **4** (1A **50**)
Cunningham Cl. PO2: Ports . . . 1H **41**
Cunningham Ct. *PO5: S'sea . . . 5D 50*
(off Collingwood Rd.)
Cunningham Dr. PO13: Gos . . . 2D **38**
Cunningham Rd. PO7: W'lle . . . 4F **19**
PO8: Horn . . . 6C **6**
Curdridge Cl. PO9: Hav . . . 4G **21**
Curie Rd. PO6: Cosh . . . 2A **30**
Curlew Cl. PO10: Ems . . . 3C **34**
Curlew Dr. PO16: Portc . . . 3F **27**
Curlew Gdns. PO8: Cowp . . . 3H **9**
Curlew Path PO4: S'sea . . . 2H **51**
Curlew Wlk. PO13: Gos . . . 2A **38**
Curtis Mead PO2: Ports . . . 1B **42**
Curtiss Gdns. PO12: Gos . . . 3B **48**
Curve, The PO8: Love . . . 1H **9**
PO13: Gos . . . 2B **38**
Curzon Howe Rd. PO1: Ports . . . 2C **4** (2A **50**)
Curzon Rd. PO7: W'lle . . . 2G **19**
(not continuous)
Cuthbert Rd. PO1: Ports . . . 1F **51**
Cutlers La. PO14: Stub . . . 2E **37**
Cygnet Ct. PO16: Portc . . . 3F **27**
Cygnet Ho. PO12: Gos . . . 6H **39**
Cygnet Rd. PO6: Farl . . . 4H **31**
Cypress Cres. PO8: Horn . . . 2A **10**
Cyprus Rd. PO2: Ports . . . 5A **42**

D

Dairymoor PO17: Wick . . . 1A **14**
Daisy La. PO12: Gos . . . 3C **48**
Daisy Mead PO7: W'lle . . . 3A **20**
Dale, The PO7: Wid . . . 1E **31**
Dale Dr. PO13: Gos . . . 6B **26**
Dale Pk. Ho. PO1: Ports . . . 2G **5** (2C **50**)
Dale Rd. PO14: Stub . . . 2F **37**
Dalewood Rd. PO15: Fare . . . 2F **25**
Dallington Cl. PO14: Stub . . . 4E **37**
Damask Gdns. PO7: W'lle . . . 6B **10**
Dame Elizabeth Kelly Ct. *PO2: Ports . . . 1A 42*
(off Phoenix Sq.)
Dampier Cl. PO13: Gos . . . 6C **38**
Danbury Ct. PO10: Ems . . . 1E **35**
Dances Way PO11: H Isl . . . 3A **54**
Dandelion Cl. PO13: Gos . . . 3B **38**
Dando Rd. PO7: Den . . . 3C **8**
Danebury Cl. PO9: Hav . . . 3E **21**
Danesbrook La. PO7: W'lle . . . 2A **20**
Danes Rd. PO16: Portc . . . 1H **27**
Daniels Cl. PO12: Gos . . . 3A **48**
Dark Hollow GU32: Pet . . . 3C **56**
Darlington Rd. PO4: S'sea . . . 4E **51**
Darren Cl. PO14: Stub . . . 1F **37**
Darren Ct. PO16: Fare . . . 1B **26**
Dartmouth Cl. PO12: Gos . . . 6A **40**
Dartmouth Ct. *PO12: Gos . . . 6A 40*
(off Dartmouth Cl.)
Dartmouth M. PO5: S'sea . . . 6E **5** (4B **50**)
Dartmouth Rd. PO3: Ports . . . 3C **42**
Darwin Cl. PO13: Lee S . . . 6H **37**
Darwin Ho. PO1: Ports . . . 2H **5**
Darwin Way PO13: Gos . . . 1H **47**
Daubney Gdns. PO9: Hav . . . 3D **20**
Daulston Rd. PO1: Ports . . . 6B **42**
Davenport Cl. PO13: Gos . . . 1G **47**
Daventry La. PO3: Ports . . . 1E **43**
Davidia Ct. PO7: W'lle . . . 3A **20**
David Lloyd Leisure
Port Solent . . . 5F **29**
David Newberry Dr.
PO13: Lee S . . . 1E **47**
Davidson Ct. PO1: Ports . . . 3C **4**
Davis Cl. PO13: Gos . . . 5C **38**
Davis Way PO14: Fare . . . 5A **26**
Daw La. PO11: H Isl . . . 5B **44**
Dayshes Cl. PO13: Gos . . . 2B **38**
Dayslondon Rd. PO7: Purb . . . 4F **19**
D-Day Mus. & Overlord Embroidery . . . 6C **50**
Deal Cl. PO14: Stub . . . 1E **37**
Deal Rd. PO6: Cosh . . . 2A **30**
Deane Ct. PO9: Hav . . . 4H **21**
Deane Gdns. PO13: Lee S . . . 1D **46**
Deane's Pk. Rd. PO16: Fare . . . 2D **26**
Dean Farm Est. PO17: Fare . . . 4A **14**
Dean Rd. PO6: Cosh . . . 3C **30**
Deans Ga. PO14: Stub . . . 4E **37**
Dean St. PO1: Ports . . . 3C **4** (2A **50**)
Deanswood Dr. PO7: W'lle . . . 6G **9**
Dean Vs. PO17: K Vil . . . 3G **13**
Debney Lodge PO7: W'lle . . . 2H **19**
Deep Dell PO8: Horn . . . 2B **10**
Deeping Ga. PO7: W'lle . . . 2A **20**
Deerhurst Cres. PO6: Cosh . . . 2E **29**
Deer Leap PO15: Fun . . . 4F **13**
Delamere Rd. PO4: S'sea . . . 4E **51**
Delaval Ho. PO1: Ports . . . 2C **4**
Delft Gdns. PO8: Cowp . . . 5F **9**
De Lisle Cl. PO2: Ports . . . 1B **42**
Delius Wlk. PO7: W'lle . . . 4G **19**
Dell, The PO9: Bed . . . 1B **32**
PO16: Fare . . . 2D **26**
Dell Cl. PO7: Wid . . . 1D **30**
Dellcrest Path PO6: Cosh . . . 2D **30**
(not continuous)
PO7: Wid . . . 1D **30**
Dellfield Cl. PO6: Cosh . . . 2E **29**
Dell Piece E. PO8: Horn . . . 2D **10**
Dell Piece W. PO8: Horn . . . 1B **10**
Dell Quay Cl. PO13: Gos . . . 3B **38**
Delme Ct. PO16: Fare . . . 2A **26**
Delme Dr. PO16: Fare . . . 1D **26**
Delme Sq. PO16: Fare . . . 2B **26**
Delphi Way PO7: Purb . . . 1H **31**
Delta Bus. Pk. PO16: Fare . . . 4B **26**
Denbigh Dr. PO16: Fare . . . 1H **25**
Dene Hollow PO6: Dray . . . 3F **31**
Denham Cl. PO14: Stub . . . 3D **36**
Denhill Cl. PO11: H Isl . . . 2A **54**
DENMEAD . . . 2B **8**
Denmead Cvn. Pk. PO7: Den . . . 3C **8**
Denmead Ho. PO1: Ports . . . 1H **5** (1D **50**)
Denmead La. PO7: Den . . . 1D **8**
Denning M. PO5: S'sea . . . 3G **5** (2C **50**)
Denville Av. PO16: Portc . . . 5B **28**
Denville Cl. PO6: Farl . . . 3H **31**
Denville Cl. Path PO6: Farl . . . 3H **31**
DENVILLES . . . 1H **33**
Denvilles Cl. PO9: Hav . . . 1H **33**
Derby Ct. PO13: Gos . . . 1G **47**
Derby Rd. PO2: Ports . . . 4H **41**
Derlyn Rd. PO16: Fare . . . 2A **26**
Dersingham Cl. PO6: Cosh . . . 2A **30**
Derwent Cl. PO8: Horn . . . 3C **6**
PO14: Stub . . . 1F **37**
Derwent Rd. PO13: Lee S . . . 2D **46**
Desborough Cl. PO6: Cosh . . . 2E **29**
Deverell Pl. PO7: Wid . . . 6E **19**
Devon Rd. PO3: Ports . . . 2C **42**
Devonshire Av. PO4: S'sea . . . 3F **51**
Devonshire Sq. PO4: S'sea . . . 3F **51**
Devonshire Way PO14: Fare . . . 3E **25**
Dhekelia Ct. PO1: Ports . . . 1D **50**
Diamond St. PO5: S'sea . . . 6E **5** (4B **50**)
Diana Cl. PO10: Ems . . . 5C **22**
PO12: Gos . . . 3A **48**
Dibden Cl. PO9: Hav . . . 5C **20**
Dickens Cl. PO2: Ports . . . 6H **41**
Dickens Ho. PO4: S'sea . . . 3H **51**
Dickins La. GU31: Pet . . . 2E **57**
Dickinson Rd. PO4: S'sea . . . 2F **51**
Dickson Pk. PO17: Wick . . . 1A **14**
Dieppe Cres. PO2: Ports . . . 1A **42**
Dieppe Gdns. PO12: Gos . . . 3B **48**
Dight Rd. PO12: Gos . . . 5E **49**
Discovery Cen.
Gosport . . . 3F 49
(off High St.)
Discovery Cl. PO14: Stub . . . 6E **25**

A-Z Portsmouth 65

Ditcham Cres. PO9: Hav 5E 21
Ditton Cl. PO14: Stub 2E 37
Dockenfield Cl. PO9: Hav 5C 20
Dock Mill Cotts. PO5: S'sea 5D 50
Dock Rd. PO12: Gos 3E 49
Dockyard Apprentice Exhibition Mus.
. . . . .2A 4 (2H 49)
Dogwood Dell PO7: W'lle 4H 19
Dolman Rd. PO12: Gos 4E 49
Dolphin Ct. PO4: S'sea 6F 51
PO13: Lee S 1C 46
PO14: Stub 1D 36
Dolphin Cres. PO12: Gos 4E 49
Dolphin Quay PO10: Ems 3E 35
Dolphin Way PO12: Gos 6F 49
Dominie Wlk. PO13: Lee S 1D 46
Domum Rd. PO2: Ports 3B 42
Domvilles App. PO2: Ports 4F 41
Donaldson Rd. PO6: Cosh 5B 30
Donnelly St. PO12: Gos 1C 48
Don Styler Physical Training Cen. 3G 39
Dorcas Cl. PO7: W'lle 6A 10
Dore Av. PO16: Portc 3H 27
Doric Cl. PO10: S'urne 2H 35
Dorking Cres. PO6: Cosh 4B 30
Dormington Rd. PO6: Cosh 2G 29
Dormy Way PO13: Gos 4B 38
Dorney Ct. PO6: Cosh 4C 30
Dornmere La. PO7: W'lle 2A 20
Dorothy Ct. PO5: S'sea 4D 50
Dorothy Dymond St.
PO1: Ports 3F 5 (2C 50)
Dorrien Rd. PO12: Gos 6H 39
Dorrita Av. PO8: Cowp 3A 10
Dorrita Cl. PO4: S'sea 5F 51
Dorset Cl. PO8: Horn 1B 10
Dorstone Rd. PO6: Cosh 2G 29
Douglas Gdns. PO9: Hav 5G 21
Douglas Rd. PO3: Ports 6C 42
Dove Cl. PO8: Cowp 3H 9
Dover Cl. PO14: Stub 2D 36
Dover Ct. PO11: H Isl 2A 54
Dovercourt Rd. PO6: Cosh 5C 30
Dover Rd. PO3: Ports 5C 42
Dowley Ct. PO14: Titch 3B 24
DOWNEND 2E 27
Down End PO6: Dray 2E 31
Down End Rd. PO6: Dray 2E 31
Downend Rd. PO16: Fare 2F 27
PO17: Fare 2F 27
Down Farm Pl. PO8: Horn 4C 6
Downham Ct. PO8: Cowp 4H 9
Downhouse Rd.
PO8: Cath, Clan . . . . .1A 6 & 2E 7
Downley Point PO9: Hav 5H 21
Downley Rd. PO9: Hav 6H 21
Down Rd. PO8: Horn 4C 6
Downs Cl. PO7: Purb 6H 19
Downside PO13: Gos 3D 38
Downside Rd. PO7: Wid 6E 19
Downsway, The PO16: Portc 3A 28
(not continuous)
Downton Ho. PO6: Cosh 2G 29
Downwood Way PO8: Horn 4C 6
Doyle Av. PO2: Ports 1A 42
Doyle Cl. PO2: Ports 1A 42
Doyle Ct. PO2: Ports 2A 42
Doyle Ho. PO9: Bed 6B 20
Dragon Est. PO6: Farl 4G 31
Dragon St. GU31: Pet 4D 56
Dragon Street Gallery 4D 56
Drake Ho. PO1: Ports 2B 4 (2A 50)
Drake Rd. PO13: Lee S 6F 37
Draycote Rd. PO8: Cath 2C 6
DRAYTON 4E 31
Drayton La. PO6: Dray 2D 30
Drayton Rd. PO2: Ports 4A 42
Dreadnought Rd. PO14: Fare 6H 25
Dresden Dr. PO8: Cowp 4F 9
Drift, The PO9: R Cas 6H 11
Drift Rd. PO8: Clan 2F 7
PO16: Fare 1D 26
Driftwood Gdns. PO4: S'sea 5A 52
Drill Shed Rd. PO2: Ports 4F 41
Drive, The PO9: Hav 6F 21
PO10: S'urne 3H 35
PO13: Gos .3A 38
PO16: Fare 2A 26
Driveway, The PO4: S'sea 2A 52
Droke, The PO6: Cosh 8B 30
(not continuous)

Drove Rd. PO17: S'wick 5E 17
Droxford Cl. PO12: Gos 3B 48
Droxford Rd. PO17: Wick 1B 14
Drum La. GU32: Pet 3D 56
Drum Mead GU32: Pet 4C 56
Drummond Rd. PO1: Ports 1H 5 (1D 50)
PO15: Seg .5A 12
Dryden Av. PO6: Cosh 2C 28
Dryden Cl. PO7: W'lle 5G 9
PO16: Fare 1H 25
Drysdale M. PO4: S'sea 5H 51
Duckpond La. PO8: Blen 5E 7
Duck Stile La. PO8: Blen 5E 7
Duckworth Ho. PO1: Ports 3C 4 (2A 50)
Dudleston Heath Dr.
PO8: Cowp 5B 10
Dudley Rd. PO3: Ports 6C 42
Duffield La. PO10: Wood 6H 23
Dugald Drummond St.
PO1: Ports 3F 5 (2C 50)
Duisburg Way PO5: S'sea 4B 50
Duke Cres. PO1: Ports 6H 41
Duke of Edinburgh Ho.
PO1: Ports 1D 4
Dukes Cl. GU32: Pet 3B 56
Dukes Ct. PO10: Westb 6F 23
Dukes Rd. PO12: Gos 1C 48
Dukes Wlk. PO7: W'lle 2G 19
Duke Ter. PO9: Hav 5D 20
Dumbarton Cl. PO2: Ports 5H 41
Dummer Ct. PO9: Hav 3D 20
Dunbar Rd. PO4: S'sea 3H 51
Duncan Cooper Ho. PO7: W'lle 2F 19
Duncan Rd. PO5: S'sea 5D 50
Duncans Dr. PO14: Fare 3D 24
Duncton Rd. PO8: Clan 2H 7
Duncton Way PO13: Gos 2C 38
Dundas Cl. PO3: Ports 3D 42
Dundas La. PO3: Ports 4D 42
Dundas Spur PO3: Ports 3D 42
Dundee Cl. PO15: Fare 6G 13
Dundonald Cl. PO11: H Isl 2C 54
Dunhurst Cl. PO9: Hav 6G 21
Dunkeld Rd. PO12: Gos 6F 39
Dunlin Cl. PO4: S'sea 2B 52
Dunn Cl. PO4: S'sea 4H 51
Dunnock Cl. PO9: R Cas 6H 11
Dunsbury Way PO9: Hav 3E 21
Dunsmore Cl. PO5: S'sea 5F 5 (3C 50)
Dunstable Wlk. PO14: Fare 3F 25
Dupree Dr. PO4: S'sea 4G 51
Durban Homes PO1: Ports 1H 5 (1D 50)
Durban Rd. PO1: Ports 6B 42
Durford Cl. PO9: Hav 3D 20
Durford Rd. GU31: Pet 4F 57
Durham Gdns. PO7: W'lle 4H 19
Durham St. PO1: Ports 2G 5 (2C 50)
PO12: Gos .1C 48
Durland Rd. PO8: Horn 5C 6
Durley Av. PO8: Cowp 4G 9
Durley Rd. PO12: Gos 1B 48
DURRANTS 1H 21
Durrants Gdns. PO9: Hav 1H 21
Durrants Rd. PO9: R Cas 2H 21
Dursley Cres. PO6: Cosh 3G 29
Dymchurch Ho. PO6: Cosh 3A 30
Dymoke St. PO10: Ems 5C 22
Dymond Ho. PO4: S'sea 3H 51
Dysart Av. PO6: Cosh 4D 30

E

Eagle Av. PO8: Cowp 3F 9
Eagle Cl. PO16: Portc 3F 27
Eagle Rd. PO13: Lee S 6F 37
Earl Godwin Cl. PO16: Fare 2D 26
Earlsdon St. PO5: S'sea 4F 5 (3C 50)
Earls Rd. PO16: Fare 4B 26
Earnley Rd. PO11: H Isl 5H 55
Eastbourne Av. PO12: Gos 5F 39
Eastbourne Rd. PO3: Ports 5C 42
Eastbrook Cl. PO12: Gos 5F 39
E. Cams Cl. PO16: Fare 2F 27
Eastcliff Cl. PO13: Lee S 6H 37
E. Copsey Path PO6: Dray 3F 31
E. Cosham Rd. PO6: Cosh 2D 30
East Ct. PO1: Ports 6A 42
PO6: Cosh .3D 30
Eastcroft Rd. PO12: Gos 2B 48
Eastern Av. PO4: S'sea 1H 51

Eastern Ind. Cen. PO6: Farl 5E 31
Eastern Pde. PO4: S'sea 6F 51
PO16: Fare 4B 26
Eastern Rd. PO2: Ports 3F 41
PO3: Ports 2H 51
PO6: Farl .5F 31
PO9: Hav .1F 33
Eastern Vs. Rd. PO4: S'sea 6D 50
Eastern Way PO16: Fare 2C 26
Eastfield Av. PO14: Fare 5H 25
Eastfield Rd. PO4: S'sea 4G 51
PO17: S'wick 1F 29
East Ga. PO1: Ports 6G 41
East Hayling Light Railway 5C 54
East Hill Cl. PO16: Fare 1D 26
East Ho. Av. PO14: Stub 3F 37
Eastlake Cl. GU31: Pet 4G 57
Eastlake Hgts. PO4: S'sea 4B 52
EASTLAND GATE .2F 9
Eastland Ga. Cotts. PO8: Love 1F 9
Eastleigh Rd. PO9: Hav 6A 22
East Lodge PO13: Lee S 1C 46
PO15: Fare 2E 25
E. Lodge Pk. PO6: Farl 3H 31
E. Meon Rd. PO8: Clan 1E 7
East M. PO17: K Vil 2G 13
EASTNEY 4H 51
Eastney Esplanade PO4: S'sea 5G 51
Eastney Farm Rd. PO4: S'sea 4A 52
Eastney Pumping Station Mus. 4A 52
Eastney Rd. PO4: S'sea 3H 51
East No. PO4: S'sea 3H 51
Eastney Swimming Pool 5A 52
EASTOKE 5E 55
Eastoke Av. PO11: H Isl 6F 55
Eastover Ct. PO9: Hav 3D 20
East Pallant PO9: Hav 2F 33
East Rd. PO17: S'wick 3E 17
East St. PO1: Ports 5A 4 (4H 49)
PO9: Hav .2F 33
PO10: Westb 6F 23
PO14: Titch 3B 24
PO16: Fare 2C 26
PO16: Portc 3B 28
E. Surrey St. PO1: Ports 2G 5 (2C 50)
Eastwood Cl. PO11: H Isl 3D 54
Eastwood Rd. PO2: Ports 1A 42
Ebery Gro. PO3: Ports 1H 51
Ecton La. PO3: Ports 2E 43
Edenbridge Rd. PO4: S'sea 2H 51
Eden Path PO6: Dray 2E 31
Eden Ri. PO16: Fare 3B 26
Eden St. PO1: Ports 1G 5 (1C 50)
Edgar Cres. PO16: Portc 5B 28
Edgbaston Ho. PO5: S'sea 4G 5 (3C 50)
Edgecombe Rd. PO13: Gos 5C 38
Edgefield Gro. PO7: W'lle 6C 10
Edgell Rd. PO10: Westb 5F 23
Edgeware Rd. PO4: S'sea 2G 51
Edinburgh Rd. PO1: Ports 2E 5 (2B 50)
Edmund Rd. PO4: S'sea 4E 51
Edneys La. PO7: Den 3D 8
Education Path PO6: Cosh 4A 30
Edward Gdns. PO9: Bed 2C 32
Edward Gro. PO16: Portc 2C 28
Edwards Cl. PO6: Cosh 2F 29
PO8: Cowp 5H 9
Egan Cl. PO2: Ports 2B 42
Eglantine Cl. PO8: Cowp 3B 10
Eglantine Wlk. PO8: Cowp 3B 10
Eileen Beard Ho. PO9: Hav 4G 21
Elaine Gdns. PO8: Cowp 2H 9
Elderberry Cl. PO8: Clan 1D 6
Elderberry Way PO8: Horn 3B 10
Elderfield Cl. PO10: Ems 6E 23
Elderfield Rd. PO9: Hav 2D 20
Elder Rd. PO9: Hav 6H 21
Eldon Cl. PO5: S'sea 5F 5 (3C 50)
Eldon St. PO5: S'sea 5F 5 (3C 50)
Eleanors Wood PO16: Portc 2H 27
Elettra Av. PO7: W'lle 1E 19
Elgar Cl. PO6: Cosh 3C 28
PO12: Gos .5C 48
Elgar Wlk. PO7: W'lle 4H 19
(not continuous)
Elgin Cl. PO15: Fare 1H 25
Elgin Rd. PO6: Cosh 5B 30
Eling Ct. PO9: Hav .3D 20
Elizabeth Cl. PO17: Wick 1A 14

Elizabeth Ct. PO6: Cosh 3B 30
PO12: Gos 1C 48
PO14: Fare 4H 25
Elizabeth Gdns. PO4: S'sea 5F 51
Elizabeth Ho. PO7: W'lle 1G 19
Elizabeth Rd. PO7: W'lle 4G 19
PO14: Stub 3F 37
PO17: Wick 1A 14
Eliza Pl. PO12: Gos 2E 49
Elkstone Rd. PO6: Cosh 2F 29
Ellachie Gdns. PO12: Gos 6D 48
Ellachie M. PO12: Gos 6D 48
Ellachie Rd. PO12: Gos 6D 48
Ellerslie Cl. PO14: Stub 4C 36
Ellesmere Orchard PO10: Westb 5F 23
Elliots Cvn. Est. PO11: H Isl 5G 55
Ellisfield Rd. PO9: Hav 5E 21
Ellison Gdns. PO14: Fare 3F 25
Elm Cl. PO11: H Isl 4C 54
Elm Cl. Est. PO11: H Isl 4B 54
Elmdale GU31: Pet 3E 57
Elm Dr. GU31: Pet 6C 56
Elmeswelle Rd. PO8: Horn 1A 10
Elm Gro. PO5: S'sea 6F 5 (4C 50)
PO11: H Isl 4C 54
PO12: Gos 2D 48
Elmhurst Bus. Pk. *PO12: Gos* *3E 49*
(off Elmhurst Rd.)
Elmhurst Rd. PO12: Gos 3E 49
PO16: Fare 3B 26
Elm La. PO9: Hav 2F 33
Elmleigh Rd. PO9: Hav 1F 33
Elm Lodge PO5: S'sea 6H 5
Elmore Av. PO13: Lee S 2D 46
Elmore Cl. PO13: Lee S 2D 46
Elmore Rd. PO13: Lee S 3D 46
Elm Pk. Rd. PO9: Hav 1F 33
Elm Rd. PO9: Hav 3G 33
Elms Rd. PO16: Fare 4B 26
Elm St. PO5: S'sea 6E 5 (4C 50)
Elmtree Rd. PO6: Farl 3G 31
Elmwood Av. PO7: W'lle 3G 19
Elmwood Lodge PO16: Fare 1B 26
Elmwood Rd. PO2: Ports 1A 42
Elphinstone Rd. PO5: S'sea 5C 50
Elsfred Rd. PO14: Stub 4C 36
Elsie Fudge Ho. PO7: Purb 6H 19
ELSON 5G 39
Elson La. PO12: Gos 5G 39
Elson Rd. PO12: Gos 5F 39
Elstead Gdns. PO7: Purb 5E 19
Elwell Grn. PO11: H Isl 4B 54
Ely Ct. PO13: Gos 2H 47
Emanuel St. PO2: Ports 6H 41
Embassy Ct. PO4: S'sea 3E 51
Emerald Cl. PO7: W'lle 2A 20
Empire Ct. PO9: Hav 2F 33
Empshott Rd. PO4: S'sea 3F 51
Empson Wlk. PO13: Lee S 6H 37
Emsbrook Dr. PO10: Ems 1D 34
EMSWORTH 3D 34
Emsworth By-Pass PO10: Ems 2A 34
Emsworth Cen., The PO10: Ems 3D 34
Emsworth Comn. Rd. PO9: Ems 4B 22
PO10: Ems 4B 22
PO10: Westb 3D 22
Emsworth Ho. PO10: Ems 2B 34
Emsworth Ho. Cl. PO10: Ems 2C 34
Emsworth Mus. 3D 34
Emsworth Rd. PO2: Ports 4A 42
PO9: Hav, Warb 2G 33
PO10: T Isl 6F 35
Emsworth Station (Rail) 2D 34
Endeavour Cl. PO12: Gos 3F 49
Enderleigh Ho. PO9: Hav 2E 33
Endofield Cl. PO14: Fare 5H 25
Ennerdale Cl. PO8: Horn 3C 6
Ennerdale Rd. PO14: Stub 1F 37
Ensign Dr. PO13: Gos 1H 47
Enterprise Ho. PO1: Ports 3F 5
Enterprise Ind. Est. PO8: Horn 5C 6
Enterprise Rd. PO8: Horn 5C 6
Eperston Rd. PO8: Horn 1A 10
Epworth Rd. PO2: Ports 4B 42
Erica Cl. PO8: Cowp 4B 10
Erica Way PO8: Cowp 3B 10
Eric Rd. PO14: Stub 3E 37
Eric Taplin Ct. PO4: S'sea 4E 51
Ernest Cl. PO10: Ems 2D 34
Ernest Rd. PO1: Ports 6A 42
PO9: Bed 6C 20
Escur Cl. PO2: Ports 1B 42
Esher Gro. PO7: W'lle 5E 9
Eskdale Cl. PO8: Horn 3C 6
Esmond Cl. PO10: Ems 3D 34
Esmonde Cl. PO13: Lee S 1D 46
Esplanade PO13: Lee S 2C 46
Esplanade, The PO12: Gos 3G 49
Esplanade Gdns. PO4: S'sea 5A 52
Essex Rd. PO4: S'sea 3G 51
Esslemont Rd. PO4: S'sea 4F 51
Estancia Cl. PO13: Lee S 6H 37
Estella Rd. PO2: Ports 5H 41
Ethel Rd. PO1: Ports 1E 51
Eton Rd. PO5: S'sea 3E 51
Euryalus Rd. PO14: Fare 5H 25
Euston Rd. PO4: S'sea 2H 51
Eva Allaway Ct. PO1: Ports 3C 4
Evans Cl. PO2: Ports 3F 41
Evans Rd. PO4: S'sea 3G 51
Evelegh Rd. PO6: Farl 3F 31
Everdon La. PO3: Ports 1D 42
Everell Ct. PO4: S'sea 6D 50
Everglades Av. PO8: Cowp 4H 9
Evergreen Cl. PO7: W'lle 2F 19
Eversley Cres. PO9: Hav 5E 21
Ewart Rd. PO1: Ports 6A 42
Ewhurst Cl. PO9: Hav 5D 20
Exbury Rd. PO9: Hav 4G 21
Excellent Rd. PO14: Fare 6H 25
Exchange Rd. PO1: Ports 3E 5 (2B 50)
Exeter Cl. PO10: Ems 6D 22
Exeter Ct. PO13: Gos 1G 47
Exeter Rd. PO4: S'sea 5F 51
Exmouth Rd. PO5: S'sea 5D 50
PO12: Gos 5G 39
Explosion
(The Mus. of Naval Fire Power) 6B 40
Exton Gdns. PO16: Portc 1A 28
Exton Rd. PO9: Hav 4H 21

F

Faber Cl. PO9: Hav 5G 21
Fabian Cl. PO7: W'lle 1A 20
Fairacre Ri. PO14: Fare 3D 24
Fairacre Wlk. PO14: Fare 4D 24
Fairbourne Cl. PO8: Cowp 5G 9
Fairfield Av. PO14: Fare 4G 25
Fairfield Cl. PO10: Ems 1D 34
Fairfield Rd. PO9: Hav 2F 33
Fairfield Sq. PO6: Cosh 3A 30
Fairfield Ter. *PO9: Hav* *2F 33*
(off Fairfield Rd.)
Fairhome Cl. PO12: Gos 6G 39
Fair Isle Cl. PO14: Stub 2D 36
Fairlead Dr. PO13: Gos 1H 47
Fairlea Rd. PO10: Ems 6D 22
Fairlight Chalets PO11: H Isl 4D 54
Fairmead Ct. PO11: H Isl 4A 54
Fairmead Wlk. PO8: Cowp 4A 10
Fair Oak Ct. PO12: Gos 4H 47
Fair Oak Dr. PO9: Hav 6F 21
Fair Oak Rd. PO4: S'sea 3A 52
Fairthorne Gdns. PO12: Gos 3C 48
Fairview Ct. PO12: Gos 3A 48
Fairwater Cl. PO13: Gos 4B 38
Fairway, The PO9: R Cas 5H 11
PO13: Gos 4C 38
PO16: Portc 3A 28
Fairway Bus. Cen. PO3: Ports 3D 42
Fairy Cross Way PO8: Cowp 4B 10
Falcon Cl. PO12: Gos 6A 40
PO16: Portc 3F 27
Falcon Grn. PO6: Farl 4H 31
Falcon Rd. PO8: Horn 6A 6
Falklands Cl. PO13: Lee S 6H 37
Falklands Rd. PO2: Ports 1A 42
Falmouth Rd. PO6: Cosh 2D 28
FAREHAM 2B 26
Fareham Ent. Cen. PO14: Fare 5A 26
Fareham Hgts. PO16: Fare 6D 14
Fareham Ind. Pk. PO16: Fare 6D 14
Fareham Leisure Cen. 1A 26
Fareham Pk. Rd. PO15: Fare 5E 13
Fareham Rd. PO13: Gos 6B 26
PO17: S'wick 4C 16
PO17: Wick 2A 14
Fareham Shop. Cen. PO16: Fare 2B 26
Fareham Station (Rail) 2H 25
Farleigh Cl. PO9: Hav 4D 20
FARLINGTON 3G 31
Farlington Av. PO6: Dray 2E 31
Farlington Marshes (Nature Reserve) 6G 31
Farlington Rd. PO2: Ports 4B 42
Far Mdw. Way PO10: Ems 3B 34
Farm Edge Rd. PO14: Stub 4E 37
Farm Ho. Cl. PO14: Stub 6E 25
Farmhouse Way PO8: Horn 2A 10
Farm La. Cl. PO7: W'lle 3F 19
Farmlea Rd. PO6: Cosh 3E 29
Farm Rd. PO14: Titch 1A 24
Farmside Gdns. PO3: Ports 1B 42
Farm Vw. PO10: Ems 6D 22
Farm Vw. Av. PO8: Clan 2F 7
Faroes Cl. PO14: Stub 2D 36
Farriers Ct. PO5: S'sea 5D 50
Farriers Wlk. *PO12: Gos* *2F 49*
(off Clarence Rd.)
Farriers Way PO7: W'lle 6C 10
Farrier Way PO16: Fare 5B 26
Farringdon Rd. PO9: Hav 5G 21
Farthingale Ter. *PO1: Ports* *6C 4*
(off Peacock La.)
Farthing La. PO1: Ports 6C 4 (4A 50)
Farthings Cl. PO12: Gos 2C 48
Farthings Ga. PO7: Purb 6G 19
Fastnet Ho. PO5: S'sea 6D 50
Fastnet Way PO14: Stub 2D 36
Fathoms Reach PO11: H Isl 3A 54
Fawcett Rd. PO4: S'sea 3E 51
Fawley Ct. PO9: Hav 4H 21
Fawley Rd. PO2: Ports 6A 30
Fay Cl. PO14: Stub 3E 37
Fayre Rd. PO16: Fare 4A 26
Fearon Rd. PO2: Ports 3A 42
Felix Rd. PO12: Gos 6H 39
Fell Dr. PO13: Lee S 6H 37
Feltons Pl. PO3: Ports 6B 30
Fen Av. PO16: Fare 5B 26
Fennell Cl. PO7: W'lle 6F 9
Fern Cl. GU31: Pet 4G 57
Ferncroft Cl. PO14: Stub 4E 37
Ferndale PO7: W'lle 2H 19
Ferndale M. PO13: Gos 1B 38
Fern Dr. PO9: Hav 1G 33
Ferneham Hall 2C 26
Ferneham Rd. PO15: Fare 1E 25
Fernhurst Cl. PO11: H Isl 4H 53
Fernhurst Rd. PO4: S'sea 3F 51
Fernie Cl. PO14: Stub 3D 36
Fern Way PO15: Seg 6A 12
Fernwood Ho. PO8: Cowp 5A 10
Ferrol Rd. PO12: Gos 1E 49
Ferry Rd. PO4: S'sea 4B 52
(not continuous)
PO11: H Isl 3D 52
Festing Gro. PO4: S'sea 5F 51
Festing M. PO4: S'sea 5F 51
Festing Rd. PO4: S'sea 5F 51
Fey Rd. PO12: Gos 2E 49
Field Cl. PO13: Gos 6B 26
Fielder Dr. PO14: Fare 5B 26
Fielders Ct. PO7: Purb 5E 19
Fieldfare Cl. PO8: Clan 1C 6
Fieldhouse Dr. PO13: Lee S 5H 37
Fieldmore Rd. PO12: Gos 6H 39
Field Way PO7: Den 3B 8
Fifth Av. PO6: Cosh 3A 30
PO9: Hav 1H 33
Fifth St. PO1: Ports 6B 42
Filmer Cl. PO13: Gos 5D 38
Finchdean Rd. PO9: Hav 5D 20
Finch Rd. PO4: S'sea 4B 52
Finchwood Farm Ind. Units PO11: H Isl 4D 44
Findon Rd. PO12: Gos 5H 39
Finisterre Cl. PO14: Stub 1D 36
Fir Copse Rd. PO7: Purb 6F 19
Firefly Cl. PO13: Lee S 2E 47
Firgrove Cres. PO3: Ports 6B 30
Firlands Ri. PO9: Bed 2A 32
Firs, The PO13: Gos 4D 38
Firs Av. PO8: Cowp 5H 9
Firs Pk. GU31: Pet 4G 57
First Av. PO6: Cosh 3B 30
PO6: Farl 3F 31
PO8: Cath 2C 6
PO9: Hav 1H 33
PO10: S'urne 3H 35
Fir Tree Gdns. PO8: Horn 2C 10
Fir Tree Rd. PO11: H Isl 4C 54
Fisgard Rd. PO12: Gos 6H 39

Fisher Cl. PO14: Stub 2D **36**
Fishermans, The PO10: Ems 3E **35**
Fisherman's Wlk. PO11: H Isl 5G **55**
PO16: Portc 4B **28**
Fisher Rd. PO13: Gos 2C **38**
Fishers Cvn. Pk. PO11: H Isl 5E **55**
Fishers Gro. PO6: Farl 4G **31**
Fishers Hill PO15: Fare 1C **24**
Fishery Creek Cvn. & Camping Pk.
PO11: H Isl 5F **55**
Fishery La. PO11: H Isl 5E **55**
Fitness First
Fareham **2F 27**
Portsmouth **2F 51**
Waterlooville **2G 19**
Fitzhamon Ho. *GU31: Pet* *4E* ***57***
(off Herne Rd.)
Fitzherbert Rd. PO6: Farl 4F **31**
Fitzherbert Spur PO6: Farl 4G **31**
Fitzherbert St. PO1: Ports 1C **50**
Fitzpatrick Ct. PO6: Cosh 2H **29**
Fitzroy Dr. PO13: Lee S 6H **37**
Fitzroy Wlk. PO1: Ports 1D **50**
Fitzwilliam Av. PO14: Stub 3C **36**
Fitzwygram Cres. PO9: Hav 6F **21**
Five Heads Rd. PO8: Cath, Horn 5A **6**
Five Post La. PO12: Gos 1D **48**
Flag Staff Grn. PO12: Gos 1F **49**
Flag Wlk. PO8: Cowp 2H **9**
Flamingo Ct. PO16: Portc 3F **27**
Flanders Ho. PO14: Fare 3G **25**
Flathouse Quay PO2: Ports 6G **41**
Flathouse Rd. PO1: Ports 1D **4** (1B **50**)
(Anchor Ga. Rd.)
PO1: Ports 6G **41**
(Victory Retail Pk.)
FLEET **5C 44**
Fleet Cl. PO13: Gos 4D **38**
Fleet End Cl. PO9: Hav 3E **21**
Fleet Farm Camping & Cvn. Site
PO11: H Isl 5C **44**
FLEETLANDS **6C 26**
Fleet Way PO1: Ports 1D **4** (1B **50**)
Fleming Cl. PO15: Seg 5A **12**
Flexford Gdns. PO9: Hav 6G **21**
(not continuous)
Flinders Ct. PO4: S'sea 5H **51**
Flint Ho. Path PO6: Dray 5E **31**
Flint St. PO5: S'sea 6E **5** (4B **50**)
Flora Twort Gallery **4D 56**
Florence Rd. PO5: S'sea 6D **50**
Florentine Way PO7: W'lle 1A **20**
Florins, The PO7: Purb 6G **19**
Flying Bull Cl. *PO2: Ports* *5H* ***41***
(off Flying Bull La.)
Flying Bull La. PO2: Ports 5H **41**
Foley Ho. PO1: Ports 1G **5** (1D **50**)
Folkestone Rd. PO3: Ports 6C **42**
Folly La. GU31: Pet 4D **56**
Fontley La. PO15: Titch 6C **12**
Fontley Rd. PO15: Titch 5C **12**
Fontwell M. PO7: W'lle 6B **10**
Fontwell Rd. PO5: S'sea 5D **50**
Forbes Ct. PO2: Ports 2A **42**
Forbury Rd. PO5: S'sea 4H **5** (3D **50**)
Fordingbridge Rd. PO4: S'sea 4H **51**
Ford Rd. PO12: Gos 1B **48**
Foreland Ct. PO11: H Isl 5E **55**
Foremans Cotts. PO12: Gos 5F **49**
Forest Av. PO8: Cowp 4H **9**
Forest Cl. PO8: Cowp 4H **9**
Forest End PO7: W'lle 2F **19**
Forest End Rdbt. PO7: W'lle 2G **19**
FOREST GATE **1A 8**
Forest La. PO17: Fare 1C **14**
Forest Mead PO7: Den 4B **8**
Forest Rd. PO7: Den 3A **8**
Forestside Av. PO9: Hav 4G **21**
Forest Way PO13: Gos 3D **38**
Forneth Gdns. PO15: Fare 3D **24**
Forsythia Cl. PO9: Hav 5H **21**
Fort Brockhurst **4F 39**
Fort Cumberland Rd. PO4: S'sea 4B **52**
Fort Fareham Ind. Site PO14: Fare 5A **26**
Fort Fareham Rd. PO14: Fare 5H **25**
Forth Cl. PO14: Stub 2D **36**
Forties Cl. PO14: Stub 1D **36**
Fort Nelson **6H 15**
FORTON **2D 48**
Forton Rd. PO1: Ports 1E **51**
PO12: Gos 1C **48**
Fort Purbrook **1F 31**
Fort Rd. PO12: Gos 6C **48**
Fortune Ho. PO12: Gos 2C **48**
Fortunes Way PO9: Bed 2H **31**
Fort Wallington Ind. Est.
PO16: Fare 1D **26**
Fort Widley **1B 30**
Forum, The PO9: Hav 1E **33**
Foster Cl. PO14: Stub 1E **37**
Foster Rd. PO1: Ports 1D **50**
PO12: Gos 4C **48**
Founders Way PO13: Gos 3D **38**
Foundry Ct. PO1: Ports 2C **4** (2A **50**)
Fountain Sq. PO11: H Isl 3A **54**
Fountain St. PO1: Ports 2F **5** (2C **50**)
Four Marks Grn. PO9: Hav 3H **21**
Fourth Av. PO6: Cosh 3A **30**
PO9: Hav 1H **33**
Fourth St. PO1: Ports 1F **51**
Fowey Ct. *PO12: Gos* *5A* ***40***
(off Hayling Cl.)
Foxbury PO13: Gos 1D **38**
Foxbury Gro. PO16: Portc 4H **27**
Foxbury La. PO10: Westb, Wood 6F **23**
PO13: Gos 1D **38**
(not continuous)
Foxcote Ho. PO6: Cosh 1D **28**
Foxcott Gro. PO9: Hav 4F **21**
Foxes Cl. PO7: W'lle 3G **19**
Foxgloves PO16: Fare 6C **14**
Foxlea Gdns. PO12: Gos 6H **39**
Foxley Dr. PO3: Ports 1D **42**
Frances Rd. PO7: Purb 6F **19**
Francis Av. PO4: S'sea 4F **51**
Francis Cl. PO13: Lee S 2E **47**
Francis Pl. PO14: Stub 3F **37**
Francis Rd. PO8: Horn 2C **6**
Frank Judd Ct. PO1: Ports 3C **4**
Frankland Ter. PO10: Ems 3E **35**
Franklin Rd. PO13: Gos 6C **38**
Frank Miles Ho. PO5: S'sea 5G **5**
Franktoon Way PO12: Gos 2F **49**
Frarydene PO10: S'urne 3H **35**
Fraser Gdns. PO10: S'urne 1H **35**
Fraser Rd. PO2: Ports 3F **41**
PO5: S'sea 4H **5** (3D **50**)
PO9: Bed 1D **32**
PO13: Gos 1C **38**
FRATER **3E 39**
Frater La. PO12: Gos 5G **39**
(not continuous)
FRATTON **2E 51**
Fratton Ct. *PO1: Ports* *2E* ***51***
(off Penhale Rd.)
Fratton Ind. Est. PO4: S'sea 2G **51**
Fratton Pk. **2G 51**
Fratton Rd. PO1: Ports 2E **51**
Fratton Station (Rail) **2E 51**
Fratton Way PO4: S'sea 3F **51**
Frederick St. PO1: Ports 1C **50**
Freefolk Grn. PO9: Hav 3H **21**
Freemantle Rd. PO12: Gos 6H **39**
Freestone Rd. PO5: S'sea 5D **50**
Frenchies Vw. PO7: Den 3A **8**
Frenchman's Rd. GU32: Pet 3C **56**
French St. PO1: Ports 6B **4** (4A **50**)
Frendstaple Rd. PO7: W'lle 2H **19**
Frensham Ct. PO4: S'sea 3F **51**
Frensham Rd. PO4: S'sea 3F **51**
Freshfield Gdns. PO7: W'lle 1G **19**
Freshwater Ct. PO13: Lee S 1C **46**
Freshwater Ho. PO14: Fare 3E **25**
Freshwater Rd. PO6: Cosh 4A **30**
Friars Pond Rd. PO15: Fare 2E **25**
Friary, The PO5: S'sea 5C **50**
Friary Cl. PO5: S'sea 5D **50**
PO12: Gos 6E **49**
Friendly Societies Homes
PO4: S'sea 4H **51**
Friendship Ho. PO5: S'sea 6G **5**
Frigate Rd. PO1: Ports 1A **50**
Frobisher Cl. PO13: Gos 1G **47**
Frobisher Gdns. PO10: Ems 3D **34**
Frobisher Gro. PO16: Portc 4A **28**
Frobisher Ho. PO1: Ports 2B **4** (2A **50**)
Froddington Rd. PO5: S'sea 4H **5** (3D **50**)
Frogham Grn. PO9: Hav 3C **20**
Frog La. PO14: Titch 3C **24**
Frogmore PO14: Fare 3E **25**
Frogmore La. PO8: Cowp 2H **9**
PO8: Horn 1A **10**
Frogmore Rd. PO4: S'sea 3G **51**
Frosthole Cl. PO15: Fare 6G **13**
Frosthole Cres. PO15: Fare 6G **13**
Froude Av. PO12: Gos 5E **49**
Froude Rd. PO12: Gos 5E **49**
Froxfield Gdns. PO16: Portc 2A **28**
Froxfield Ho. *PO1: Ports* *1H* ***5***
(off Buriton St.)
Froxfield Rd. PO9: Hav 4H **21**
Froyle Ct. PO9: Hav 4H **21**
Fulflood Rd. PO9: Hav 4E **21**
Fullerton Cl. PO9: Hav 4H **21**
Fulmar Wlk. PO13: Gos 2A **38**
Fulmer Wlk. PO8: Cowp 3G **9**
Fun City **6C 14**
Funlands Amusements **5B 54**
Funtington Rd. PO2: Ports 5B **42**
FUNTLEY **4G 13**
Funtley Ct. PO16: Fun 5G **13**
Funtley Hill PO16: Fun 5G **13**
Funtley La. PO17: Fun 4G **13**
Funtley Rd. PO15: Fun 3F **13**
PO17: Fun 3F **13**
Furdies PO7: Den 3A **8**
Furlonge Ho. PO10: Ems 2C **34**
Furneaux Gdns. PO16: Fare 6B **14**
Furness Rd. PO5: S'sea 6D **50**
Furniss Way PO11: H Isl 3H **53**
Furston Gro. PO10: S'urne 2H **35**
Fury Way PO14: Stub 2D **36**
Furzedown Cres. PO9: Hav 4G **21**
Furze Hall PO16: Fare 5B **14**
Furzehall Av. PO16: Fare 6B **14**
Furze La. PO4: S'sea 3B **52**
FURZELEY CORNER **5B 8**
Furzeley Rd. PO7: Den 5B **8**
Furze Way PO8: Cowp 3B **10**
Furzley Ct. PO9: Hav 3C **20**
Fushia Cl. PO9: Hav 5A **22**
Fyning St. PO1: Ports 1H **5** (1D **50**)

G

GABLE HEAD **3C 54**
Gable M. PO11: H Isl 3C **54**
Gainsborough Ho. PO4: S'sea 5E **51**
Gainsborough M. PO14: Titch 3B **24**
Gains Rd. PO4: S'sea 5E **51**
Galaxie Rd. PO8: Cowp 3B **10**
Gale Moor Av. PO12: Gos 4H **47**
Galleon Pl. PO12: Gos 1F **49**
Galt Rd. PO6: Farl .3G **31**
Gamble Rd. PO2: Ports 5H **41**
Gammon Cl. GU31: Pet 3E **57**
Gannets, The PO14: Stub 2D **36**
Garden Cl. PO11: H Isl 4B **54**
Garden Ct. PO16: Portc 3B **28**
Gardenia Dr. PO15: Seg 6A **12**
Garden La. PO5: S'sea 6F **5** (4C **50**)
Garden M. GU31: Pet 4D **56**
Gardens, The PO9: Warb 2H **33**
PO16: Fare 6C **14**
Garden Ter. PO5: S'sea 5D **50**
Gardner Rd. PO14: Titch 4B **24**
Garfield Rd. PO2: Ports 5H **41**
Garland Av. PO10: Ems 6D **22**
Garland Ct. PO12: Gos 2D **48**
Garnett Cl. PO14: Stub 1E **37**
Garnier Pk. PO17: Wick 1A **14**
Garnier St. PO1: Ports 2D **50**
Garrick Ho. PO2: Ports 1B **42**
Garsons Rd. PO10: S'urne 3H **35**
Garstons Cl. PO14: Titch 3B **24**
Garstons Rd. PO14: Titch 3B **24**
Gatcombe Av. PO3: Ports 3B **42**
Gatcombe Dr. PO2: Ports 2B **42**
Gatcombe Gdns. PO14: Fare 3D **24**
Gate Ho. Rd. PO16: Portc 4G **27**
Gaulter Cl. PO9: Hav 6G **21**
Gawn Pl. PO12: Gos 5E **49**
Gaylyn Way PO14: Fare 3D **24**
Gaza Ho. PO15: Fare 6E **13**
Gazebo Garden **2F 33**
Gazelle Cl. PO13: Gos 2H **47**
Geddes Way GU31: Pet 3G **57**
Genoa Ho. PO6: P Sol 4E **29**
Geoffrey Av. PO7: Wid 1D **30**
Geoffrey Cres. PO16: Fare 4B **26**
George Byng Way PO2: Ports 5G **41**
George Ct., The PO1: Ports 6C **4**

George St. PO1: Ports 6A 42
PO2: Ports 6A 42
PO12: Gos 2E 49
Georgia Cl. PO9: Hav 6E 21
PO13: Lee S 6H 37
Geranium Gdns. PO7: Den 3C 8
Gerard Ho. PO2: Ports 1A 42
Gibraltar Cl. PO15: Fare 1F 25
Gibraltar Rd. PO4: S'sea 4B 52
PO14: Fare 5H 25
Gibson Cl. PO13: Lee S 6H 37
(not continuous)
PO15: White 3A 12
Gifford Cl. PO15: Fare 6G 13
Gilbert Cl. PO13: Gos 5D 38
Gilbert Mead PO11: H Isl 3A 54
Gilbert Way PO7: W'lle 4G 19
Giles Cl. PO12: Gos 1C 48
PO16: Fare 6B 14
Gilkicker Rd. PO12: Gos 6E 49
Gillies, The PO16: Fare 2A 26
(not continuous)
Gillman Rd. PO6: Farl 2G 31
Gisors Rd. PO4: S'sea 3H 51
Gitsham Gdns. PO7: Wid 6E 19
Glade, The PO7: W'lle 1A 20
PO11: H Isl 5E 55
PO15: Fare 5F 13
Glade Holiday Home Pk., The
PO11: H Isl 5G 55
Gladstone Gdns. PO16: Portc 4A 28
Gladstone Pl. PO2: Ports 5H 41
Gladstone Rd. PO12: Gos 6G 39
Gladys Av. PO2: Ports 3H 41
PO8: Cowp 3A 10
Glamis Cl. PO7: W'lle 1A 20
Glamis Ct. PO14: Stub 2E 37
Glamorgan Rd. PO8: Cath 3B 6
Glasgow Rd. PO4: S'sea 4H 51
Glasspool PO7: Den 2A 8
Glebe, The PO14: Stub 4E 37
Glebe Cl. PO11: H Isl 2A 54
Glebe Cnr. PO17: Wick 2B 14
Glebe Dr. PO13: Gos 4C 38
Glebefield Gdns. PO6: Cosh 3A 30
Glebe Gdns. PO9: Warb 2H 33
Glebe Ho. PO10: S'urne 3H 35
Glebe Pk. Av. PO9: Bed 2A 32
Glen, The PO13: Gos 4E 39
Glenbrook Wlk. PO14: Fare 3E 25
Glencoe Rd. PO1: Ports 6B 42
Gleneagles Dr. PO7: W'lle 5B 10
Glenelg PO15: Fare 1H 25
Glenesha Gdns. PO15: Fare 5B 30
Glenleigh Av. PO6: Cosh 4B 30
Glenleigh Pk. PO9: Warb 1H 33
Glenmore Gdns. PO8: Cowp 5H 9
Glenny Cl. PO13: Lee S 1E 47
Glenthorne Cl. PO14: Stub 4F 37
Glenthorne Rd. PO3: Ports 4C 42
Glenwood Gdns. PO8: Cowp 4H 9
Glenwood Rd. PO10: S'urne 2H 35
Glidden Cl. PO1: Ports 2H 5
Gloucester Cl. GU32: Pet 4B 56
Gloucester Ct. GU32: Pet 3D 56
Gloucester Ho. PO12: Gos 3E 49
(off Holly St.)
Gloucester M. PO5: S'sea 5F 5 (3C 50)
Gloucester Pl. PO5: S'sea 6F 5 (4C 50)
Gloucester Rd. PO1: Ports 1B 4 (1A 50)
PO7: W'lle 3H 19
Gloucester Ter. PO5: S'sea 6F 5 (4C 50)
Gloucester Vw. PO5: S'sea 5F 5 (4C 50)
Glyn Dr. PO14: Stub 3E 37
Glyn Way PO14: Stub 3E 37
Godiva Lawn PO11: H Isl 4A 52
Godwin Cl. PO10: Ems 6C 22
Godwin Cres. PO8: Cath 1C 6
Godwit Cl. PO12: Gos 5H 39
Godwit Rd. PO4: S'sea 1A 52
Gofton Av. PO6: Cosh 4D 30
Goldcrest Cl. PO8: Horn 6A 6
PO16: Portc 3E 27
Golden Ct. PO7: W'lle 2G 19
Goldfinch La. PO13: Lee S 6H 37
Goldring Cl. PO11: H Isl 4C 54
Goldsmith Av. PO4: S'sea 3E 51
Gold St. PO5: S'sea 6E 5 (4B 50)
Gomer Ct. PO12: Gos 4A 48
Gomer La. PO12: Gos 3A 48
Goodsell Cl. PO14: Stub 3D 36

Goodwood Cl. PO8: Cowp 6B 10
PO12: Gos 5H 39
Goodwood Ct. PO10: S'urne 3H 35
Goodwood Rd. PO5: S'sea 4E 51
PO12: Gos 5H 39
Goose Grn. Cvn. Pk. PO11: H Isl 5G 55
Gordon Rd. PO1: Ports 4B 50
PO7: W'lle 3F 19
PO10: S'urne 4F 35
PO12: Gos 3C 48
PO16: Fare 2A 26
Goring Av. PO8: Clan 2H 7
Gorley Ct. PO9: Hav 3D 20
Gorran Av. PO13: Gos 4C 38
Gorselands Way PO13: Gos 5D 38
Gorse Rd. GU31: Pet 4G 57
Gorseway, The PO11: H Isl 4H 53
GOSPORT 3F 49
Gosport Bus. Cen. PO13: Gos 3E 39
Gosport Gallery 3F 49
Gosport Ho. PO9: Hav 4H 21
Gosport Ice Rink 4E 39
Gosport Rd. PO13: Lee S 2D 46
PO14: Stub 1B 46
PO16: Fare 4B 26
GOSPORT WAR MEMORIAL HOSPITAL . .3C 48
Gothic Bldgs. PO5: S'sea 6H 5 (4D 50)
Goyda Ho. PO12: Gos 1B 48
Grafton Cl. PO12: Gos 6A 40
Grafton St. PO2: Ports 6G 41
Graham Rd. PO4: S'sea 4E 51
PO12: Gos 1C 48
Granada Cl. PO8: Cowp 4A 10
Granada Rd. PO4: S'sea 6E 51
Grand Division Row PO4: S'sea 4H 51
Grand Pde. PO1: Ports 6B 4 (4A 50)
PO11: H Isl 5C 54
GRANGE .1H 47
Grange, The PO10: Ems 1D 34
(off New Brighton Rd.)
Grange Cl. PO9: Hav 1H 33
PO12: Gos 1B 48
Grange Cres. PO12: Gos 1B 48
Grange La. PO13: Gos 5C 38
(not continuous)
Grange Rd. GU32: Pet 5C 56
PO2: Ports 4H 41
PO13: Gos 3H 47
Grant Rd. PO6: Farl 3F 31
Granville Cl. PO9: Warb 2G 33
Grasmere Ho. PO6: Cosh 2F 29
Grasmere Way PO14: Stub 1F 37
Grassmere Way PO7: W'lle 6B 10
Grateley Cres. PO9: Hav 5C 20
Grayland Cl. PO11: H Isl 3A 54
Grays Cl. PO12: Gos 4A 48
Grays Ct. PO1: Ports 5C 4 (3A 50)
Grayshott Rd. PO4: S'sea 3F 51
PO12: Gos 3B 48
Grayson Cl. PO13: Lee S 1E 47
Gt. Copse Dr. PO9: Hav 3E 21
Greater Horseshoe Way PO17: K Vil . . .1G 13
Greatfield Way PO9: R Cas 4H 11
Great Gays PO14: Stub 4C 36
Great Hanger GU31: Pet 4F 57
Great Mead PO7: Den 4C 8
GREAT POSBROOK 4B 24
Gt. Southsea St. PO5: S'sea 6F 5 (4C 50)
Grebe Cl. PO8: Cowp 3G 9
PO10: Westb 5F 23
PO16: Portc 3F 27
Green, The PO1: Ports 2B 4 (2A 50)
PO7: Den 2A 8
PO9: R Cas 5H 11
Greenacre Gdns. PO7: Purb 5F 19
Greenbanks Gdns. PO16: Fare 1D 26
Green Cres. PO13: Gos 4C 38
Greendale, The PO15: Fare 5F 13
Greendale Cl. PO15: Fare 5F 13
Green Farm Gdns. PO3: Ports 1B 42
PO8: Horn 2C 10
Greenfield Ri. PO8: Cowp 4B 10
Greenhaven Cvn. Pk. PO11: H Isl 6G 55
Green Hollow Cl. PO16: Fare 5H 13
Green La. PO3: Ports 2B 42
PO7: Den 2A 8
PO8: Clan . . . . .1C 6 & 2G 7
PO11: H Isl 4A 54
PO12: Gos 5C 48
(Anglesey Rd., not continuous)

Green La. PO12: Gos 5A 40
(St Helier Rd.)
Greenlea Cl. PO7: Wid 1D 30
Greenlea Gro. PO12: Gos 6F 39
Green Link PO13: Lee S 2D 46
Green Pond Cnr. PO9: Warb 2H 33
Green Rd. PO5: S'sea 6F 5 (4C 50)
PO12: Gos 5C 48
PO14: Stub 1E 37
Green Wlk. PO15: Fare 6G 13
Greenway, The PO10: Ems 5D 22
Greenway Rd. PO12: Gos 1D 48
Greenwood Av. PO6: Cosh 3H 29
Greenwood Cl. PO16: Fare 5A 14
Greetham St. PO5: S'sea 3G 5 (2C 50)
Gregson Av. PO13: Gos 2C 38
Gregson Cl. PO13: Gos 2C 38
Grenehurst Way GU31: Pet 4D 56
Grenfield Cl. PO10: Ems 6D 22
Grenville Ho. PO1: Ports 3C 4
Grenville Rd. PO4: S'sea 4E 51
Grevillea Av. PO15: Seg 6A 12
Greville Grn. PO10: Ems 5C 22
Greyfriars Ct. PO5: S'sea 4C 50
Greyfriars Rd. PO15: Fare 1E 25
Greyshott Av. PO14: Fare 3E 25
Greywell Rd. PO9: Hav 4F 21
Greywell Shop. Cen. PO9: Hav 4F 21
Greywell Sq. PO9: Hav 4F 21
Griffin Wlk. PO13: Gos 1G 47
Grindle Cl. PO16: Portc 2A 28
Gritanwood Rd. PO4: S'sea 4H 51
Grosvenor Ct. PO14: Stub 3F 37
Grosvenor Ho. PO5: S'sea 5G 5 (3C 50)
Grosvenor M. PO12: Gos 2E 49
Grosvenor St. PO5: S'sea 4G 5 (3C 50)
Grove, The PO10: Westb 6F 23
PO14: Stub 3D 36
Grove Av. PO12: Gos 2E 49
PO16: Portc 5A 28
Grove Bldgs. PO12: Gos 3E 49
Grove Ct. PO9: Hav 2F 33
Grove Ho. PO5: S'sea 6H 5 (4D 50)
(Cottage Gro.)
PO5: S'sea 6G 5
(Elm Gro.)
Grove Rd. PO6: Dray 4E 31
PO9: Hav 2F 33
PO12: Gos 1D 48
PO13: Lee S 1C 46
PO16: Fare 2A 26
Grove Rd. Nth. PO5: S'sea 6G 5 (4D 50)
Grove Rd. Sth. PO5: S'sea 6G 5 (5C 50)
Gruneisen Rd. PO2: Ports 3G 41
Guardhouse Rd. PO1: Ports 6F 41
Guardroom Rd. PO2: Ports 4F 41
Gudge Heath La. PO15: Fare 6F 13
Guelders, The PO7: Purb 6G 19
Guessens La. PO14: Titch 3B 24
Guessens Path PO14: Titch 3B 24
Guildford Cl. PO10: S'urne 2H 35
Guildford Ct. PO13: Gos 2H 47
Guildford Rd. PO1: Ports 1E 51
(not continuous)
Guildhall Sq. PO1: Ports 3F 5 (2C 50)
Guildhall Wlk. PO1: Ports 4E 5 (3C 50)
Guillemot Gdns. PO13: Gos 2B 38
Gull Cl. PO13: Gos 3B 38
Gunners Bldgs. Ind. Est. PO3: Ports . . .1B 42
Gunners Row PO4: S'sea 5H 51
Gunners Way PO12: Gos 5F 39
Gunstore Rd. PO3: Ports 1C 42
Gunwharf Quays PO1: Ports 4B 4 (3A 50)
Gunwharf Rd. PO1: Ports 5B 4 (3A 50)
Gurnard Rd. PO6: Cosh 4A 30
Gurney Rd. PO4: S'sea 3H 51
Gutner La. PO11: H Isl 4E 45
Gwatkin Cl. PO9: Bed 6C 20
Gwynn Way PO17: Wick 1A 14
Gypsy La. PO8: Cowp 2H 9

H

Hackett Way PO14: Fare 5A 26
(off Sharlands Rd.)
Haddon Cl. PO14: Fare 2G 25
Hadleigh Rd. PO6: Cosh 3H 29
Haig Ct. PO2: Ports 2A 42
Hale Ct. PO1: Ports 6A 42
Halesowen Ho. PO5: S'sea 5F 5

Hale St. Nth.—Henley Rd.

Hale St. Nth. PO1: Ports . . . 1D **50**
Hale St. Sth. PO1: Ports . . . 1H **5** (1D **50**)
Half Moon St. PO1: Ports . . . 2B **4** (2A **50**)
Halfpenny La. PO1: Ports . . . 6C **4** (4A **50**)
Halifax Ri. PO7: W'lle . . . 2H **19**
Hallett Rd. PO9: Hav . . . 1H **33**
Halletts Cl. PO14: Stub . . . 2E **37**
Halliards, The PO16: Fare . . . 4B **26**
Halliday Cl. PO12: Gos . . . 2D **48**
Halliday Cres. PO4: S'sea . . . 4A **52**
Hallowell Ho. PO1: Ports . . . 1C **50**
Halsey Cl. PO12: Gos . . . 4B **48**
Halstead Rd. PO6: Cosh . . . 3H **29**
Halyard Cl. PO13: Gos . . . 6D **38**
Hamble Ct. PO8: Cowp . . . 3H **9**
PO14: Stub . . . 2D **36**
Hambledon Pde. PO7: W'lle . . . 5E **9**
Hambledon Rd. PO7: Den . . . 1A **8**
PO7: W'lle . . . 5E **9**
(not continuous)
PO8: Clan . . . 1E **7**
Hamble Ho. PO16: Fare . . . 4A **26**
Hamble La. PO7: W'lle . . . 4G **19**
Hamble Rd. PO12: Gos . . . 3B **48**
Hambrook Rd. PO12: Gos . . . 1C **48**
Hambrook St. PO5: S'sea . . . 6E **5** (4B **50**)
Hamfield Dr. PO11: H Isl . . . 3A **54**
Hamilton Cl. PO9: Lang . . . 3F **33**
Hamilton Ct. PO5: S'sea . . . 5C **50**
Hamilton Ent. Cen. PO6: Farl . . . 4G **31**
Hamilton Gro. PO13: Gos . . . 3B **38**
Hamilton Ho. *PO1: Ports . . . 1E 51*
(off Clive Rd.)
Hamilton Rd. PO5: S'sea . . . 5D **50**
PO6: Cosh . . . 3C **28**
Ham La. PO8: Cath . . . 5A **6**
PO10: S'urne . . . 4H **35**
PO12: Gos . . . 5G **39**
Hamlet Way PO12: Gos . . . 4G **39**
Hammond Ct. PO12: Gos . . . 3G **49**
Hammond Ind. Pk. PO14: Stub . . . 4F **37**
Hammond Rd. PO15: Fare . . . 1F **25**
Hampage Grn. PO9: Hav . . . 2D **20**
Hampshire St. PO1: Ports . . . 6A **42**
Hampshire Ter. PO1: Ports . . . 5E **5** (3B **50**)
Hampton Cl. PO7: W'lle . . . 2A **20**
Hampton Gro. PO15: Fare . . . 2D **24**
Hanbidge Cres. PO13: Gos . . . 1D **38**
Hanbidge Wlk. PO13: Gos . . . 1D **38**
Hanbury Sq. GU31: Pet . . . 2E **57**
Handley Rd. PO12: Gos . . . 1B **48**
Handsworth Ho. PO5: S'sea . . . 4H **5** (3D **50**)
Hanger Way GU31: Pet . . . 4F **57**
Hannah Gdns. PO7: W'lle . . . 1H **19**
Hannington Rd. PO9: Hav . . . 2D **20**
Hanover Ct. PO1: Ports . . . 5C **4** (4A **50**)
Hanover Gdns. PO16: Fare . . . 6B **14**
Hanover Ho. PO13: Gos . . . 6B **26**
Hanover St. PO1: Ports . . . 2B **4** (2A **50**)
Hanway Rd. PO1: Ports . . . 5H **41**
PO2: Ports . . . 5A **42**
Ha'penny Dell PO7: Purb . . . 6G **19**
Harbourgate Bus. Pk. PO6: Cosh . . . 3G **29**
Harbour Rd. PO11: H Isl . . . 3G **53**
PO12: Gos . . . 2F **49**
Harbourside PO9: Lang . . . 5F **33**
Harbour Side Cvn. & Camping Site
PO3: Ports . . . 4F **43**
Harbour Twr. PO12: Gos . . . 3G **49**
Harbour Vw. PO16: Portc . . . 5A **28**
Harbour Way PO2: Ports . . . 3G **41**
PO10: Ems . . . 3E **35**
Harbridge Ct. PO9: Hav . . . 2D **20**
Harcourt Cl. PO8: Cowp . . . 3A **10**
Harcourt Rd. PO1: Ports . . . 6A **42**
PO12: Gos . . . 2C **48**
PO14: Fare . . . 4D **24**
Hard, The PO1: Ports . . . 2B **4** (2A **50**)
Harding Rd. PO12: Gos . . . 1B **48**
Hard Interchange, The
PO1: Ports . . . 3B **4** (2A **50**)
Hardman Ct. PO3: Ports . . . 1D **42**
HARDWAY . . . 5H **39**
Hardway Sailing Club . . . 5A **40**
Hardy Av. GU31: Pet . . . 2E **57**
Hardy Cl. PO13: Gos . . . 2C **38**
Hardy Rd. PO6: Farl . . . 3G **31**
Harebell Cl. PO16: Fare . . . 6C **14**
Harestock Rd. PO9: Bed . . . 6D **20**
Harkness Dr. PO7: W'lle . . . 1B **20**
Harlequin Ct. PO12: Gos . . . 2F **49**
Harlequin Gro. PO15: Fare . . . 2H **25**
Harleston Rd. PO6: Cosh . . . 2H **29**
Harley Wlk. PO1: Ports . . . 1D **50**
Harman Rd. PO13: Gos . . . 2C **38**
Harold Rd. PO4: S'sea . . . 4E **51**
PO10: Westb . . . 5F **23**
PO11: H Isl . . . 5D **54**
PO14: Stub . . . 2F **37**
Harold Ter. PO10: Ems . . . 2D **34**
Harper Way PO16: Fare . . . 2B **26**
Harrier Cl. PO8: Horn . . . 6A **6**
PO13: Lee S . . . 1D **46**
Harrier Way GU31: Pet . . . 5G **57**
Harriet Cl. PO14: Stub . . . 3D **36**
Harrison Ho. PO2: Ports . . . 3H **41**
Harrison Rd. PO16: Fare . . . 1B **26**
Harris Rd. PO13: Gos . . . 2D **38**
Harrow La. GU32: Pet . . . 1D **56**
Harrow Rd. PO5: S'sea . . . 3E **51**
Harry Law Hall PO1: Ports . . . 3F **5** (2C **50**)
Harry Sotnick Ho. PO1: Ports . . . 1F **51**
Hartford Ho. PO1: Ports . . . 6E **5** (4B **50**)
Harting Cl. PO8: Clan . . . 1D **6**
Harting Down GU31: Pet . . . 4F **57**
Harting Gdns. PO16: Portc . . . 2A **28**
Hartington Rd. PO12: Gos . . . 1B **48**
Hartland Ct. PO10: S'urne . . . 2H **35**
Hartland's Rd. PO16: Fare . . . 2B **26**
Hartley Rd. PO2: Ports . . . 2H **41**
Hart Plain Av. PO8: Cowp . . . 3F **9**
(not continuous)
Harts Farm Way PO9: Hav . . . 3B **32**
Hartwell Rd. PO3: Ports . . . 1D **42**
Hartwood Gdns. PO8: Cowp . . . 5G **9**
Harvard Cl. PO13: Lee S . . . 2E **47**
Harvester Dr. PO15: Fare . . . 2D **24**
Harvestgate Wlk. PO9: Hav . . . 3D **20**
Harvest Rd. PO7: Den . . . 2A **8**
Harvey Brown Ho. PO11: H Isl . . . 2C **54**
Harvey Rd. PO6: Cosh . . . 2A **30**
Harwich Rd. PO6: Cosh . . . 2H **29**
Harwood Cl. PO13: Gos . . . 1C **38**
Harwood Rd. PO13: Gos . . . 1C **38**
Haselworth Dr. PO12: Gos . . . 6D **48**
Haslar Cres. PO7: W'lle . . . 5E **9**
Haslar Jetty Rd. PO12: Gos . . . 5F **49**
Haslar Rd. PO12: Gos . . . 3G **49**
(not continuous)
Haslar Sea Wall PO12: Gos . . . 6F **49**
Haslar Ter. PO12: Gos . . . 5F **49**
Haslegrave Ho. *PO2: Ports . . . 5H 41*
(off Nessus St.)
Haslemere Gdns. PO11: H Isl . . . 5H **55**
Haslemere Rd. PO4: S'sea . . . 4F **51**
PO10: S'urne . . . 1H **35**
Hassocks, The PO7: W'lle . . . 2A **20**
Hastings Av. PO12: Gos . . . 5F **39**
Hastings Ho. PO2: Ports . . . 3G **41**
Hatch Ct. PO9: Hav . . . 2C **20**
Hatch Moor Rd. PO7: Den . . . 3A **8**
Hatfield Rd. PO4: S'sea . . . 4G **51**
Hathaway Gdns. PO7: W'lle . . . 6B **10**
Hatherley Cres. PO16: Portc . . . 3G **27**
Hatherley Dr. PO16: Portc . . . 3H **27**
Hatherley Rd. PO6: Cosh . . . 2E **29**
HAVANT . . . 2F **33**
Havant & Waterlooville FC . . . 4G **21**
Havant Bus. Cen. PO9: Hav . . . 3D **32**
Havant By-Pass PO6: Cosh, Farl . . . 5C **30**
PO9: Hav . . . 3C **32**
PO9: Hav, Warb . . . 3G **33**
Havant Farm Cl. PO9: Hav . . . 6F **21**
Havant Leisure Cen. . . . 1F **33**
Havant Mus. & Arts Cen. . . . 2G **33**
Havant Retail Pk. PO9: Bed . . . 2B **32**
Havant Rd. PO2: Ports . . . 4A **42**
PO6: Dray, Farl, Cosh . . . 3B **30**
PO8: Horn . . . 6D **6**
PO9: Bed . . . 3F **31**
PO9: R Cas . . . 6D **6**
PO10: Ems . . . 3A **34**
PO11: H Isl . . . 2B **44**
Havant Station (Rail) . . . 1F **33**
Havant St. PO1: Ports . . . 2B **4** (2A **50**)
HAVANT WAR MEMORIAL HOSPITAL . . . 1E **33**
Havelock Mans. PO5: S'sea . . . 3E **51**
Havelock Rd. PO5: S'sea . . . 3D **50**
Haven, The PO4: S'sea . . . 2H **51**
PO12: Gos . . . 5D **48**
Haven Cres. PO14: Stub . . . 4B **36**
Haven Rd. PO11: H Isl . . . 6G **55**
Havisham Rd. PO2: Ports . . . 6H **41**
Hawk Cl. PO14: Stub . . . 3D **36**
Hawke St. PO1: Ports . . . 2B **4** (2A **50**)
Hawkewood Av. PO7: W'lle . . . 5F **9**
Hawkins Rd. PO13: Gos . . . 3D **38**
Hawkley Cl. PO9: Hav . . . 3E **21**
Hawkwell PO16: Portc . . . 2F **27**
Hawstead Grn. PO9: Hav . . . 3D **20**
Hawthorn Cl. PO16: Portc . . . 2H **27**
Hawthorn Ct. GU31: Pet . . . 4G **57**
Hawthorn Cres. PO6: Cosh . . . 5B **30**
Hawthorne Gro. PO11: H Isl . . . 3C **54**
Hawthorn Rd. PO7: Den . . . 3A **8**
PO8: Horn . . . 3C **6**
Hawthorn Wlk. PO13: Lee S . . . 1D **46**
Haydock M. PO7: W'lle . . . 6B **10**
Hayes Cl. PO15: Fare . . . 6F **13**
Hayes Ct. PO5: S'sea . . . 6H **5** (4D **50**)
Hayling Av. PO3: Ports . . . 6C **42**
Hayling Billy Bus. Cen.
PO11: H Isl . . . 3H **53**
Hayling Cl. PO12: Gos . . . 5A **40**
PO14: Fare . . . 3F **25**
Hayling Island Lifeboat Station & Mus.
. . . 5H **55**
Hayling Island Sailing Club . . . 4H **55**
Hayward Bus. Cen. PO9: Hav . . . 6H **21**
Haywards Ct. PO1: Ports . . . 5C **4** (3A **50**)
Hazelbank Cl. GU31: Pet . . . 3F **57**
Hazel Ct. PO4: S'sea . . . 3F **51**
Hazeldean Ct. PO9: R Cas . . . 6H **11**
Hazeldean Dr. PO9: R Cas . . . 6H **11**
Hazeley Grn. *PO9: Hav . . . 4H 21*
(off Sharps Rd.)
Hazel Gro. PO8: Clan . . . 2G **7**
Hazelholt Dr. PO9: Bed . . . 6D **20**
Hazel Rd. PO8: Clan . . . 2G **7**
Hazel Wlk. GU31: Pet . . . 6D **56**
Hazelwood PO14: Stub . . . 6D **24**
Hazelwood Av. PO9: Bed . . . 6B **20**
Hazleton Ind. Est. PO8: Horn . . . 1C **10**
Hazleton Way PO8: Cowp . . . 4B **10**
PO8: Horn . . . 2B **10**
Head Down GU31: Pet . . . 4F **57**
Headley Cl. PO13: Lee S . . . 1D **46**
Heath, The PO7: Den . . . 3C **8**
Heath Cl. PO8: Horn . . . 6B **6**
Heathcote Rd. PO2: Ports . . . 4B **42**
Heath Ct. GU31: Pet . . . 5D **56**
Heather Cl. PO7: W'lle . . . 3H **19**
PO13: Gos . . . 3B **38**
Heather Gdns. PO15: Fare . . . 6F **13**
Heatherley Ct. PO5: S'sea . . . 4D **50**
Heather Rd. GU31: Pet . . . 4G **57**
Heatherton M. PO10: Ems . . . 6D **22**
HEATHFIELD . . . 2F **25**
Heathfield Av. PO15: Fare . . . 2F **25**
Heathfield Rd. GU31: Pet . . . 4G **57**
PO2: Ports . . . 5H **41**
Heath La. PO14: Titch . . . 4A **24**
Heath Lawns PO15: Fare . . . 2F **25**
Heath Rd. GU31: Pet . . . 4D **56**
Heath Rd. E. GU31: Pet . . . 6F **57**
Heath Rd. W. GU31: Pet . . . 5E **57**
Heaton Rd. PO12: Gos . . . 6F **39**
Hebrides Cl. PO14: Stub . . . 2D **36**
Heckfield Cl. PO9: Hav . . . 4H **21**
Hector Cl. PO7: Purb . . . 1G **31**
Hector Rd. PO14: Fare . . . 5A **26**
Hedge End Wlk. PO9: Hav . . . 3A **22**
Hedgerow Gdns. PO10: Ems . . . 6D **22**
Heidelberg Rd. PO4: S'sea . . . 3F **51**
Heidi Cl. PO12: Gos . . . 1D **48**
Heights, The PO16: Fare . . . 1D **26**
Helena Rd. PO4: S'sea . . . 5F **51**
Hellyer Rd. PO4: S'sea . . . 4G **51**
Helm Cl. PO13: Gos . . . 1H **47**
Helsby Cl. PO14: Fare . . . 3G **25**
Helsted Cl. PO12: Gos . . . 3A **48**
Helston Dr. PO10: Ems . . . 6C **22**
Helston Rd. PO6: Cosh . . . 2D **28**
Hemlock Rd. PO8: Cowp . . . 3F **9**
Hempsted Path PO6: Cosh . . . 2F **29**
Hempsted Rd. PO6: Cosh . . . 2F **29**
Hemsley Wlk. PO8: Cowp . . . 3A **10**
Henderson Pk. Mobile Homes
PO4: S'sea . . . 4A **52**
Henderson Rd. PO4: S'sea . . . 4H **51**
Hendy Cl. PO5: S'sea . . . 6G **5** (4C **50**)
Henley Gdns. PO15: Fare . . . 5F **13**
Henley Rd. PO4: S'sea . . . 5F **51**

Henry Cort Dr. PO15: Fare 6E **13**
Henry Player Av. PO12: Gos 2F **49**
Henry St. PO12: Gos 3E **49**
Henville Cl. PO13: Gos 5D **38**
Henwood Down GU31: Pet 4E **57**
Herbert Rd. PO4: S'sea 5E **51**
 PO12: Gos 2B **48**
Herbert St. PO1: Ports 6G **41**
Hercules St. PO2: Ports 5H **41**
Hereford Ct. *PO5: S'sea* *4D 50*
 (off Hereford Rd.)
 PO13: Gos 1G **47**
Hereford Rd. PO5: S'sea 4D **50**
Heritage Bus. Pk. PO12: Gos 4F **39**
Heritage Gdns. PO16: Portc 4G **27**
Heritage Way PO12: Gos 4G **39**
 PO12: Gos 4E **39**
Hermes Ct. PO12: Gos 5A **40**
Hermes Rd. PO13: Lee S 6F **37**
HERMITAGE 2E **35**
Hermitage, The PO10: S'urne 2E **35**
Hermitage Cl. PO9: Hav 5E **21**
Hermitage Gdns. PO7: W'lle 1H **19**
Hermitage Way PO12: Gos 5H **39**
Herne Farm Leisure Cen., The 4E **57**
Herne Rd. GU31: Pet 4E **57**
 PO6: Cosh 3A **30**
Heron Cl. PO4: S'sea 5E **51**
Heron Ho. PO5: S'sea 5E **51**
Heron Quay PO10: S'urne 4E **35**
Herons Cl. PO14: Stub 1E **37**
Heron Way PO13: Gos 2B **38**
Herriot Ho. PO8: Cowp 4A **10**
Herriott Cl. PO8: Cowp 2A **10**
Hertford Pl. PO1: Ports 6H **41**
Hester Rd. PO4: S'sea 3H **51**
Heston Wlk. PO12: Gos 4A **48**
Hewett Cl. PO14: Titch 4B **24**
Hewett Ho. PO14: Titch 4B **24**
Hewett Rd. PO2: Ports 3A **42**
 PO14: Titch 4B **24**
Hewitt Cl. PO12: Gos 1C **48**
Hewlett Ct. PO16: Fare 2C **26**
Heyshott Gdns. PO8: Clan 1D **6**
Heyshott Rd. PO4: S'sea 3F **51**
Heyward Rd. PO4: S'sea 4E **51**
Heywood Gdns. PO9: Hav 3D **20**
Hickley Path PO16: Fare 1C **26**
Highbank Av. PO7: Wid 6D **18**
Highbury Bldgs. PO6: Cosh 5B **30**
Highbury College Community Sports Cen.
 . . . . .5C **30**
Highbury Gro. PO6: Cosh 5B **30**
Highbury St. PO1: Ports 5C **4** (3A **50**)
Highbury Way PO6: Cosh 5B **30**
Highclere Av. PO9: Hav 5D **20**
Highcliffe Rd. PO12: Gos 3B **48**
High Ct. PO4: S'sea 4G **51**
Highcroft Ind. Est. PO8: Horn 5C **6**
Highcroft La. PO8: Horn 5C **6**
High Dr. PO13: Gos 4C **38**
Highfield Av. PO7: W'lle 6H **9**
 PO14: Fare 3H **25**
Highfield Cl. PO7: W'lle 6H **9**
Highfield Pde. PO7: W'lle 6A **10**
Highfield Rd. GU32: Pet 3D **56**
 PO1: Ports 2H **5** (2D **50**)
 PO12: Gos 1B **48**
Highgate Rd. PO3: Ports 4C **42**
Highgrove Ind. Pk. PO3: Ports 2D **42**
Highgrove Rd. PO3: Ports 5D **42**
Highland Cl. PO10: Ems 3C **34**
Highland Rd. PO4: S'sea 5F **51**
 PO10: Ems 2C **34**
Highlands Pk. PO15: Fare 6G **13**
Highlands Rd. PO6: Dray 3F **31**
 PO15: Fare 3D **24**
 PO16: Fare 3D **24**
Highland St. PO4: S'sea 5G **51**
Highland Ter. PO4: S'sea 4F **51**
High Lawn Way PO9: Hav 4E **21**
High Mead PO15: Fare 6G **13**
High St. GU31: Pet 4D **56**
 GU32: Pet 4D **56**
 PO1: Ports 6B **4** (4A **50**)
 PO6: Cosh 4B **30**
 PO10: Ems 3D **34**
 PO12: Gos 3F **49**
 PO13: Lee S 1C **46**
 PO14: Titch 3B **24**
 PO16: Fare 2C **26**

High St. PO17: S'wick 3D **16**
High Trees PO7: W'lle 1H **19**
High Vw. GU32: Pet 3D **56**
 PO16: Portc 2A **28**
High Wlk. PO15: Fare 6G **13**
Highwood Lawn PO9: Hav 2D **20**
Highwood Rd. PO13: Gos 6C **38**
Higworth Cvn. Pk. PO11: H Isl 2B **54**
Higworth La. PO11: H Isl 2B **54**
Hilary Av. PO6: Cosh 4C **30**
Hilary Ct. PO13: Gos 1H **47**
Hilda Gdns. PO7: Den 4C **8**
Hillary Cl. PO16: Fare 1H **25**
Hillborough Cl. PO5: S'sea 4D **50**
Hillborough Cres. PO5: S'sea 4D **50**
Hill Brow Cl. PO9: R Cas 6H **11**
Hillbrow Cl. PO15: Fare 6F **13**
Hill Coppice Rd. PO15: White 3A **12**
Hill Cft. PO15: Seg 6A **12**
Hilldowns Av. PO2: Ports 3G **41**
Hill Dr. PO15: Fare 6F **13**
Hiller Wlk. PO13: Lee S 1D **46**
HILL HEAD 5D **36**
Hill Head Rd. PO14: Stub 4C **36**
Hill Head Sailing Club 5D **36**
Hillmead Gdns. PO9: Bed 1B **32**
HILL PARK 6F **13**
Hill Pk. Rd. PO12: Gos 1B **48**
 PO15: Fare 5F **13**
Hill Rd. PO16: Portc 2B **28**
Hillside Av. PO7: Wid 1D **30**
Hillside Cl. PO8: Cath 2C **6**
Hillside Cres. PO6: Cosh 2D **28**
Hillside Ind. Est. PO8: Horn 5C **6**
Hillsley Rd. PO6: Cosh 1D **28**
Hillson Dr. PO15: Fare 6E **13**
Hillson Ho. PO15: Fare 6F **13**
Hilltop Cres. PO6: Cosh 1E **31**
Hilltop Gdns. PO8: Horn 2D **6**
Hilltop Rd. PO17: S'wick 1E **29**
Hillview PO8: Horn 2C **10**
Hill Vw. Rd. PO16: Portc 2A **28**
Hill Wlk. PO15: Fare 6F **13**
Hillway, The PO16: Portc 3A **28**
HILSEA 6A **30**
Hilsea Cres. PO2: Ports 6A **30**
Hilsea Lido 6A **30**
HILSEA LINES 6C **30**
Hilsea Mkt. PO2: Ports 6A **30**
Hilsea Station (Rail) 1C **42**
Hiltingbury Rd. PO9: Hav 4G **21**
Hilton Rd. PO12: Gos 4E **49**
Hinton Cl. PO9: Hav 5C **20**
Hinton Mnr. La.
 PO8: Cath, Clan, Love . . . . . . .2A **6** & 2E **7**
Hipley Rd. PO9: Hav 6G **21**
Hither Grn. PO10: S'urne 1H **35**
Hitherwood Cl. PO7: W'lle 6B **10**
HMS Alliance 4G **49**
 PO13: Gos 2G **47**
HMS Daedalus Cvn. Pk.
 PO13: Gos 2G **47**
HM Sub Holland 1 . . . . .4G **49**
HMS Victory 1A **4** (1H **49**)
HMS Warrior 3A **4** (2H **49**)
Hoadlands GU31: Pet 3E **57**
Hobbs Pas. PO12: Gos 3G **49**
Hobbs Sq. GU31: Pet 2E **57**
Hobby Cl. PO3: Ports 1C **42**
 PO8: Cowp 3G **9**
Hockham Ct. PO9: Hav 2C **20**
Hockley Cl. PO6: Cosh 3H **29**
Hockley Path PO6: Cosh 3A **30**
Hodges Cl. PO9: Hav 6G **21**
Hoe, The PO13: Gos 4E **39**
Hoeford Cl. PO16: Fare 5B **26**
Hoggarth Cl. GU31: Pet 3E **57**
Holbeach Cl. PO6: Cosh 2A **30**
Holbrook Recreation Cen. 4E **39**
Holbrook Rd. PO1: Ports 1H **5** (1D **50**)
 PO5: S'sea 1D **50**
 PO16: Fare 3B **26**
Holbury Ct. PO9: Hav 4H **21**
Holcot La. PO3: Ports 1E **43**
Holdenby Ct. PO3: Ports 6E **31**
Holdenhurst Cl. PO8: Horn 4C **6**
Hollam Cl. PO14: Fare 3D **24**
Hollam Cres. PO14: Fare 3D **24**
Hollam Dr. PO14: Fare 3D **24**
Hollam Rd. PO4: S'sea 2H **51**
Holland Pl. PO13: Gos 3D **38**
Holland Rd. PO4: S'sea 3E **51**

Hollies, The PO8: Horn 3C **6**
Hollies Cvn. Pk., The PO11: H Isl 5G **55**
Hollow La. PO11: H Isl 4B **54**
HOLLYBANK 1G **33**
Hollybank PO13: Lee S 2D **46**
Hollybank Cl. PO8: Horn 2C **10**
Hollybank La. PO10: Ems 5D **22**
Holly Dr. PO7: W'lle 3A **20**
Holly Gro. PO16: Fare 5G **13**
Holly St. PO12: Gos 3E **49**
Hollywell Dr. PO6: P Sol 4F **29**
Holman Cl. PO8: Cowp 5A **10**
Holmbush Cl. PO5: S'sea 4C **50**
Holm Ct. PO11: H Isl 5B **54**
Holmdale Rd. PO12: Gos 6F **39**
Holmefield Av. PO14: Fare 5H **25**
Holne Ct. PO4: S'sea 4A **52**
Holst Way PO7: W'lle 4G **19**
Holt Cl. PO13: Lee S 1E **47**
 PO17: Wick 1A **14**
Holt Down GU31: Pet 4F **57**
Holt Gdns. PO9: R Cas 4H **11**
Holybourne Rd. PO9: Hav 6F **21**
Holyrood Cl. PO7: W'lle 2A **20**
Homefayre Ho. PO16: Fare 2B **26**
Homefield Path PO6: Dray 4E **31**
Homefield Rd. PO6: Dray 4E **31**
 PO10: Westb 5F **23**
Homefield Way PO8: Clan 1F **7**
Homefort Ho. *PO12: Gos* *3D 48*
 (off Stoke Rd.)
Homegrove Ho. PO5: S'sea 6H **5** (4D **50**)
Homeheights PO5: S'sea 5C **50**
Home Mead PO7: Den 4B **8**
Homer Cl. PO8: Cowp 5G **9**
 PO13: Gos 5B **38**
Homerose Ho. PO5: S'sea 5G **5** (3C **50**)
Homeryde Ho. PO13: Lee S 2C **46**
Homesea Ho. PO5: S'sea 5G **5** (4C **50**)
Homewater Ho. PO7: W'lle 1G **19**
Home Way GU31: Pet 4G **57**
Homewell PO9: Hav 2F **33**
Honey La. PO15: Fun 4F **13**
Honeysuckle Cl. PO13: Gos 2B **38**
Honeysuckle Ct. PO7: W'lle 4H **19**
Honeywood Cl. PO3: Ports 1B **42**
Hook's Farm Way PO9: Bed 6D **20**
Hook's La. PO9: Bed 6C **20**
 (not continuous)
Hope St. PO1: Ports 1C **50**
Hopfield Cl. PO7: W'lle 2G **19**
Hopfield Ho. PO7: W'lle 3G **19**
Hopfield M. PO7: W'lle 3G **19**
Hopkins Cl. PO6: Cosh 3C **28**
Hopkins Ct. PO4: S'sea 5H **51**
Horatia Ho. PO5: S'sea 4E **5** (3B **50**)
Hordle Rd. PO9: Hav 5B **20**
Hornbeam Rd. PO9: Hav 6H **21**
HORNDEAN 6B **6**
Horndean Cvn. Site PO8: Horn 4C **6**
Horndean Cen. 6B **6**
 (off Barton Cross)
Horndean Ho. PO1: Ports 1H **5** (1D **50**)
Horndean Pct. PO8: Horn 6D **6**
Horndean Rd. PO8: Blen 5E **7**
 PO10: Ems 5B **22**
Hornet Cl. PO12: Gos 4E **49**
 PO15: Fare 1F **25**
Hornetide Ho. PO13: Lee S 2C **46**
Hornet Rd. PO14: Fare 6H **25**
Horsea La. PO2: Ports 1H **41**
Horsea Rd. PO2: Ports 1A **42**
Horsebridge Rd. PO9: Hav 5G **21**
Horse Sands Cl. PO4: S'sea 4B **52**
Horton Rd. PO13: Gos 1C **38**
Hoskins Ho. PO1: Ports 1D **4**
Hospital La. PO16: Portc 5C **28**
Houghton Cl. PO9: Hav 3H **21**
House Farm Rd. PO12: Gos 3A **48**
Hove Cl. PO13: Lee S 1C **46**
Hoverfly Cl. PO13: Gos 2E **47**
Howard Cl. PO13: Lee S 6A **38**
Howard Lodge PO5: S'sea 5C **50**
Howard Rd. PO2: Ports 1A **42**
 PO6: Cosh 4B **30**
Howe Rd. PO13: Gos 1G **47**
Hoylake Cl. PO13: Gos 4C **38**
Hoylake Rd. PO6: Dray 2E **31**
Hoylecroft Cl. PO15: Fare 6G **13**
Hubert Rd. Rdbt. PO7: W'lle 1G **19**
Hudson Cl. PO13: Gos 1G **47**
Hudson Rd. PO5: S'sea 5H **5** (3D **50**)

Hulbert Rd. PO7: Hav, W'lle 1G 19
(not continuous)
PO9: Bed, Hav 5B 20
Humber Cl. PO14: Stub 2D 36
Hundred, The PO7: W'lle 6F 9
Hunter Cl. PO13: Gos 6D 38
Hunter Rd. PO4: S'sea 4F 51
PO6: Cosh 2B 30
Hunters Lodge PO15: Fare 2D 24
Hunters Ride PO7: W'lle 3G 19
Huntley Cl. PO6: Cosh 2F 29
Huntsman Cl. PO8: Cowp 2H 9
Hurn Ct. PO9: Hav 3H 21
Hursley Rd. PO9: Hav 4D 20
Hurstbourne Cl. PO9: Hav 3D 20
Hurst Cl. PO14: Stub 4C 36
Hurst Grn. PO13: Gos 3B 38
Hurst Grn. Cl. PO8: Cowp 5B 10
Hurstville Dr. PO7: W'lle 3H 19
(not continuous)
Hurstwood Av. PO10: S'urne 2H 35
Hussar Ct. PO7: W'lle 6E 9
Hutfield Ct. PO12: Gos 2D 48
(off Lees La.)
Hyde Pk. Ho. PO5: S'sea 4G 5 (3C 50)
Hyde Pk. Rd. PO5: S'sea 4G 5 (3C 50)
Hyde St. PO5: S'sea 6F 5 (4C 50)
Hylton Rd. GU32: Pet 4D 56
Hythe Rd. PO6: Cosh 2A 30

I

Ian Gibson Ct. PO5: S'sea 3H 5
Ibsley Gro. PO9: Bed 6D 20
Icarus Pl. PO7: Purb 1H 31
Idsworth Cl. PO8: Horn 1D 10
Idsworth Down GU31: Pet 4E 57
Idsworth Ho. PO1: Ports 1G 5
Idsworth Rd. PO3: Ports 5C 42
PO8: Cowp 5B 10
Iford Ct. PO9: Hav 3H 21
Ilex Wlk. PO11: H Isl 4E 55
Illustrious Rd. PO14: Stub 4D 36
Implacable Rd. PO13: Lee S 6F 37
Ingledene Cl. PO9: Bed 1D 32
PO12: Gos 3D 48
Ingleside Cl. PO14: Fare 3D 24
Inglis Rd. PO5: S'sea 4E 51
Inhams La. PO7: Den 3A 8
Inhurst Av. PO7: W'lle 6A 10
Inhurst Rd. PO2: Ports 3A 42
Inkpen Wlk. PO9: Hav 2D 20
Inmans La. GU32: Pet 2F 57
Invergordon Av. PO6: Cosh 4D 30
Inverkip Cl. PO13: Lee S 6G 37
Inverness Av. PO15: Fare 6G 13
Inverness Rd. PO1: Ports 6A 42
PO12: Gos 1C 48
Invincible Rd. PO14: Stub 4D 36
Iping Av. PO9: Hav 4E 21
Ireland Way PO7: W'lle 4G 19
Ironbridge La. PO4: S'sea 3A 52
Iron Mill Cl. PO15: Fare 6F 13
Ironmill La. PO15: Titch 4D 12
Irvine Cl. PO16: Fare 6A 14
Irwin Hgts. PO12: Gos 5G 39
Isambard Brunel Rd. PO1: Ports . . .3F 5 (2C 50)
Island Cl. PO11: H Isl 2C 44
Island Vw. Ter. PO2: Ports 4G 41
Island Vw. Wlk. PO16: Portc 2A 28
Islay Gdns. PO6: Cosh 2B 30
Isle of Wight Ferry Terminal (Vehicular) . . .5B 4
Isle of Wight Hovercraft Terminal 5A 50
Itchen Cl. GU31: Pet 5C 56
Itchen Ct. PO8: Cowp 3H 9
Itchenor Rd. PO11: H Isl 5H 55
Itchen Rd. PO9: Hav 3H 21
Ithica Cl. PO11: H Isl 3C 54
Ivy Ct. PO7: Purb 5F 19
Ivydene Gdns. PO8: Cowp 3A 10
Ivy Ho. PO12: Gos 3E 49
Ivy La. PO1: Ports 1B 4 (1A 50)
Ivy Orchard PO8: Clan 1F 7

J

Jacana Ct. PO12: Gos 2F 49
Jacaranda Cl. PO15: Seg 5E 13
Jack Cockerill Way PO5: S'sea 6D 50

Jackdaw Cl. PO8: Cowp 3G 9
Jackson Cl. PO6: Farl 5E 31
Jacobs Cl. PO8: Clan 2G 7
Jacobs Ct. PO9: Hav 2E 33
Jacob's St. PO1: Ports 1G 5 (1C 50)
Jacomb Pl. PO13: Gos 3D 38
Jacqueline Av. PO7: Purb 5F 19
Jade Ct. PO7: W'lle 1G 19
PO13: Gos 1G 47
Jago Rd. PO1: Ports 1A 4 (1H 49)
Jamaica Pl. PO12: Gos 3E 49
Jamaica Rd. PO12: Gos 2F 49
James Butcher Ct. PO5: S'sea 6D 50
(off Eastern Villas Rd.)
James Callaghan Dr. PO6: Cosh 1D 28
PO17: S'wick 1D 28
James Cl. PO11: H Isl 3A 54
PO13: Gos 1C 38
James Copse Rd. PO8: Love 2H 9
James Howell Ct. PO7: Den 3B 8
James Rd. PO9: Bed 1E 33
PO13: Gos 1C 38
James Watson Hall PO1: Ports 3E 5
Japonica Way PO9: Hav 6A 22
Jarndyce Wlk. PO2: Ports 6H 41
Jasmine Ct. PO13: Gos 1G 47
Jasmine Gro. PO7: W'lle 3A 20
Jasmine Wlk. PO14: Fare 3G 25
Jasmine Way PO8: Clan 2G 7
Jasmond Rd. PO6: Cosh 5B 30
Jason Pl. PO7: Horn 1G 31
Jason Way PO12: Gos 5F 39
Jay Cl. PO8: Horn 6A 6
PO14: Stub 6D 24
Jellicoe Av. PO12: Gos 5B 48
Jellicoe Ho. PO1: Ports 1H 5
Jellicoe Way PO2: Ports 4F 41
Jenkins Gro. PO3: Ports 6D 42
Jenner Rd. PO6: Cosh 2B 30
Jerram Cl. PO12: Gos 4B 48
Jersey Cl. PO14: Stub 4F 37
Jersey Rd. PO2: Ports 5A 42
Jervis Dr. PO12: Gos 1D 48
Jervis Rd. PO2: Ports 3G 41
Jessica Cl. PO7: W'lle 6B 10
Jessie Rd. PO4: S'sea 3E 51
PO9: Bed .6C 20
PO12: Gos 3C 48
Jodrell Cl. PO8: Horn 6C 6
John Marshall Ct. PO2: Ports 5H 41
Johnson Vw. PO15: White 3A 12
Johns Rd. PO16: Fare 4B 26
Jolliffe Ct. GU32: Pet 4D 56
(off Hylton Rd.)
Jonathan Rd. PO15: Fare 2G 25
Joseph Nye Ct. PO1: Ports 3C 4
Joseph St. PO12: Gos 3E 49
Joslin Cl. PO12: Gos 1F 49
Jubilee Av. PO6: Cosh 2C 28
Jubilee Ct. PO14: Fare 4A 26
Jubilee Ho. PO10: Ems 2C 34
Jubilee M. PO10: S'urne 3G 35
Jubilee Path PO9: Bed 2D 32
Jubilee Rd. PO4: S'sea 4F 51
PO7: W'lle 6F 9
PO12: Gos 2D 48
PO16: Portc 3B 28
Jubilee Ter. PO5: S'sea 6E 5 (4B 50)
Julie Av. PO15: Fare 2G 25
Juliet Ct. PO7: W'lle 1A 20
Juniper Rd. PO8: Horn 4C 6
Juniper Sq. PO9: Hav 3F 33
Jupiter Cl. PO1: Ports 4B 4 (3A 50)
Jura Cl. PO6: Cosh 2C 30
Justin Cl. PO14: Fare 3G 25
Jute Cl. PO16: Portc 2H 27
Juventu Cl. PO9: Hav 5G 21

K

Karen Av. PO6: Dray 5E 31
Kassassin St. PO4: S'sea 5G 51
Kassel Cl. PO7: W'lle 1B 20
Katrina Gdns. PO11: H Isl 2C 54
Kealy Rd. PO12: Gos 1C 48
Kearsney Av. PO2: Ports 2A 42
Keast Wlk. PO13: Gos 1D 38
Keats Av. PO6: Cosh 2C 28
Keats Cl. PO8: Cowp 3H 9

Keats Ho. PO9: Hav 5E 21
Keelan Ct. PO5: S'sea 5D 50
Keel Cl. PO3: Ports 2E 43
PO13: Gos 6D 38
Keep, The PO16: Portc 3B 28
Kefford Ct. PO8: Horn 1B 10
Keith Cl. PO12: Gos 1D 48
Keith Ho. PO1: Ports 2C 4
Kelly Ct. PO4: S'sea 4E 51
PO16: Fare 1B 26
Kelly Rd. PO7: W'lle 4G 19
Kelsey Av. PO10: S'urne 2H 35
Kelsey Head PO6: P Sol 4E 29
Kelvin Gro. PO16: Portc 3B 28
Kempenfelt Ho. PO1: Ports 2C 4
Kempton Pk. PO7: W'lle 6B 10
Kemshott Ct. PO9: Hav 3D 20
Ken Berry Ct. PO9: Hav 3H 21
Kench, The PO11: H Isl 3D 52
Kenchester Cl. PO6: Cosh 3G 29
Kendal Av. PO3: Ports 4C 42
Kendal Cl. PO8: Cowp 3A 10
Kenilworth Cl. PO13: Lee S 6H 37
Kenilworth Rd. PO5: S'sea 6D 50
Kennedy Av. PO15: Fare 6G 13
Kennedy Cl. PO7: Purb 5F 19
Kennedy Cres. PO12: Gos 5A 48
Kennet Cl. PO12: Gos 6D 48
Kennet Rd. GU31: Pet 5C 56
Kensington Ho. PO11: H Isl 3A 54
Kensington Rd. PO2: Ports 3B 42
PO12: Gos 4E 49
Kent Gro. PO16: Portc 5A 28
Kentidge Rd. PO7: Purb 4F 19
Kent Rd. PO5: S'sea 4B 50
PO13: Gos 1B 38
Kent St. PO1: Ports 3C 4 (2A 50)
Kenwood Bus. Pk. PO9: Hav 1G 33
Kenwood Rd. PO16: Portc 5B 28
Kenya Rd. PO16: Portc 4H 27
Kenyon Rd. PO2: Ports 3B 42
Kestrel Cl. PO8: Clan 1C 6
PO14: Stub 1D 36
Kestrel Pl. PO6: Farl 4H 31
Kestrel Rd. PO3: Ports 1C 42
Keswick Av. PO3: Ports 5C 42
Kettering Ter. PO2: Ports 5G 41
Keydell Av. PO8: Horn 2A 10
Keydell Cl. PO8: Horn 2A 10
Keyes Cl. PO13: Gos 2C 38
Keyes Ct. PO5: S'sea 5D 50
(off Albert Rd.)
Keyhaven Cl. PO13: Gos 2C 38
Keyhaven Dr. PO9: Hav 3A 38
Khandala Gdns. PO7: Purb 4C 20
Kidmore La. PO7: Den 5H 19
Kielder Gro. PO13: Gos 1B 8
Kilbride Path PO2: Ports 3D 38
Kilderkin Dr. PO8: Horn 5H 41
Kilmeston Cl. PO9: Hav 6D 6
Kilmiston Cl. PO1: Ports 3F 21
Kilmiston Dr. PO16: Portc 6A 42
Kiln Acre Ind. Site 2H 27
PO16: Fare 6B 14
Kiln Rd. PO3: Ports 4C 42
PO16: Fare 5H 13
Kilnside PO7: Den 4B 8
Kilpatrick Cl. PO2: Ports 5H 41
Kilwich Way PO16: Portc 5H 27
Kimberley Rd. PO4: S'sea 5G 51
Kimbers GU32: Pet 3C 56
Kimbolton Rd. PO3: Ports 1G 51
Kimbridge Cres. PO9: Hav 3G 21
Kimpton Cl. PO13: Lee S 1D 46
Kimpton Ct. PO9: Hav 3H 21
King Albert Ct. PO1: Ports 1E 51
King Albert St. PO1: Ports 1D 50
King Arthurs Ct. PO6: Dray 3F 31
King Charles St. PO1: Ports 5B 4 (3A 50)
Kingcome Ho. PO1: Ports 1D 50
(off Staunton St.)
King Edward's Cres. PO2: Ports 3H 41
Kingfisher Cvn. Pk. PO13: Lee S 4G 47
Kingfisher Cl. PO8: Cowp 3G 9
PO9: R Cas 6H 11
PO11: H Isl 5E 55
Kingfisher Ct. PO3: Ports 1C 42
PO9: Hav .6H 21
Kingfisher Dr. PO10: Westb 5F 23
Kingfishers PO16: Portc 3F 27

King George Av.—Lester Av.

King George Av. GU32: Pet 3D 56
King George M. *GU32: Pet* *3D 56*
(off King George Av.)
King George Rd. PO16: Portc 4A 28
King Henry I St. PO1: Ports 3E 5 (2B 50)
King James's Gate 4D 4
King James Ter. PO1: Ports 6B 4
King John Av. PO16: Portc 4H 27
King Richard I Rd. PO1: Ports 3E 5 (2B 50)
King Richard Cl. PO6: Cosh 3H 29
Kings Bench All. PO1: Ports 2C 4 (2A 50)
Kingsbury Ct. PO8: Clan 1F 7
Kingsclere Av. PO9: Hav 3D 20
Kings Cl. PO9: R Cas 5G 11
Kingscote Ho. PO6: Cosh 1D 28
Kingscote Rd. PO6: Cosh 1D 28
PO8: Cowp 4F 9
Kingscroft Ct. PO9: Hav 2D 32
Kings Cft. La. PO9: Bed 2C 32
Kingsdown Pl. PO1: Ports 2E 51
Kingsdown Rd. PO7: W'lle 5E 9
Kingsey Av. PO10: Ems 3C 34
Kingsfernsden La. GU32: Pet 2E 57
Kingsland Cl. PO6: Cosh 2G 29
Kingsley Grn. PO9: Hav 3E 21
Kingsley Ho. PO10: Ems 3C 34
Kingsley Rd. PO4: S'sea 4H 51
PO12: Gos 6F 39
Kingsmead Av. PO14: Stub 4F 37
Kings Mede PO8: Horn 2A 10
Kings M. PO5: S'sea 5D 50
Kingsmill Cl. PO12: Gos 4B 48
Kings Rd. GU32: Pet 3B 56
PO5: S'sea 6E 5 (4B 50)
PO8: Cowp 4H 9
PO10: Ems 3C 34
PO11: H Isl 1C 54
PO12: Gos 3D 48
PO13: Lee S 6G 37
PO16: Fare 2B 26
King's Ter. PO5: S'sea 6E 5 (4B 50)
PO10: Ems 3D 34
King's Theatre 5D 50
KINGSTON 1F 51
Kingston Cres. PO2: Ports 5H 41
Kingston Gdns. PO15: Fare 5F 13
Kingston Rd. PO1: Ports 5H 41
PO2: Ports 5H 41
PO12: Gos 2B 48
King St. PO5: S'sea 5E 5 (3B 50)
(not continuous)
PO10: Ems 3E 35
PO10: Westb 6F 23
PO12: Gos 2F 49
Kings Way PO9: R Cas 6G 11
Kingsway PO11: H Isl 2C 44
Kingsway, The PO16: Portc 3A 28
Kingswell Path PO1: Ports 1F 5 (1C 50)
Kingswell St. PO1: Ports 2F 5 (2C 50)
Kingswood Pl. PO17: K Vil 2G 13
Kingsworthy Rd. PO9: Hav 6F 21
King William St. PO1: Ports 1C 4 (1A 50)
Kinnell Cl. PO10: Ems 3D 34
Kinross Cres. PO6: Cosh 4D 30
Kintyre Rd. PO6: Cosh 2B 30
Kipling Rd. PO2: Ports 2A 42
Kirby Ct. PO2: Ports 3A 42
Kirby Rd. PO2: Ports 3A 42
Kirkstall Rd. PO4: S'sea 6E 51
Kirpal Rd. PO3: Ports 1H 51
Kirtley Cl. PO6: Dray 5E 31
Kirton Rd. PO6: Dray 4E 31
Kite Cl. PO8: Cowp 3G 9
Kite's Cft. Bus. Pk. PO14: Titch 2A 24
Kittiwake Cl. PO13: Gos 3B 38
Kitwood Grn. PO9: Hav 4H 21
Kneller Ct. PO16: Fare 5H 13
PO17: Fare 5H 13
Knight Gdns. PO6: Farl 4G 31
Knighton Cnr. PO8: Horn 6C 6
Knights Bank Rd. PO14: Stub 4B 36
Knightstone Ct. PO2: Ports 1B 42
Knightwood Av. PO9: Hav 4G 21
Knollys Ho. PO1: Ports 1E 51
Knowle Av. PO17: K Vil 2F 13
Knowle Rd. PO17: Fare 2H 13
KNOWLE VILLAGE 2G 13
Knowle Village Bus. Pk.
PO17: K Vil 1F 13
Knowsley Cres. PO6: Cosh 4C 30
Knowsley Rd. PO6: Cosh 4B 30
Knox Rd. PO2: Ports 4G 41
PO9: Hav 2D 32
Kynon Cl. PO12: Gos 5A 40
Kyoto Wlk. PO9: Hav 6G 21

L

Laburnum Av. PO6: Dray 4E 31
Laburnum Gro. PO2: Ports 4A 42
PO11: H Isl 3D 54
Laburnum Path PO6: Dray 3E 31
Laburnum Rd. PO7: W'lle 3F 19
PO16: Fare 4B 26
Ladram Rd. PO12: Gos 3A 48
Lady Betty's Dr. PO15: White 3A 12
Ladybridge Rd. PO7: Purb 5E 19
Ladywood Ho. PO5: S'sea 4G 5 (3C 50)
LA Fitness
Fareham *2B 26*
(off Market Quay)
Lake Rd. PO1: Ports 1G 5 (1C 50)
Lakeside PO13: Lee S 3D 46
PO17: Fun 4G 13
Lakeside Av. PO3: Ports 6D 42
Lakeside Ct. PO4: S'sea 5F 51
Lakeside Gdns. PO9: Hav 1G 33
Lakeside Holiday Village PO11: H Isl 5F 55
Lakesmere Rd. PO8: Horn 1C 10
Lambert Cl. PO7: W'lle 4G 19
Lambourn Cl. PO14: Fare 3F 25
Lampeter Av. PO6: Dray 3D 30
Lancaster Cl. PO13: Lee S 3F 47
PO16: Portc 2H 27
Lancaster Way PO7: W'lle 3H 19
Landguard Rd. PO4: S'sea 4G 51
Landon Ct. PO12: Gos 5C 48
Landon Rd. PO13: Gos 5D 38
LANDPORT 1D 50
Landport Gate 5C 4
Landport St. PO1: Ports 5E 5 (3B 50)
(Crasswell St.)
PO1: Ports 1H 5 (1D 50)
(Landport Ter.)
PO5: S'sea 5E 5 (3B 50)
Landport Ter. PO1: Ports 5E 5 (3B 50)
Landport Vw. PO1: Ports 1G 5 (1C 50)
Lane, The PO4: S'sea 5F 51
PO12: Gos 6C 48
Lane End Dr. PO10: Ems 3D 34
Lanes End PO14: Stub 3E 37
Langbrook Cl. PO9: Lang 3F 33
Langdale Av. PO6: Cosh 4D 30
Langford Ct. *PO16: Fare* *2B 26*
(off Queens Rd.)
Langford Rd. PO1: Ports 6B 42
Langley Rd. PO2: Ports 5A 42
Langrish Cl. PO9: Hav 3G 21
LANGSTONE 4F 33
Langstone Av. PO9: Lang 4F 33
Langstone Bri. PO9: Lang 6G 33
PO11: H Isl 6G 33
Langstone High St. PO9: Lang 5F 33
Langstone Ho. PO9: Hav 6G 21
PO16: Fare 4A 26
Langstone Marina Hgts. PO4: S'sea 4B 52
Langstone Rd. PO3: Ports 1G 51
PO9: Lang 3F 33
Langstone Sailing Club 5F 33
Langstone Technology Pk. PO9: Lang 3E 33
Langstone Wlk. PO13: Gos 3B 38
PO14: Fare 3F 25
Langstone Way PO4: S'sea 2H 51
Langton Cl. PO13: Lee S 1E 47
Langton Farm Gdns. PO1: Ports 6A 42
Lansdowne Av. PO7: Wid 6D 18
PO16: Portc 5B 28
Lansdowne Ho. PO12: Gos 1C 48
Lansdowne St. PO5: S'sea 5E 5 (3B 50)
Lansdown Ter. PO10: Westb 4F 23
Lantana Cl. PO7: W'lle 3H 19
Lanyard Dr. PO13: Gos 1H 47
Lapthorn Cl. PO13: Gos 1B 38
Lapwing Cl. PO8: Horn 6B 6
PO12: Gos 6H 39
Lapwing Gro. PO16: Portc 3F 27
Lapwing Rd. PO4: S'sea 2A 52
Larch Cl. PO13: Lee S 2E 47
Larch Ct. PO1: Ports 1D 50
Larches Gdns. PO15: Fare 2E 25
Larchfield Way PO8: Horn 2C 10
Larchwood Av. PO9: Bed 5B 20
Larcombe Rd. GU32: Pet 5B 56
Larkhill Rd. PO3: Ports 1B 42
Lark Way PO10: Westb 5F 23
Larkwhistle Wlk. PO9: Hav 2C 20
Lasham Grn. *PO9: Hav* *4H 21*
(off Newnham Ct.)
Lasham Wlk. PO14: Fare 3F 25
Latchmore Forest Gro. PO8: Cowp 4A 10
Latchmore Gdns. PO8: Cowp 4G 9
Latimer Ct. PO3: Ports 1D 42
Lauder Cl. PO10: S'urne 1H 35
Launceston Cl. PO12: Gos 6A 40
Laurel Cl. PO12: Gos 6A 40
Laurel Rd. PO8: Horn 3C 10
Laurence Grn. PO10: Ems 5D 22
Lauren M. *PO11: H Isl* *5A 54*
(off Sea Front)
Laurus Cl. PO7: W'lle 4A 20
Laurus Wlk. PO13: Lee S 1D 46
Lavant Cl. PO8: Cowp 6B 10
Lavant Ct. GU32: Pet 3C 56
Lavant Dr. PO9: Hav 6F 21
Lavant St. GU32: Pet 3C 56
Lavender Ct. PO15: White 1A 12
Lavender Rd. PO7: W'lle 3A 20
Laverock Lea PO16: Portc 2A 28
Lavey's La. PO15: Fun 3C 12
Lavinia Rd. PO12: Gos 2D 48
Lawn Cl. PO13: Gos 5D 38
(not continuous)
Lawnswood Cl. PO8: Cowp 5H 9
Lawrence Av. PO8: Cowp 5G 9
Lawrence Mans. PO5: S'sea 4E 51
Lawrence Rd. PO5: S'sea 4E 51
PO15: Fare 1H 25
Lawrence Sq. *PO12: Gos* *3F 49*
(off Walpole Rd.)
Lawrence Wlk. PO13: Gos 1H 47
Lawson Rd. PO5: S'sea 3E 51
Layton Rd. PO13: Gos 2C 38
Lazy Acre PO10: S'urne 3H 35
Leafy La. PO15: White 3A 12
Lealand Gro. PO6: Dray 3F 31
Lealand Rd. PO6: Dray 4F 31
Leamington Cres. PO13: Lee S 6H 37
Leamington Ho. PO5: S'sea 4F 5 (3C 50)
Leander Dr. PO12: Gos 6A 40
Lea-Oak Gdns. PO15: Fare 6F 13
Lear Rd. PO12: Gos 2D 48
Leaway, The PO16: Portc 3B 28
Lechlade Gdns. PO15: Fare 5G 13
Leckford Cl. PO16: Portc 1A 28
Leckford Rd. PO9: Hav 3G 21
Ledbury Rd. PO6: Cosh 2G 29
Lederle La. PO13: Gos 6C 26
Ledwell Ct. PO12: Gos 1F 49
LEE GROUND 4B 12
LEE-ON-THE-SOLENT 1C 46
Lee-on-the-Solent Sailing Club 3D 46
Leep La. PO12: Gos 5D 48
Lee Rd. PO12: Gos 1C 48
Leesland Rd. PO12: Gos 2C 48
Lees La. PO12: Gos 2D 48
Lees La. Nth. PO12: Gos 2D 48
Legion Rd. PO11: H Isl 3C 54
Leicester Ct. PO13: Gos 2H 47
LEIGH PARK 3E 21
Leigh Pk. Gdns. 3G 21
Leigh Pk. Shop. Cen. *PO9: Hav* *4F 21*
(off Greywell Sq.)
Leigh Rd. PO9: Hav 1F 33
PO16: Fare 1A 26
Leisure, The PO13: Gos 1D 38
Leith Av. PO16: Portc 2B 28
Lendorber Av. PO6: Cosh 3C 30
Lennox Cl. PO12: Gos 6E 49
Lennox Ct. *PO5: S'sea* *5D 50*
(off Lennox Rd. Nth.)
Lennox Rd. Nth. PO5: S'sea 5D 50
Lennox Rd. Sth. PO5: S'sea 5D 50
Lennox Row PO1: Ports 1C 4 (1A 50)
Lensyd Gdns. PO8: Love 1H 9
Leofric Ct. PO4: S'sea 4A 52
Leominster Ho. PO6: Cosh 2F 29
Leominster Rd. PO6: Cosh 2F 29
Leonard Rd. PO12: Gos 2E 49
Leopold St. PO4: S'sea 5E 51
Lerryn Rd. PO13: Gos 3D 38
Lesser Horseshoe Cl. PO17: K Vil 1G 13
Lester Av. PO9: Bed 1C 32

Lester Rd.—Magister Dr.

Lester Rd. PO12: Gos 2B **48**
Letcombe Pl. PO8: Horn 1D **10**
Leventhorpe Ct. PO12: Gos 3E **49**
Leveret Cl. PO12: Gos 5A **40**
Leveson Cl. PO12: Gos 4B **48**
Leviathan Cl. PO14: Stub 3F **37**
Lewis Rd. PO10: Ems 6E **23**
Lexden Gdns. PO11: H Isl 3A **54**
Leyland Cl. PO12: Gos 4D **48**
Liam Cl. PO9: Hav .5G **21**
Liberty, The PO7: Den 4A **8**
Library Gdns. PO9: Hav 6E **21**
Lichfield Ct. *PO13: Gos* *2H 47*
(off Gazelle Cl.)
Lichfield Dr. PO12: Gos 6A **40**
Lichfield Rd. PO3: Ports 1G **51**
Liddiards Way PO7: Purb 6G **19**
Lidiard Gdns. PO4: S'sea 5H **51**
Lightfoot Lawn PO4: S'sea 4A **52**
Lilac Cl. PO9: Hav .6A **22**
Lily Av. PO7: Wid 1D **30**
Limberline Rd. PO3: Ports 1C **42**
Limberline Spur PO3: Ports 6C **30**
Lime Gro. PO6: Cosh 2F **29**
PO11: H Isl .3G **53**
Limes, The PO9: Lang 3F **33**
PO13: Gos 4D **38**
Lincoln Ct. PO13: Gos 2H **47**
Lincoln Ri. PO8: Cowp 3A **10**
Lincoln Rd. PO1: Ports 2E **51**
Linda Gro. PO8: Cowp 4H **9**
Lindbergh Cl. PO13: Gos 2H **47**
Lindbergh Ri. PO15: White 3A **12**
Lind Cl. PO7: Purb .6H **19**
Linden Gro. PO11: H Isl 4C **54**
PO12: Gos 4D **48**
Linden Lea PO16: Portc 2H **27**
Lindens Cl. PO10: Ems 1D **34**
Linden Way PO8: Horn 2C **10**
PO9: Hav 6F **21**
Lindisfarne Cl. PO6: Cosh 3C **30**
Lindley Av. PO4: S'sea 5G **51**
Lindon Ct. PO4: S'sea 3F **51**
Lind Rd. PO12: Gos 6E **49**
Lindsey Ho. *PO5: S'sea* *5D 50*
(off Richmond Rd.)
Linford Ct. PO9: Hav 2D **20**
Lingfield Ct. PO1: Ports 6D **4** (4B **50**)
Link, The PO7: W'lle 6A **10**
Linkenholt Way PO9: Hav 4C **20**
Linklater Path PO1: Ports 6H **41**
Linklater Rd. PO1: Ports 6H **41**
Link Rd. PO17: S'wick 1F **29**
Links, The PO13: Gos 4C **38**
Links Cl. PO9: R Cas 6H **11**
Links La. PO9: R Cas 5H **11**
PO11: H Isl 4G **53**
Link Way PO14: Stub 4E **37**
Linnet Cl. GU31: Pet 5G **57**
PO8: Cowp 3G **9**
Linnet Ct. PO12: Gos 1B **48**
Linnets, The PO16: Portc 3F **27**
Lion Brewery, The PO2: Ports 5H **41**
Lion Rd. PO1: Ports 6D **40**
Lion St. PO1: Ports 2D **4** (2B **50**)
Lion Ter. PO1: Ports 3D **4** (2B **50**)
(not continuous)
Liphook Ho. PO9: Hav 4H **21**
Lisle Way PO10: Ems 6C **22**
Liss Rd. PO4: S'sea 3F **51**
Lister Rd. PO6: Cosh 3B **30**
Lith Av. PO8: Horn .5C **6**
Lith Cres. PO8: Horn 4C **6**
Lith La. PO8: Cath .5A **6**
PO8: Horn 4B **6**
Little Anglesey PO12: Gos 5D **48**
Lit. Anglesey Rd. PO12: Gos 5C **48**
Lit. Arthur St. PO2: Ports 6A **42**
Little Cl. PO13: Gos 1C **38**
Lit. Coburg St. PO1: Ports 2D **50**
Little Cnr. PO7: Den 4B **8**
Little Gays PO14: Stub 3C **36**
Lit. George St. PO1: Ports 6A **42**
Little Green PO12: Gos 5C **48**
Littlegreen Av. PO9: Hav 5G **21**
Lit. Grn. Orchard PO12: Gos 4C **48**
Lit. Hambrook St. PO5: S'sea 6E **5** (4B **50**)
Lit. Hyden La. PO8: Clan 1F **7**
Little La. PO12: Gos 5C **48**
Little Mead PO7: Den 4C **8**
Littlepark Av. PO9: Bed 6B **20**
Littlepark Ho. PO9: Bed 6B **20**
LITTLE POSBROOK 6B **24**
Lit. Southsea St. PO5: S'sea 6E **5** (4B **50**)
Littleton Gro. PO9: Hav 5F **21**
Lit. Woodham La. PO13: Gos 2G **47**
Liverpool Ct. PO13: Gos 2H **47**
Liverpool Rd. PO1: Ports 2E **51**
PO14: Fare 5H **25**
Livesay Gdns. PO3: Ports 1F **51**
Livingstone Ct. PO13: Gos 1H **47**
Livingstone Rd. PO5: S'sea 4D **50**
Livingwell Fitness Club
Farlington .5F **31**
Lobelia Ct. PO7: W'lle 3A **20**
Locarno Rd. PO3: Ports 3C **42**
Lock App. PO6: P Sol 4E **29**
Lockerley Rd. PO9: Hav 6G **21**
LOCKS HEATH .5A **12**
Locksheath Cl. PO9: Hav 3D **20**
Locks Sailing Club 3B **52**
Locksway Rd. PO4: S'sea 3H **51**
Lock Vw. PO6: P Sol 4E **29**
Lodge, The PO7: W'lle 3A **20**
Lodge Av. PO6: Cosh 3C **30**
Lodgebury Cl. PO10: S'urne 3H **35**
Lodge Gdns. PO12: Gos 4C **48**
Lodge Rd. PO9: Bed 2B **32**
Lodsworth Cl. PO8: Clan 1D **6**
Lodsworth Ho. PO1: Ports 1D **50**
Lombard Ct. PO1: Ports 6C **4**
Lombard St. PO1: Ports 6B **4** (4A **50**)
Lombardy Cl. PO13: Gos 3E **39**
Lombardy Ri. PO7: W'lle 4H **19**
Lomond Cl. PO2: Ports 5H **41**
Londesborough Rd. PO4: S'sea 4E **51**
London Av. PO2: Ports 3H **41**
London Mall PO2: Ports 3A **42**
London Rd. GU31: Pet 2F **57**
PO2: Ports 6A **30**
PO6: Cosh 3B **30**
PO7: Cowp, Purb, W'lle 3E **19**
PO7: Wid 1D **30**
PO8: Clan, Horn . . . . .4D **6** & 2H **7**
(not continuous)
PO8: Cowp 4A **10**
Lone Valley PO7: Wid 6E **19**
Long Acre Ct. PO1: Ports 6A **42**
Longbridge Ho. PO5: S'sea 4E **5**
Long Copse Ct. PO10: Ems 5D **22**
Long Copse La. PO10: Ems, Westb 5D **22**
Longcroft PO9: Hav 2E **33**
Long Curtain Rd. PO5: S'sea 5A **50**
Longdean Cl. PO6: Cosh 2E **29**
Longdon Dr. PO13: Lee S 6H **37**
Long Down GU31: Pet 3F **57**
Long Dr. PO13: Gos 4C **38**
Longfield Av. PO14: Fare 4F **25**
Longfield Cl. PO4: S'sea 2A **52**
Longfield Rd. PO10: Ems 6C **22**
Longlands Rd. PO10: S'urne 3H **35**
Longmead Ct. PO9: Lang 4F **33**
Longmead Gdns. PO9: Lang 4F **33**
Longmynd Dr. PO14: Fare 3F **25**
Long Rd. GU32: Pet 2E **57**
Longshore Way PO4: S'sea 3B **52**
Longs La. PO14: Stub 2F **37**
Longstaff Gdns. PO16: Fare 6H **13**
Longstock Rd. PO9: Hav 3H **21**
Longs Wlk. PO1: Ports 6H **41**
Long Water Dr. PO12: Gos 6E **49**
Longwood Av. PO8: Cowp 4H **9**
Lonsdale Av. PO6: Cosh 4C **30**
PO16: Portc .5B **28**
Lordington Cl. PO6: Dray 3D **30**
Lord Montgomery Way
PO1: Ports 4E **5** (3B **50**)
Lords Ct. PO1: Ports 1D **50**
Lord's St. PO1: Ports 1H **5** (1D **50**)
Loring Ho. PO2: Ports 1A **42**
Lorne Rd. PO5: S'sea 4E **51**
Louis Flagg Ho. PO5: S'sea 5G **5** (3C **50**)
Lovage Way PO8: Horn 4C **6**
Lovatt Gro. PO15: Fare 6F **13**
LOVEDEAN 1G **9**
Lovedean La. PO8: Cath, Love . . . . . .4A **6** & 1G **9**
PO8: Cowp 2H **9**
Love La. GU31: Pet 3E **57**
Lovett Rd. PO3: Ports 2B **42**
Lowcay Rd. PO5: S'sea 5E **51**
Lower Bellfield PO14: Titch 4B **24**
Lwr. Bere Wood PO7: W'lle 2H **19**
Lwr. Brookfield Rd. PO1: Ports 1E **51**
Lwr. Church Path PO1: Ports 2G **5** (2C **50**)
Lwr. Derby Rd. PO2: Ports 4G **41**
Lwr. Drayton La. PO6: Dray 4E **31**
(not continuous)
Lwr. Farlington Rd. PO6: Farl 3G **31**
Lwr. Farm Dr. PO6: Cosh 4A **30**
Lwr. Forbury Rd. PO5: S'sea 4H **5** (3D **50**)
Lower Gro. Rd. PO9: Hav 2G **33**
Lower Heyshott GU31: Pet 4E **57**
Lower Mead GU31: Pet 4F **57**
Lower Quay PO16: Fare 3B **26**
Lwr. Quay Cl. PO16: Fare 3B **26**
Lwr. Quay Rd. PO16: Fare 3B **26**
Lower Rd. PO9: Bed 2B **32**
Lwr. Tye Cvn. & Camping Cen.
PO11: H Isl 4D **44**
Lower Wardown GU31: Pet 3F **57**
(not continuous)
Lwr. Wingfield St. PO1: Ports 1D **50**
Lowestoft Rd. PO6: Cosh 2H **29**
Lowland Rd. PO7: Den 3A **8**
Loxwood Rd. PO8: Love 1H **9**
Luard Ct. PO9: Warb 2H **33**
Lucerne Av. PO7: W'lle 5E **9**
Lucknow St. PO1: Ports 2E **51**
Lucky Tree Farm Cvn. Pk. PO8: Cath 5A **6**
Ludcombe PO7: Den 2B **8**
Ludlow Rd. PO6: Cosh 2F **29**
Lugano Cl. PO7: W'lle 5F **9**
Luker Dr. GU31: Pet 2E **57**
Lulworth Cl. PO11: H Isl 2C **54**
Lulworth Rd. PO13: Lee S 2C **46**
LUMLEY 2E **35**
Lumley Gdns. PO10: S'urne 3E **35**
Lumley Path PO10: Ems 2E **35**
Lumley Rd. PO10: S'urne 2E **35**
Lumley Ter. PO10: Ems 2E **35**
PO10: S'urne 2E **35**
Lumsden Rd. PO4: S'sea 4B **52**
Lundy Wlk. PO14: Stub 2D **36**
Lutman St. PO10: Ems 5C **22**
Luxor Pk. PO9: Hav 4E **33**
Lychgate Dr. PO8: Horn 5B **6**
Lychgate Grn. PO14: Stub 6E **25**
Lydden Ct. PO13: Gos 3D **38**
Lydney Cl. PO6: Cosh 3G **29**
LYE HEATH 3H **17**
Lymbourn Rd. PO9: Hav 2G **33**
Lynden Cl. PO14: Fare 3D **24**
Lynden Ct. PO11: H Isl 3A **54**
Lyndhurst Cl. PO11: H Isl 5C **54**
Lyndhurst Ho. PO9: Hav 3E **21**
Lyndhurst Rd. PO2: Ports 3B **42**
PO12: Gos 3C **48**
Lyndum Cl. GU32: Pet 3D **56**
Lyne Pl. PO8: Horn .1B **10**
Lynn Rd. PO2: Ports 5B **42**
Lynton Gdns. PO16: Fare 6H **13**
Lynton Ga. PO5: S'sea 5C **50**
Lynton Gro. PO3: Ports 5C **42**
Lynton Rd. GU32: Pet 3C **56**
Lynwood Av. PO8: Cowp 4F **9**
Lynx Ho. PO6: Cosh 5A **30**
Lysander Ct. PO1: Ports 4B **4** (3A **50**)
Lysander Way PO7: W'lle 1A **20**
Lysses Ct. PO16: Fare 2C **26**
Lysses Path PO16: Fare 2C **26**

M

Mabey Cl. PO12: Gos 5E **49**
Mablethorpe Rd. PO6: Cosh 2A **30**
Macaulay Av. PO6: Cosh 2D **28**
Madden Cl. PO12: Gos 4B **48**
Madeira Rd. PO2: Ports 2A **42**
Madeira Wlk. PO11: H Isl 4B **54**
Madeline Rd. GU31: Pet 3D **56**
Madison Cl. PO13: Gos 5E **39**
Madison Ct. PO16: Fare 2C **26**
Madocks Way PO8: Cowp 3G **9**
Mafeking Rd. PO4: S'sea 4F **51**
Magdala Rd. PO6: Cosh 4B **30**
PO11: H Isl 4A **54**
Magdalen Ct. PO2: Ports 2A **42**
Magdalen Rd. PO2: Ports 2H **41**
Magdalen Row GU32: Pet 4C **56**
Magennis Cl. PO13: Gos 6D **38**
Magenta Ct. PO13: Gos 1G **47**
Magister Dr. PO13: Lee S 2E **47**

Magnolia Cl. PO14: Fare 3G **25**
Magnolia Way PO8: Cowp 3C **10**
Magpie Cl. PO16: Portc 3E **27**
Magpie La. PO13: Lee S 6H **37**
Magpie Rd. PO8: Ids 2H **11**
Magpie Wlk. PO8: Cowp 3F **9**
PO8: Horn 3G **11**
Maidford Gro. PO3: Ports 1E **43**
Maidstone Cres. PO6: Cosh 2A **30**
Main Dr. PO17: S'wick 3E **17**
Main Rd. PO1: Ports 1A **4** (1H **49**)
PO10: S'urne .3E **35**
PO13: Gos 1D **38**
Mainsail Dr. PO16: Fare 3B **26**
Maisemore Gdns. PO10: Ems 3B **34**
Maitland St. PO1: Ports 6H **41**
Maizemore Wlk. PO13: Lee S 1D **46**
Malcolm Ho. PO2: Ports 1B **42**
Maldon Rd. PO6: Cosh 3H **29**
Malin Cl. PO14: Stub 2D **36**
Malins Rd. PO2: Ports 6H **41**
Mall, The PO2: Ports 4H **41**
Mallard Gdns. PO13: Gos 3B **38**
Mallard Rd. PO4: S'sea 2H **51**
PO9: R Cas 6H **11**
Mallards, The PO9: Lang 4F **33**
PO16: Fare 6A **14**
Mallard Way PO10: Westb 5G **23**
Mallory Cres. PO16: Fare 6A **14**
Mallow Cl. PO6: Cosh 3B **30**
PO7: W'lle 3H **19**
Malmesbury Lawn PO9: Hav 3C **20**
Maloney M. PO11: H Isl 6F **55**
Malta Rd. PO2: Ports 5A **42**
Malthouse La. PO16: Fare 2B **26**
Malthouse Rd. PO2: Ports 5H **41**
Maltings, The GU31: Pet 4D **56**
PO16: Fare 1D **26**
Malus Cl. PO14: Fare 4H **25**
Malvern Av. PO14: Fare 4G **25**
Malvern M. PO10: Ems 2D **34**
Malvern Rd. PO5: S'sea 6D **50**
PO12: Gos 2B **48**
Malwood Cl. PO9: Hav 3G **21**
Manchester Ct. PO13: Gos 2H **47**
Manchester Rd. PO1: Ports 2E **51**
Mancroft Av. PO14: Stub 3E **37**
Mandarin Way PO13: Gos 1G **47**
Manners La. PO4: S'sea 3E **51**
Manners Rd. PO4: S'sea 3E **51**
Manor Cl. PO9: Hav 2F **33**
PO17: Wick 2A **14**
Manor Ct. PO9: Hav 2E **33**
Manor Cres. PO6: Dray 4D **30**
Manor Gdns. PO10: S'urne 2G **35**
Mnr. Lodge Rd. PO9: R Cas 5G **11**
Manor M. PO6: Dray 3E **31**
Manor Pk. Av. PO3: Ports 5C **42**
Manor Rd. PO1: Ports 6A **42**
PO10: S'urne .2H **35**
PO11: H Isl 3A **54**
Manor Vs. PO17: Wick 2A **14**
Manor Way PO10: S'urne 2H **35**
PO11: H Isl 5C **54**
PO13: Lee S 1C **46**
Mansfield Rd. PO13: Gos 5C **38**
Mansion Ct. PO4: S'sea 6E **51**
Mansion Rd. PO4: S'sea 6E **51**
Mansvid Av. PO6: Cosh 4D **30**
Mantle Cl. PO13: Gos 6D **38**
Mantle Sq. PO2: Ports 3F **41**
Maple Cl. PO10: Ems 1D **34**
PO13: Lee S 2E **47**
PO15: Fare 2E **25**
Maple Cres. PO8: Clan 1G **7**
Maple Dr. PO7: Den 4C **8**
Maple Ho. PO9: Hav 1G **33**
Maple Rd. PO5: S'sea 5D **50**
Mapletree Av. PO8: Horn 2C **10**
Maple Wlk. GU31: Pet 6D **56**
Maple Wood PO9: Bed 2B **32**
Maralyn Av. PO7: W'lle 3G **19**
Marchesi Ct. PO14: Stub 1E **37**
Marchwood Ct. *PO12: Gos 4H 47*
(off Broadsands Dr.)
Marchwood Rd. PO9: Hav 3E **21**
Marden Way GU31: Pet 4E **57**
Margaret Cl. PO7: W'lle 6F **9**
Margaret Rule Hall PO1: Ports 3G **5**
Margarita Rd. PO15: Fare 1G **25**
Margate Rd. PO5: S'sea 5G **5** (3D **50**)
Margery's Ct. PO1: Ports 3C **4** (2A **50**)
Marie Ct. PO7: W'lle 1G **19**
Marigold Cl. PO15: Fare 1G **25**
Marina Bldgs. *PO12: Gos 3D 48*
(off Stoke Rd.)
Marina Cl. PO10: Ems 4E **35**
Marina Gro. PO3: Ports 6D **42**
PO16: Portc 4A **28**
Marina Keep PO6: P Sol 5E **29**
Marine Cotts. PO12: Gos 2D **48**
Marine Ct. PO4: S'sea 5G **51**
Marine Pde. E. PO13: Lee S 2C **46**
Marine Pde. W. PO13: Lee S 6F **37**
Mariners Wlk. PO4: S'sea 2H **51**
Mariners Way PO12: Gos 4F **49**
Marine Wlk. PO11: H Isl 4E **55**
Marion Rd. PO4: S'sea 6E **51**
Marjoram Cres. PO8: Cowp 4B **10**
Marjoram Way PO15: White 2A **12**
Mark Anthony Ct. PO11: H Isl 4A **54**
Mark Cl. PO3: Ports 1B **42**
Mark Ct. PO7: W'lle 1G **19**
Market Pde. PO9: Hav 2F **33**
Market Quay PO16: Fare 2B **26**
Market Way PO1: Ports 1F **5** (1C **50**)
Mark's Rd. PO14: Stub 3G **37**
Marks Tey Rd. PO14: Stub 6E **25**
Markway Cl. PO10: Ems 2B **34**
Marlands Lawn PO9: Hav 3C **20**
Marlborough Cl. PO7: W'lle 4F **19**
Marlborough Gro. PO16: Portc 4A **28**
Marlborough Pk. PO9: Hav 6H **21**
Marlborough Rd. PO12: Gos 1B **48**
Marlborough Row PO1: Ports 1B **4** (1A **50**)
Marldell Cl. PO9: Hav 4G **21**
Marles Cl. PO13: Gos 5D **38**
Marlin Cl. PO13: Gos 1H **47**
Marlow Cl. PO15: Fare 5G **13**
Marlowe Ct. PO7: W'lle 6F **9**
Marmion Av. PO5: S'sea 5D **50**
Marmion Rd. PO5: S'sea 5C **50**
Marne Ho. PO14: Fare 3G **25**
Marples Way PO9: Hav 2D **32**
Marrels Wood Gdns. PO7: Purb 5E **19**
Marsden Rd. PO6: Cosh 3F **29**
Marshall Rd. PO11: H Isl 5E **55**
Marsh Cl. PO6: Dray 5E **31**
Marshfield Ho. PO6: Dray 4F **31**
Marshlands Rd. PO6: Farl 4F **31**
Marshlands Spur PO6: Farl 4G **31**
Marsh La. PO14: Stub 3C **36**
Marshwood Av. PO7: W'lle 2A **20**
Marston La. PO3: Ports 1D **42**
Martello Cl. PO12: Gos 4H **47**
Martells Ct. PO1: Ports 5C **4** (3A **50**)
Martin Av. PO7: Den 3C **8**
PO14: Stub 3F **37**
Martin Cl. PO13: Lee S 6H **37**
Martinet Dr. PO13: Lee S 2E **47**
Martin Rd. PO3: Ports 5C **42**
PO9: Hav 5G **21**
PO14: Stub 3F **37**
Martin Snape Ho. PO12: Gos 3F **49**
Martlet Cl. PO13: Lee S 2E **47**
Marvic Ct. PO9: Hav 3E **21**
Mary Coombs Ct. PO11: H Isl 4C **54**
Mary Rose Cl. PO15: Fare 6G **13**
Mary Rose Mus. 2A **4** (2H **49**)
Mary Rose Ship Hall 1A **4** (1H **49**)
Mary Rose St., The PO1: Ports 3F **5** (2C **50**)
Marzan Rd. PO3: Ports 3D **42**
Masefield Av. PO6: Cosh 2D **28**
Masefield Cres. PO8: Cowp 4H **9**
Masten Cres. PO13: Gos 5C **38**
Matapan Rd. PO2: Ports 1H **41**
Matrix Pk. PO15: Titch 6A **12**
Matthews Cl. PO9: Bed 6C **20**
Matthews Pl. PO7: W'lle 3G **19**
Maurepas Way PO7: W'lle 1F **19**
Maurice Rd. PO4: S'sea 3A **52**
Mavis Cres. PO9: Hav 1F **33**
Maxstoke Cl. PO5: S'sea 3H **5** (2D **50**)
Maxwell Rd. PO4: S'sea 4G **51**
Maydman Sq. PO3: Ports 1G **51**
Mayfield Cl. PO14: Stub 2F **37**
Mayfield Rd. PO2: Ports 3A **42**
PO12: Gos 4E **49**
Mayflower Cl. PO14: Stub 4E **37**
Mayflower Dr. PO4: S'sea 2A **52**
Mayhall Rd. PO3: Ports 4C **42**
Maylands Av. PO4: S'sea 2G **51**
Maylands Rd. PO9: Bed 1B **32**
Mayles Cl. PO17: Wick 2A **14**
Mayles Cnr. PO17: K Vil 1F **13**
Mayles La. PO15: K Vil 3F **13**
PO17: K Vil, Wick . . . . .3F **13** & 2A **14**
Mayles Rd. PO4: S'sea 2H **51**
Maylings Farm Rd. PO16: Fare 6H **13**
Maynard Cl. PO13: Gos 1C **38**
Maynard Pl. PO8: Horn 6B **6**
Mayo Cl. PO1: Ports 6H **41**
May's La. PO14: Stub 2E **37**
Maytree Gdns. PO8: Cowp 4G **9**
Maytree Rd. PO8: Cowp 4G **9**
PO16: Fare 2A **26**
Mead, The GU32: Pet 5B **56**
PO13: Gos 2B **38**
MEAD END 4B **8**
Meadend Cl. PO9: Hav 4H **21**
Mead End Rd. PO7: Den 4C **8**
Meadow, The PO7: Den 3B **8**
Meadowbank Rd. PO15: Fare 2F **25**
Meadow Cl. PO11: H Isl 2B **44**
Meadow Ct. PO10: Ems 3D **34**
Meadow Edge PO7: Wid 1D **30**
Meadow Lands GU32: Pet 5C **56**
Meadowlands PO9: R Cas 4H **11**
PO9: Warb 2G **33**
Meadow Ri. PO8: Cowp 4B **10**
Meadows, The PO7: W'lle 1E **19**
PO16: Fare 6C **14**
Meadowside Leisure Cen. 1A **12**
Meadow St. PO5: S'sea 6E **5** (4B **50**)
Meadowsweet PO7: W'lle 6B **10**
Meadowsweet Way PO6: Cosh 2H **29**
Meadow Wlk. PO1: Ports 1F **5** (1C **50**)
PO13: Gos 6B **26**
Mead Way PO16: Fare 6B **14**
Meadway PO7: W'lle 6A **10**
Meath Cl. PO11: H Isl 6E **55**
Medina Ct. PO13: Lee S 6F **37**
Medina Ho. PO14: Fare 4A **26**
Medina Rd. PO6: Cosh 3H **29**
Medstead Rd. PO9: Hav 6F **21**
Megan Ct. PO6: Cosh 4B **30**
Megson Dr. PO13: Lee S 6A **38**
Melbourne Ho. PO1: Ports 2G **5** (1C **50**)
Melbourne Pl. PO5: S'sea 4E **5** (3B **50**)
Mellor Cl. PO6: Cosh 3H **29**
Melrose Cl. PO4: S'sea 3H **51**
Melrose Gdns. PO12: Gos 6F **39**
Melville Rd. PO4: S'sea 5B **52**
PO12: Gos 6G **39**
Melvin Jones Ho. PO14: Stub 1E **37**
Memorial Sq. PO1: Ports 3F **5** (2C **50**)
Mendips Rd. PO14: Fare 3G **25**
Mendips Wlk. PO14: Fare 3F **25**
MENGHAM 4C **54**
Mengham Av. PO11: H Isl 5C **54**
Mengham Ct. PO11: H Isl 4D **54**
Mengham House .4D **54**
Mengham La. PO11: H Isl 4C **54**
Mengham Rd. PO11: H Isl 4C **54**
Mengham Rythe Sailing Club 4F **55**
Menin Ho. PO15: Fare 1E **25**
MEON 1A **36**
Meon Cl. GU32: Pet 3C **56**
PO8: Clan 1D **6**
PO13: Gos 3B **38**
Meon Ho. PO16: Fare 4A **26**
Meon Rd. PO4: S'sea 3G **51**
PO14: Titch 1A **36**
Meonside Ct. PO17: Wick 2A **14**
Merchants Row *PO1: Ports 6B 4*
(off White Hart Rd.)
Merchistoun Rd. PO8: Horn 6B **6**
Mercury Pl. PO7: Purb 1G **31**
Mere Cft. PO15: Seg 6A **12**
Meredith Lodge PO7: W'lle 2H **19**
Meredith Rd. PO2: Ports 2A **42**
Merganser Cl. PO12: Gos 6H **39**
Meriden Rd. PO5: S'sea 4E **5** (3B **50**)
Meridian Cen. PO9: Hav 2F **33**
Merlin Cl. PO8: Cowp 3G **9**
Merlin Dr. PO3: Ports 1C **42**
Merlin Gdns. PO16: Portc 2H **27**
Mermaid Rd. PO14: Fare 6H **25**
Merrivale Ct. PO10: S'urne 2H **35**
Merrivale Rd. PO2: Ports 2A **42**
Merrow Cl. PO16: Portc 3G **27**
Merryfield Av. PO9: Hav 4D **20**
Merryfield Rd. GU31: Pet 3F **57**

Merstone Rd. PO13: Gos . . . 3C **38**
Merthyr Av. PO6: Dray . . . 2D **30**
Merton Av. PO16: Portc . . . 5B **28**
Merton Ct. PO5: S'sea . . . 4D **50**
Merton Cres. PO16: Portc . . . 5A **28**
Merton Rd. PO5: S'sea . . . 4C **50**
Meryl Rd. PO4: S'sea . . . 3A **52**
Metcalfe Av.
PO14: Stub . . . 2F **37**
Methuen Rd. PO4: S'sea . . . 4G **51**
Mews, The GU31: Pet . . . 3D **56**
PO1: Ports . . . 1E 51
(off Clive Rd.)
PO5: S'sea . . . 5D 50
(off Collingwood Rd.)
PO9: Hav . . . 5E **21**
(Riders La.)
PO9: Hav . . . 2F **33**
(The Pallant)
PO12: Gos . . . 3G **49**
Mewsey Ct. PO9: Hav . . . 2D **20**
Mey Cl. PO7: W'lle . . . 2A **20**
Meyrick Ho. PO2: Ports . . . 4G **41**
Meyrick Rd. PO2: Ports . . . 4G **41**
PO9: Hav . . . 2D **32**
Micawber Ho. PO1: Ports . . . 6H **41**
Michael Crook Cl.
PO9: Bed . . . 6C **20**
Midas Cl. PO7: Purb . . . 5H **19**
Middle Ct. *PO1: Ports . . . 6A 42*
(off Inverness Rd.)
Middlecroft La. PO12: Gos . . . 1B **48**
Middle Mead PO14: Fare . . . 3D **24**
Middle Pk. Way PO9: Hav . . . 5D **20**
Middlesex Rd. PO4: S'sea . . . 4H **51**
Middle St. PO5: S'sea . . . 4F **5** (3C **50**)
Middleton Cl. PO14: Fare . . . 4G **25**
Middleton Ri. PO8: Clan . . . 1D **6**
Middleton Wlk. PO14: Fare . . . 4G **25**
Midfield Cl. PO14: Fare . . . 4H **25**
Midhurst Ho. PO1: Ports . . . 1H **5** (1D **50**)
Midhurst Rd. GU31: Pet . . . 2H **57**
Midway Rd. PO2: Ports . . . 6A **30**
Midways PO14: Stub . . . 4E **37**
Milbeck Cl. PO8: Cowp . . . 4A **10**
Milebush Rd. PO4: S'sea . . . 2A **52**
Mile End Rd. PO1: Ports . . . 6G **41**
PO2: Ports . . . 5H **41**
Miles Ct. PO11: H Isl . . . 6F **55**
Milestone Point *PO9: Hav . . . 2F 33*
(off West St.)
Milford Cl. PO9: Bed . . . 6D **20**
Milford Ct. PO4: S'sea . . . 3H **51**
PO12: Gos . . . 4H **47**
Milford Rd. PO1: Ports . . . 2H **5** (2D **50**)
Military Rd. PO1: Ports . . . 1B **50**
PO3: Ports . . . 6B **30**
PO6: Dray . . . 2E **31**
PO12: Gos . . . 6C **48**
(Fort Rd., not continuous)
PO12: Gos . . . 3G **39**
(Gunners Way)
PO12: Gos . . . 3A **48**
(Privett Rd.)
PO13: Lee S . . . 4G **47**
PO16: Fare . . . 1D **26**
Milk La. PO7: W'lle . . . 3E **19**
Millam Ct. PO11: H Isl . . . 3A **54**
Millbrook Dr. PO9: Hav . . . 3G **21**
Mill Cl. PO7: Den . . . 3D **8**
PO11: H Isl . . . 3B **44**
Mill End PO10: S'urne . . . 3E **35**
Millennium Cl. PO7: W'lle . . . 4G **19**
Millennium Ct. PO7: W'lle . . . 4G **19**
Miller Dr. PO16: Fare . . . 6H **13**
(not continuous)
Millers Quay Ho. *PO16: Fare . . . 3B 26*
(off Lwr. Quay Rd.)
Mill Ga. Ho. *PO1: Ports . . . 3C 4*
(off St George's Sq.)
Mill La. GU32: Pet . . . 1F **57**
PO1: Ports . . . 6G **41**
PO7: Purb . . . 1A **30**
PO9: Bed . . . 2C **32**
PO9: Lang . . . 4E **33**
PO10: S'urne, Westb . . . 2E **35**
PO12: Gos . . . 1D **48**
PO15: Titch . . . 2C **24**
PO17: Wick . . . 1A **14**
Mill Pond Rd. PO12: Gos . . . 1D **48**
Mill Quay PO10: S'urne . . . 4E **35**
Mill Rd. PO7: Den . . . 3C **8**
PO7: W'lle . . . 3F **19**
PO10: Westb . . . 5F **23**
PO12: Gos . . . 1C **48**
PO16: Fare . . . 3A **26**
Mill Rythe Holiday Village PO11: H Isl . . . 1E **55**
Mill Rythe La. PO11: H Isl . . . 6C **44**
Mills Rd. PO2: Ports . . . 4H **41**
Mill St. PO14: Titch . . . 3C **24**
MILTON . . . 3G **51**
Milton Ct. PO4: S'sea . . . 2G **51**
Milton La. PO4: S'sea . . . 2F **51**
Milton Locks PO4: S'sea . . . 3B **52**
Milton Pde. PO8: Cowp . . . 5G **9**
Milton Pk. Av. PO4: S'sea . . . 3H **51**
Milton Rd. PO3: Ports . . . 1G **51**
PO4: S'sea . . . 2G **51**
PO7: W'lle . . . 6F **9**
PO8: Cowp . . . 5G **9**
Milverton Ho. PO5: S'sea . . . 5G **5** (3C **50**)
Milvil Ct. PO13: Lee S . . . 1C **46**
Milvil Rd. PO13: Lee S . . . 1C **46**
Mimosa Cl. PO15: Seg . . . 6A **12**
Minden Ho. PO14: Fare . . . 3H **25**
Minerva Cl. PO7: Purb . . . 1G **31**
Minerva Cres. PO1: Ports . . . 5B **4** (3A **50**)
Minerva Dr. PO12: Gos . . . 6A **40**
Minley Ct. PO9: Hav . . . 4H **21**
Minnitt Rd. PO12: Gos . . . 3G **49**
Minstead Rd. PO4: S'sea . . . 4H **51**
Minster Cl. PO15: Fare . . . 1E **25**
Minter's Lepe PO7: Purb . . . 6G **19**
Mission La. PO8: Cowp . . . 4A **10**
Mitchell Rd. PO9: Bed . . . 6B **20**
Mitchell Way PO3: Ports . . . 2D **42**
Mizen Way PO13: Gos . . . 1H **47**
Mizzen Ho. PO6: P Sol . . . 4E **29**
Moat Ct. PO12: Gos . . . 4H **47**
Moat Dr. PO12: Gos . . . 4H **47**
Moat Wlk. PO12: Gos . . . 4H **47**
Mobile Home Pk. PO8: Horn . . . 2D **6**
Moggs Mead GU31: Pet . . . 4E **57**
Mole Hill PO7: W'lle . . . 4H **19**
Molesworth Rd. PO12: Gos . . . 3E **49**
(not continuous)
Mollison Ri. PO15: White . . . 3A **12**
Monarch Cl. PO7: W'lle . . . 2A **20**
Monckton Rd. PO3: Ports . . . 3C **42**
PO12: Gos . . . 6D **48**
Moneyfield Av. PO3: Ports . . . 5C **42**
Moneyfield La. PO3: Ports . . . 5C **42**
Moneyfield Path PO3: Ports . . . 4D **42**
Monks Hill PO10: Westb . . . 3E **23**
PO13: Lee S . . . 5E **37**
Monks Orchard GU32: Pet . . . 2D **56**
Monks Wlk. PO12: Gos . . . 4G **39**
Monks Way PO14: Stub . . . 4D **36**
Monks Wood GU32: Pet . . . 2D **56**
Monkwood Cl. PO9: Hav . . . 4D **20**
Monmouth Rd. PO2: Ports . . . 3H **41**
Monroe Cl. PO12: Gos . . . 4A **48**
Monson Ho. PO1: Ports . . . 1E **51**
Montagu Cl. PO12: Gos . . . 5A **40**
Montague Gdns. GU31: Pet . . . 4G **57**
Montague Rd. PO2: Ports . . . 4A **42**
Montague Wallis Ct.
PO1: Ports . . . 3C **4** (2A **50**)
Montana Ct. PO7: W'lle . . . 3H **19**
Monterey Dr. PO9: Hav . . . 5G **21**
Montgomerie Rd. PO5: S'sea . . . 4H **5** (3D **50**)
Montgomery Rd. PO9: Hav . . . 2G **33**
PO13: Gos . . . 1C **38**
Montgomery Wlk. PO7: W'lle . . . 4F **19**
Montrose Av. PO16: Portc . . . 2C **28**
Montserrat Rd. PO13: Lee S . . . 1C **46**
Monument La. PO17: Boar, Fare . . . 4H **15**
Monxton Grn. PO9: Hav . . . 3H **21**
Moody Rd. PO14: Stub . . . 4D **36**
Moore Gdns. PO12: Gos . . . 3B **48**
Moorgreen Rd. PO9: Hav . . . 4G **21**
Moorings, The PO16: Fare . . . 4B **26**
Moorings Way PO4: S'sea . . . 2H **51**
Moorland Rd. PO1: Ports . . . 1E **51**
Moor Pk. PO7: W'lle . . . 6B **10**
Moortown Av. PO6: Dray . . . 2E **31**
Moraunt Cl. PO12: Gos . . . 5A **40**
Moraunt Dr. PO16: Portc . . . 4H **27**
Morcumb Pk. Homes PO10: S'urne . . . 3F **35**
Morecombe Ct. PO5: S'sea . . . 4H **5** (3D **50**)
Moreland Rd. PO12: Gos . . . 2D **48**
Morelands Ct. PO7: Purb . . . 5H **19**
Morelands Rd. PO7: Purb . . . 5G **19**
Moresby Ct. PO16: Fare . . . 2B **26**
Morgan Rd. PO4: S'sea . . . 3A **52**
Morgan's Dr. PO14: Stub . . . 6E **25**
Morley Cres. PO8: Cowp . . . 4A **10**
Morley Rd. PO4: S'sea . . . 5G **51**
Morningside Av. PO16: Portc . . . 2C **28**
Morris Cl. PO13: Gos . . . 6B **26**
Morshead Cres. PO16: Fare . . . 6H **13**
Mortimer Lawn PO9: Hav . . . 2D **20**
Mortimer Rd. PO6: Cosh . . . 2G **29**
Mortimore Rd. PO12: Gos . . . 1B **48**
Mosdell Rd. PO10: S'urne . . . 3H **35**
Moulin Av. PO5: S'sea . . . 5E **51**
Mound Cl. PO12: Gos . . . 4C **48**
Mount, The PO13: Gos . . . 4E **39**
Mountbatten Bus. Pk. PO6: Farl . . . 4F **31**
(not continuous)
Mountbatten Cen., The . . . 2H **41**
Mountbatten Cl. PO13: Gos . . . 1C **38**
Mountbatten Dr. PO7: W'lle . . . 3E **19**
Mountbatten Gallery . . . 3F **5** (2C **50**)
Mountbatten Ho. PO1: Ports . . . 1B **4** (1A **50**)
Mountbatten Sq. PO4: S'sea . . . 5H **51**
Mountbatten Way PO1: Ports . . . 6F **41**
Mount Dr. PO15: Fare . . . 3D **24**
Mountjoy Ct. PO1: Ports . . . 6B **4** (4A **50**)
Mt. Pleasant Rd. PO12: Gos . . . 5D **48**
Mountview Av. PO16: Portc . . . 2C **28**
Mountwood Rd. PO10: S'urne . . . 2H **35**
Mousehole Rd. PO6: Cosh . . . 2D **28**
Muccleshell Cl. PO9: Hav . . . 5G **21**
Mulberry Av. PO6: Cosh . . . 3C **30**
PO14: Stub . . . 4E **37**
Mulberry Cl. PO12: Gos . . . 3D **48**
Mulberry La. PO6: Cosh . . . 4C **30**
Mulberry Path PO6: Cosh . . . 4C **30**
Mullion Cl. PO6: P Sol . . . 4F **29**
Mumby Rd. PO12: Gos . . . 2F **49**
Mundays Row PO8: Horn . . . 4C **6**
Munster Rd. PO2: Ports . . . 3H **41**
Murefield Rd. PO1: Ports . . . 2D **50**
Muriel Rd. PO7: W'lle . . . 1G **19**
Murray Cl. PO15: Fare . . . 1G **25**
Murray Rd. PO8: Horn . . . 1B **10**
Murray's La. PO1: Ports . . . 1A **4** (1H **49**)
Murrills Est. PO16: Portc . . . 3C **28**
Muscliffe Ct. PO9: Hav . . . 4H **21**
Museum Rd. PO1: Ports . . . 5D **4** (3B **50**)
My Lord's La. PO11: H Isl . . . 4D **54**
Myrtle Av. PO16: Portc . . . 4B **28**
Myrtle Cl. PO13: Gos . . . 2C **38**
Myrtle Gro. PO3: Ports . . . 6D **42**

N

Nailsworth Rd. PO6: Cosh . . . 2F **29**
Naish Ct. PO9: Hav . . . 2C **20**
Naish Dr. PO12: Gos . . . 4G **39**
Nancy Rd. PO1: Ports . . . 2E **51**
Napier Cl. PO13: Gos . . . 2H **47**
Napier Cres. PO15: Fare . . . 2E **25**
Napier Rd. PO5: S'sea . . . 5D **50**
PO8: Horn . . . 1C **10**
Narvik Rd. PO2: Ports . . . 1H **41**
Naseby Cl. PO6: Cosh . . . 2E **29**
Nashe Cl. PO15: Fare . . . 6F **13**
Nashe Ho. PO15: Fare . . . 6E **13**
Nashe Way PO15: Fare . . . 6E **13**
Nasmith Cl. PO12: Gos . . . 3A **48**
Nat Gonella Sq. *PO12: Gos . . . 3F 49*
(off Walpole Rd.)
Navy Rd. PO1: Ports . . . 1A **50**
Needles Ho. PO16: Fare . . . 4A **26**
Neelands Gro. PO6: Cosh . . . 3C **28**
Nelson Av. PO2: Ports . . . 3H **41**
PO16: Portc . . . 4H **27**
Nelson Cen., The PO3: Ports . . . 3D **42**
Nelson Cl. PO10: S'urne . . . 3E **35**
Nelson Ct. PO14: Fare . . . 5H **25**
Nelson Cres. PO8: Horn . . . 6C **6**
Nelson Dr. GU31: Pet . . . 2E **57**
PO4: S'sea . . . 2A **52**
(not continuous)
Nelson Ho. *PO12: Gos . . . 3G 49*
(off South St.)
Nelson La. PO17: Fare . . . 6A **16**
Nelson Rd. PO1: Ports . . . 6H **41**
PO5: S'sea . . . 4C **50**
PO12: Gos . . . 3D **48**

Nepean Cl.—Odeon Cinema

Nepean Cl. PO12: Gos 6D **48**
Neptune Ct. PO1: Ports 5B **4** (3A **50**)
PO13: Gos 3D **38**
Neptune Rd. PO14: Fare 6H **25**
PO15: Fare 1E **25**
Nerissa Cl. PO7: W'lle 1A **20**
Nesbitt Cl. PO13: Gos 2B **38**
Nessus St. PO2: Ports 5H **41**
Nest Bus. Pk. PO9: Hav 5H **21**
Netherfield Cl. PO9: Warb 2G **33**
Netherton Rd. PO12: Gos 6F **39**
Netley Ct. PO12: Gos 5A **40**
Netley Pl. *PO5: S'sea 5C 50*
(off Netley Ter.)
Netley Rd. PO5: S'sea 5C **50**
Netley Ter. PO5: S'sea 5C **50**
Nettlecombe Av. PO4: S'sea 6E **51**
Nettlestone Rd. PO4: S'sea 5G **51**
Neville Av. PO16: Portc 5B **28**
Neville Ct. PO12: Gos 2D **48**
Neville Gdns. PO10: Ems 6C **22**
Neville Rd. PO3: Ports 6C **42**
Nevil Shute Rd. PO3: Ports 2C **42**
New Barn Farm La. PO8: Blen . . . . 2D **6** & 3E **7**
Newbarn Rd. PO9: Bed 6B **20**
Newbolt Cl. PO8: Cowp 4G **9**
Newbolt Rd. PO6: Cosh 2C **28**
NEW BRIGHTON 6D **22**
New Brighton Rd. PO10: Ems 2D **34**
Newbroke Rd. PO13: Gos 5D **38**
Newcomen Ct. PO2: Ports 3G **41**
Newcomen Rd. PO2: Ports 3G **41**
Newcome Rd. PO1: Ports 1E **51**
New Cut PO11: H Isl 2B **44**
New Down La. PO7: Purb 1C **30**
Newgate La. PO14: Fare 2A **38**
Newgate La. Ind. Est. PO14: Fare 5B **26**
(not continuous)
New Hampshire Blvd.
PO1: Ports 4B **4** (3A **50**)
Newlands PO15: Fare 2E **25**
Newlands Av. PO12: Gos 3C **48**
Newlands La. PO7: Den, Purb 5B **8**
Newlands Rd. PO7: Purb 4F **19**
New La. PO9: Hav 1G **33**
Newlease Rd. PO7: W'lle 4H **19**
Newlyn Way PO6: P Sol 4E **29**
Newmer Ct. PO9: Hav 3C **20**
Newney Cl. PO2: Ports 1B **42**
Newnham Ct. PO9: Hav 4H **21**
New Pde. PO16: Portc 3B **28**
Newport Rd. PO12: Gos 2B **48**
New Rd. PO2: Ports 6A **42**
PO8: Clan 1C **6**
PO8: Love 1G **9**
PO9: Bed 1D **32**
PO10: S'urne 3H **35**
PO10: Westb 6F **23**
PO16: Fare 2A **26**
New Rd. E. PO2: Ports 5B **42**
New Royal Theatre 3E 5 (2C 50)
News Cen., The PO3: Ports 6B **30**
Newton Cl. PO14: Stub 1E **37**
Newton Pl. PO13: Lee S 6G **37**
NEWTOWN
PO11 . . . . 3A **54**
PO12 . . . . 3E **49**
New Town PO16: Portc 3B **28**
Newtown La. PO11: H Isl 3A **54**
NHS WALK-IN CENTRE
(ST MARY'S, PORTSMOUTH) *1G 51*
(within grounds of St Mary's Hospital)
Nicholas Ct. PO11: H Isl 4A **54**
PO13: Lee S 2C **46**
Nicholas Cres. PO15: Fare 1H **25**
Nicholl Pl. PO13: Gos 3C **38**
Nicholson Gdns. PO1: Ports 2H **5**
Nicholson Way PO9: Hav 6E **21**
Nickel St. PO5: S'sea 6E **5** (4B **50**)
Nickleby Ho. PO1: Ports 6H **41**
Nickleby Rd. PO8: Clan 1F **7**
Nightingale Cl. PO9: R Cas 6G **11**
PO12: Gos 1B **48**
Nightingale Ct. PO6: Cosh 3D **30**
PO10: Westb 5F **23**
Nightingale Pk. PO9: Warb 2H **33**
Nightingale Rd. GU32: Pet 5C **56**
PO5: S'sea 5B **50**
PO6: Cosh 2B **30**
Nightjar Cl. PO8: Horn 6A **6**
Nile St. PO10: Ems 3D **34**
Nimrod Dr. PO13: Gos 6D **38**
(not continuous)
Nine Elms La. PO17: Fare 5D **14**
Ninian Pk. Rd. PO3: Ports 3C **42**
Ninian Path PO3: Ports 3C **42**
Niton Cl. PO13: Gos 3C **38**
Nobbs La. PO1: Ports 5C **4** (3A **50**)
Nobes Av. PO13: Gos 2C **38**
Nobes Cl. PO13: Gos 3D **38**
Noctule Ct. PO17: K Vil 1F **13**
Nook, The PO13: Gos 4E **39**
Nore Cres. PO10: Ems 2B **34**
Nore Farm Av. PO10: Ems 2B **34**
Noreuil Rd. GU32: Pet 4B **56**
Norfolk Cres. PO11: H Isl 5H **53**
Norfolk Ho. PO9: Hav 2G **33**
Norfolk M. PO11: H Isl 4A **54**
Norfolk Rd. PO12: Gos 6F **39**
Norfolk St. PO5: S'sea 6F **5** (4C **50**)
Norgett Way PO16: Portc 5H **27**
Norland Rd. PO4: S'sea 4E **51**
Norley Cl. PO9: Hav 4E **21**
Norman Cl. PO16: Portc 5B **28**
Norman Ct. PO4: S'sea 5E **51**
Normandy Ct. PO17: Wick 1B **14**
Normandy Gdns. PO12: Gos 3B **48**
Normandy Rd. PO2: Ports 1H **41**
Norman Rd. PO4: S'sea 4E **51**
PO11: H Isl 5D **54**
PO12: Gos 2C **48**
Norman Way PO9: Bed 1C **32**
Norris Gdns. PO9: Warb 3G **33**
Norrish Ct. *PO1: Ports 6A 42*
(off Inverness Rd.)
Norset Rd. PO15: Fare 1E **25**
Northam M. PO1: Ports 2H **5** (2D **50**)
Northam St. PO1: Ports 1H **5** (1D **50**)
Northarbour Rd. PO6: Cosh 4H **29**
Northarbour Spur PO6: Cosh 3H **29**
North Av. PO2: Ports 6A **30**
Nth. Battery Rd. PO2: Ports 3F **41**
Northbrook Cl. PO1: Ports 6H **41**
North Cl. PO9: Hav 3G **33**
PO12: Gos 3B **48**
Northcote Rd. PO4: S'sea 4E **51**
Northcott Cl. PO12: Gos 4B **48**
North Ct. PO1: Ports 6A **42**
North Cres. PO11: H Isl 4D **54**
Northcroft Rd. PO12: Gos 1B **48**
Nth. Cross St. PO12: Gos 3F **49**
North Dr. PO17: S'wick 3D **16**
NORTH END 4H **41**
North End Av. PO2: Ports 3H **41**
North End Gro. PO2: Ports 3H **41**
Northern Pde. PO2: Ports 2H **41**
Northern Rd. PO6: Cosh 5B **30**
Northesk Ho. PO1: Ports 1D **50**
NORTH FAREHAM 5B **14**
Northfield Av. PO14: Fare 4H **25**
Northfield Cvn. Pk. PO16: Portc 1H **27**
Northfield Cl. PO8: Horn 3C **6**
Northfield Pk. PO16: Portc 2H **27**
Northgate Av. PO2: Ports 5B **42**
North Gro. Ho. PO5: S'sea 6H **5** (4D **50**)
NORTH HARBOUR 5F **29**
Nth. Harbour Bus. Pk.
PO6: Cosh 4G **29**
NORTH HAYLING 2E **45**
North Hill PO16: Fare 6B **14**
PO17: S'wick 1F **29**
North La. PO8: Clan 1F **7**
NORTHNEY 1E **45**
Northney La. PO11: H Isl 1E **45**
Northney Rd. PO11: H Isl 6G **33**
Northover Rd. PO3: Ports 5D **42**
North Pk. Bus. Cen. PO17: K Vil 1F **13**
North Rd. GU32: Pet 3D **56**
PO8: Horn 3C **6**
PO17: S'wick 1E **29**
North Rd. E. PO17: S'wick 3E **17**
North Rd. W. PO17: S'wick 3E **17**
Nth. Shore Rd. PO11: H Isl 3H **53**
North Sq. PO17: K Vil 2G **13**
North St. PO1: Ports 1D **50**
(Cornwallis Cres.)
PO1: Ports 2C **4** (2A **50**)
(Queen St.)
PO9: Bed 1D **32**
PO9: Hav 2F **33**
PO10: Ems 2D **34**
PO10: Westb 4F **23**
North St. PO12: Gos 3F **49**
(not continuous)
North St. Arc. PO9: Hav 2F **33**
Northumberland Rd. PO5: S'sea 3E **51**
NORTH WALLINGTON 1D **26**
North Wallington PO16: Fare 1C **26**
North Way PO9: Hav 2E **33**
Northway PO13: Gos 1C **38**
PO15: Titch 6A **12**
Northways PO14: Stub 3F **37**
Northwood La. PO11: H Isl 4C **44**
Northwood Rd. PO2: Ports 1A **42**
Northwood Sq. PO16: Fare 1B **26**
Norton Cl. PO7: W'lle 2F **19**
PO17: S'wick 3D **16**
Norton Dr. PO16: Fare 6A **14**
Norton Rd. PO17: S'wick 3D **16**
Norway Rd. PO3: Ports 1B **42**
Norwich Pl. PO13: Lee S 6G **37**
Norwich Rd. PO6: Cosh 2H **29**
Nottingham Pl. PO13: Lee S 6G **37**
Novello Gdns. PO7: W'lle 3G **19**
Nursery Cl. PO10: Ems 6D **22**
PO13: Gos 2B **38**
Nursery Gdns. PO8: Horn 2A **10**
Nursery La. PO14: Stub 3E **37**
Nursery Rd. PO9: Bed 1C **32**
Nursling Cres. PO9: Hav 4G **21**
Nutbourne Ho. PO6: Farl 4F **31**
Nutbourne Rd. PO6: Farl 4F **31**
PO11: H Isl 5G **55**
Nutfield Pl. PO1: Ports 1D **50**
Nuthatch Cl. PO9: R Cas 6H **11**
Nutley Rd. PO9: Hav 4D **20**
Nutwick Rd. PO9: Hav 6H **21**
Nyewood Av. PO16: Portc 2B **28**
Nyria Way PO12: Gos 3F **49**

O

Oakapple Gdns. PO6: Farl 3G **31**
Oak Cl. PO8: Cowp 5G **9**
Oak Ct. PO15: Fare 1E **25**
Oakcroft La. PO14: Stub 6E **25**
Oakdene PO13: Gos 4D **38**
Oakdene Rd. PO4: S'sea 3A **52**
Oakdown Rd. PO14: Stub 2F **37**
Oak Dr. GU31: Pet 6C **56**
Oakes, The PO14: Stub 1D **36**
Oakfield Ct. PO9: Hav 4H **21**
Oakhurst Dr. PO7: W'lle 1A **20**
Oakhurst Gdns. PO7: Wid 1D **30**
Oaklands PO7: W'lle 3A **20**
Oaklands Gro. PO8: Cowp 4F **9**
Oaklands Ho. PO6: Cosh 1D **28**
Oaklands Rd. GU32: Pet 3C **56**
PO9: Hav 2G **33**
Oaklea Cl. PO7: Wid 1D **30**
Oakley Ho. PO5: S'sea 6F **5** (4C **50**)
Oakley Rd. PO9: Hav 4D **20**
Oak Lodge PO2: Ports 3G **41**
Oakmeadow Cl. PO10: Ems 6E **23**
Oakmont Dr. PO8: Cowp 5H **9**
Oak Pk. Dr. PO9: Hav 6G **21**
Oak Pk. Ind. Est. PO6: Cosh 3H **29**
Oak Rd. PO8: Clan 2G **7**
PO15: Fare 1F **25**
Oaks, The PO8: Cowp 5A **10**
Oaks Coppice PO8: Horn 1A **10**
Oakshott Dr. PO9: Hav 4G **21**
Oak St. PO12: Gos 3E **49**
Oakthorn Cl. PO13: Gos 1G **47**
Oak Tree Dr. PO10: Ems 5C **22**
Oakum Ho. PO3: Ports 1G **51**
Oakwood Av. PO9: Bed 6B **20**
Oakwood Cen., The PO9: Hav 5H **21**
Oakwood Rd. PO2: Ports 1A **42**
PO11: H Isl 4B **54**
Oberon Cl. PO7: W'lle 1A **20**
Occupation La. PO14: Titch 3A **24**
Ocean Cl. PO15: Fare 1F **25**
Ocean Ct. PO11: H Isl 5A **54**
Ocean Pk. PO3: Ports 3D **42**
Ocean Rd. PO14: Fare 6H **25**
Ockendon Cl. PO5: S'sea 5F **5** (3C **50**)
Octavius Ct. PO7: W'lle 6B **10**
Odell Cl. PO16: Fare 6H **13**
Odeon Cinema
North End 4H **41**
Port Solent 5F **29**

A-Z Portsmouth 77

Officers Quarters, The PO12: Gos 2F 49
O'Jays Ind. Pk. PO3: Ports 3C 42
Olave Cl. PO13: Lee S 1C 46
Old Barn Gdns. PO8: Love 1H 9
Old Bri. Rd. PO4: S'sea 5E 51
Oldbury Ho. PO5: S'sea 5F 5
Oldbury Way PO14: Fare 3E 25
Old Canal PO4: S'sea 3H 51
Old Canal, The PO4: S'sea 3H 51
Old Commercial Rd. PO1: Ports 6G 41
Old Copse Rd. PO9: Hav 1G 33
Old Dairy Workshops PO10: Westb 6F 23
Old Farm La. PO10: Westb 6F 23
PO14: Stub 4E 37
Old Farm Way PO6: Farl 4G 31
Old Flour Mill, The PO10: Ems 3E 35
Oldgate Gdns. PO2: Ports 1B 42
Old Gosport Rd. PO16: Fare 3B 26
Old La. PO8: Cath 3B 6
Old London Rd. PO2: Ports 1B 42
Old Manor Farm PO9: Bed 2B 32
Old Manor Way PO6: Cosh 4D 30
Old Mill La. GU31: Pet 2F 57
PO8: Love 1D 8
OLD PORTSMOUTH 6B 4 (4A 50)
Old Rectory Cl. PO10: Westb 6E 23
Old Rectory Rd. PO6: Farl 3G 31
Old Reservoir Rd. PO6: Farl 4F 31
Old River PO7: Den 4B 8
Old Rd. PO12: Gos 4E 49
Old Rd., The PO6: Cosh 5B 30
Old School Dr. PO11: H Isl 5D 54
Old Star Pl. PO1: Ports 2B 4 (2A 50)
Old St. PO14: Stub 4C 36
(not continuous)
Old Timbers PO11: H Isl 4B 54
Old Turnpike PO16: Fare 6B 14
Old Van Diemans Rd.
PO7: Purb 4E 19
Old Wymering La. PO6: Cosh 3A 30
Olinda St. PO1: Ports 1E 51
Olive Cres. PO16: Portc 5B 28
Olive Leaf Ct. PO11: H Isl 2D 54
Oliver Rd. PO4: S'sea 4G 51
Olivers Ct. PO2: Ports 5A 42
Olivia Cl. PO7: W'lle 6A 10
Omega Ho. PO5: S'sea 3H 5 (2D 50)
Omega St. PO5: S'sea 3H 5 (2D 50)
Onslow Rd. PO5: S'sea 6D 50
Ophir Rd. PO2: Ports 3H 41
Oracle Dr. PO7: Purb 6G 19
Orange Gro. PO13: Gos 4D 38
Orange Row PO10: Ems 3D 34
Orchard, The PO6: Cosh 4B 30
PO7: Den 3B 8
Orchard Cl. PO8: Horn 1C 10
PO11: H Isl 5B 54
PO12: Gos 4G 39
Orchard Gro. PO8: Cowp 4H 9
PO16: Portc 4G 27
Orchard La. PO10: S'urne 3E 35
Orchard Rd. PO4: S'sea 3E 51
PO9: Hav 3F 33
PO11: H Isl 5C 54
Orchid Cl. PO17: K Vil 2F 13
Ordnance Ct. PO3: Ports 6C 30
Ordnance Rd. PO12: Gos 3F 49
Ordnance Row PO1: Ports 3B 4 (2A 50)
Orford Ct. PO6: Cosh 4B 30
Oriel Rd. PO2: Ports 3H 41
Orion Av. PO12: Gos 6A 40
Orion Cl. PO14: Stub 3F 37
Orkney Rd. PO6: Cosh 2B 30
Ormsby Rd. PO5: S'sea 4C 50
Ornamental Farm 3G 21
Orpine Cl. PO15: Titch 6B 12
Orsmond Cl. PO7: W'lle 3H 19
Orwell Cl. PO12: Gos 6A 40
Orwell Rd. GU31: Pet 5C 56
Osborn Ct. PO3: Ports 1D 42
Osborn Cres. PO13: Gos 1B 38
Osborne Cl. PO7: W'lle 2A 20
Osborne Rd. GU32: Pet 3D 56
PO5: S'sea 5C 50
PO12: Gos 2F 49
PO13: Lee S 1C 46
Osborne Vw. Rd. PO14: Stub 4C 36
Osborn Mall PO16: Fare 2C 26
Osborn Rd. PO16: Fare 2B 26
Osborn Rd. Sth. PO16: Fare 2B 26
Osborn Sq. PO16: Fare 2C 26
Osier Cl. PO2: Ports 3G 41
Osier Rd. GU32: Pet 5B 56
Osprey Cl. PO6: Farl 4H 31
Osprey Ct. PO16: Portc 3F 27
Osprey Dr. PO11: H Isl 4D 54
Osprey Gdns. PO13: Lee S 1D 46
Osprey Quay PO10: S'urne 4F 35
Othello Dr. PO7: W'lle 1A 20
Otterbourne Cres. PO9: Hav 4D 20
Otter Cl. PO13: Gos 2H 47
Outram Rd. PO5: S'sea 6H 5 (4D 50)
Oval Gdns. PO12: Gos 3B 48
Oven Camp Site, The PO11: H Isl 2B 54
Overton Cres. PO9: Hav 4D 20
Overton Rd. PO10: S'urne 2H 35
Owen Cl. PO13: Gos 6C 38
Owen Ho. *PO3: Ports* 1F 51
(off Whitcombe Gdns.)
Owen St. PO4: S'sea 5G 51
Owslebury Gro. PO9: Hav 4F 21
Oxenwood Grn. PO9: Hav 3D 20
Oxford Cl. PO16: Fare 1H 25
Oxford Rd. PO5: S'sea 4E 51
PO12: Gos 2B 48
Oxleys Cl. PO14: Fare 3D 24
Oxted Ct. PO4: S'sea 2H 51
Oysell Gdns. PO16: Fare 2F 27
Oyster Est., The PO6: Farl 4F 31
Oyster M. PO1: Ports 6B 4 (4A 50)
Oyster Quay PO6: P Sol 4F 29
Oyster St. PO1: Ports 6B 4 (4A 50)
Oyster Vw. PO13: Lee S 6F 37

P

Padbury Cl. PO2: Ports 1B 42
Paddington Rd. PO2: Ports 4B 42
Paddock, The PO12: Gos 4C 48
PO14: Stub 1E 37
Paddock End PO7: Den 4B 8
Paddock Wlk. PO6: Cosh 3E 29
Paddock Way GU32: Pet 5B 56
Padnell Av. PO8: Cowp 4A 10
Padnell Pl. PO8: Cowp 5B 10
Padnell Rd. PO8: Cowp 4A 10
Padwick Av. PO6: Cosh 3C 30
Padwick Ct. PO11: H Isl 4A 54
Paffard Cl. PO13: Gos 6C 38
Paget Rd. PO12: Gos 5C 48
Pagham Cl. PO10: S'urne 3E 35
Pagham Gdns. PO11: H Isl 5H 55
Paignton Av. PO3: Ports 5C 42
Pain's Rd. PO5: S'sea 5H 5 (3D 50)
Painswick Cl. PO6: Cosh 3G 29
Painter Cl. PO3: Ports 2D 42
Palk Rd. PO9: Bed 1D 32
Pallant, The PO9: Hav 2F 33
Pallant Gdns. PO16: Fare 1D 26
Palm Ct. PO5: S'sea 5C 50
Palmer's Rd. PO10: Ems 2D 34
Palmers Rd. Ind. Est. PO10: Ems 2D 34
Palmerston Av. PO16: Fare 2B 26
Palmerston Bus. Pk. PO14: Fare 4A 26
Palmerston Ct. *PO5: S'sea* 5C 50
(off Clarence Pde.)
Palmerston Dr. PO14: Fare 4A 26
Palmerston Indoor Bowls Club 4A 26
Palmerston Mans. *PO5: S'sea* 5C 50
(off Palmerston Rd.)
Palmerston Rd. PO5: S'sea 5C 50
PO11: H Isl 3C 54
Palmerston Way PO12: Gos 5A 48
Palmyra Rd. PO12: Gos 6G 39
Pamela Av. PO6: Cosh 2D 28
Pangbourne Av. PO6: Cosh 4D 30
Pannall Rd. PO12: Gos 6G 39
Pan St. PO1: Ports 1G 5 (1C 50)
Panton Cl. PO10: Ems 6C 22
Parade, The PO1: Ports 1B 4 (1A 50)
PO13: Gos 2B 38
PO14: Stub 2E 37
Parade Ct. PO2: Ports 6A 30
Paradise La. PO10: Westb 5F 23
PO16: Fare 2E 27
(not continuous)
Paradise St. PO1: Ports 1G 5 (1C 50)
Parchment, The PO9: Hav 2F 33
Parham Rd. PO12: Gos 1E 49
Park App. PO17: K Vil 2G 13
Park Av. PO7: Purb, Wid 1E 31
Park Cl. PO12: Gos 1B 48
Park Ct. PO5: S'sea 6F 5 (4C 50)
Park Cres. PO10: Ems 2B 34
Parker Cl. PO12: Gos 4G 39
Parker Gdns. PO7: Wid 1E 31
Pk. Farm Av. PO15: Fare 5E 13
Park Farm Cl. PO15: Fare 6F 13
Park Farm Rd. PO7: Purb 5F 19
Parkfield Ho. PO6: Cosh 1D 28
Park Gro. PO6: Cosh 4B 30
Park Ho. PO5: S'sea 5C 50
Pk. House Farm Way PO9: Hav 5B 20
Parklands PO7: Den 4B 8
Parklands Av. PO8: Cowp 2A 10
PO8: Horn 2A 10
Parklands Bus. Pk. PO7: Den 4B 8
Parklands Cl. PO12: Gos 1D 48
Park La. PO6: Cosh 3C 30
PO8: Cowp 5A 10
PO9: Bed 1C 32
PO9: Hav 1C 20
PO10: R Cas 1F 23
PO14: Stub 2E 37
PO16: Fare 6B 14
Park Mans. PO6: Cosh 4C 30
Park Pde. PO9: Hav 5E 21
Park Rd. GU32: Pet 4D 56
PO1: Ports 4C 4 (3A 50)
PO7: Den 2B 8
PO7: Purb 5E 19
PO11: H Isl 3G 53
PO12: Gos 5D 48
Park Rd. Nth. PO9: Hav 1E 33
Park Rd. Sth. PO9: Hav 2F 33
Park Royal PO2: Ports 2A 42
Parkside PO9: Bed 1C 32
Parkstone Av. PO4: S'sea 6E 51
Parkstone La. PO4: S'sea 5E 51
Park St. PO5: S'sea 5E 5 (3B 50)
PO12: Gos 2D 48
Park Terraces PO12: Gos 3E 49
Park Vw. PO9: R Cas 1H 21
Park Vw. Ho. PO16: Fare 5B 14
Park Wlk. PO15: Fare 6F 13
Park Way PO9: Hav 2E 33
Parkway PO15: White 2A 12
PO16: Fare 6B 14
Parkway, The PO13: Gos 3B 38
Parkwood Cen. PO7: W'lle 1G 19
Parr Rd. PO6: Cosh 3H 29
Parry Cl. PO6: Cosh 3C 28
Parsonage Cl. GU32: Pet 2F 57
Parsons Cl. PO3: Ports 1B 42
Partridge Cl. PO16: Portc 3E 27
Partridge Gdns. PO8: Cowp 3F 9
Passfield Wlk. PO9: Hav 4H 21
Passingham Wlk. PO8: Cowp 3A 10
Pasteur Rd. PO6: Cosh 3A 30
Pastures, The PO7: Den 4A 8
Patchway Dr. PO14: Fare 3E 25
Patrick Howard Dobson Ct. PO8: Cowp 3H 9
Patterdale Ho. PO6: Cosh 2F 29
Pattersons La. PO8: Blen 1E 11
PAULSGROVE 3F 29
Paulsgrove Enterprise Cen. PO6: Cosh 3F 29
Paulsgrove Ind. Cen. PO6: Cosh 3F 29
Paulsgrove Rd. PO2: Ports 5B 42
Pavilion Way PO12: Gos 2F 49
Paxton Rd. PO14: Fare 2H 25
Peacock Cl. PO16: Portc 3E 27
Peacock La. PO1: Ports 6C 4 (4A 50)
Peak, The PO9: R Cas 4H 11
Peak Dr. PO14: Fare 3F 25
Peakfield PO7: Den 3A 8
Peak La. PO14: Fare 3F 25
Peak Rd. PO8: Clan 2E 7
Pearce Ct. PO12: Gos 2E 49
Peartree Cl. PO14: Stub 2F 37
Pebble Cl. PO11: H Isl 5D 54
Pebble Ct. PO11: H Isl 6F 55
Pebmarsh Rd. PO6: Cosh 3H 29
Pedam Cl. PO4: S'sea 4G 51
PEEL COMMON 3A 38
Peel Pl. PO5: S'sea 5F 5 (3C 50)
Peel Rd. PO12: Gos 2E 49
Pegasus Cl. PO13: Gos 2H 47
Peggotty Ho. PO1: Ports 6H 41
Pegham Ind. Pk. PO15: Fun 3E 13
Pelham Rd. PO5: S'sea 6G 5 (4C 50)
PO12: Gos 2D 48
Pelham Rd. Pas. PO5: S'sea 6G 5 (4C 50)

Pelham Ter. PO10: Ems 3E **35**
Pelican Cl. PO15: Fare 1F **25**
Pelican Rd. PO14: Fare 6H **25**
Pembroke Chambers
PO1: Ports 6C **4**
Pembroke Cl. PO1: Ports 6C **4** (4A **50**)
Pembroke Ct. PO13: Gos 4C **38**
Pembroke Cres. PO14: Stub 3C **36**
Pembroke Rd. PO1: Ports . . 6C **4** & 6D **4** (4A **50**)
(not continuous)
Pembury Rd. PO9: Warb 3G **33**
PO14: Stub 1F **37**
Penarth Av. PO6: Dray 3D **30**
Pendennis Rd. PO6: Cosh 2D **28**
Penhale Rd. PO1: Ports 2E **51**
Penhurst Rd. PO9: Bed 1B **32**
Penjar Av. PO7: Purb 5E **19**
Penk Ridge PO9: Bed 3H **31**
Pennant Hills PO9: Bed 1B **32**
Pennant Pk. PO16: Fare 6C **14**
Pennerly Ct. PO9: Hav 2D **20**
Penner Rd. PO9: Hav 4E **33**
Pennine Wlk. PO14: Fare 4G **25**
Pennine Way PO13: Lee S 3E **47**
Pennington Way PO15: Fare 6F **13**
Penns Pl. GU31: Pet 4H **57**
Penns Rd. GU32: Pet 3C **56**
Penn Way PO12: Gos 4A **48**
Penny La. PO10: S'urne 3F **35**
Penny Pl. PO7: Purb 6G **19**
Penny St. PO1: Ports 6B **4** (4A **50**)
Penrhyn Av. PO6: Dray 3D **30**
Penrose Cl. PO2: Ports 3H **41**
Pentere Rd. PO8: Horn 1A **10**
Pentland Ri. PO16: Portc 2B **28**
Penton Ct. PO9: Hav 3H **21**
Penwood Grn. PO9: Hav 4H **21**
Peper Harow PO8: Horn 1B **10**
Pepper Cl. PO11: H Isl 2C **54**
Pepys Cl. PO4: S'sea 4F **51**
PO12: Gos 6D **48**
Percival Cl. PO13: Lee S 2E **47**
Percival Rd. PO2: Ports 5B **42**
Percy Chandler St. PO1: Ports 1H **5** (1D **50**)
Percy Rd. PO4: S'sea 3E **51**
PO12: Gos 3E **49**
Peregrines, The PO16: Portc 3F **27**
Perkins Ho. PO1: Ports 2D **4**
Peronne Cl. PO3: Ports 6B **30**
Peronne Rd. PO3: Ports 6B **30**
Perseus Pl. PO7: Purb 6G **19**
Perseus Ter. PO1: Ports 5B **4** (3A **50**)
Perth Ho. PO1: Ports 2H **5** (2D **50**)
Perth Rd. PO4: S'sea 3H **51**
PO13: Gos 2D **38**
Pervin Rd. PO6: Cosh 3B **30**
Peter Ashley Activity Cen. 2F **31**
Peter Ashley La. PO6: Dray 2F **31**
Peterborough Ct. *PO13: Gos 2H 47*
(off Anson Cl.)
Peterborough Rd. PO6: Cosh 2A **30**
PETERSFIELD 4D **56**
Petersfield Bus. Pk. GU32: Pet 4B **56**
PETERSFIELD HOSPITAL 4C **56**
Petersfield Ho. PO1: Ports 1H **5**
Petersfield Mus. 4D **56**
Petersfield Rd. PO8: Clan 1G **7**
PO9: Hav 1E **33**
Petersfield Station (Rail) 3C **56**
Petersfield Swimming Pool 4E **57**
Petersham Cl. PO7: W'lle 6F **9**
Petersham Ho. *PO5: S'sea 6D 50*
(off Clarendon Rd.)
Petrel Wlk. PO13: Gos 3B **38**
Petrie Rd. PO13: Lee S 1D **46**
Pettycot Cres. PO13: Gos 2B **38**
Petworth Rd. PO3: Ports 1H **51**
Philip Rd. PO7: W'lle 4H **19**
Phoenix Bldgs. PO3: Ports 3C **42**
Phoenix Sq. PO2: Ports 1A **42**
Phoenix Way PO13: Gos 4C **38**
Physic Garden, The 4D **56**
Pickwick Ho. PO1: Ports 6H **41**
Picton Ho. PO5: S'sea 4G **5** (3C **50**)
Pier Head Rd. PO2: Ports 5E **41**
Pier Rd. PO5: S'sea 5B **50**
Pier St. PO13: Lee S 1C **46**
Pigeonhouse La. PO7: Purb 3H **17**
Pilbrow Ct. PO12: Gos 3B **48**
Pilgrims Way PO14: Stub 4D **36**
Pilning Cl. PO14: Fare 3E **25**
Pine Ct. PO10: Ems 5D **22**
Pine Dr. PO8: Clan 2G **7**
Pine Gro. PO9: Hav 2G **33**
Pinehurst Cl. PO7: W'lle 5C **10**
Pines, The PO16: Fare 2G **27**
Pine Tree Gdns. PO8: Cowp 5A **10**
Pine Trees Cl. PO14: Fare 3F **25**
Pinewood PO13: Gos 4E **39**
Pinewood Av. PO9: Bed 6B **20**
Pinewood Cl. PO14: Stub 1F **37**
Pinewood Lodge *PO16: Fare 1B 26*
(off Northwood Sq.)
Pink Rd. PO2: Ports 5A **42**
Pinks Hill PO16: Fare 1D **26**
Pinsley Dr. PO17: S'wick 3D **16**
Pipers Mead PO8: Clan 2E **7**
Pipers Wood Ind. Est.
PO7: W'lle 1E **19**
Pipistrelle Wlk. PO17: K Vil 1G **13**
Pipit Cl. PO8: Horn 1A **10**
PO12: Gos 6H **39**
Pitcairn M. PO4: S'sea 5H **51**
Pitcroft La. PO2: Ports 5H **41**
(not continuous)
Pitcroft Rd. PO2: Ports 4H **41**
Pitreavie Rd. PO6: Cosh 5B **30**
Pitt Lane Gymnastics Cen. 1C **50**
Pitymoor La. PO17: S'wick 5F **17**
Place Cres. PO7: W'lle 4H **19**
Place Ho. Cl. PO15: Fare 2E **25**
Plaitford Gro. PO9: Hav 5B **20**
Playfair Rd. PO5: S'sea 5H **5** (3D **50**)
Pleasant Rd. PO4: S'sea 3H **51**
Plover Cl. PO14: Stub 3D **36**
Plover Reach PO4: S'sea 2H **51**
Plovers Rd. PO8: Horn 6A **6**
Plumley Wlk. PO9: Hav 2D **20**
Plumpton Gdns. PO3: Ports 2D **42**
Plumpton Gro. PO7: W'lle 6B **10**
Plymouth Dr. PO14: Stub 3C **36**
Plymouth St. PO5: S'sea 4G **5** (3C **50**)
Poinsettia Cl. PO15: Seg 6A **12**
Pompey Cen., The PO4: S'sea 2F **51**
Pond La. PO8: Clan 1F **7**
Pond Piece PO7: Den 4B **8**
Ponsonby Ho. PO5: S'sea 4G **5** (3C **50**)
Pook La. PO9: Warb 4G **33**
(not continuous)
PO17: Fare 5B **14**
Popham Ct. PO9: Hav 3C **20**
Poplar Dr. PO14: Fare 3G **25**
Poplar Gro. PO11: H Isl 3C **54**
Poplar Wlk. GU31: Pet 6C **56**
Portsmouth Stadium (Greyhound) 2G **41**
Portal Rd. PO13: Gos 2C **38**
PORTCHESTER 3A **28**
Portchester Castle 5D **28**
Portchester Crematorium
PO16: Portc 2H **27**
Portchester Hgts. PO16: Portc 2B **28**
Portchester La. PO17: Fare, S'wick 6B **16**
Portchester Rd. PO2: Ports 5A **42**
PO16: Portc 2F **27**
Portchester Station (Rail) 3B **28**
Portcreek Cotts. PO6: Cosh 6D **30**
Portfield Ind. Est. PO3: Ports 2C **42**
Portfield Rd. PO3: Ports 2C **42**
Portland Bldgs. PO12: Gos 3E **49**
Portland Dr. PO12: Gos 4H **47**
Portland Ho. PO12: Gos 3F **49**
Portland Rd. PO5: S'sea 5C **50**
PO7: W'lle 2G **19**
Portlands Cl. GU32: Pet 2F **57**
Portland St. PO1: Ports 3D **4** (2B **50**)
PO16: Fare 2B **26**
Portland Ter. PO5: S'sea 5C **50**
Portobello Gro. PO16: Portc 2B **28**
Port Royal St. PO5: S'sea 3H **5** (2D **50**)
Port Royal St. Ind. Est.
PO5: S'sea 3H **5** (2D **50**)
Portsbridge Rdbt. PO6: Cosh 5A **30**
Portsdown Av. PO6: Dray 3E **31**
Portsdown Hill Rd. PO6: Cosh, Dray 1H **29**
PO9: Bed 2D **30**
PO17: Fare 6H **15**
Portsdown Rd. PO6: Cosh 2C **28**
PO16: Portc 2C **28**
PORTSEA 2B **4** (2A **50**)
PORTSMOUTH 2A **50**
Portsmouth & Southsea Station (Rail)
. . . . . 2F **5** (2C **50**)
PORTSMOUTH BUPA HOSPITAL 4B **22**
Portsmouth Cathedral 6B **4** (4A **50**)
Portsmouth Enterprise Cen.
PO3: Ports 2D **42**
Portsmouth FC 2G **51**
Portsmouth Harbour Station (Rail)
. . . . . 3A **4** (2H **49**)
Portsmouth Indoor Tennis Cen.
. . . . . 4D **4** (3B **50**)
Portsmouth Rd. PO6: Cosh 5B **30**
PO8: Horn 2B **10**
PO13: Lee S 3D **46**
PORT SOLENT 4E **29**
Portsview Av. PO16: Portc 2B **28**
Portsview Gdns. PO16: Portc 2B **28**
Portswood Rd. PO2: Ports 6A **30**
PO9: Hav 3D **20**
Port Way PO6: P Sol 3E **29**
Posbrooke Rd. PO4: S'sea 3G **51**
Posbrook La. PO14: Titch 6A **24**
Postern Cl. PO16: Portc 3B **28**
Post Office Rd. PO7: Purb 4E **19**
Potash Ct. PO9: Hav 2E **33**
Potash Ter. PO9: Hav 1E **33**
Potteries, The PO16: Fare 6B **14**
Potters Av. PO16: Fare 5A **14**
Potwell Ct. PO7: W'lle 4G **19**
Potwell La. PO7: Purb 5A **18**
Poulner Ct. PO9: Hav 3C **20**
Pound Cl. PO13: Gos 5D **38**
Pound Lea PO11: H Isl 2C **54**
Pound Rd. PO17: S'wick 1F **29**
Pounds Ter. PO1: Ports 1C **4** (1A **50**)
Power Rd. PO1: Ports 1E **51**
Powerscourt Rd. PO2: Ports 5A **42**
Poyner Cl. PO16: Fare 1B **26**
Poynings Pl. PO1: Ports 6C **4** (4B **50**)
Precinct, The PO7: W'lle 2G **19**
PO11: H Isl 4C **54**
PO12: Gos 3F **49**
Premier Bus. Pk. PO14: Fare 5B **26**
Preston Rd. PO2: Ports 5B **42**
Pretoria Rd. PO4: S'sea 4F **51**
Prideaux-Brune Av. PO13: Gos 1C **38**
Primate Rd. PO14: T Cmn 1A **24**
Primrose Cl. PO13: Gos 6C **26**
Primrose Ct. PO7: W'lle 3A **20**
Prince Albert Rd. PO4: S'sea 4G **51**
Prince Alfred St. PO12: Gos 4D **48**
Prince George St. PO1: Ports 2C **4** (2A **50**)
PO9: Hav 2F **33**
Prince of Wales Cl. PO7: W'lle 2A **20**
Prince of Wales Rd.
PO12: Gos 3E **49**
Prince Regent Ct. PO5: S'sea 5F **5**
Prince Rd. PO14: Fare 5H **25**
Princes Ct. PO1: Ports 6H **41**
Princes Dr. PO7: W'lle 6A **10**
Princes Ho. *PO5: S'sea 6E 5*
(off King's Ter.)
Prince's Pl. PO1: Ports 6G **41**
Princes Rd. GU32: Pet 3B **56**
Princess Gdns. PO8: Horn 6B **6**
Prince's St. PO1: Ports 6H **41**
Prinstead Ct. PO10: S'urne 3H **35**
PRINSTED 3H **35**
Prinsted Cres. PO6: Farl 4F **31**
Prinsted La. PO10: S'urne 3G **35**
Prinsted Wlk. PO14: Fare 3F **25**
Priors Cl. PO10: S'urne 2H **35**
Priorsdean Av. PO3: Ports 1G **51**
Priorsdean Cres. PO9: Hav 5D **20**
Priory Ct. PO4: S'sea 3E **51**
PO6: Cosh 3C **28**
Priory Cres. PO4: S'sea 3G **51**
Priory Gdns. PO7: W'lle 6G **9**
PO16: Portc 4A **28**
Priory Rd. PO4: S'sea 5G **51**
PO12: Gos 5H **39**
PO15: Fare 1F **25**
PO17: S'wick 3E **17**
Priory School Sports Hall 3E **51**
PRIVETT 3A **48**
Privett Ho. PO1: Ports 1C **4** (1A **50**)
Privett Pl. PO12: Gos 3A **48**
Privett Rd. PO7: Wid 6F **19**
PO12: Gos 3A **48**
PO13: Lee S 4G **47**
PO15: Fare 1E **25**
Prochurch Rd. PO8: Cowp 3B **10**
Proctor La. PO1: Ports 2F **51**

Promenade—Roads Hill

Promenade PO1: Ports 4A **50**
PO5: S'sea 5A **50**
PO12: Gos 6B **48**
PO13: Lee S 6F **37**
Promenade, The PO2: Ports 4H **41**
PO10: Ems 4D **34**
Promenade Ct. PO13: Lee S 1C **46**
Prospect La. PO9: Hav, R Cas 4H **21**
Prospect Rd. PO1: Ports 6G **41**
Protea Gdns. PO14: Titch 2C **24**
Providence Ct. PO1: Ports 6H **41**
Puffin Cres. PO14: Stub 1D **36**
Puffin Gdns. PO13: Gos 2B **38**
Puffin Wlk. PO8: Cowp 3F **9**
Pulens Cres. GU31: Pet 3G **57**
Pulens La. GU31: Pet 2F **57**
Pump La. PO8: Horn 2A **10**
PO13: Gos 4C **38**
Purbeck Dr. PO14: Fare 3F **25**
Purbeck Wlk. PO14: Fare 3F **25**
PURBROOK 5E **19**
Purbrook Chase Pct. PO7: Purb 6G **19**
Purbrook Gdns. PO7: Purb 4E **19**
Purbrook Heath Rd. PO7: Purb 4B **18**
Purbrook Rd. PO1: Ports 2E **51**
Purbrook Way PO7: Purb 5H **19**
PO9: Hav 5B **20**
Purcell Cl. PO7: W'lle 4G **19**
Purrocks, The GU32: Pet 2D **56**
Purslane Gdns. PO15: Titch 6A **12**
Pycroft Cl. PO11: H Isl 2E **45**
Pye St. PO1: Ports 1G **5** (1C **50**)
Pyle Cl. PO8: Cowp 3A **10**
Pyle La. PO8: Horn 2E **11**
Pyramid Cen. PO3: Ports 2D **42**
Pyramid Pk. PO9: Hav 4E **33**
Pyramids Leisure Cen., The 6D **50**
Pyrford Cl. PO7: W'lle 5G **9**
PO12: Gos 4A **48**
Pytchley Cl. PO14: Stub 3C **36**

Q

Quail Way PO8: Horn 1A **10**
Quandra Point PO3: Ports 2D **42**
Quarely Rd. PO9: Hav 3C **20**
Quarterdeck, The PO12: Gos 2G **49**
Quarterdeck Av. PO2: Ports 4F **41**
Quartremaine Rd. PO3: Ports 2D **42**
Quartremaine Rd. Ind. Est. PO3: Ports 3D **42**
Quay La. PO12: Gos 4H **39**
(Elson)
PO12: Gos 3G **49**
(Gosport)
Quay Point PO6: Cosh 3G **29**
Quayside Commerce Cen. *PO16: Fare* *3B* ***26***
(off Old Gosport Rd.)
Quay St. PO16: Fare 3C **26**
(not continuous)
QUEEN ALEXANDRA HOSPITAL 3B **30**
Queen Anne's Dr. PO9: Bed 1C **32**
Queen Elizabeth The Queen Mother Hall
PO4: S'sea 2B **52**
Queen Mary Rd. PO16: Portc 4B **28**
Queen Rd. PO14: Fare 5H **25**
Queens Cl. PO13: Lee S 1C **46**
Queens Ct. PO12: Gos 3E **49**
Queens Cres. PO5: S'sea 4C **50**
PO8: Horn 6B **6**
PO14: Stub 2F **37**
Queens Ga. *PO5: S'sea* *5B* ***50***
(off Osborne Rd.)
Queens Gro. PO5: S'sea 5C **50**
PO7: Purb 4F **19**
Queens Keep PO5: S'sea 5C **50**
Queen's Mall, The PO1: Ports 3F **5** (2C **50**)
Queen's Pde. PO7: W'lle 2G **19**
PO12: Gos 3A **48**
Queen's Pl. PO5: S'sea 4C **50**
Queens Rd. GU32: Pet 3B **56**
PO1: Ports 1A **4** (1H **49**)
PO2: Ports 5A **42**
PO7: W'lle 5G **9**
PO12: Gos 2E **49**
PO13: Lee S 3D **46**
PO16: Fare 2B **26**
Queen's Ter. PO5: S'sea 4C **50**
Queen St. PO1: Ports 2B **4** (2A **50**)
PO10: Ems 3E **35**
Queen's Way PO5: S'sea 4C **50**
Queensway PO11: H Isl 2C **44**
Queensway, The PO16: Portc 3H **27**
Quinton Cl. PO5: S'sea 4H **5** (3D **50**)
Quinton Flds. PO10: Ems 6E **23**
Quintrell Av. PO16: Portc 3G **27**

R

Racecourse La. PO6: Cosh 3F **29**
Racton Av. PO6: Dray 3D **30**
Racton Rd. PO10: Ems 6D **22**
Radclyffe Rd. PO16: Fare 1C **26**
Radnor St. PO5: S'sea 4G **5** (3C **50**)
Raglan St. PO5: S'sea 3H **5** (2D **50**)
Raglan Ter. PO10: Ems 2E **35**
PO10: S'urne 2E **35**
Rails La. PO11: H Isl 5D **54**
Railway Flats PO1: Ports 2E **51**
Railway Triangle Ind. Est. PO6: Farl 5D **30**
Railway Vw. PO1: Ports 2H **5** (2D **50**)
Raleigh Ho. PO1: Ports 3C **4**
Raleigh Wlk. PO13: Gos 1H **47**
Rambler Dr. PO13: Gos 1G **47**
Ramblers Way PO7: W'lle 6B **10**
Ramillies Ho. *PO12: Gos* *3E* ***49***
(off The Anchorage)
PO14: Fare 4G **25**
Rampart Gdns. PO3: Ports 6B **30**
Rampart Row PO12: Gos 4G **49**
Ramsay Pl. PO13: Gos 3C **38**
Ramscote GU31: Pet 3E **57**
Ramsdale Av. PO9: Hav 4C **20**
Ramsey Rd. PO11: H Isl 4C **54**
Ramshill GU31: Pet 3D **56**
Rams Wlk. GU32: Pet 4D **56**
Randolph Rd. PO2: Ports 2A **42**
Ranelagh Rd. PO2: Ports 4G **41**
PO9: Hav 2D **32**
Range Grn. PO2: Ports 2G **41**
Rannoch Cl. PO15: Fare 6G **13**
Ransome Cl. PO14: Titch 4B **24**
Ranvilles La. PO14: Fare, Stub 3D **24**
Rapley Ct. *PO11: H Isl* *4A* ***54***
(off Stamford Av.)
Rapson Cl. PO6: Cosh 2G **29**
Ratsey La. PO1: Ports 1E **51**
Raven Cl. PO13: Gos 1G **47**
Raven Cft. PO5: S'sea 6F **5** (4C **50**)
Ravens Cl. PO14: Stub 3F **37**
Ravenswood Gdns. PO5: S'sea 5D **50**
RAVENSWOOD HOUSE 1G **13**
Rawlinson Ter. PO1: Ports 1C **4** (1A **50**)
Ray Cl. GU31: Pet 2E **57**
Raymond Rd. PO6: Cosh 2C **28**
Raynes Rd. PO13: Lee S 3D **46**
Reading Ho. PO11: H Isl 5B **54**
Readon Cl. GU31: Pet 3E **57**
Record Rd. PO10: Ems 2C **34**
Rectory Av. PO6: Farl 2H **31**
Rectory Cl. PO12: Gos 5C **48**
PO14: Stub 2E **37**
Rectory Rd. PO9: Lang 3F **33**
(not continuous)
Redan, The PO12: Gos 6E **49**
Red Barn Av. PO16: Portc 2A **28**
Red Barn La. PO15: Fare 5G **13**
PO16: Fare 5G **13**
Redbridge Gro. PO9: Bed 6D **20**
Redcar Av. PO3: Ports 4C **42**
Redcliffe Gdns. PO4: S'sea 6E **51**
RED HILL 6H **11**
Redhill Ho. PO1: Ports 1D **50**
Redhill Rd. PO9: R Cas 1H **21**
Redhouse Pk. Gdns. PO12: Gos 1A **48**
Redlands Gro. PO4: S'sea 3A **52**
Redlands La. PO10: Ems 5D **22**
(not continuous)
PO14: Fare 2H **25**
PO16: Fare 4A **26**
Redlynch Cl. PO9: Hav 5H **21**
Redmill Dr. PO13: Lee S 6G **37**
Rednal Ho. PO5: S'sea 3H **5** (2D **50**)
Redoubt Ct. PO14: Fare 5H **25**
Redshank Rd. PO8: Horn 6A **6**
Redwing Ct. PO4: S'sea 2A **52**
Redwing Rd. PO8: Clan 1C **6** & 2G **7**
Redwood Ct. PO7: W'lle 1G **19**
Redwood Dr. PO16: Portc 3H **27**
Redwood Gro. PO9: Hav 5G **21**
Redwood Lodge PO16: Fare 1B **26**
Reedling Dr. PO4: S'sea 2A **52**
Reedmace Cl. PO7: W'lle 3A **20**
Reed's Pl. PO12: Gos 2C **48**
Reeds Rd. PO12: Gos 6H **39**
Rees Hall PO5: S'sea 6E **5**
Regal Cl. PO6: Cosh 3B **30**
Regency Ct. PO1: Ports 5B **4** (3A **50**)
Regency Gdns. PO7: W'lle 3F **19**
Regency Pl. PO15: Fare 2G **25**
Regent Ct. PO1: Ports 6H **41**
Regent Pl. PO5: S'sea 4B **50**
Regents Ct. PO9: Lang 3F **33**
PO17: K Vil 2G **13**
Regents M. GU32: Pet 3B **56**
Regents Pl. PO12: Gos 1F **49**
Regents Trade Pk.
PO13: Gos 6C **26**
Regent St. PO1: Ports 6G **41**
Reginald Rd. PO4: S'sea 4G **51**
Reigate Ho. PO1: Ports 1D **50**
Relay Rd. PO7: W'lle 1F **19**
Reldas, The *PO1: Ports* *6B* ***4***
(off Oyster St.)
Renny Rd. PO1: Ports 2E **51**
Renown Gdns. PO8: Cowp 2H **9**
Renown Ho. *PO12: Gos* *3E* ***49***
(off The Anchorage)
Repton Cl. PO12: Gos 3A **48**
Reservoir La. GU32: Pet 2D **56**
Resolution Ho. *PO12: Gos* *3E* ***49***
(off The Anchorage)
Rest-a-Wyle Av. PO11: H Isl 2C **54**
Retreat, The PO5: S'sea 4C **50**
Retreat Holiday Cvn. Pk., The
PO11: H Isl 5G **55**
Revenge Cl. PO4: S'sea 1A **52**
Revenge Ho. PO12: Gos 3E **49**
Reynolds Rd. PO12: Gos 5E **49**
Rhinefield Cl. PO9: Hav 5C **20**
Rhys Ct. PO4: S'sea 3G **51**
Richard Gro. PO12: Gos 4G **39**
Riches M. PO16: Fare 2A **26**
Richmond Cl. PO11: H Isl 3H **53**
Richmond Dr. PO11: H Isl 3H **53**
Richmond Gdns. *PO7: Purb* *4E* ***19***
(off Crofton Cl.)
Richmond Pl. PO1: Ports 3D **4** (2B **50**)
PO5: S'sea 5C **50**
Richmond Ri. PO16: Portc 2A **28**
Richmond Rd. PO5: S'sea 5D **50**
PO12: Gos 3C **48**
PO13: Lee S 6F **37**
Richmond Ter. *PO5: S'sea* *5C* ***50***
(off Netley Rd.)
Riders La. PO9: Hav 5E **21**
(not continuous)
Ridge Cl. PO8: Clan 1C **6**
RIDGE COMMON 1A **56**
Ridge Comn. La.
GU32: Ste, Stro 2A **56**
Ridgeway, The PO16: Fare 2E **27**
Ridgeway Cl. PO6: Cosh 2D **28**
Ridgeway Office Pk. GU32: Pet 5B **56**
Ridgway PO9: Hav 2D **32**
Ridings, The PO2: Ports 1B **42**
Rimington Rd. PO8: Cowp 4G **9**
Ringwood Ho. PO9: Hav 4F **21**
Ringwood Rd. PO4: S'sea 4H **51**
Ripley Gro. PO3: Ports 5C **42**
Ripon Ct. PO13: Gos 2H **47**
Ripon Gdns. PO7: W'lle 6B **10**
Rise, The PO7: Wid 1F **31**
Ritchie Cl. PO11: H Isl 4C **54**
Rival Moor Rd. GU31: Pet 4G **57**
(Durford Rd.)
GU31: Pet 5F **57**
(Heath Rd. E.)
Riverdale Av. PO7: W'lle 2A **20**
Riverhead Cl. PO4: S'sea 2H **51**
River La. PO15: Fun 3E **13**
Rivermead Ct. PO10: Ems 6E **23**
Riversdale Gdns. PO9: Hav 1F **33**
Riverside Av. PO16: Fare 6D **14**
Riverside M. PO17: Wick 2A **14**
Riverside Ter. PO10: Ems 3E **35**
Riverside Wlk. GU31: Pet 4E **57**
(not continuous)
River's St. PO5: S'sea 4H **5** (3D **50**)
River St. PO10: Westb 5F **23**
River Way PO9: Hav 6G **21**
Roads Hill PO8: Cath 4A **6**

Road Vw.—St Mary's Av.

Road Vw. PO2: Ports .5G **41**
Robert Mack Ct. PO1: Ports .3C **4** (2B **50**)
Roberts Cl. PO17: Wick .1A **14**
Roberts Rd. PO12: Gos .1B **48**
Robina Cl. PO7: W'lle .2A **20**
Robin Gdns. PO8: Cowp .3F **9**
Robins Cl. PO14: Stub .2E **37**
Robinson Ct. PO16: Portc .2A **28**
Robinson Rd. PO14: Stub .4D **36**
Robinson Way PO3: Ports .3E **43**
Rochester Ct. PO13: Gos .2H **47**
Rochester Rd. PO4: S'sea .4F **51**
Rochford Rd. PO6: Cosh .3H **29**
Rockbourne Cl. PO9: Hav .5C **20**
Rockingham Way PO16: Portc .3H **27**
Rockrose Way PO6: Cosh .1E **29**
Rockville Dr. PO7: W'lle .2G **19**
Rockwood Ct. PO10: Ems .2D **34**
Rodney Cl. PO13: Gos .6C **38**
Rodney Ho. PO12: Gos .3F **49**
Rodney Rd. PO4: S'sea .2F **51**
Rodney Way PO8: Horn .1B **10**
Roebuck Av. PO15: Fun .3F **13**
Roebuck Cl. PO6: Cosh .4B **30**
Roebuck Dr. PO12: Gos .6A **40**
Rogate Gdns. PO16: Portc .2A **28**
Rogate Ho. PO1: Ports .1H **5** (1D **50**)
Rogers Cl. PO12: Gos .1D **48**
Rogers Ho. PO13: Lee S .2D **46**
Rogers Mead PO11: H Isl .2B **44**
Roko Health & Fitness .2C **42**
Roland Cl. PO8: Horn .1B **10**
Roller Skating Rink
Hilsea .6A **30**
Roman Ct. PO10: S'urne .2H **35**
Roman Grn. PO7: Den .3A **8**
Roman Gro. PO16: Portc .5B **28**
Roman Way PO9: Bed .1C **32**
Romsey Av. PO3: Ports .1H **51**
PO16: Portc .3G **27**
Romsey Rd. PO8: Horn .3C **6**
Romyns Ct. PO14: Fare .2H **25**
Rooke Ho. PO1: Ports .2C **4**
Rookery, The PO10: S'urne .2E **35**
Rookery Av. PO15: White .2A **12**
Rookes Cl. PO8: Horn .1B **10**
Rookes M. GU31: Pet .3E **57**
Rook Farm Way PO11: H Isl .3B **54**
Rooksbury Cft. PO9: Hav .4G **21**
Rooksway Gro. PO16: Portc .3F **27**
Rookwood Vw. PO7: Den .2B **8**
Rope Quays PO12: Gos .2F **49**
Rope Wlk., The PO16: Fare .3B **26**
Ropley Rd. PO9: Hav .4H **21**
Rosebay Ct. PO7: W'lle .4H **19**
Rosebery Av. PO6: Cosh .4C **30**
Rosecott PO8: Horn .6D **6**
Rosedale Cl. PO14: Titch .3B **24**
Rose Hill PO8: Cowp .1A **10**
Roselands PO8: Horn .2A **10**
Rosemary Gdns. PO15: White .1A **12**
Rosemary La. PO1: Ports .3B **4** (2A **50**)
Rosemary Wlk. PO13: Lee S .1D **46**
Rosemary Way PO8: Horn .3B **10**
Rosery, The PO12: Gos .6D **48**
Rosetta Rd. PO4: S'sea .3H **51**
Rosewood PO13: Gos .4E **39**
Rosewood Gdns. PO8: Clan .2G **7**
Rosina Cl. PO7: W'lle .1B **20**
Roslyn Ho. PO5: S'sea .6G **5** (4C **50**)
Ross Way PO13: Lee S .6H **37**
Rostrevor La. PO4: S'sea .6E **51**
Rotherbrook Ct. GU32: Pet .5B **56**
Rother Cl. GU31: Pet .3G **57**
Rotherwick Cl. PO9: Hav .4H **21**
Rothesay Rd. PO12: Gos .6G **39**
Rothwell Cl. PO6: Cosh .2E **29**
Roundhouse Ct. PO11: H Isl .5D **54**
Roundhouse Mdw. PO10: S'urne .4E **35**
Round Tower, The .6A **4** (4H **49**)
Roundway PO7: W'lle .1H **19**
Rowallan Av. PO13: Gos .5C **38**
Rowan Av. PO8: Cowp .5B **10**
Rowan Cl. PO13: Lee S .2D **46**
Rowan Ct. PO4: S'sea .3F **51**
Rowan Rd. PO9: Hav .6H **21**
ROWANS HOSPICE, THE .5D **18**
Rowan Way PO14: Fare .3D **24**
Rowbury Rd. PO9: Hav .3D **20**
Rowena Ct. *PO5: S'sea* .*4D* **50**
(off Outram Rd.)
Rowes All. PO1: Ports .5A **4** (3H **49**)
Rowin Cl. PO11: H Isl .5F **55**
Rowland Rd. PO6: Cosh .2C **28**
PO15: Fare .1H **25**
Rowlands Av. PO7: W'lle .6G **9**
ROWLAND'S CASTLE .5H **11**
Rowlands Castle Rd.
PO8: Horn, Ids .1D **10**
ROWNER .4C **38**
Rowner Cl. PO13: Gos .4C **38**
Rowner La. PO13: Gos .3C **38**
Rowner Rd. PO13: Gos .3A **38**
(not continuous)
Rowner Swimming Cen. .1G **47**
Rowner Wlk. PO13: Gos .5C **38**
(not continuous)
Rownhams Rd. PO9: Hav .4D **20**
Row Wood La. PO13: Gos .4B **38**
Royal Albert Wlk. PO4: S'sea .5E **51**
Royal Apartments PO11: H Isl .5A **54**
Royal Armouries Mus. of Artillery .6H **15**
Royal Gdns. PO9: R Cas .6G **11**
Royal Garrison Church .*6C* **4**
(off Penny St.)
Royal Ga. PO4: S'sea .5H **51**
ROYAL HOSPITAL HASLAR .5F **49**
Royal Marines Mus. .5H **51**
Royal Naval Cotts. PO17: S'wick .3D **16**
Royal Naval Mus. .1A **4** (1H **49**)
Royal Navy Submarine Mus. .4G **49**
Royal Sovereign Av. PO14: Fare .6A **26**
Royal Way PO7: W'lle .2A **20**
Rudgwick Cl. PO16: Portc .3H **27**
Rudmore Ct. PO2: Ports .4G **41**
Rudmore Rd. PO2: Ports .5G **41**
Rudmore Rdbt. PO2: Ports .5H **41**
Rudmore Sq. PO2: Ports .5G **41**
Rudolph Ct. PO7: Purb .4E **19**
Rugby Rd. PO5: S'sea .3E **51**
Runnymede PO15: Fare .5F **13**
Rushes Farm GU32: Pet .3C **56**
Rushes Rd. GU32: Pet .3C **56**
Rushmere Wlk. PO9: Hav .3D **20**
Ruskin Rd. PO4: S'sea .3G **51**
Ruskin Way PO8: Cowp .3H **9**
Russell Churcher Ct. PO12: Gos .6F **39**
Russell Cl. PO13: Lee S .1D **46**
Russell Pl. PO16: Fare .2A **26**
Russell Rd. PO9: Hav .6F **21**
PO13: Lee S .2D **46**
Russell St. PO12: Gos .1C **48**
Russell Way GU31: Pet .5E **57**
Russet Gdns. PO10: S'urne .3F **35**
Rustington Ho. PO1: Ports .2G **5**
Rydal Cl. PO6: Cosh .2F **29**
Rydal Ho. PO6: Cosh .2F **29**
Rydal Rd. PO12: Gos .5G **39**
Ryde Pl. PO13: Lee S .3E **47**
Ryecroft PO9: Warb .2H **33**
Ryefield Cl. GU31: Pet .4G **57**

S

Sackville St. PO5: S'sea .5F **5** (3C **50**)
(not continuous)
Sadlers Wlk. PO10: S'urne .3E **35**
Saffron Way PO15: White .2A **12**
Sage Cl. PO7: W'lle .3A **20**
Sainsbury Lodge *PO1: Ports* .*2E* **51**
(off Lucknow St.)
St Agathas Way PO1: Ports .1F **5** (1C **50**)
St Albans Ct. PO13: Gos .2H **47**
St Alban's Rd. PO4: S'sea .4F **51**
PO9: Hav .5G **21**
St Andrew Cl. PO8: Horn .3C **6**
St Andrews Ct. PO1: Ports .4E **5** (3B **50**)
St Andrew's Rd. PO5: S'sea .6H **5** (4D **50**)
PO6: Farl .3H **31**
PO11: H Isl .5D **54**
PO12: Gos .3D **48**
St Anne's Gro. PO14: Fare .4H **25**
St Ann's Cres. PO12: Gos .1C **48**
St Ann's Rd. PO4: S'sea .4F **51**
PO8: Horn .6C **6**
St Aubin's Pk. PO11: H Isl .4H **53**
St Augustine Rd. PO4: S'sea .5F **51**
St Barbara Way PO2: Ports .1B **42**
St Bartholomew's Gdns.
PO5: S'sea .6H **5** (4D **50**)
St Catherines Ct. PO11: H Isl .4G **53**
St Catherine's Rd. PO11: H Isl .4G **53**
St Catherine St. PO5: S'sea .6D **50**
St Catherines Way PO16: Fare .2E **27**
St Chad's Av. PO2: Ports .3A **42**
St Christopher Av. PO16: Fare .6B **14**
St Christophers Gdns. PO13: Gos .3C **38**
ST CHRISTOPHER'S HOSPITAL .6B **14**
St Christophers Rd. PO9: Bed .5C **20**
St Clares Av. PO9: Hav .2D **20**
St Clares Ct. PO9: Hav .3D **20**
St Colman's Av. PO6: Cosh .3C **30**
St Davids Ct. PO13: Gos .1G **47**
St David's Rd. PO5: S'sea .5H **5** (3D **50**)
PO8: Clan .2G **7**
St Denys Wlk. PO9: Hav .3D **20**
St Edmondsbury Ct. *PO13: Gos* .*2H* **47**
(off Anson Cl.)
St Edwards Rd. PO5: S'sea .6F **5** (4C **50**)
PO12: Gos .3D **48**
St Edwards Ter. PO12: Gos .1C **48**
St Faith's Cl. PO12: Gos .2C **48**
St Faith's Rd. PO1: Ports .1H **5** (1D **50**)
St Francis Ct. PO2: Ports .1A **42**
St Francis Pl. PO9: Hav .6E **21**
St Francis Rd. PO12: Gos .6E **49**
St Georges Av. PO9: Warb .2H **33**
St George's Bus. Cen.
PO1: Ports .3C **4** (2A **50**)
St George's Ct. PO5: S'sea .6E **5** (4B **50**)
PO16: Fare .3B **26**
St George's Ind. Cen.
PO4: S'sea .2G **51**
St George's Rd. PO1: Ports .4C **4** (3A **50**)
PO4: S'sea .5G **51**
PO6: Cosh .3B **30**
PO11: H Isl .4H **53**
St George's Sq. PO1: Ports .3C **4** (2A **50**)
St Georges Wlk. *PO7: W'lle* .*2G* **19**
(off Hambledon Rd.)
PO12: Gos .2F **49**
St George's Way PO1: Ports .3C **4** (2A **50**)
St Giles Way PO8: Horn .3C **6**
St Helena Way PO16: Portc .3A **28**
St Helen's Cl. PO4: S'sea .5F **51**
St Helen's Ct. *PO4: S'sea* .*6E* **51**
(off St Helen's Pde.)
St Helens Ho. PO14: Fare .3E **25**
St Helen's Pde. PO4: S'sea .6E **51**
St Helens Rd. PO11: H Isl .4H **53**
PO12: Gos .4A **48**
St Helier Rd. PO12: Gos .5A **40**
St Hellen's Rd. PO6: Dray .3F **31**
St Herman's Cvn. Est.
PO11: H Isl .5E **55**
St Herman's Rd. PO11: H Isl .5E **55**
St Hilda Av. PO8: Horn .3C **6**
St Hubert Rd. PO8: Horn .3C **6**
St James Cl. PO8: Clan .1C **6**
ST JAMES HOSPITAL .2A **52**
St James' Rd. PO10: Ems .2D **34**
St James's Rd. PO5: S'sea .5F **5** (3C **50**)
St James's St. PO1: Ports .2D **4** (2B **50**)
St James Way PO16: Portc .3A **28**
St John's Av. PO7: Purb .5G **19**
St Johns Cl. PO11: H Isl .5A **54**
PO12: Gos .2D **48**
St John's Ct. PO2: Ports .4G **41**
St Johns M. PO5: S'sea .6H **5** (4D **50**)
St John's Rd. PO6: Cosh .3B **30**
PO9: Bed .5C **20**
PO10: S'urne .2H **35**
St John's Sq. PO12: Gos .2D **48**
St John the Evangelist Roman Catholic Cathedral .2E **5** (2B **50**)
St Judes Cl. PO5: S'sea .4C **50**
St Kitts Ho. PO6: Cosh .1D **28**
St Leonard's Av. PO11: H Isl .3C **54**
St Leonards Cl. PO15: Seg .6A **12**
St Lucia Ho. PO6: Cosh .1D **28**
St Luke's Community Sports Cen. .3G **5** (2C **50**)
St Luke's Rd. PO12: Gos .1C **48**
St Margarets La. PO14: Titch .2A **24**
St Margaret's Rd. PO11: H Isl .4C **54**
St Mark's Cl. PO12: Gos .6D **48**
St Marks Ct. PO12: Gos .2B **48**
St Mark's Pl. PO12: Gos .5D **48**
St Mark's Rd. PO2: Ports .4H **41**
PO12: Gos .6C **48**
St Martin's Ho. PO5: S'sea .6D **50**
St Mary's Av. PO12: Gos .5C **48**

ST MARY'S HOSPITAL 1F **51**
St Mary's Ho. PO3: Ports 1F **51**
St Mary's Rd. PO1: Ports 1E **51**
　　PO3: Ports 1E **51**
　　PO11: H Isl .4B **54**
　　PO14: Stub 1E **37**
St Matthew's Ct. PO12: Gos 2F **49**
St Matthew's Rd. PO6: Cosh 3B **30**
St Michaels Ct. PO6: Cosh 2F **29**
St Michael's Gro. PO14: Fare 4H **25**
St Michael's Ho. PO14: Fare 3H **25**
St Michael's Rd. PO1: Ports 4E **5** (3B **50**)
　　PO9: Bed 5C **20**
St Michaels Way PO8: Horn 3C **6**
St Nicholas Av. PO13: Gos 5B **38**
St Nicholas Rd. PO9: Bed 6C **20**
St Nicholas Row PO17: Wick 2A **14**
St Nicholas St. PO1: Ports 6C **4** (4A **50**)
St Paul's Rd. PO5: S'sea 5E **5** (3B **50**)
St Paul's Sq. PO5: S'sea 5E **5** (3B **50**)
St Peter's Av. PO11: H Isl 3E **45**
St Peters Ct. *GU32: Pet* *4D 56*
　　　　　　　　　　　　　　　(off Hylton Rd.)
　　PO10: Ems *3E 35*
　　　　　　　　　　　　　　　(off High St.)
St Peters Gro. PO5: S'sea 6H **5** (4D **50**)
St Peter's Rd. GU32: Pet 4D **56**
　　PO11: H Isl .1E **45**
St Peter's Sq. PO10: Ems 3D **34**
St Piran's Av. PO3: Ports 6C **42**
St Quentin Ho. *PO14: Fare* *4G 25*
　　　　　　　　　　　　　(off Bishopsfield Rd.)
St Richards Gdns. *PO7: Purb* *4E 19*
　　　　　　　　　　　　　(off Campbell Cres.)
St Ronan's Av. PO4: S'sea 5E **51**
St Ronan's Rd. PO4: S'sea 6E **51**
St Sebastian Cres. PO16: Fare 6B **14**
St Simon's Rd. PO5: S'sea 5D **50**
St Stephen's Rd. PO2: Ports 5A **42**
St Swithun's Rd. PO2: Ports 3B **42**
St Theresa's Cl. PO9: Bed 6C **20**
St Thomas Av. PO11: H Isl 4H **53**
St Thomas Cl. PO16: Fare 6C **14**
St Thomas's Ct. PO1: Ports 5C **4** (3A **50**)
St Thomas's Rd. PO12: Gos 5H **39**
St Thomas's St. PO1: Ports 6B **4** (4A **50**)
St Ursula Gro. PO5: S'sea 6H **5** (4D **50**)
St Valerie Rd. PO12: Gos 4D **48**
St Vincent Cres. PO8: Horn 1B **10**
St Vincent Leisure Cen. 1D **48**
St Vincent Rd. PO5: S'sea 5D **50**
　　PO12: Gos 1D **48**
St Vincent St. PO5: S'sea 4E **5** (3C **50**)
Salcombe Av. PO3: Ports 4C **42**
Salerno Dr. PO12: Gos 3B **48**
Salerno Ho. PO14: Fare 4H **25**
Salerno Rd. PO2: Ports 1H **41**
Salet Way PO7: W'lle 6B **10**
Salisbury Rd. PO4: S'sea 5F **51**
　　PO6: Cosh 4C **30**
Salisbury Ter. PO13: Lee S 2D **46**
Salterns Av. PO4: S'sea 2H **51**
Salterns Cl. PO11: H Isl 4E **55**
Salterns Est. PO16: Fare 4B **26**
Salterns La. PO11: H Isl 4D **54**
　　PO16: Fare 4B **26**
Saltern's Rd. PO13: Lee S 5D **46**
　　PO14: Stub 5D **36**
Saltings, The PO6: Farl 4G **31**
　　PO9: Lang 5F **33**
Saltmarsh La. PO11: H Isl 2A **54**
Salvia Cl. PO7: W'lle 3A **20**
Sampson Rd. PO1: Ports 1A **4** (1H **49**)
　　PO14: Fare 5H **25**
Samson Cl. PO13: Gos 6D **38**
Samuel Rd. PO1: Ports 1F **51**
Sandcroft Cl. PO12: Gos 4A **48**
Sanderling Lodge PO12: Gos 2F **49**
Sanderling Rd. PO4: S'sea 2A **52**
Sanderlings, The PO11: H Isl 5C **54**
Sanderson Cen., The PO12: Gos 2D **48**
Sandford Av. PO12: Gos 3H **47**
Sandhill La. PO13: Lee S 5A **38**
　　　　　　　　　　　　　　(not continuous)
Sandhurst Ct. PO5: S'sea 6H **5** (4D **50**)
San Diego Rd. PO12: Gos 1D **48**
Sandisplatt PO14: Fare 3E **25**
Sandleford Rd. PO9: Hav 2D **20**
Sandlewood Cl. PO8: Clan 2G **7**
Sandown Cl. PO12: Gos 4H **47**
Sandown Hgts. PO14: Fare 3E **25**

Sandown Rd. PO6: Cosh 4A **30**
Sandpiper Cl. PO8: Horn 6A **6**
Sandpipers PO6: Farl 4G **31**
Sandport Gro. PO16: Portc 4H **27**
Sandringham La. PO1: Ports 2E **51**
Sandringham Rd. GU32: Pet 3D **56**
　　PO1: Ports 2E **51**
　　PO14: Fare 3D **24**
Sandsbury La. GU32: Stro 2A **56**
Sandy Beach Est. PO11: H Isl 6H **55**
Sandy Brow PO7: Purb 5F **19**
Sandy Cl. GU31: Pet 4G **57**
Sandyfield Cres. PO8: Cowp 4G **9**
Sandy La. PO14: Titch 3B **24**
Sandy Point PO11: H Isl 5H **55**
Sandy Point Nature Reserve 6H **55**
Sandy Point Rd. PO11: H Isl 6G **55**
　　　　　　　　　　　　　　(not continuous)
Sanross Cl. PO14: Stub 4C **36**
Sapphire Cl. PO12: Gos 6H **39**
Sapphire Ridge PO7: W'lle 2A **20**
Sarah Robinson Ho. PO1: Ports . . .2C **4** (2A **50**)
Saunders Cl. PO13: Lee S 6A **38**
Saunders Ho. PO6: Cosh 2C **28**
Saunders M. PO4: S'sea 5H **51**
Savernake Cl. PO13: Gos 3D **38**
Saville Cl. PO12: Gos 4B **48**
Saville Gdns. PO16: Fare 6A **14**
Savoy Ct. PO4: S'sea 6E **51**
Saxe Ct. PO17: K Vil 2G **13**
Saxley Ct. PO9: Hav 3C **20**
Saxon Cl. PO8: Cath 2C **6**
　　PO16: Portc .2H **27**
Scafell Av. PO14: Fare 3F **25**
Scarff Ct. PO11: H Isl 5D **54**
Scholars' Wlk. PO6: Dray 4E **31**
School La. GU32: Pet 1F **57**
　　PO2: Ports 6H **41**
　　PO7: Den 2A **8**
　　PO10: Ems 3D **34**
　　PO10: Westb 4F **23**
School Rd. PO9: Hav 2E **33**
　　PO12: Gos 4F **39**
　　PO17: Wick .2A **14**
Schooners Cl. PO13: Lee S 1D **46**
Schooner Way PO4: S'sea 1A **52**
Scimitars, The PO14: Stub 2D **36**
Scotney Ct. PO9: Hav 3H **21**
Scott Cl. PO14: Stub 1E **37**
Scott Ho. PO2: Ports 3G **41**
Scott Rd. PO1: Ports 1A **4** (1H **49**)
　　PO3: Ports 6B **30**
Scratchface La. PO7: Purb 5H **19**
　　　　　　　　　　　　　　(not continuous)
　　PO9: Bed 1A **32**
Seabird Way PO16: Fare 4B **26**
Sea Breeze Gdns. PO4: S'sea 4A **52**
Seacourt Tennis Club 5B **54**
Sea Crest Rd. PO13: Lee S 2D **46**
Seafarers Wlk. PO11: H Isl 6H **55**
SEAFIELD 4E **49**
Seafield Pk. Rd. PO14: Stub 4D **36**
Seafield Rd. PO3: Ports 4C **42**
　　PO16: Portc .4H **27**
Seafields PO10: Ems 3C **34**
Seafield Ter. PO12: Gos 4E **49**
Seafire Cl. PO13: Lee S 2E **47**
Sea Front PO11: H Isl 4G **53**
Sea Front Est. PO11: H Isl 5D **54**
Seager's Ct. PO1: Ports 6A **4** (4H **49**)
Sea Gro. Av. PO11: H Isl 5C **54**
Seagrove Rd. PO2: Ports 4H **41**
Seagull Cl. PO4: S'sea 1A **52**
Seagull La. PO10: Ems 2D **34**
　　　　　　　　　　　　　　(not continuous)
Seagulls, The PO13: Lee S 3E **47**
Seahorse Wlk. PO12: Gos 2F **49**
Sea Kings PO14: Stub 2D **36**
　　　　　　　　　　　　　　(not continuous)
Sea La. PO14: Stub 5E **37**
Sealark Rd. PO12: Gos 6H **39**
Seamead PO14: Stub 5E **37**
Sea Mill Gdns.
　　PO1: Ports 3C **4** (2A **50**)
Searle Dr. PO12: Gos 6B **40**
Seathrift Cl. PO13: Lee S 1C **46**
Seathwaite Ho. PO6: Cosh 2F **29**
Seaton Av. PO3: Ports 5C **42**
Seaton Cl. PO14: Stub 3E **37**
SEA VIEW 5C **54**
Seaview Av. PO16: Portc 2C **28**

Seaview Ct. PO12: Gos 4H **47**
　　PO13: Lee S .2D **46**
Sea Vw. Rd. PO6: Dray 2E **31**
Seaview Rd. PO11: H Isl 4E **55**
Seaward Twr. PO12: Gos 3G **49**
Seaway Cres. PO4: S'sea 3B **52**
Seaway Gro. PO16: Portc 5A **28**
Sebastian Gro. PO7: W'lle 1A **20**
Second Av. PO6: Cosh 3A **30**
　　PO6: Farl 4F **31**
　　PO9: Hav 1H **33**
　　PO10: S'urne 3H **35**
Sedgefield Cl. PO6: Cosh 3D **28**
Sedgeley Gro. PO12: Gos 5G **39**
Sedgewick Cl. PO13: Gos 5C **38**
Sedgley Cl. PO5: S'sea 4H **5** (3D **50**)
SEGENSWORTH 5A **12**
Segensworth E. Ind. Est.
　　PO15: Seg 4A **12**
　　　　　　　　　　　　　　(not continuous)
Segensworth Nth. Ind. Est.
　　PO15: Seg 4A **12**
Segensworth Rd. PO15: Seg, Titch 5A **12**
　　　　　　　　　　　　　　(not continuous)
Selangor Av. PO10: Ems 2A **34**
Selborne Av. PO9: Hav 4D **20**
Selborne Cl. GU32: Pet 2D **56**
Selborne Gdns. PO12: Gos 3B **48**
Selbourne Rd. PO9: Hav 2E **33**
Selbourne Ter. PO1: Ports 2E **51**
Selhurst Ho. PO1: Ports 1D **50**
Selma Cl. PO5: S'sea 5D **50**
Selsey Av. PO4: S'sea 5G **51**
　　PO12: Gos 5G **39**
Selsey Cl. PO11: H Isl 5H **55**
SELSMORE 4E **55**
Selsmore Av. PO11: H Isl 5E **55**
Selsmore Rd. PO11: H Isl 4C **54**
Sennen Pl. PO6: P Sol 4E **29**
Sentinel Cl. PO7: W'lle 6B **10**
Serotine Cl. PO17: K Vil 2G **13**
Serpentine Rd. PO4: S'sea 5C **50**
　　　　　　　　　　　　　　(Clarence Pde.)
　　PO5: S'sea 5C **50**
　　　　　　　　　　　　　　(Osborne Rd.)
　　PO7: Wid 6E **19**
　　PO16: Fare 6B **14**
Service Rd. PO6: Cosh 3H **29**
Settlers Cl. PO1: Ports 1H **5** (1D **50**)
Sevenoaks Rd. PO6: Cosh 3A **30**
Severn Cl. PO6: Cosh 2F **29**
　　　　　　　　　　　　　　(not continuous)
　　PO16: Portc .3G **27**
Seymour Cl. PO2: Ports 6H **41**
Seymour Rd. PO13: Lee S 3D **46**
Shackleton Ho. PO2: Ports 3A **42**
Shackleton Rd. PO13: Gos 5D **38**
Shadwell Cl. PO2: Ports 3G **41**
Shadwell Rd. PO2: Ports 3H **41**
Shaftesbury Av. PO7: Purb, W'lle 5F **19**
Shaftesbury Rd. PO5: S'sea 5C **50**
　　PO12: Gos 3E **49**
　　　　　　　　　　　　　　(not continuous)
Shakespeare Gdns. PO8: Cowp 4G **9**
Shakespeare M. *PO14: Titch* *3C 24*
　　　　　　　　　　　　　　　(off East St.)
Shakespeare Rd. PO1: Ports 1E **51**
Shakespeare Ter. PO1: Ports 6C **4**
Shalbourne Rd. PO12: Gos 6G **39**
Shaldon Rd. PO9: Hav 3H **21**
Shamrock Cl. PO12: Gos 3F **49**
Shamrock Enterprise Cen. PO12: Gos 4F **39**
Shanklin Pl. PO14: Fare 3E **25**
Shanklin Rd. PO4: S'sea 3E **51**
Shannon Cl. PO15: Fare 1F **25**
Shannon Ct. *PO12: Gos* *5A 40*
　　　　　　　　　　　　　　(off Hayling Cl.)
Shannon Rd. PO14: Fare 5A **26**
　　PO14: Stub 1D **36**
Sharlands Rd. PO14: Fare 5A **26**
Sharon Ct. PO12: Gos 2E **49**
Sharpness Cl. PO14: Fare 3E **25**
Sharps Cl. PO3: Ports 2D **42**
Sharps Rd. PO9: Hav 4H **21**
Shawcross Ind. Pk. PO3: Ports 6C **30**
Shawfield Rd. PO9: Hav 2G **33**
Shawford Gro. PO9: Hav 4C **20**
Shearer Rd. PO1: Ports 6A **42**
Shear Hill GU31: Pet 2F **57**
Shearwater Av. PO16: Portc 2E **27**
Shearwater Cl. PO13: Gos 3B **38**

Shearwater Dr. PO6: Farl . . . 4H **31**
Sheep St. GU32: Pet . . . 4D **56**
Sheepwash La. PO7: Den . . . 6A **8**
Sheepwash Rd. PO8: Cowp . . . 4C **10**
(not continuous)
PO8: Horn . . . 1D **10**
Sheerwater Ct. PO11: H Isl . . . 6F **55**
SHEET . . . 1F **57**
Sheffield Ct. PO13: Gos . . . 1G **47**
Sheffield Rd. PO1: Ports . . . 2E **51**
Shelford Rd. PO4: S'sea . . . 2H **51**
Shelley Av. PO6: Cosh . . . 2C **28**
Shelley Gdns. PO8: Cowp . . . 4G **9**
Shenley Cl. PO15: Fare . . . 1E **25**
Shepards Cl. PO14: Fare . . . 3E **25**
Shepheard's Way PO12: Gos . . . 5E **49**
Sheppard Cl. PO8: Horn . . . 1A **10**
Sherbrooke Cl. PO13: Lee S . . . 1E **47**
Sherfield Av. PO9: Hav . . . 4G **21**
Sheringham Rd. PO6: Cosh . . . 2H **29**
Sherland Pl. *PO14: Fare . . . 4G 25*
(off Longfield Av.)
Sherwin Wlk. PO12: Gos . . . 4C **48**
Sherwood Rd. PO12: Gos . . . 3C **48**
Shetland Cl. PO6: Cosh . . . 2B **30**
Shillinglee PO7: Purb . . . 5G **19**
Shipbuilding Rd. PO1: Ports . . . 1H **49**
Ship Leopard St. PO1: Ports . . . 2B **4** (2A **50**)
Shipton Grn. PO9: Hav . . . 3D **20**
Shire Cl. PO7: W'lle . . . 6B **10**
Shirley Av. PO4: S'sea . . . 3A **52**
Shirley Rd. PO5: S'sea . . . 5E **51**
Shirrel Ct. PO12: Gos . . . 4H **47**
Sholing Ct. PO9: Hav . . . 3D **20**
Shoot La. PO13: Lee S . . . 5H **37**
Shore Av. PO4: S'sea . . . 1H **51**
Shorehaven PO6: Cosh . . . 3D **28**
Short Rd. PO14: Stub . . . 3C **36**
Short Row PO1: Ports . . . 1B **4** (1A **50**)
Shrubbery, The PO12: Gos . . . 6F **39**
Shrubbery Cl. PO16: Portc . . . 4A **28**
Sibland Cl. PO14: Fare . . . 3F **25**
Sidlesham Cl. PO11: H Isl . . . 5H **55**
Sidmouth Av. PO3: Ports . . . 5C **42**
Silchester Rd. PO3: Ports . . . 6D **42**
Silhouette Ct. PO11: H Isl . . . 6E **55**
Silkstead Av. PO9: Hav . . . 3F **21**
Silver Birch Av. PO14: Fare . . . 3G **25**
Silverdale Dr. PO7: W'lle . . . 5E **9**
Silverlock Cl. PO2: Ports . . . 5H **41**
Silverlock Pl. PO10: Westb . . . 4F **23**
Silversands Ct. PO11: H Isl . . . 4B **54**
Silver Sands Gdns. PO11: H Isl . . . 5D **54**
Silver St. PO5: S'sea . . . 6E **5** (4B **50**)
Silverthorne Way PO7: W'lle . . . 1F **19**
Silvertrees PO10: Ems . . . 1D **34**
Silvester Rd. PO8: Cowp . . . 4G **9**
Simmons Grn. PO11: H Isl . . . 4E **55**
Simpson Cl. PO16: Portc . . . 2A **28**
Simpson Rd. PO2: Ports . . . 4G **41**
PO6: Cosh . . . 2B **30**
Sinah La. PO11: H Isl . . . 4G **53**
SINAH WARREN . . . 3F **53**
Sinah Warren Holiday & Leisure Club
PO11: H Isl . . . 3F **53**
Singleton Gdns. PO8: Clan . . . 1D **6**
Sirius Ct. PO5: S'sea . . . 5F **5** (3C **50**)
Sirius Ho. PO5: S'sea . . . 5D **50**
Siskin Gro. PO7: W'lle . . . 3A **20**
Siskin Rd. PO4: S'sea . . . 2A **52**
Sissinghurst Rd. PO16: Portc . . . 4G **27**
Siward Ho. GU32: Pet . . . 4C **56**
Sixth Av. PO6: Cosh . . . 3A **30**
Skew Rd. PO16: Portc . . . 1A **28**
PO17: Fare . . . 1A **28**
Skipper Way PO13: Lee S . . . 1D **46**
Skye Cl. PO6: Cosh . . . 2B **30**
Skylark Ct. PO4: S'sea . . . 2A **52**
Skylark Mdws. PO15: Titch . . . 4B **12**
Slater App. PO2: Ports . . . 4F **41**
(not continuous)
Slindon Cl. PO8: Clan . . . 2H **7**
Slindon Gdns. PO9: Hav . . . 2F **33**
Slindon St. PO1: Ports . . . 2G **5** (2C **50**)
Slingsby Cl. PO1: Ports . . . 6D **4** (4B **50**)
Slipper Cvn. Pk. PO10: S'urne . . . 3E **35**
Slipper Mill PO10: S'urne . . . 4E **35**
Slipper Rd. PO10: S'urne . . . 3E **35**
Slipway, The PO6: P Sol . . . 4E **29**
Sloane Stanley Ct. PO12: Gos . . . 1D **48**
Slocum Ho. PO12: Gos . . . 3E **49**
Small Cl. GU31: Pet . . . 2E **57**
Smallcutts Av. PO10: S'urne . . . 2H **35**
Smeaton Cl. PO15: Seg . . . 5A **12**
Smeaton St. PO2: Ports . . . 3G **41**
Smeeton Rd. PO13: Lee S . . . 1D **46**
Smith St. PO12: Gos . . . 3C **48**
Smithy, The PO7: Den . . . 3A **8**
Snape Cl. PO13: Gos . . . 5C **38**
Snowberry Cres. PO9: Hav . . . 6H **21**
Snowdon Dr. PO14: Fare . . . 3G **25**
SOAKE . . . 4D **8**
Soake Rd. PO7: Den . . . 4D **8**
Soberton Dr. GU31: Pet . . . 2E **57**
Soberton Ho. PO1: Ports . . . 1H **5**
Soberton Rd. PO9: Hav . . . 5E **21**
Soccer City . . . 6C **14**
Soldridge Cl. PO9: Hav . . . 3H **21**
Solent 27 PO6: Farl . . . 5E **31**
Solent Bus. Pk. PO15: White . . . 2A **12**
Solent Cen. PO15: White . . . 2A **12**
Solent Ct. PO14: Stub . . . 3E **37**
Solent Dr. PO4: S'sea . . . 3H **51**
PO11: H Isl . . . 5B **54**
Solent Hgts. PO4: S'sea . . . 4C **52**
PO13: Lee S . . . 2C **46**
Solent Ho. PO9: Hav . . . 6G **21**
PO16: Fare . . . 4A **26**
Solent Rd. PO6: Dray . . . 3E **31**
PO9: Hav . . . 2D **32**
PO14: Stub . . . 4C **36**
Solent Vw. PO13: Lee S . . . 6F **37**
PO16: Portc . . . 2H **27**
Solent Village PO15: White . . . 3A **12**
Solent Way PO12: Gos . . . 4A **48**
Somborne Dr. PO9: Hav . . . 4F **21**
Somerset Rd. PO5: S'sea . . . 6D **50**
Somers Rd. PO5: S'sea . . . 5G **5** (3C **50**)
(not continuous)
Somers Rd. Nth. PO1: Ports . . . 2D **50**
Somerston Flats PO9: Hav . . . 2G **33**
SOMERS TOWN . . . 5G **5** (3C **50**)
Somervell Cl. PO12: Gos . . . 5C **48**
Somervell Dr. PO16: Fare . . . 6H **13**
Somerville Pl. PO2: Ports . . . 3G **41**
Sonata Ho. PO6: P Sol . . . 4E **29**
Sonnet Way PO7: W'lle . . . 1B **20**
Sopley Ct. PO9: Hav . . . 3H **21**
Sorrel Cl. PO7: W'lle . . . 3A **20**
Sorrel Dr. PO15: White . . . 2A **12**
Southampton Hill PO14: Titch . . . 2B **24**
Southampton Ho. PO9: Hav . . . 4G **21**
Southampton Rd. PO6: Cosh . . . 3C **28**
PO14: Titch . . . 1A **24**
PO16: Fare . . . 1B **26**
Southampton Row PO1: Ports . . . 2C **4** (2A **50**)
South Av. PO2: Ports . . . 1A **42**
SOUTHBOURNE . . . 3H **35**
Southbourne Av. PO6: Dray . . . 3D **30**
PO10: S'urne . . . 3F **35**
Southbourne Ind. Est.
PO10: S'urne . . . 2H **35**
Southbourne Station (Rail) . . . 3H **35**
Southbrook Cl. PO9: Lang . . . 3F **33**
Southbrook Rd. PO9: Lang . . . 3F **33**
Southcliff PO13: Lee S . . . 6G **37**
South Cl. PO9: Hav . . . 3G **33**
PO12: Gos . . . 5B **48**
Southcroft Rd. PO12: Gos . . . 2B **48**
Sth. Cross St. PO12: Gos . . . 3F **49**
Southdown Rd. PO6: Cosh . . . 3C **30**
PO8: Horn . . . 3C **6**
(not continuous)
Southdown Vw. PO7: W'lle . . . 5E **9**
Southernhay PO7: Den . . . 3B **8**
Southfield Wlk. PO9: Hav . . . 2C **20**
SOUTH HAYLING . . . 5A **54**
Southlands PO6: Cosh . . . 3C **30**
South La. PO8: Blen, Chal . . . 4G **7**
PO8: Clan . . . 2F **7**
PO10: S'urne . . . 1H **35**
PO10: Westb, Wood . . . 6H **23**
Southleigh Gro. PO11: H Isl . . . 3B **54**
Southleigh Rd. PO9: Hav, Warb . . . 2H **33**
PO10: Ems . . . 6C **22**
South Lodge PO15: Fare . . . 2D **24**
Southmead Rd. PO15: Fare . . . 2F **25**
Southmoor La. PO9: Hav . . . 3D **32**
South Normandy
PO1: Ports . . . 5C **4** (3A **50**)
South Pde. PO4: S'sea . . . 6D **50**
PO5: S'sea . . . 6D **50**
South Pl. PO13: Lee S . . . 3E **47**
South Rd. PO1: Ports . . . 6A **42**
PO6: Dray . . . 4F **31**
PO8: Horn . . . 4C **6**
(not continuous)
PO11: H Isl . . . 4B **54**
PO17: S'wick . . . 1E **29**
(Hilltop Rd.)
PO17: S'wick . . . 3E **17**
(Main Dr.)
SOUTHSEA . . . 5C **50**
Southsea Cvn. Activity Pk.
PO4: S'sea . . . 5B **52**
Southsea Castle & Mus. . . . 6C **50**
Southsea Esplanade PO4: S'sea . . . 6F **51**
Southsea Model Village . . . 6F **51**
Southsea Ter. PO5: S'sea . . . 4B **50**
Southsea Works Ind. Est. PO4: S'sea . . . 2G **51**
South Spur PO17: S'wick . . . 1F **29**
South Sq. PO17: K Vil . . . 2G **13**
South St. PO5: S'sea . . . 6E **5** (4C **50**)
PO9: Hav . . . 3F **33**
PO10: Ems . . . 3D **34**
PO12: Gos . . . 4D **48**
PO14: Titch . . . 3B **24**
South Ter. PO1: Ports . . . 2B **4** (2A **50**)
South Vw. PO8: Cowp . . . 3A **10**
Southwater PO13: Lee S . . . 1B **46**
Southway PO13: Gos . . . 2C **38**
PO15: Titch . . . 6A **12**
Southways PO14: Stub . . . 3F **37**
SOUTHWICK . . . 3C **16**
Southwick Av. PO16: Portc . . . 2C **28**
Southwick By-Pass PO17: S'wick . . . 3B **16**
Southwick Ct. PO14: Fare . . . 5A **26**
Southwick Hill Rd. PO6: Cosh . . . 1H **29**
Southwick Ho. PO1: Ports . . . 1H **5**
Southwick Rd. PO6: Cosh . . . 4D **16**
PO7: Den . . . 3A **8**
PO17: S'wick . . . 4D **16**
PO17: Wick . . . 2B **14**
Southwood Rd. PO2: Ports . . . 1A **42**
PO11: H Isl . . . 5E **55**
Sovereign Av. PO12: Gos . . . 6A **40**
Sovereign Cl. PO4: S'sea . . . 2B **52**
Sovereign Dr. PO4: S'sea . . . 2A **52**
Sovereign Ga. *PO1: Ports . . . 1C 50*
(off Staunton St.)
Sovereign La. PO7: Purb . . . 6G **19**
Spain, The GU32: Pet . . . 4C **56**
Sparrow Cl. PO8: Cowp . . . 3H **9**
Sparrow Ct. PO13: Lee S . . . 6H **37**
Sparrowhawk Cl. PO3: Ports . . . 1C **42**
Sparsholt Cl. PO9: Hav . . . 4C **20**
Spartan Cl. PO14: Stub . . . 6F **25**
Specks La. PO4: S'sea . . . 2G **51**
Speedfield Pk. Retail Pk.
PO14: Fare . . . 6B **26**
Spencer Cl. PO11: H Isl . . . 4C **54**
Spencer Ct. PO5: S'sea . . . 5D **50**
PO14: Stub . . . 3G **37**
Spencer Dr. PO13: Lee S . . . 2D **46**
Spencer Gdns. PO8: Cowp . . . 3G **9**
Spencer Rd. PO4: S'sea . . . 5F **51**
PO10: Ems . . . 5C **22**
Spenlow Cl. PO2: Ports . . . 6H **41**
Spice Quay PO1: Ports . . . 6A **4** (4A **50**)
Spicer Ho. PO1: Ports . . . 1D **4**
Spicer St. PO1: Ports . . . 1G **5** (1C **50**)
Spicewood PO15: Fare . . . 1G **25**
Spindle Cl. PO9: Hav . . . 6A **22**
Spindle Warren PO9: Hav . . . 6A **22**
Spinnaker Cl. PO11: H Isl . . . 3A **54**
PO13: Gos . . . 6D **38**
Spinnaker Dr. PO2: Ports . . . 1H **41**
Spinnaker Grange
PO11: H Isl . . . 1E **45**
Spinnaker Ho. PO6: P Sol . . . 4E **29**
Spinnaker Tower . . . 4A **4** (3H **49**)
Spinnaker Vw. PO9: Bed . . . 2A **32**
Spinney, The PO7: Den . . . 4B **8**
PO8: Horn . . . 1A **10**
PO13: Gos . . . 4D **38**
PO16: Fare . . . 2F **27**
Spinney Cl. PO8: Cowp . . . 4G **9**
Spithead Av. PO12: Gos . . . 6E **49**
Spithead Hgts. PO4: S'sea . . . 4C **52**
Spithead Ho. PO16: Fare . . . 4A **26**
Spring, The PO7: Den . . . 4B **8**
Spring Ct. PO13: Lee S . . . 2D **46**
Springcroft PO13: Gos . . . 6B **26**

Springfield Cl. PO9: Bed 1B 32
  PO17: Wick 1A 14
Springfield Way PO14: Stub 4E 37
Spring Gdn. La. PO12: Gos 2E 49
Spring Gdns. PO1: Ports 3E 5 (2C 50)
  PO10: Ems 3D 34
Springles La. PO15: Titch 4B 12
Spring St. PO1: Ports 2F 5 (2C 50)
Spring Va. PO8: Cowp 3B 10
Spring Wlk. PO1: Ports 1F 5 (1C 50)
Springwell PO9: Hav 2F 33
Springwood Av. PO7: W'lle 3H 19
Spruce Av. PO7: W'lle 2A 20
Spruce Wlk. PO13: Lee S 1D 46
Spur, The PO12: Gos 5B 48
  PO17: Wick 1A 14
Spurlings Ind. Est. PO17: Fare 6E 15
Spurlings Rd. PO17: Fare 5D 14
Spur Rd. PO6: Cosh 3B 30
  PO7: W'lle 2G 19
           (not continuous)
Square, The GU32: Pet 4D 56
  PO10: Westb 6F 23
  PO12: Gos 5A 40
  PO14: Titch 3B 24
  PO17: Wick 2A 14
           (not continuous)
Square Tower, The 6A 4 (4H 49)
Stable La. GU31: Pet 4D 56
          (off Bowen La.)
Stacey Ct. PO9: Hav 2D 20
Stafford Rd. GU32: Pet 2D 56
  PO5: S'sea 6H 5 (4D 50)
Staffwise Bus. Cen. PO6: Cosh 4B 30
Stagshorn Rd. PO8: Horn 6C 6
Stag Way PO15: Fun 4F 13
STAKES 4G 19
Stakes Hill Rd. PO7: Purb, W'lle 2G 19
Stakes Rd. PO7: Purb 4E 19
Stallard Cl. PO10: Ems 2C 34
Stamford Av. PO11: H Isl 4A 54
Stamford St. PO1: Ports 1E 51
Stampsey Ct. PO2: Ports 3H 41
STAMSHAW .3H 41
Stamshaw & Tipner Leisure Cen. 3G 41
Stamshaw Prom. PO2: Ports 1H 41
Stamshaw Rd. PO2: Ports 3H 41
Stanbridge Rd. PO9: Hav 6H 21
Standard Way PO16: Fare 6C 14
Stanford Cl. PO6: Cosh 3H 29
Stanford Ct. PO9: Hav 4H 21
Stanhope Ga. PO5: S'sea 5C 50
Stanhope Rd. PO1: Ports 2F 5 (2C 50)
Stanley Av. PO3: Ports 5D 42
Stanley Cl. PO12: Gos 4G 39
  PO15: Fare 2G 25
Stanley La. PO5: S'sea 5C 50
Stanley Rd. PO2: Ports 4G 41
  PO10: Ems 3E 35
Stanley St. PO5: S'sea 5C 50
STANSTED 1E 23
Stansted Cl. PO9: R Cas 5H 11
Stansted Cres. PO9: Hav 3H 21
STANSTED PARK 1G 23
Stansted Rd. PO5: S'sea 3D 50
Stanswood Rd. PO9: Hav 3D 20
Stanton Rd. GU32: Pet 3C 56
Staple Cl. PO7: W'lle 6F 9
Staplers Reach PO13: Gos 3B 38
Stapleton Rd. PO3: Ports 5C 42
Stares Cl. PO13: Gos 6C 38
Starina Gdns. PO7: W'lle 1B 20
Starling Way PO13: Lee S 6H 37
Station App. PO1: Ports 3B 4 (2A 50)
  PO10: Ems 2D 34
  PO16: Fare 2A 26
Station Cl. PO17: Wick 1A 14
Station Rd. GU32: Pet 3C 56
  PO3: Ports 5C 42
  PO6: Dray 5E 31
  PO11: H Isl 3H 53
  PO12: Gos 6F 39
  PO16: Portc 3B 28
  PO17: Wick 1A 14
Station St. PO1: Ports 2F 5 (2C 50)
Station Theatre 3H 53
Staunton Av. PO11: H Isl 4H 53
Staunton Country Pk. 3G 21
Staunton Country Pk. Vis. Cen. 3F 21
Staunton Hgts. PO9: Hav 4E 21
Staunton Rd. PO9: Hav 1E 33

Staunton St. PO1: Ports 1C 50
Stead Cl. PO11: H Isl 4D 54
Steel St. PO5: S'sea 6E 5 (4B 50)
STEEP 1B 56
Steep Cl. PO16: Portc 2A 28
Steerforth Cl. PO2: Ports 5H 41
Stein Rd. PO10: S'urne 1H 35
Stephen Cl. PO8: Cowp 5B 10
Stephen Lodge PO5: S'sea 4C 50
Stephen Rd. PO15: Fare 2H 25
Stephenson Cl. PO12: Gos 5C 48
Stephenson Rd. PO15: Titch 1A 24
Stewart Pl. PO1: Ports 6A 42
Stirling Av. PO7: W'lle 2H 19
Stirling Cl. PO15: Fare 6G 13
Stirling St. PO2: Ports 5H 41
Stockbridge Cl. PO9: Hav 4H 21
Stocker Pl. PO13: Gos 4D 38
STOCKHEATH 5F 21
Stockheath La. PO9: Hav 1E 33
Stockheath Rd. PO9: Hav 5E 21
Stockheath Way PO9: Hav 6F 21
STOKE 4C 44
Stoke Gdns. PO12: Gos 3E 49
Stoke Rd. PO12: Gos 3D 48
Stokes Bay Mobile Home Pk.
  PO12: Gos 5H 47
          (not continuous)
Stokes Bay Rd. PO12: Gos 5H 47
Stokes Bay Sailing Club 6B 48
Stokeway PO12: Gos 3E 49
Stonechat Cl. GU31: Pet 5G 57
Stonechat Rd. PO8: Horn 1A 10
Stonecross Ho. PO2: Ports 5H 41
Stoneham Cl. GU32: Pet 3B 56
Stoneham Pk. GU32: Pet 3B 56
Stone La. PO12: Gos 3D 48
          (not continuous)
Stoneleigh Cl. PO16: Portc 3H 27
Stoners Cl. PO13: Gos 2B 38
Stone Sq. PO9: Hav 5F 21
Stone St. PO5: S'sea 6E 5 (4B 50)
Stony La. PO1: Ports 1A 4 (1H 49)
Storrington Rd. PO8: Clan 2H 7
Stour Cl. GU31: Pet 5C 56
Stow Cres. PO15: Fare 1F 25
Stowe Rd. PO4: S'sea 3A 52
Stradbrook PO13: Gos 4B 38
Strand, The PO4: S'sea 6D 50
  PO11: H Isl 6E 55
Stratfield Gdns. PO9: Hav 2D 20
Stratfield Pk. PO7: W'lle 1E 19
Stratford Ho. PO5: S'sea 5F 5 (3C 50)
Stratford Rd. PO7: W'lle 1A 20
Strathmore Rd. PO12: Gos 3E 49
Stratton Cl. PO6: Cosh 3G 29
Stride Av. PO3: Ports 1G 51
Strode Rd. PO2: Ports 3G 41
Stroud Cl. PO6: Cosh 2E 29
Strouden Ct. PO9: Hav 2D 20
Strouden Ct. Pct. PO9: Hav 2D 20
Stroud Grn. La. PO14: Stub 6F 25
Stroudley Av. PO6: Dray 5E 31
Stroudwood Rd. PO9: Hav 6F 21
Stuart Cl. PO14: Stub 3E 37
Stuart Ct. PO6: Cosh 3B 30
STUBBINGTON 2F 37
Stubbington Av. PO2: Ports 4A 42
Stubbington Grn. PO14: Stub 2E 37
Stubbington La. PO13: Lee S 5E 37
  PO14: Stub 2F 37
Studland Rd. PO13: Lee S 1C 46
Sudbury Rd. PO6: Cosh 3H 29
Suffolk Cotts. PO12: Gos 4D 48
Suffolk Rd. PO4: S'sea 4G 51
Sullivan Cl. PO6: Cosh 3C 28
Sullivan Way PO7: W'lle 4G 19
Sultan Rd. PO1: Ports 6G 41
  PO2: Ports 6H 41
  PO10: Ems 2D 34
Sumar Cl. PO14: Stub 6F 25
Summerhill Rd. PO8: Cowp 4H 9
Summerlands Wlk. PO9: Hav 4H 21
Summerleigh Wlk. PO14: Stub 6F 25
Sunbeam Way PO12: Gos 4D 48
Sunbury Ct. PO15: Fare 5G 13
Sun Ct. PO5: S'sea 4H 5
Suncourt Vs. PO12: Gos 5F 39
Sunderton La. PO8: Clan 2F 7
Sundridge Cl. PO6: Cosh 3A 30
Sunningdale Cl. PO13: Gos 4C 38

Sunningdale Rd. PO3: Ports 1G 51
  PO16: Portc 4B 28
Sunnyheath PO9: Hav 5E 21
Sunnymead Dr. PO7: W'lle 5E 9
Sunnyside Wlk. PO9: Hav 2D 20
Sunny Wlk. PO1: Ports 2A 4 (2H 49)
Sunshine Av. PO11: H Isl 5D 54
Sun St. PO1: Ports 3C 4 (2A 50)
Suntrap Gdns. PO11: H Isl 5D 54
Sunwood Rd. PO9: Hav 4D 20
Surrey St. PO1: Ports 2F 5 (2C 50)
Sussex Cl. PO5: S'sea 4C 50
  PO12: Gos 5A 40
Sussex Gdns. GU31: Pet 5D 56
Sussex Pl. PO1: Ports 1C 50
  PO5: S'sea 4C 50
Sussex Rd. GU31: Pet 5D 56
  PO5: S'sea 4C 50
Sussex Ter. PO5: S'sea 4C 50
Sutherland Rd. PO4: S'sea 4E 51
Sutton Cl. PO3: Ports 1D 42
  PO8: Cowp 4F 9
Sutton Ct. PO14: Fare 2H 25
Sutton Rd. PO8: Cowp 4F 9
Swallow Cl. PO9: Hav 6H 21
  PO13: Lee S 1F 7
Swallow Ct. PO8: Cowp 4F 9
  PO13: Lee S 6H 37
Swallow Wood PO16: Fare 5B 14
Swanage Rd. PO13: Lee S 1C 46
Swan Cl. PO10: Ems 3E 35
Swancote PO16: Portc 3F 27
Swan Ct. GU32: Pet 4D 56
  PO13: Gos 1B 38
Swanmore Rd. PO9: Hav 2D 20
Swan Quay PO16: Fare 3D 26
Swan St. GU32: Pet 4D 56
Swans Wlk. PO11: H Isl 4E 55
Swanton Cl. PO14: Stub 2F 37
Swarraton Rd. PO9: Hav 6G 21
Sway Ct. PO9: Hav 4H 21
Swaythling Rd. PO9: Hav 3D 20
Sweetbriar Gdns. PO7: W'lle 4H 19
Swift Cl. PO8: Horn 6A 6
  PO13: Lee S 6H 37
Swinburn Gdns. PO8: Cowp 3H 9
Swiss Rd. PO7: W'lle 2G 19
Swivelton La. PO17: Boar 5G 15
Sword Cl. PO8: Clan 2F 7
  PO12: Gos 5A 48
Swordfish Cl. PO13: Lee S 5E 37
Sword Sands Path PO3: Ports 6E 43
Sword Sands Rd. PO3: Ports 6E 43
Sycamore Cl. PO8: Clan 2H 7
  PO8: Cowp 4G 9
  PO12: Gos 4E 39
Sycamore Dr. PO11: H Isl 3A 54
Sycamore Wlk. GU31: Pet 6C 56
Sydenham Ct. PO1: Ports 2D 50
Sydenham Ter. PO1: Ports 2D 50
  PO10: Westb 4F 23
Sydmonton Ct. PO9: Hav 3H 21
Sydney Ho. PO1: Ports 1H 5 (1C 50)
Sydney Rd. PO12: Gos 3D 48
Sylvan Vw. PO7: W'lle 3H 19
Sywell Cres. PO3: Ports 2D 42

T

Tagdell La. PO8: Love 5A 6
Tait Pl. PO13: Gos 4D 38
Talbot Cl. PO9: Bed 6D 20
Talbot M. PO4: S'sea 3E 51
Talbot Rd. PO4: S'sea 2D 20
  PO9: Bed 6D 20
  PO15: Titch 1A 24
Tamar Cl. PO16: Portc 2G 27
Tamar Down PO7: W'lle 2A 20
Tamarisk Cl. PO4: S'sea 4A 52
  PO7: W'lle 4A 20
  PO14: Stub 4E 37
Tammy's Turn PO14: Fare 3D 24
Tamworth Ct. PO12: Gos 4D 48
Tamworth Rd. PO3: Ports 1G 51
Tanfield Cl. PO17: Wick 2A 14
Tanfield Pk. PO17: Wick 2A 14
Tangier Rd. PO3: Ports 6C 42
Tanglewood PO16: Fare 6A 14
Tanglewood Pk. PO7: Purb 5E 19
Tangley Wlk. PO9: Hav 4H 21
Tangyes Cl. PO14: Stub 2F 37

Tankerton Cl. PO6: Cosh 3A 30
Tanneries, The PO9: Hav 2E 33
  PO14: Titch 3C 24
Tanner La. PO14: Fare 5G 25
Tanner's La. PO7: Den 2B 8
Tanner's Ridge PO7: Purb 6G 19
Tansy Cl. PO7: W'lle 3A 20
Tarbery Cres. PO8: Horn 6C 6
Target Rd. PO2: Ports 2G 41
Tarius Cl. PO13: Gos 2D 38
Tarleton Rd. PO6: Cosh 2F 29
Tarn Ri. PO8: Horn 3C 6
Taro Leisure Cen. 4G 57
Tarrant Gdns. PO9: Bed 6D 20
Taswell Rd. PO5: S'sea 5D 50
Tattershall Cres. PO16: Portc 4H 27
Tavistock Gdns. PO9: Warb 2H 33
Tawny Owl Cl. PO14: Stub 1D 36
Taylor Rd. PO12: Gos 5E 49
Teal Cl. PO8: Horn 6A 6
  PO11: H Isl 4D 54
  PO16: Portc 3F 27
Teal Wlk. PO13: Gos 2B 38
Teapot Row PO4: S'sea 5H 51
Teazle Cl. GU31: Pet 5G 57
Tebourba Dr. PO12: Gos 4C 48
Tebourba Ho. PO14: Fare 3G 25
Tedder Rd. PO13: Gos 2D 38
Teddington Rd. PO4: S'sea 4G 51
Ted Kelly Ct. PO1: Ports 3C 4 (2A 50)
Tegdown GU31: Pet 3F 57
Teglease Grn. PO9: Hav 2D 20
Teignmouth Rd. PO3: Ports 5C 42
  PO12: Gos 6F 39
Telephone Rd. PO4: S'sea 3E 51
Telford Rd. PO2: Ports 2A 42
Tempest Av. PO7: W'lle 2A 20
Templemere PO14: Fare 4D 24
Temple St. PO1: Ports 1G 5 (1C 50)
Templeton Cl. PO2: Ports 2A 42
Tennyson Cres. PO7: W'lle 5F 9
Tennyson Gdns. PO12: Gos 3E 49
  (off Jamaica Pl.)
  PO16: Fare 1A 26
Tennyson Rd. PO2: Ports 5B 42
Tensing Cl. PO16: Fare 6A 14
Terminus Ind. Est.
  PO1: Ports 2G 5 (2C 50)
Tern Wlk. PO4: S'sea 2H 51
  PO13: Gos 2B 38
Terrace Gdns. PO4: S'sea 5E 51
Test Cl. GU31: Pet 5C 56
Testcombe Rd. PO12: Gos 4C 48
Testwood Rd. PO9: Hav 4D 20
Tewkesbury Av. PO12: Gos 6G 39
  PO15: Fare 6E 13
Tewkesbury Cl. PO6: Cosh 3H 29
Thackeray Mall PO16: Fare 2B 26
  (off Fareham Shop. Cen.)
Thackeray Sq. PO16: Fare 2B 26
Thames Dr. PO15: Fare 3C 24
Thamesmead Cl. PO12: Gos 6F 39
The . . . . . .
  Names prefixed with 'The' for example
  'The I O Cen.' are indexed under the main
  name such as 'I O Cen., The'
Theatre M. PO5: S'sea 5D 50
Theseus Rd. PO13: Lee S 6F 37
Thetford Rd. PO12: Gos 6F 39
Thicket, The PO5: S'sea 6G 5 (4D 50)
  PO7: Wid 1F 31
  PO13: Gos 4E 39
  PO16: Fare 2F 27
Third Av. PO6: Cosh 3A 30
  PO9: Hav 1G 33
Thirlmere Cl. PO14: Stub 1F 37
Thirlmere Ho. PO6: Cosh 2F 29
Thistledown PO8: Horn 2B 10
Thistledown Gdns. PO10: S'urne 3F 35
Thomas Grant Av. GU31: Pet 2F 49
Thomas Rd. GU31: Pet 2E 57
Thornbrake Rd. PO12: Gos 4E 49
Thornbury Cl. PO14: Fare 3E 25
Thornbury Ho. PO6: Cosh 1D 28
Thornby Cl. PO3: Ports 1D 42
Thorncliffe Cl. PO2: Ports 1B 42
Thorn Cl. GU31: Pet 5G 57
Thorncroft Rd. PO1: Ports 2E 51
Thorney Cl. PO14: Fare 3F 25
Thorney Rd. PO10: S'urne 3F 35
Thorney Vw. PO11: H Isl 3E 45

Thornfield Cl. PO8: Horn 3C 6
Thorngate Ct. PO12: Gos 2C 48
Thorngate Way PO12: Gos 3F 49
Thornham La. PO10: S'urne 5F 35
Thorn Av. PO15: Fare 6E 13
Thornton Cl. PO7: Wid 1D 30
Thornton Rd. PO12: Gos 5H 39
Thorrowgood Ho. PO2: Ports 5H 41
Three Acres PO7: Den 4C 8
Three Tun Cl. PO1: Ports 3C 4 (2A 50)
Thresher Cl. PO7: W'lle 6C 10
Thrush Wlk. PO8: Cowp 4G 9
Thruxton Rd. PO9: Hav 4C 20
Thurbern Rd. PO2: Ports 3A 42
Tichborne Gro. PO9: Hav 4D 20
Tichborne Way PO13: Gos 3D 38
Tidcombe Grn. PO9: Hav 2C 20
Tideway Gdns. PO4: S'sea 3A 52
Tidworth Rd. PO9: Hav 5F 21
Tiffield Cl. PO3: Ports 1E 43
Tiger Moth Cl. PO13: Lee S 1E 47
Tiger Rd. PO1: Ports 6D 40
Tilford Rd. PO8: Love 1H 9
Tillington Gdns. PO8: Clan 1D 6
TILMORE GARDENS 2D 56
Tilmore Gdns. GU32: Pet 2D 56
Tilmore Rd. GU32: Pet 3D 56
Timberlane PO7: Purb 5F 19
Timberley Ho. PO1: Ports 2H 5
Timbers, The PO15: Fare 2E 25
Timpson Rd. PO1: Ports 1E 51
Timsbury Cres. PO9: Bed 6E 21
Tintagel Way PO6: P Sol 4F 29
Tintern Cl. PO6: Cosh 2E 29
Tintern Rd. PO12: Gos 3C 48
TIPNER 2F 41
Tipner Grn. PO2: Ports 2G 41
Tipner La. PO2: Ports 2F 41
Tipner Rd. PO2: Ports 3G 41
Tiptoe Grn. PO9: Hav 3H 21
  (off Sopley Ct.)
Tipton Ho. PO5: S'sea 4G 5 (3C 50)
Tisted Ct. PO9: Hav 4H 21
TITCHFIELD 3C 24
Titchfield Abbey 1C 24
Titchfield By-Pass PO14: Titch 2B 24
Titchfield Haven Nature Reserve 3B 36
Titchfield Haven Nature Reserve Vis. Cen.
.....................................4B 36
Titchfield Hill PO14: Titch 3C 24
  (not continuous)
Titchfield Industries
  PO14: Titch 3C 24
Titchfield La. PO15: Titch, Wick 1E 13
TITCHFIELD PARK 6A 12
Titchfield Pk. Rd. PO15: Seg 6A 12
Titchfield Rd. PO14: Stub, Titch 3C 24
Tithe, The PO7: Den 4B 8
Titus Gdns. PO7: W'lle 1A 20
Tiverton Ct. PO16: Fare 1B 26
Tivoli Cl. PO2: Ports 5B 42
Tobys Gdn. GU31: Pet 4D 56
Toby St. PO1: Ports 1G 5 (1C 50)
Todhurst Rd. PO1: Ports 3H 5 (2D 50)
Tokar St. PO4: S'sea 5G 51
Tokio Rd. PO3: Ports 4C 42
Tollgate, The PO16: Fare 1B 26
Tonbridge St. PO5: S'sea 5C 50
Tonnant Cl. PO14: Stub 3F 37
Topaz Gro. PO7: W'lle 1B 20
Torberry Dr. GU31: Pet 5F 57
Tor Cl. PO7: Purb 6H 19
Torfrida Ct. PO4: S'sea 4A 52
Toronto Pl. PO10: Gos 2D 48
Toronto Rd. PO12: Gos 6A 42
Torquay Av. PO12: Gos 5G 39
Torrington Rd. PO2: Ports 2A 42
Tortworth Cl. PO14: Fare 3F 25
Torway GU31: Pet 4D 56
Totland Rd. PO6: Cosh 4A 30
  PO13: Gos 3C 38
Totsome Cotts. PO17: K Vil 6G 13
Tottenham Rd. PO1: Ports 1E 51
Totton Wlk. PO9: Hav 3D 20
Tourist Info. Cen.
  Fareham 2B 26
  Petersfield 4D 56
  Portsmouth 2A 4 (2A 50)
  Southsea 5B 50
Tournerbury La. PO11: H Isl 3C 54

Tower Cl. PO12: Gos 4H 47
  (not continuous)
Tower Gdns. PO9: Lang 5F 33
Tower Rd. PO4: S'sea 4F 51
Tower St. PO1: Ports 6A 4 (4H 49)
  PO10: Ems 3D 34
Town Hall Rd. PO9: Hav 2F 33
Town La. GU32: Pet 2F 57
Town Quay PO1: Ports 5A 4 (3A 50)
Towpath Mead PO4: S'sea 3A 52
Trafalgar Cl. PO10: S'urne 3H 35
Trafalgar Ct. PO5: S'sea 5D 50
  (off Richmond Rd.)
  PO14: Fare 4H 25
Trafalgar Hall PO5: S'sea 4F 5
Trafalgar Pl. PO1: Ports 1E 51
Trafalgar Ri. PO8: Clan 2F 7
Trafalgar Sq. PO12: Gos 2D 48
Tranmere Rd. PO4: S'sea 3H 51
Treadgold Mus. 2C 4 (2A 50)
Treadwheel Rd. PO8: Ids 1G 11
Tredegar Rd. PO4: S'sea 4F 51
Treeside Way PO7: W'lle 6G 9
Trefoil Cl. PO7: W'lle 2H 19
Tregaron Av. PO6: Cosh 3D 30
Treloar Rd. PO11: H Isl 6H 55
Trent Wlk. PO16: Portc 3G 27
Trent Way PO13: Lee S 2D 46
Trevis Rd. PO4: S'sea 3A 52
Trevor Rd. PO4: S'sea 4E 51
Trevose Cl. PO13: Gos 4C 38
Triangle, The PO11: H Isl 5G 55
Triangle La. PO14: Titch 1A 36
Tribe Rd. PO12: Gos 2C 48
Trimmer's Ct. PO1: Ports 5A 4 (4A 50)
Trinidad Ho. PO6: Cosh 1C 28
Trinity Cl. PO12: Gos 3F 49
Trinity Gdns. PO16: Fare 2A 26
Trinity Grn. PO12: Gos 3G 49
Trinity St. PO16: Fare 1B 26
Triumph Cl. PO15: Fare 1F 25
Triumph Rd. PO14: Fare 6H 25
Trojan Way PO7: Purb 6H 19
Troon Cres. PO6: Dray 2E 31
Trosnant Rd. PO9: Hav 1E 33
Truro Ct. PO13: Gos 1G 47
Truro Rd. PO6: Cosh 2D 28
Tudor Av. PO10: Ems 5C 22
Tudor Cl. PO11: H Isl 5B 54
  PO13: Gos 5D 38
  PO16: Portc 2H 27
Tudor Ct. PO5: S'sea 6D 50
  PO6: Cosh 3B 30
  PO14: Fare 4A 26
Tudor Cres. PO6: Cosh 5B 30
Tukes Av. PO13: Gos 1B 38
Tulip Gdns. PO9: Bed 1C 32
Tunstall Rd. PO9: Cosh 2H 29
Tunworth Ct. PO9: Hav 4H 21
Tupman Ho. PO1: Ports 6H 41
Tuppenny La. PO10: S'urne 3G 35
Turner Av. PO13: Gos 4D 38
Turner Rd. PO1: Ports 6H 41
Turnpike Gallery, The 4D 56
Turtle Cl. PO14: Stub 1D 36
Turvy King Ct. PO7: Den 3B 8
Tuscany Way PO7: W'lle 1B 20
Tweed Ct. PO9: Hav 5E 21
Twittens Way PO9: Hav 2F 33
Two Acres Cvn. Pk.
  PO11: H Isl 5G 55
Twyford Av. PO2: Ports 2H 41
  (not continuous)
Twyford Dr. PO13: Lee S 6H 37
TYE 4E 45
Tyler Ct. PO9: Hav 4E 21
Tynedale Cl. PO12: Gos 5F 39
Tynefield Cvn. Site
  PO15: Titch 5B 12
Tyrrel Lawn PO9: Hav 2D 20
Tyseley Rd. PO5: S'sea 4G 5 (2C 50)
Tytherley Grn. PO9: Hav 3H 21

U

Ullswater Ho. PO6: Cosh 2F 29
Underdown Av. PO7: Wid 1F 31
Unicorn Ga. PO1: Ports 1B 50
Unicorn Rd. PO1: Ports 1E 5 (1B 50)
  PO13: Lee S 6F 37

Union Pl. PO1: Ports 1H **5** (1D **50**)
Union Rd. PO9: Hav 2E **33**
Union St. PO1: Ports 2C **4** (2A **50**)
   PO16: Fare .2C **26**
University of Portsmouth
   Frewen Library 5D **4** (3B **50**)
   Langstone Campus 2B **52**
   Marine Sciences 3C **52**
   Mercantile House 4E **5** (3B **50**)
   Omega Cen. 3H **5** (2D **50**)
   St George's Building 5D **4** (3A **50**)
   St Michael's Rd. 4E **5** (3B **50**)
   St Paul's Gymnasium 4E **5**
   University House 4E **5** (3B **50**)
   University House Lodge 4E **5**
   University Quarter 2D **4** (2B **50**)
   Wiltshire Building 4E **5** (3B **50**)
UPLANDS 6A **14**
Uplands Cres. PO16: Fare 6B **14**
Uplands Rd. PO6: Dray 2E **31**
   PO7: Den 1A **8**
Up. Arundel St. PO1: Ports 2G **5** (2C **50**)
Up. Bere Wood PO7: W'lle 3H **19**
Up. Cornaway La. PO16: Portc 1H **27**
   (not continuous)
Upper Heyshott GU31: Pet 4E **57**
Up. House Ct. PO17: Wick 2A **14**
Up. Old St. PO14: Stub 1D **36**
Upper Piece PO7: Den 4C **8**
Up. St Michael's Gro.
   PO14: Fare 3H **25**
Upper Wardown GU31: Pet 3F **57**
Upper Wharf PO16: Fare 3C **26**
Upton Cl. PO9: Hav 2D **20**
Usborne Cl. PO13: Lee S 6H **37**

V

Vadne Gdns. PO12: Gos 1D **48**
Vale, The PO5: S'sea 5C **50**
   PO8: Horn .4C **6**
Vale Gro. PO12: Gos 6G **39**
Valentine Cl. PO15: Fare 6E **13**
Valentine Cl. PO7: W'lle 1A **20**
Valerian Av. PO15: Titch 6B **12**
Valetta Pk. PO10: Ems 3C **34**
Valiant Gdns. PO2: Ports 1H **41**
Valley Cl. PO7: Wid 6E **19**
Valley Pk. Dr. PO8: Clan 1D **6**
Valsheba Dr. PO14: Stub 4D **36**
Vanguard Ct. PO4: S'sea 4B **52**
Vanguard Rd. PO12: Gos 5A **40**
Vanstone Rd. PO13: Gos 5D **38**
Varos Cl. PO12: Gos 1C **48**
Vauxhall Way GU32: Pet 4C **56**
Vectis Rd. PO12: Gos 4A **48**
Vectis Way PO6: Cosh 4B **30**
Velder Av. PO4: S'sea 2G **51**
Venerable Rd. PO14: Fare 6A **26**
Vengeance Rd. PO13: Lee S 6G **37**
Venice Cl. PO7: W'lle 1A **20**
Ventnor Rd. PO4: S'sea 3E **51**
   PO13: Gos .2B **38**
Ventnor Way PO16: Fare 2E **27**
Venture Ct. PO3: Ports 6C **30**
Venture Ind. Pk. PO3: Ports 6C **30**
   PO13: Gos .2D **38**
Venture Sidings PO4: S'sea 2F **51**
Verbena Cres. PO8: Cowp 3B **10**
Vernon Av. PO4: S'sea 2G **51**
   (not continuous)
Vernon Cl. PO12: Gos 2C **48**
Vernon Ct. PO2: Ports 3A **42**
Vernon M. PO4: S'sea 2G **51**
Vernon Rd. PO3: Ports 3C **42**
   PO12: Gos .2C **48**
Verwood Rd. PO9: Hav 3H **21**
Veryan PO14: Fare 2G **25**
Vian Cl. PO13: Gos 1C **38**
Vian Rd. PO7: W'lle 3F **19**
Vicarage La. PO14: Stub 2E **37**
Vicarage Ter. PO12: Gos 5F **39**
Victoria Av. PO7: Wid 6D **18**
   PO11: H Isl .4B **54**
VICTORIA COTTAGE HOSPITAL 3D **34**
Victoria Gro. PO5: S'sea 6H **5** (4D **50**)
Victoria M. PO17: K Vil 2G **13**
Victoria Pl. PO12: Gos 3D **48**
Victoria Rd. PO1: Ports 1H **49**
   PO7: W'lle .2G **19**

Victoria Rd. PO10: Ems 2C **34**
   PO11: H Isl .3B **44**
Victoria Rd. Nth. PO5: S'sea 6H **5** (4D **50**)
Victoria Rd. Sth. PO5: S'sea 6H **5** (5D **50**)
Victoria Sq. PO13: Lee S 1C **46**
Victoria St. PO1: Ports 6G **41**
   PO12: Gos .2E **49**
Victoria Swimming Cen. 2E **5** (2B **50**)
Victoria Ter. PO6: Cosh 4B **30**
   PO10: Ems .2E **35**
   PO10: S'urne 2E **35**
   (Lumley Rd.)
   PO10: S'urne 3G **35**
   (Prinsted La.)
Victor Rd. PO3: Ports 6B **42**
Victory Av. PO8: Horn 1A **10**
Victory Ct. PO13: Gos 4D **38**
Victory Ga. PO1: Ports 2A **4** (2A **50**)
Victory Grn. PO2: Ports 3G **41**
Victory Ho. PO6: P Sol 4E **29**
Victory Indoor Bowls Club 2H **41**
Victory Retail Pk. PO1: Ports 6G **41**
Victory Rd. PO1: Ports 3B **4** (2A **50**)
   PO14: Stub .3F **37**
Victory Trad. Est. PO3: Ports 3C **42**
Viking Cl. PO14: Stub 2D **36**
Viking Ct. PO14: Stub 2D **36**
Viking Way PO8: Horn 2C **6**
Villa Gdns. PO7: W'lle 1G **19**
Village Cl. PO14: Stub 3E **37**
Village Ga. PO14: Titch 2B **24**
Village Rd. PO12: Gos 5B **48**
Village St. GU32: Pet 1F **57**
Ville De Paris Rd.
   PO14: Fare 6A **26**
Villiers Cl. PO5: S'sea 5C **50**
Villiers Rd. PO5: S'sea 5C **50**
   (not continuous)
Vimy Ho. PO14: Fare 3G **25**
Vincent Gro. PO16: Portc 4A **28**
Vine Coppice PO7: W'lle 5G **19**
Vineside PO13: Gos 4E **39**
Violet Av. PO14: Stub 3D **36**
Virginia Pk. Rd. PO12: Gos 1B **48**
Vita Rd. PO2: Ports 2A **42**
Vivash Rd. PO1: Ports 2E **51**
Vixen Cl. PO14: Stub 3D **36**
Vue Cinema
   Portsmouth 4B **4**
Vulcan, The PO1: Ports 4B **4** (3A **50**)

W

Wade Ct. Rd. PO9: Hav 3G **33**
Wade La. PO9: Hav 4G **33**
Wadham Rd. PO2: Ports 3H **41**
Wagtail Rd. PO8: Horn 6A **6**
Wagtail Way PO16: Portc 3F **27**
Wainscott Rd. PO4: S'sea 5G **51**
Wainwright Cl. PO6: Dray 5E **31**
Wait End Rd. PO7: W'lle 3G **19**
Wakefield Av. PO16: Fare 6H **13**
Wakefield Ct. PO7: Purb 6H **19**
Wakefield Pl. PO12: Gos 5C **48**
   (off Stephenson Cl.)
Wakefords Way PO9: Hav 3G **21**
Wake Lawn PO4: S'sea 4A **52**
Walberant Bldgs. PO3: Ports 1B **42**
Walberton Av. PO6: Cosh 3C **30**
Walberton Ct. PO6: Cosh 3C **30**
Walburton Way PO8: Clan 1D **6**
Walden Gdns. PO8: Horn 6B **6**
Walden Rd. PO2: Ports 3G **41**
Walford Rd. PO6: Cosh 2G **29**
Walker Pl. PO13: Gos 4D **38**
Walker Rd. PO2: Ports 3G **41**
Wallace Rd. PO2: Ports 5B **42**
WALLINGTON 1D **26**
Wallington Ct. PO14: Fare 4H **25**
   PO16: Fare .6D **14**
Wallington Hill PO16: Fare 1C **26**
Wallington Orchard PO16: Fare 6D **14**
Wallington Rd. PO2: Ports 4B **42**
Wallington Shore Rd. PO16: Fare 1C **26**
   (not continuous)
Wallington Way PO16: Fare 1C **26**
Wallisdean Av. PO3: Ports 6D **42**
   PO14: Fare .3H **25**
Wallis Gdns. PO7: W'lle 6G **9**
Wallis Rd. PO7: W'lle 6G **9**
Wallrock Wlk. PO10: Ems 5D **22**

Walmer Rd. PO1: Ports 2E **51**
Walnut Dr. PO14: Stub 3D **36**
Walnut Tree Cl. PO11: H Isl 4B **54**
Walnut Tree Dr. PO10: Wood 6H **23**
Walpole Rd. PO12: Gos 3F **49**
Walpole Ter. PO12: Gos 4D **48**
Walsall Rd. PO3: Ports 1G **51**
Walsingham Cl. PO6: Cosh 2H **29**
Waltham Cl. PO16: Portc 2A **28**
Waltham St. PO5: S'sea 4E **5** (3B **50**)
Walton Cl. PO7: W'lle 4G **19**
   PO12: Gos .3C **48**
Walton Ct. PO1: Ports 5C **4**
   PO15: Fare .5F **13**
Walton Rd. PO6: Farl 5D **30**
   PO12: Gos .3C **48**
Walton Rd. Ind. Est. PO6: Farl 5E **31**
Wandesford Pl. PO12: Gos 4G **39**
Warbler Cl. PO8: Horn 6A **6**
WARBLINGTON 2H **33**
Warblington Av. PO9: Warb 2H **33**
Warblington Ct. PO1: Ports 5C **4** (3A **50**)
Warblington Rd. PO10: Ems 4C **34**
Warblington Station (Rail) 1H **33**
Warblington St. PO1: Ports 5C **4** (3A **50**)
Warbrook Ct. PO9: Hav 4H **21**
Ward Cl. PO11: H Isl 4A **54**
Ward Cres. PO10: Ems 6E **23**
Wardens Cl. PO11: H Isl 2B **54**
Warders Ct. PO12: Gos 2D **48**
Ward Ho. PO1: Ports 1C **4** (1B **50**)
Ward Rd. PO4: S'sea 5G **51**
Wardroom Rd. PO2: Ports 4F **41**
Warfield Av. PO7: W'lle 2G **19**
Warfield Cres. PO7: W'lle 2G **19**
Warnborough Ct. PO9: Hav 3H **21**
Warnford Cl. PO12: Gos 3B **48**
Warnford Cres. PO9: Hav 4D **20**
Warren Av. PO4: S'sea 2G **51**
Warren Cl. PO11: H Isl 3G **53**
WARREN PARK 3C **20**
Warrior Bus. Cen., The
   PO6: Farl 4G **31**
Warrior Ct. PO12: Gos 3G **49**
Warsash Cl. PO9: Hav 3E **21**
Warsash Gro. PO13: Gos 3B **38**
Warsash Rd. PO14: Titch, T Cmn 3A **24**
Warships by Water Tour 2A **4** (2H **49**)
Warspite Cl. PO2: Ports 1H **41**
Warwick Cl. PO13: Lee S 3E **47**
Warwick Ct. PO10: Ems 3D **34**
   (off High St.)
Warwick Cres. PO5: S'sea 5G **5** (3C **50**)
Warwick Way PO17: Wick 1A **14**
Wasdale Cl. PO8: Horn 3C **6**
Washbrook Rd. PO6: Cosh 3H **29**
Washington Rd. PO2: Ports 5H **41**
   PO10: Ems .2D **34**
Washington Ter. PO10: Ems 2D **34**
Waterberry Dr. PO7: W'lle 6E **9**
Watergate PO12: Gos 3G **49**
Waterlock Gdns. PO4: S'sea 3B **52**
Waterloo Cl. PO8: Cowp 4F **9**
Waterloo Rd. PO9: Hav 1F **33**
   PO12: Gos .6E **49**
Waterloo St. PO5: S'sea 4F **5** (3C **50**)
WATERLOOVILLE 2G **19**
Waterlooville Leisure Cen. 6E **9**
Waterman Ter. PO5: S'sea 4E **51**
   (off Boulton Rd.)
Watermead Rd. PO6: Farl 4G **31**
Watermill Ct. PO9: Hav 2F **33**
Waters, The PO17: Fun 4G **13**
Water's Edge PO13: Lee S 3D **46**
Watersedge PO17: Wick 1A **14**
Waters Edge Cvn. Pk.
   PO11: H Isl .5G **55**
Watersedge Gdns. PO10: Ems 3D **34**
Watersedge Rd. PO6: Cosh 3E **29**
Waterside Gdns. PO16: Fare 1D **26**
Waterside La. PO16: Portc 5C **28**
Watersmeet PO16: Fare 4B **26**
Waterworks Rd. GU32: Pet 1E **57**
   PO6: Farl 3F **31**
Watland Cl. PO7: W'lle 3F **19**
Watts Rd. PO1: Ports 6H **41**
Wavell Rd. PO13: Gos 2D **38**
Waveney Cl. PO13: Lee S 1D **46**
Waverley Gro. PO4: S'sea 5E **51**
   PO5: S'sea .5E **51**
Waverley Path PO12: Gos 4A **48**

Waverley Rd. PO5: S'sea 6D 50
  PO6: Dray 3E 31
Wayfarer Cl. PO4: S'sea 2A 52
Wayfarers PO13: Gos 6D 48
Wayte St. PO6: Cosh 4B 30
Weavers Grn. PO9: Hav 6A 22
Webb Cl. PO11: H Isl 5C 54
Webbers Way PO12: Gos 5E 49
Webb La. PO11: H Isl 5C 54
Webb Rd. PO16: Portc 5B 28
WECOCK 3H 9
Wedgewood Cl. PO14: Stub 3E 37
Wedgwood Way PO8: Cowp 5G 9
Weevil La. PO12: Gos 1F 49
Welch Rd. PO4: S'sea 5E 51
  PO12: Gos 6G 39
Welchwood Cl. PO8: Love 1H 9
Well Copse Cl. PO8: Horn 4C 6
Weller Ho. PO1: Ports 6H 41
Wellesley Cl. PO7: W'lle 2G 19
Wellington Cl. PO8: Horn 1D 10
Wellington Ct. PO9: Hav 1F 33
Wellington Dr. PO13: Lee S 2E 47
Wellington Gro. PO16: Portc 4A 28
Wellington Retail Pk. PO7: W'lle 1G 19
Wellington St. PO5: S'sea 4F 5 (3C 50)
Wellington Ter. PO2: Ports 6A 42
  (off Arthur St.)
Wellington Way PO7: W'lle 2G 19
Well Mdw. PO9: Hav 3E 21
Wellow Cl. PO9: Bed 6D 20
Wells Cl. PO3: Ports 1H 51
Wellsworth La. PO9: Ids, R Cas 4H 11
Wembley Gro. PO6: Cosh 5C 30
Wendover Rd. PO9: Hav 1E 33
Wensley Gdns. PO10: Ems 6D 22
Wentworth Dr. PO8: Horn 6B 6
  PO10: S'urne 1H 35
Wesermarsch Rd. PO8: Cowp 3A 10
Wesley Cl. PO1: Ports 2E 51
Wesley Gro. PO3: Ports 2B 42
Wessex Cl. PO13: Lee S 1E 47
Wessex Gdns. PO16: Portc 4H 27
Wessex Ga. Ind. Est. PO8: Horn 1C 10
Wessex Rd. PO8: Horn 2C 6
W. Battery Rd. PO2: Ports 4F 41
Westborn Rd. PO16: Fare 2B 26
WESTBOURNE .6F 23
Westbourne Av. PO10: Ems 1D 34
Westbourne Cvn. Pk. PO10: Westb 5H 23
Westbourne Cl. PO10: Ems 1E 35
Westbourne Ct. PO9: Hav 1E 33
Westbourne Rd. PO2: Ports 5B 42
  PO10: Ems, Westb 6E 23
Westbrook Cen., The PO7: W'lle 6B 10
Westbrooke Cl. PO8: Horn 1B 10
Westbrook Gro. PO7: Purb 4F 19
Westbrook Rd. PO16: Portc 5B 28
Westbury Cl. PO6: Cosh 2F 29
Westbury Mall PO16: Fare 2B 26
Westbury Manor Mus. 2B 26
Westbury Rd. PO16: Fare 2B 26
Westbury Sq. PO16: Fare 2B 26
Westcliff Cl. PO13: Lee S 6H 37
West Ct. PO1: Ports 6A 42
  PO4: S'sea 4G 51
Westcroft Rd. PO12: Gos 2B 48
W. Downs Cl. PO16: Fare 5A 14
WEST END 4G 25
Westerham Cl. PO6: Cosh 3A 30
Western Av. PO10: Ems 3B 34
Western Ct. PO16: Fare 2A 26
Western Pde. PO5: S'sea 4B 50
  PO10: Ems 4C 34
Western Rd. PO6: Cosh 3G 29
  (not continuous)
  PO9: Hav 1E 33
  PO16: Fare 2B 26
Western Ter. PO2: Ports 3G 41
Western Way PO12: Gos 4A 48
  PO16: Fare 2A 26
WESTFIELD 4B 54
Westfield Av. PO11: H Isl 4B 54
  PO14: Fare 3H 25
Westfield Ind. Est. PO8: Horn 6D 6
  PO12: Gos 3C 48
Westfield Oaks PO11: H Isl 4B 54
Westfield Rd. PO4: S'sea 4G 51
  PO12: Gos 2B 48
Westgate PO14: Stub 4E 37
W. Haye Rd. PO11: H Isl 6F 55

WEST HILL PARK 3A 24
Westland Dr. PO7: Purb 5G 19
  PO13: Lee S .2E 47
Westland Gdns. PO12: Gos 4C 48
Westlands Gro. PO16: Portc 4A 28
West La. PO11: H Isl 3A 54
WEST LEIGH 4G 21
West Leigh Pk. .5G 21
Westley Gro. PO14: Fare 3H 25
West Lodge PO13: Lee S 6F 37
Westmead Cl. PO11: H Isl 4H 53
West M. PO17: K Vil 2G 13
Westminster Pl. PO1: Ports 6H 41
WESTON 6A 56
Weston Av. PO4: S'sea 3H 51
Weston Ct. PO1: Ports 3H 5
Weston Ho. GU32: Pet 4C 56
Weston La. GU32: W'ton 6A 56
Weston Rd. GU31: Pet 4E 57
Westover Rd. PO3: Ports 5D 42
West Point PO13: Lee S 1C 46
West Rd. PO10: Ems 3B 34
  PO17: S'wick 3E 17
Westside Vw. PO7: W'lle 6E 9
West St. PO1: Ports 6A 4 (4H 49)
  PO9: Bed, Hav 1D 32
  PO10: Ems 3D 34
  PO14: Titch 3B 24
  PO16: Fare 2A 26
  (not continuous)
  PO16: Portc .3H 27
  (not continuous)
  PO17: S'wick 3C 16
WEST TOWN 4A 54
West Vw. Cotts. PO10: S'urne 1H 35
Westway PO15: Titch 6A 12
Westways PO9: Bed 3H 31
  PO14: Stub 3F 37
Westwood Cl. PO10: Ems 1E 35
Westwood Rd. PO2: Ports 1A 42
Wetherdown GU31: Pet 4E 57
Weyhill Cl. PO9: Hav 4D 20
  PO16: Portc .2A 28
Weymouth Av. PO12: Gos 5F 39
Weymouth Rd. PO2: Ports 4H 41
Whaddon Chase PO14: Stub 3D 36
Whaddon Ct. PO9: Hav 3C 20
Whale Island Way PO2: Ports 4G 41
Whaley Rd. PO2: Ports 4F 41
Wharf Rd. PO2: Ports 5G 41
Wheatcroft Rd. PO13: Lee S 1D 46
Wheatear Dr. GU31: Pet 4E 57
Wheatlands Av. PO11: H Isl 6G 55
Wheatlands Cres. PO11: H Isl 6G 55
Wheatley Grn. PO9: Hav 3C 20
Wheatsheaf Dr. PO8: Horn 4F 9
Wheatstone Rd. PO4: S'sea 4E 51
Wheeler Cl. PO12: Gos 1D 48
Wherwell Ct. PO9: Hav 4H 21
Whichers Cl. PO9: R Cas 1H 21
Whichers Ga. Rd. PO9: R Cas 1H 21
Whimbrel Cl. PO4: S'sea 2B 52
Whinchat Cl. PO15: Fare 5E 13
Whippingham Cl. PO6: Cosh 3H 29
Whitcombe Gdns. PO3: Ports 1F 51
Whiteacres Cl. PO12: Gos 2D 48
Whitebeam Cl. PO8: Horn 2C 10
White Beam Ri. PO8: Clan 2G 7
Whitechimney Row PO10: Westb 6F 23
Whitecliffe Av. PO3: Ports 6C 42
Whitecliffe Ct. PO12: Gos 3H 47
White Cloud Pk. PO4: S'sea 4F 51
White Cloud Pl. PO4: S'sea 4F 51
Whitecross Gdns. PO2: Ports 2B 42
Whitedell La. PO17: Fare 5D 14
White Dirt La. PO8: Cath 3B 6
White Hart All. PO1: Ports 6B 4 (4A 50)
White Hart La. PO16: Portc 4H 27
White Hart Rd. PO1: Ports 6B 4 (4A 50)
  PO12: Gos 3D 48
Whitehaven PO8: Horn 1D 10
  PO16: Portc .4H 27
White Horse La. PO7: Den 1C 8
White Ho. GU32: Pet 4C 56
White Ladies Cl. PO9: Hav 2G 33
Whiteley Farm Rdbt. PO15: White 1A 12
Whiteley La. PO15: Titch 6B 12
  PO15: White .1A 12
Whiteley Village Shop. Cen.
  PO15: White .1A 12

Whiteley Way PO15: White 1A 12
White Lion Wlk. PO12: Gos 2F 49
White Lodge Gdns. PO16: Fare 5G 13
White Oak Wlk. PO9: Hav 4H 21
Whites Cl. PO2: Ports 4H 41
Whites Pl. PO12: Gos 2D 48
White Swan Rd. PO1: Ports 3E 5 (2B 50)
Whitethorn Rd. PO11: H Isl 4D 54
White Wings Ho. PO7: Den 4B 8
Whitley Cl. PO10: Westb 4F 23
Whitley Row PO4: S'sea 2A 52
Whitsbury Rd. PO9: Hav 4G 21
Whitstable Rd. PO6: Cosh 3A 30
Whittington Ct. PO10: Ems 3D 34
Whitwell Rd. PO4: S'sea 6E 51
Whitworth Cl. PO12: Gos 3D 48
Whitworth Rd. PO2: Ports 5B 42
  PO12: Gos 3C 48
Whyke Cl. PO9: Hav 1E 33
WICKHAM 1A 14
Wickham Cl. PO12: Gos 4H 47
Wickham Cft. PO17: Wick 2A 14
Wickham Rd. PO16: Fare 5B 14
  PO17: Fare 3B 14
Wickham St. PO1: Ports 2B 4 (2A 50)
Wickor Cl. PO10: Ems 1E 35
Wickor Way PO10: Ems 6E 23
Wicor Mill La. PO16: Portc 4H 27
Wicor Path PO16: Portc 5B 28
  (Bayly Av.)
  PO16: Portc .4G 27
  (Cador Dr.)
Widgeon Cl. PO12: Gos 6H 39
Widgeon Ct. PO16: Portc 3F 27
WIDLEY 1E 31
Widley Ct. PO14: Fare 5A 26
Widley Ct. Dr. PO6: Cosh 4C 30
Widley Gdns. PO7: Wid 6F 19
Widley Rd. PO2: Ports 3G 41
  PO6: Cosh 3C 30
Widley Wlk. PO7: Purb 1B 30
Wield Cl. PO9: Hav 5C 20
Wigan Cres. PO9: Bed 1B 32
Wight Vw. PO13: Lee S 6F 37
Wigmore Ho. PO1: Ports 1D 50
Wilberforce Rd. PO5: S'sea 6F 5 (4C 50)
  PO12: Gos 6E 49
Wilby La. PO3: Ports 1E 43
Wild Grounds Nature Reserve 6B 38
Wildmoor Wlk. PO9: Hav 4H 21
Wild Ridings PO14: Fare 3D 24
Wilkins Cl. PO8: Clan 1F 7
Willersley Cl. PO6: Cosh 2G 29
William Booth Ho. PO1: Ports 1D 4 (2B 50)
William Cl. PO14: Stub 4F 37
William George Ct. PO13: Lee S 2C 46
William Price Gdns. PO16: Fare 1B 26
Williams Cl. PO13: Gos 6D 38
Williams Rd. PO3: Ports 2D 42
Willis Rd. PO1: Ports 2F 5 (2C 50)
  PO12: Gos 3E 49
  (not continuous)
Willow Cl. PO9: Hav 2G 33
Willow Ct. PO14: Fare 2F 25
Willowdene Cl. PO9: Bed 5B 20
Willow Dr. GU31: Pet 6D 56
Willow Gdns. PO10: Westb 5F 23
Willow Pl. PO12: Gos 2D 48
Willows, The PO2: Ports 3G 41
  PO7: Den 3A 8
Willow Tree Av. PO8: Cowp 5B 10
Willow Tree Gdns. PO14: Fare 3G 25
Willow Wood Rd. PO11: H Isl 4C 54
Wilmcote Gdns. PO5: S'sea 4H 5
Wilmcote Ho. PO5: S'sea 4H 5 (2D 50)
Wilmott Cl. PO12: Gos 2B 48
Wilmott La. PO12: Gos 2B 48
Wilson Gro. PO5: S'sea 4D 50
Wilson Rd. PO2: Ports 3G 41
Wilton Cl. PO12: Gos 3B 48
Wilton Dr. PO8: Horn 2A 10
Wilton Pl. PO5: S'sea 5D 50
Wilton Ter. PO5: S'sea 5D 50
Wiltshire St. PO5: S'sea 4E 5 (3B 50)
Wilverley Av. PO9: Hav 5G 21
Wimbledon Pk. PO5: S'sea 5D 50
Wimbledon Pk. Sports Cen. 5D 50
Wimborne Rd. PO4: S'sea 3G 51
Wimpole Cl. PO1: Ports 1E 51
Wimpole St. PO1: Ports 1D 50
Wincanton Way PO7: W'lle 6B 10

Winchcombe Rd. PO6: Cosh . . . 2F **29**
Winchester Ct. PO13: Gos . . . 2H **47**
Winchester Ho. PO9: Hav . . . 4G **21**
Winchester Rd. GU32: Stro . . . 3A **56**
PO2: Ports . . . 5A **42**
PO17: Wick . . . 1A **14**
Winchfield Cres. PO9: Hav . . . 5B **20**
Winchfield Ho. PO12: Gos . . . 3G **49**
Windermere Av. PO14: Stub . . . 1F **37**
Windermere Ho. PO6: Cosh . . . 3F **29**
Windermere Rd. PO2: Ports . . . 2B **42**
Windmill Cl. PO8: Clan . . . 1G **7**
Windmill Fld. PO7: Den . . . 3C **8**
Windmill Gro. PO16: Portc . . . 5H **27**
Windrush Gdns. PO7: W'lle . . . 2F **19**
Windsor Ct. PO6: Cosh . . . 3B **30**
Windsor Ho. PO1: Ports . . . 2H **5** (2D **50**)
Windsor La. PO5: S'sea . . . 5H **5** (3D **50**)
Windsor Rd. GU32: Pet . . . 3D **56**
PO6: Cosh . . . 4B **30**
PO7: W'lle . . . 5F **9**
PO12: Gos . . . 3C **48**
PO16: Portc . . . 5B **28**
Winfield Way PO10: Ems . . . 5D **22**
Wingate Rd. PO12: Gos . . . 4F **39**
Wingfield St. PO1: Ports . . . 6H **41**
Winifred Rd. PO7: W'lle . . . 1G **19**
Winkfield Row PO8: Horn . . . 2B **10**
Winkton Cl. PO9: Bed . . . 6D **20**
Winnham Dr. PO16: Portc . . . 2G **27**
Winnington PO15: Fare . . . 5F **13**
Winnington Cl. PO15: Fare . . . 5F **13**
Winscombe Av. PO8: Cowp . . . 5A **10**
Winslade Rd. PO9: Hav . . . 4D **20**
Winslow Ct. PO6: Dray . . . 3F **31**
Winsor Cl. PO11: H Isl . . . 6F **55**
Winstanley Rd. PO2: Ports . . . 4G **41**
Winston Churchill Av.
PO1: Ports . . . 4F **5** (3C **50**)
PO5: S'sea . . . 4F **5** (3C **50**)
Winston Cl. PO11: H Isl . . . 4A **54**
Winterbourne Rd. PO6: Cosh . . . 2D **28**
Winterhill Rd. PO6: Cosh . . . 3H **29**
Winter Rd. PO4: S'sea . . . 4G **51**
Winterslow Dr. PO9: Hav . . . 3E **21**
Winton Ct. GU32: Pet . . . 4D **56**
Winton Rd. GU32: Pet . . . 3D **56**
PO2: Ports . . . 3B **42**
Wisborough Rd. PO5: S'sea . . . 5E **51**
Wises All. PO12: Gos . . . 3G **49**
Wises Ct. PO12: Gos . . . 3G **49**
Wish Pl. PO5: S'sea . . . 4E **51**
Wisteria Gdns. PO9: Hav . . . 5H **21**
Witchampton Cl. PO9: Hav . . . 4G **21**
Witherbed La. PO15: Seg . . . 5A **12**
(not continuous)
Withies Rd. PO13: Gos . . . 5D **38**
Withington Cl. PO6: Cosh . . . 2F **29**
Witley Rd. PO8: Love . . . 1H **9**
Wittering Rd. PO11: H Isl . . . 5H **55**
Woburn Ct. PO13: Lee S . . . 3D **46**
Wode Cl. PO8: Horn . . . 2C **6**
Wolverton Rd. PO9: Hav . . . 4E **21**
Wonston Ct. PO9: Hav . . . 3H **21**
Woodberry La. PO9: R Cas . . . 1C **22**
PO10: R Cas, Westb . . . 1C **22**
Woodbourne Cl. PO15: Fare . . . 2F **25**
Woodbury Av. GU32: Pet . . . 2C **56**
PO9: Lang . . . 3F **33**
Woodbury Gro. PO8: Cowp . . . 2H **9**
WOODCOT . . . 1B **38**
Woodcot Cvn. Pk. PO11: H Isl . . . 5F **55**
Woodcot Cres. PO9: Hav . . . 3G **21**
Woodcote La. PO14: Fare . . . 2A **38**
Woodcroft Gdns. PO8: Cowp . . . 2H **9**
Woodcroft La. PO8: Cowp . . . 2H **9**
Woodcutters Dr. PO8: Cowp . . . 3G **9**
Woodfield Av. PO6: Farl . . . 2G **31**
Woodfield Ho. PO2: Ports . . . 2A **42**
Woodfield Pk. Rd. PO10: S'urne . . . 2F **35**
Woodgaston La. PO11: H Isl . . . 4E **45**
Woodgreen Av. PO9: Bed . . . 1D **32**
Woodhall Way PO15: Fare . . . 6G **13**
Woodhay Wlk. PO9: Hav . . . 3H **21**
Woodhouse La. PO8: Ids . . . 1G **11**
PO8: Ids, R Cas . . . 3H **11**
PO9: R Cas . . . 3H **11**
Woodington Cl. PO9: Hav . . . 3G **21**
Woodlands PO16: Fare . . . 1D **26**
Woodlands Av. PO10: Ems . . . 6C **22**
Woodlands Cl. PO13: Gos . . . 1G **47**
Woodlands Gro. PO7: Purb . . . 4F **19**
Woodlands La. PO11: H Isl . . . 2A **54**
Woodland St. PO1: Ports . . . 1E **51**
Woodlands Wlk. PO4: S'sea . . . 2A **52**
Woodlands Way PO9: Hav . . . 5F **21**
Woodland Vw. PO8: Love . . . 1H **9**
Wood La. PO17: S'wick . . . 3E **17**
Woodlark Gdns. GU31: Pet . . . 4G **57**
Woodleigh Cl. PO9: Hav . . . 6A **22**
Woodley Rd. PO12: Gos . . . 3E **49**
Woodmancote La. PO10: Wood . . . 4H **23**
Woodmancote Rd. PO4: S'sea . . . 3G **51**
Woodpath PO5: S'sea . . . 6G **5** (4C **50**)
Woodpath Ho. PO5: S'sea . . . 6G **5** (4C **50**)
Woodpecker Cl. PO9: Warb . . . 2H **33**
Woodpecker Way PO3: Ports . . . 1C **42**
Woodroffe Wlk. PO10: Ems . . . 5D **22**
Woodrow PO7: Den . . . 3A **8**
Woodsedge PO7: W'lle . . . 3A **20**
Woodside PO5: S'sea . . . 4C **50**
PO13: Gos . . . 6B **26**
Woodstock Av. PO8: Horn . . . 2A **10**
Woodstock Cl. PO14: Fare . . . 2G **25**
Woodstock Rd. PO9: Bed . . . 1C **32**
PO12: Gos . . . 4E **49**
Woodvale PO15: Fare . . . 1F **25**
Woodville Dr. PO1: Ports . . . 6D **4** (4B **50**)
Woodville Rd. PO9: Bed . . . 1B **32**
Woodward Cl. PO12: Gos . . . 3B **48**
Woofferton Rd. PO6: Cosh . . . 2E **29**
Woolmer Ct. PO9: Hav . . . 4H **21**
Woolmer St. PO10: Ems . . . 5C **22**
Woolner Av. GU32: Pet . . . 3D **56**
PO6: Cosh . . . 3C **30**
Woolston Ct. PO12: Gos . . . 4A **48**
Woolston Rd. PO9: Hav . . . 3C **20**
Wootton Rd. PO13: Lee S . . . 3E **47**
Wootton St. PO6: Cosh . . . 4B **30**
Worcester Cl. PO5: S'sea . . . 5H **5** (3D **50**)
Worcester Ct. PO13: Gos . . . 1G **47**
Wordsworth Av. PO6: Cosh . . . 2C **28**
Workshop Rd. PO17: S'wick . . . 1E **29**
Worldham Rd. PO9: Hav . . . 3H **21**
Worsley Rd. PO5: S'sea . . . 4C **50**
Worsley St. PO4: S'sea . . . 5G **51**
Worthing Av. PO12: Gos . . . 5F **39**
Worthing Rd. PO5: S'sea . . . 5D **50**
Worthy Ct. PO9: Hav . . . 4H **21**
Wraysbury Pk. Dr. PO10: Ems . . . 5D **22**
Wren Cen., The PO10: Ems . . . 6E **23**
Wrenway PO16: Portc . . . 3F **27**
Wrexham Gro. PO8: Cath . . . 2B **6**
Wright Cl. PO15: White . . . 3B **12**
Wyborn Cl. PO11: H Isl . . . 5C **54**
Wych La. PO13: Gos . . . 1B **38**
Wycote Rd. PO13: Gos . . . 1B **38**
Wyeford Ct. PO9: Hav . . . 3H **21**
Wykeham Av. PO2: Ports . . . 4A **42**
Wykeham Fld. PO17: Wick . . . 2A **14**
Wykeham Rd. PO2: Ports . . . 4A **42**
Wylds La. GU32: W'ton . . . 6A **56**
Wyllie Rd. PO2: Ports . . . 1A **42**
WYMERING . . . 2H **29**
Wymering La. PO6: Cosh . . . 3A **30**
Wymering Mnr. Cl. PO6: Cosh . . . 3H **29**
Wymering Rd. PO2: Ports . . . 5A **42**
Wyndcliffe Rd. PO4: S'sea . . . 4E **51**
Wyndham Cl. PO8: Cowp . . . 3B **10**
Wyndham M.
PO1: Ports . . . 6C **4** (4A **50**)
Wyn Sutcliffe Ct. PO4: S'sea . . . 4G **51**
Wynton Way PO15: Fare . . . 6E **13**

Y

Yaldhurst Ct. PO9: Hav . . . 3H **21**
Yapton St. PO1: Ports . . . 2G **5** (2C **50**)
Yarborough Rd. PO5: S'sea . . . 6F **5** (4C **50**)
Yardlea Cl. PO9: R Cas . . . 6H **11**
Yardley Cl. PO3: Ports . . . 1E **43**
Yateley Cl. PO9: Hav . . . 4C **20**
Yeo Ct. PO4: S'sea . . . 3A **52**
Yews, The PO8: Horn . . . 6D **6**
Yewside PO13: Gos . . . 4D **38**
Yew Tree Av. PO8: Cowp . . . 5B **10**
Yew Tree Gdns. PO7: Den . . . 3A **8**
Yew Tree Rd. PO11: H Isl . . . 5C **44**
Yoells Cres. PO8: Love . . . 1H **9**
Yoells La. PO8: Love . . . 1H **9**
York Cl. GU32: Pet . . . 4B **56**
York Cres. PO13: Lee S . . . 3E **47**
Yorke St. PO5: S'sea . . . 5E **5** (3B **50**)
York Gdns. PO16: Portc . . . 5C **28**
York Ho. PO12: Gos . . . 3F **49**
York Pl. PO1: Ports . . . 2D **4** (1B **50**)
York Ter. PO3: Ports . . . 6B **30**
Youngbridge Ct. PO16: Fare . . . 4A **26**
Yves M. PO5: S'sea . . . 5D **50**

Z

Zetland Path PO6: Farl . . . 4F **31**
Zetland Rd. PO6: Farl . . . 4F **31**
PO12: Gos . . . 2D **48**
Zeus La. PO7: Purb . . . 6H **19**
Zurich Cen., The PO15: White . . . 2A **12**